1940 | 1950 | 1960

1947
Max Horkheimer and Theodor Adorno, *Dialectic of Enlightenment*

1952
Frantz Fanon, *Black Skin/White Masks*
1957
Roland Barthes, *Mythologies*
1958
Raymond Williams, *Culture and Society*

1962
Claude Lévi-Strauss, *The Savage Mind*; Rachel Carson, *Silent Spring*
1964
Marshall McLuhan, *Understanding Media*
1967
Guy Debord, *Society of the Spectacle*
1969
Richard Hoggart, *Contemporary Cultural Studies*

1946
NBA founded; First game between the Toronto Huskies and the New York Knickerbockers

1951
Debut of *I Love Lucy*
1953
Elvis records at Sun Studios, 1953-4
1955
Disneyland Theme Park opens
1956
The Quiz Show scandals
1958
Canada Broadcast Corporation (CBC) begins Canada-wide broadcast
1959
First Barbie doll launched

1960
Alfred Hitchcock's *Psycho* released; First Paralympic Games held in Rome
1962
The Beatles release their first single, **"Love Me Do"**; Production of first videogame, *Spacewar!*; Andy Warhol's first solo exhibition; The first James Bond movie, *Dr. No*, released
1964
Bob Dylan's *The Times They Are a-Changin'* released

1966
Original series of *Star Trek* broadcast
1967
Rolling Stone magazine founded
1969
The Woodstock music festival

1944
The world's first global financial system, the Bretton Woods Agreements, comes into force
1945
World War II ends
1947
South Asia achieves independence; Hundreds of thousands die and millions are displaced in violence following India/Pakistan partition; In the USA, the House Un-American Committee begins its investigations into communist presence in the film industry
1948
Universal Declaration of Human Rights adopted by the UN General Assembly

1954
Segregation in US schools deemed unconstitutional in the Brown vs. Board of Education decision
1956
Defeat of Hungarian Revolution against Soviet rule

1960
John F. Kennedy and Richard Nixon take part in the first televised presidential debate; Canada approved the sale of the birth control pill
1962
Cuban Missile Crisis
1967
San Francisco becomes the epicentre of the Hippy movement during the Summer of Love

1968
Massive student and leftist protests bring down the De Gaulle government in France
1969
Neil Armstrong walks on the moon: the event is televised; Stonewall Riots; Homosexuality legalised in Canada; First Earth Day celebrated

---

1943
The founding of IKEA
1945
First ballpoint pens go on sale in New York City
1946
Demonstration of first full-colour television; First bikinis go on sale in Paris
1947
First microwaves go on sale
1948
McDonalds establishes their "Speedee Service System"; First drive-through opens at In-and-Out Burger in California

1950
Diners Group, the first credit card, launched
1956
The invention of the pulltab can in Thunder Bay, Ontario

1962
Wal-Mart founded
1964
First Tim Hortons opens in Hamilton, Ontario

Popular
Culture

A USER'S GUIDE

SECOND EDITION

Susie O'Brien
McMaster University

Imre Szeman
University of Alberta

NELSON / EDUCATION

NELSON / EDUCATION

Popular Culture: A User's Guide,
Second Edition

by Susie O'Brien and Imre Szeman

**Associate Vice President,
Editorial Director:**
Evelyn Veitch

**Editor-in-Chief,
Higher Education:**
Anne Williams

Executive Editor:
Laura Macleod

Marketing Manager:
Amanda Henry

Senior Developmental Editor:
Linda Sparks

Photo Researcher:
Melody Tolson

Permissions Coordinator:
Melody Tolson

Production Service:
Macmillan Publishing Solutions

Copy Editor:
Elizabeth Phinney

Proofreader:
Barbara Storey

Indexer:
Patti Schiendelman

Senior Production Coordinator:
Ferial Suleman

Design Director:
Ken Phipps

Managing Designer:
Franca Amore

Interior Design:
Peter Papayanakis

Cover Design:
Carianne Bauldry

Cover Image:
Bruegel-Bosch Bus sculpture by Kim
H. Adams. Art Gallery of Hamilton,
acquired with the assistance of the
York Wilson Endowment Award at
The Canada Council for the Arts and
with funds from the E. Muriel Baker
Estate, the Russell Nelson Eden
Estate and the Walter and Duncan
Gordon Foundation, 2001.
Photograph taken by Dick
Hemingway.

Compositor:
Macmillan Publishing Solutions

Printer:
Webcom

**Library and Archives Canada
Cataloguing in Publication Data**

O'Brien, Susie
   Popular culture : a user's
guide / Susie O'Brien,
Imre Szeman. — 2nd ed.

Includes bibliographical references
and index.
ISBN 978-0-17-610467-2

   1. Popular culture—Textbooks.
I. Szeman, Imre, 1968– II. Title.

CB430.O27 2003   306
C2009-900424-0

ISBN-13: 978-0-17-610467-2
ISBN-10: 0-17-610467-4

Contents

CHAPTER 4—THE PRODUCTION OF POPULAR CULTURE   109

CHAPTER 5—THE CONSUMING LIFE   149

CHAPTER 6—IDENTITY AND THE BODY   183

Preface: A User's Guide to the *User's Guide*

The goal of *Popular Culture: A User's Guide* is to provide readers with an introduction to the critical study of popular culture. Our aim is to give readers the analytical tools to understand the everyday texts and practices that surround them, as well as their own roles as consumers of and participants in popular culture.

Why does anyone need a guidebook to popular culture? Don't we all already know not only what is meant by popular culture, but also how to consume and use it? Guidebooks are supposed to make mysterious lands with unusual customs more familiar, or help us learn how to navigate complex tasks (like building a deck or planting a good-looking garden) with greater ease. Popular culture, on the other hand, is, well, *popular*. When it comes to watching films, listening to pop music, shopping, or sucking down cups of coffee, we believe that we know exactly what we are doing and why we are doing it. Like our native tongue, popular culture is something we know how to "speak" without resorting to lessons, audiotapes, courses, or guidebooks. So what can a user's guide tell us about popular culture that we don't already know?

In many respects, it is precisely the intimacy and familiarity with which we engage in contemporary popular culture that requires critical reflection, exploration, and analysis. After all, knowing how to speak a language because we are immersed in it does not mean that we are necessarily able to read or write it, or that we understand its syntax and structure. Reading and writing take an enormous amount of effort to get right; even once we have learned how to read, we are faced with other questions, such as how written language on a page can convey information about real and imagined worlds.

As with language, so, too, with popular culture. Because we are immersed in it, popular culture is both uniquely accessible and frustratingly opaque; it is hard to get a critical purchase on something we inhabit so completely and, most of the time, more or less unconsciously. In order to help us understand the "syntax" and "grammar" of popular culture— the unacknowledged but crucial structures that give popular culture its shape, meaning, and significance—the goal of this book is to help readers to see this familiar terrain more acutely and with greater insight. Our familiarity with popular culture tends to hide some of its most important features and its relationship to broader social, political, and economic currents. *Popular Culture: A User's Guide* will help readers to see parts of the contemporary cultural landscape that they may have been looking at all along without really perceiving.

This book aims to take readers beyond the "common sense" approach to popular culture, an approach that is defined by an odd mix of cynical knowingness and complacency. We are working from the premise that readers today possess an unprecedented level of media literacy. We are all aware, for example, that certain forms of media such as advertising operate according to particular agendas that may or may not reflect our own interests, and we also believe that we are smart enough to resist. This book seeks to create a level of awareness that goes beyond that cynical complacency, not only to make readers aware of the underlying socioeconomic structures that determine the shape of media and, by extension, consciousness, but also to recognize the myriad ways that popular culture manages to manoeuvre around these structures. We want to give students the tools to understand their role not just as consumers but also as agents of popular culture.

We also want to showcase the full range of activities and practices that can be considered to be part of contemporary popular cultural experience. Unlike "high culture," which is generally understood to refer to a discrete body of books or artworks that are unified by their adherence to specific aesthetic and cultural codes, the field of popular culture is diverse and uneven, comprising texts and practices ranging from commercial media to subcultural styles to the activities of everyday life (eating, shopping, drinking coffee, recreational activities, etc.).

Many books about popular culture are actually surveys or overviews of academic or theoretical *approaches* to the study of popular culture. In other words, what such books offer is a roughly historical account of a specific academic discipline (what is now often called "cultural studies") and the individuals and theories that have been important to the development of that discipline. While we certainly discuss and make use of many of the most important theories of popular culture, we have chosen to emphasize practical strategies for understanding and interpreting the popular. Working from case studies and examples, the aim of this book is to provide readers with a critical vocabulary and methods of analysis that will allow them to perform independent readings of cultural texts extending far beyond the sampling we offer here.

The specific analyses that we provide in each chapter exemplify ways of using and adapting critical and theoretical materials to address the issues and problems at hand. The text is organized mainly around broad themes rather than specific genres or forms of popular culture (television, music, film, etc.), and is book-ended by chapters that focus on the prehistory of contemporary popular culture (Chapter 1) and on the complexities that the current historical context introduces for the study of popular culture (Chapters 9 and 10).

There are a number of other features of this book that make it a distinctive contribution to the study of popular culture. There is, first, an emphasis throughout on the politics of popular culture—that is, on the way in which popular culture is always connected to practices and discourses related to the exercise and struggle over power and recognition in contemporary society. Second, there is an emphasis on Canadian examples and situations. Why? Even though our understanding of popular culture has been shaped and influenced by writers and thinkers from around the world, our approach to and understanding of popular culture is informed by our experiences of growing up and teaching in Canada. This does not mean, of course, that everything that we talk about or make reference to in this book has been made or created in Canada. This would be a false reflection of the experience of popular culture in Canada, which has historically always included radio and television programs from the United States and the United Kingdom (and elsewhere), and film and literature from around the world—alongside and in conjunction with homegrown programming and cultural production.

Sometimes at the expense of our own cultural producers, Canadians have been (for a variety of reasons) avid consumers of pop culture produced around the world. This book reflects this diversity of pop cultural sources, but just as importantly provides an interesting, uniquely Canadian perspective on Western pop culture that emerges out of Canada's specific structural relationship to the mythical pop cultural centre of "America." Because Canada is both outside of American pop culture and also uniquely and deeply engaged with it, we hope that this book sheds an interesting and useful light on phenomena that have thus far been examined from the perspective of too few geographic locations—for the most part, from the United States, the United Kingdom, and Australia. In the study of popular culture, what you see and do not see often depends on where you are looking from.

Finally, in order to help our readers work through the *User's Guide,* we have incorporated a number of pedagogical features. Important terms and concepts are listed in a glossary at the end of the book, and are highlighted in **bold** in the text to allow readers to cross-reference with ease. Each chapter contains one or more suggested activities and questions that are intended to get readers to think further about particular subjects and to apply them to their own experiences. In course use, these Suggested Activities may form the basis of oral or written assignments. Close-Ups in each chapter clarify key concepts, theories, or movements, and may also form the basis for further study and investigation. Each chapter ends with a list of suggestions for further reading. These titles include other introductory texts that might deal with the same material in a different way or with a different emphasis, and original works by scholars and theorists referred to in the chapter. This text also has a website with more helpful resources and information, located at www.popularculture2e.nelson.com.

Like the writers of any guidebook, our hope is that readers use our maps and recommendations of places to visit and things to think about as a jumping-off point for the elaboration of their own maps of the landscape of popular culture. The authors would be the first to admit that, not only are there plenty of things that they have not seen, but there are places they do not yet know even exist.

PREFACE TO THE SECOND EDITION

In the late 1990s when we began work on the first edition of *Popular Culture: A User's Guide,* we had a good sense that the task was going to be daunting. How to produce a reasonable survey of a subject whose hugeness was only exceeded by its stubborn refusal to stop moving? In the end, we felt the book did a pretty good job of covering its topic; what merited inclusion was vast but seemed mostly containable in representative samples and case studies. In the relatively short time between the publication of the first edition (2004) and this one, what counts as popular culture has grown exponentially, and with it, the range of potential examples and case studies has expanded beyond the capacities of two authors and a team of research assistants to contain. Our experience has been a little like watching the revolving thumbnail images of videos people are watching on YouTube: every few seconds something new comes along that could potentially be interesting and illustrative of an issue or concept that would unlock the idea of popular culture for our readers, but as we pause to consider it, it's quickly replaced by something else. At certain points we've just had to stop, click the "X" in the upper-right-hand corner of our browser and word processor and take our best educated guesses about what phenomena will offer the clearest insights into the state of popular culture not just over the next few weeks. "Feist on Sesame Street?" "HYPE: The Obama Effect?" "Master Casters—Skeet Fishing"? Who is to say which of these commentaries on the state of things will imprint itself on our collective minds in a lasting way? (We hope you won't be too disappointed to know that none of these topics makes it into the book in any significant way.)

On a more pragmatic level, as we considered what to do with the second edition of this book, we had to reign in two impulses: the desire to do the whole thing over again from scratch, and the desire to add and add until there was nothing in the pop cultural universe that we hadn't discussed or at least touched upon. Assuming we had world enough and time, either of these approaches would have probably have ended up making a fatal mess of a book that we feel has done a good job of introducing students to the ins and outs of the study of popular culture. In consultation with students and instructors, and based on our (admittedly subjective) sense of what's important at the moment, this book does look different from its predecessor in some significant ways. We have expanded some sections and condensed others; for example, material in the final chapter in the first edition, which touched briefly on the history and development of the academic field of cultural studies, has been incorporated into Chapter 1. In addition to more detailed discussions of digital culture throughout, this book contains one entirely new chapter on the spaces and places of popular culture. Finally, the new edition includes a more extensive and up-to-date range of case studies.

You might ask: Why didn't they spend time talking about *Guitar Hero*? Or the cost of cell phone service in Canada? Or about the crisis that happens at the dinner table when your kids have been spending too much time watching *Ramsay's Kitchen Nightmares*? How could they have talked about *x* without thinking about *y*? No single book on popular culture—especially an introductory book like this one—can claim to be definitive: the topics and case studies that we use are meant to be supplemented by other ideas and examples. We hope we've given you fodder for spirited disagreement and recognition of all that we've left out—but we hope, too, that the book offers you helpful tools, concepts, ideas, and examples that you will continue to work with long after your academic relationship to pop culture is over.

Susie O'Brien
Imre Szeman
Hamilton, Ontario
July 2008

Acknowledgments

We would like to thank Ken Paradis and Marc Ouellette, and all of the reviewers who gave us feedback on the first edition and helped us prepare for the second. A big thanks, too, to Linda Sparks and the editorial team at Nelson Education Ltd., who did an excellent job of keeping our noses to the grindstone. Also, William Edwards, Tim Kaposy, Sarah Blacker, Nick Holm, Peter Mountford (the pop culture shizzle dizzle), and Scott Stoneman added a lot more than just their own two cents to the second edition. Thanks, guys, for all your help and ideas.

Imre thanks the students, staff and faculty who have given life and energy to the Cultural Studies and Critical Theory program at McMaster University, as well as the 3Js—Jason, Jonathan, and Joseph—masters of the Bold Street basement Wii.

Susie thanks the CSCT and English students at McMaster, as well as the students in Peter Mountford's Nelson Secondary School English classes, whose wild and wide-ranging cultural knowledge wended its way into our house where it formed weird amalgams with the nine-, five-, and one-year-old perspectives of Bridget, Thomas, and Jamie, respectively. From this nutritionally dubious but tasty stew, the book draws many of its arguments and examples.

Chapter 1

Introducing Popular Culture

APPROACHING POPULAR CULTURE

"Let's go get a coffee."

Every day, throughout North America, this phrase is uttered thousands of times, by different people—students, teachers, construction workers, lawyers, mothers, retail clerks, unemployed people, old people, young people—and in different social contexts, such as work, breaks from work, dating, interviews, therapy sessions, or hanging out. Going for a coffee is a major part of popular culture, not only in the sense that it is such a common practice, but also in that it means so much more than the literal act of tossing back a hot caffeinated beverage: in fact, "going for coffee" need not involve drinking coffee at all. So what does it mean? And what is it about coffee drinking that makes it part of popular culture while other equally common practices—like, say, yawning, or mowing the lawn—are not? Or are they part of popular culture, too?

These are the kind of questions this book sets out to answer—not by offering a comprehensive account of what fits in the category of popular culture and what does not, but by helping us to think about the question of *why* popular culture is such a critical part of contemporary life. For this reason, it might be misleading to call this book a "user's guide" to popular culture. A standard user's guide to, say, the smartphone that you may have just received for Christmas (which happens all the time in television commercials, less often in real life) tells you everything there is to know about the specific object that you have in your hands, what its functions are, and what it can and cannot do. Popular culture is not like that. For one thing, popular culture is a far more difficult "thing" to pin down than a smartphone, or an Ikea desk, or Windows Vista; it is constantly changing shape, shifting locations, assuming new identities and new tasks and functions. The goal of a user's guide to popular culture is to provide the users of it—that is, all of us—with a way to think about popular culture that is flexible and supple enough to also allow us to think about its changes and redefinitions. Let's face it: no one reads past the first few pages of the thick book of instructions that comes with a cell phone—you turn the phone on and figure it out as you go. Once again, popular culture is different. In this case, we *need* a guide precisely because we're already so familiar with the ways we use it that it's difficult to figure out what else we can do with it—we do not really understand its possibilities, and its limits.

What's at stake in the definition of popular culture? How can we learn to read and participate in—to *use*—the popular in a way that strengthens our understanding of our selves and the world we live in? These are large and exhausting questions—large and exhausting enough to make you want to, well, go get a coffee! That's why, although such questions are at the core of this book, the way in which we attempt to get at them is through the analysis of actual "texts" (objects that we can interpret just like a book) and "practices" (things that we do): seeing movies, listening to songs, watching television shows, playing sports, going shopping—and drinking coffee. The purpose of this introduction is to lay out a working definition of popular culture, to outline a few key concepts that will reappear in later discussion, and to give you a diagram of the way this book is put together—a "guide to the guide"—that should help make the task of piecing the bits of popular culture together a productive one. In other words, we'll first lay out the pieces and the tools and describe what they do before trying to fit them into the bigger picture. We also offer a rough guide to the field of Cultural Studies for readers who want to delve further into the question of how popular culture has come to be seen as something significant and tricky enough to require a user's guide. Just be forewarned: by the end of the book you will still be left with extra parts and you will likely end up with a concept of popular culture that looks different than that of your neighbours. But trust us: this is a good thing. . . .

DEFINING POPULAR CULTURE

Like most things that form a big part of our daily lives, popular culture is familiar and obvious at first glance, but very complicated as soon as you start to think about it in any detail. Before we outline the concept of popular culture that informs this book, we suggest you take a couple of minutes to try and come up with your own working definition. When we've conducted this exercise in introductory university classes, a typical range of ideas tend to come up: popular culture consists of those things—products, texts, practices, and so on—that are enjoyed by lots and lots of people; popular culture is commercial culture (as opposed to, say, "high" culture, which people today still tend to associate with the things they imagine that rich people who own yachts like to do, like listen to opera or go to the symphony); popular culture consists of the traditional practices and beliefs or way of life of a specific group; and, finally, the most wide-ranging definition of all, popular culture is simply the practices of everyday life.

What is interesting about these definitions is not just their range, but their differences—differences that are shaped to a large degree by the way we understand the terms "popular" and "culture." How does your definition fit with these? Does it accord more closely with some than others? What definitions of "popular" and "culture" are implied by your understanding of popular culture?

It is worth taking the time to think about different ways of understanding popular culture, though not so we can dismiss some of them in order to identify a correct definition. Like most other important social concepts—concepts such as "democracy," "progress," "justice," "civilization," and so on, that produce the shape of the societies that we live in—it does not really make sense to hope for a correct definition that would do something like solve the puzzle of all of these different meanings by establishing the essential one supposedly lurking in their midst. Rather, we want to suggest that popular culture is informed by *all* these perspectives, not just in the sense that each is

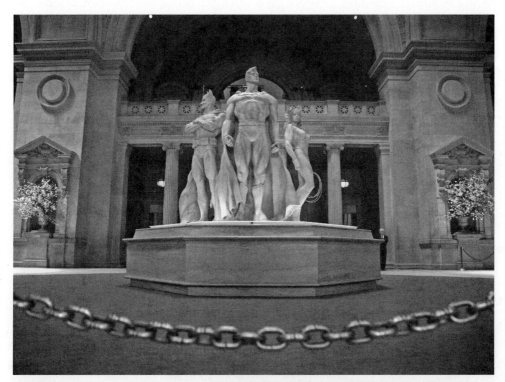

Many museums now embrace elements of popular culture. For example, the Metropolitan Museum of Art in New York recently ran an exhibit entitled "Superheroes: Fashion and Fantasy," which explored the influence of the superhero on contemporary fashion through a collection that included movie costumes, avant-garde haute couture, and high-performance sportswear.

partially true, but in the sense that the tension between them is fundamental to understanding the meaning of popular culture today. So before we erect a definition of popular culture that we can all feel comfortable inhabiting, we need to think about this tension. This may initially seem to be a frustratingly circuitous and unhelpful route to finding out the "facts." However, such meanderings are a critical part of the study of culture, in which the question of meaning is never evident, but always up for negotiation and disagreement.

What Is Culture?

When we ask our students to track the word "culture" as it is used in the media and other sources, two things tend to emerge: (1) "culture" (along with variations such as "multiculturalism") gets mentioned *a lot*, implying that it is a significant concept in our society, and one that we likely can't do without; and (2) it appears in many different, often contradictory, contexts, suggesting that exactly *how* it signifies is hard to pin down. When we talk about "culture" in the sense of building opera houses, the word obviously means something different than when we talk about "Western culture" or "youth culture," "national culture" or "business culture." "Culture" in the first sense—the one that fits with opera houses, ballet, and Shakespeare, which for convenience we'll call "capital-C Culture"—focuses on what we usually think of as high-end creative production: artistic pursuits that are enjoyed by an elite minority as opposed to more accessible leisure activities, such as sports. These kinds of cultural productions are those that have over time (they are often associated with the past) assumed an especially privileged place in the collection of ideas and artifacts that comprises a cultural *tradition*. In the context of this understanding of "Culture," which is the one generally associated with university programs in humanities or the arts, the idea of "popular culture" would seem to be a contradiction in terms. After all, you go to university to learn about John Milton, not Paris Hilton.

A second definition encompasses a much broader understanding of culture as a whole way of life of a society or a distinct subsection of society: along with art, it encompasses everyday rituals such as meals, work, religious observances, sports, sex, family, and friendship. Implicitly opposed to "nature," which we associate with biology (the things we share with the living non-human world), "culture" in this context refers to the practices that define us, collectively and in distinct groups, as human. This definition of culture, or something close to it, informs the disciplines of the social sciences—particularly anthropology, which until recently tended to focus on the cultures of preindustrial societies. When we go on vacation to experience other "cultures," it is this sense of culture that we are making reference to: a glimpse into a different way of life organized according to its own principles and around its own unique practices.

The Mass Media   Interestingly, neither the familiar humanities definition of culture nor the one employed by traditional anthropologists adequately encompasses the experience of living in a postmodern capitalist society—the experience of most of us who teach and study those subjects—which is a way of life increasingly dominated by the mass media. Not only do the mass media tend to fall outside the definitions of culture centred around elite artistic production or the practices of ordinary everyday life; they also are frequently cited as the thing that threatens to destroy "culture" in both these senses: while one set of critics laments the dumbing-down of Shakespeare to satisfy the tastes of a mass audience in Hollywood productions such as *William Shakespeare's Romeo and Juliet*, *O* (based on *Othello*), or *10 Things I Hate About You* (based on *The Taming of the Shrew*), another warns of the corruption of "authentic" grassroots cultures by the global entertainment industry, which has made it more difficult to find cultures in our travels that are all that different from our own. While they come from different places, what these criticisms have in common is an element of nostalgia, a feeling that something has been lost, that a once-pure realm of culture has become contaminated by commerce. It is the desire to understand this world-contaminated-by-commerce that motivates the relatively new discipline of *cultural studies*, into which this book fits (and whose development as an academic field is discussed in more detail later in this chapter).

Objects of Study   To avoid the limitations of earlier definitions of "culture," cultural studies defines its object of study in very broad terms. One definition, offered in *Key Concepts in Communication and Cultural Studies*, describes culture as "the social production and reproduction of sense, meaning and consciousness. The sphere of meaning, which unifies the spheres of production (economics) and social relations (politics)" (O'Sullivan et al. 68). This is a useful definition insofar as it manages to encompass a wide variety of "meaning-producing" practices and technologies, including both traditional definitions of culture—fine art and everyday practices—and mass media. Of course, while the incorporation of these diverse meanings into one functional frame might give us a quick snapshot of what it is that cultural studies actually *studies*—the kinds of things that it looks at and why it is that it looks at them—it is difficult to ignore that the different conceptions of culture that are named in this definition are historically not only different, but also *contradictory*.

Rather than seeking to smooth over these contradictions, cultural studies is interested in actively teasing them out and laying them bare. It is committed to an understanding of culture that does not just expand on earlier definitions in order to include practices, objects, and people that tended, for different reasons, to get left out (such as television game shows, science fiction novels, or skateboarding), but also thinks about why and how such inclusions and exclusions occur in the first place. This means that cultural studies thinks deeply about the connections between culture and the spheres of politics and economics, and seeks to understand how that realm of activity concerned with "meanings, pleasures, and identities" (Fiske *Understanding* 1) shapes (and is shaped by) relations of power. Among the key questions that are raised by the contradictions between the different definitions of culture cited above are: How is culture produced (made by a society) and reproduced (passed on by a society into the future)? Who makes culture? For whom is it made? This brings us to the other half of the concept of "popular culture."

What/Who Defines the Popular?

Having wrestled with the complicated problem of what constitutes "culture," the meaning of "popular" seems much more straightforward, at least initially. Derived from the Latin word *popularis*, which means "of, or belonging to the people," "popular" is often used in a contemporary context to describe something that is liked by a lot of people. For example, when an authoritative source cites *CSI: Miami* as the most popular show on television, based on ratings in 20 nations ("CSI show"), we can assume, reasonably, that a lot of us like slick crime dramas shot in glamorous settings. But when we start to look a little further into how the word "popular" is used today, it becomes obvious that it has to do with more than numbers—that the words "popular" and "the people" don't refer to absolutely everyone, but to a particular group to whom a certain quality or value is attached (Chapter 10 extends the discussion of popular culture and television in relation to the effects of globalization).

A couple of examples will serve to illustrate this. First, a number of major art museums have recently come under fire for abandoning their mandate to promote serious art in favour of "popular," blockbuster shows guaranteed to fill up the galleries (and the museum shop). Recent examples of this phenomenon include the "Art of Star Wars" exhibition that toured galleries in Japan, Singapore, Scotland, and England between 2002 and 2004, and "Diana, a Celebration," a tribute to the late Princess Diana that drew crowds at museums in Toronto, Fort Lauderdale, and Dayton, Ohio, in 2006 and 2007.

Art and museum critics are not all happy about the trend of blurring high and popular culture. As George Neubert, former director of the San Antonio Museum of Art and the Sheldon Memorial Art Gallery puts it,

Among the items on display in "Diana, A Celebration" were "Diana's fairy tale wedding gown [from her 1981 marriage to Prince Charles], complete with 25-foot train, diamond tiara, shoes and parasol." (Kenney)

a lot of museums are now torn between two extreme opposite philosophies . . . . One feels it has to compete with pop culture and mass culture to be relevant and for the big E, education, with lots of well-intentioned outreach and participatory programs. It does for a short moment bring up the numbers, but I wonder how meaningful those are in the long term.'" (Wolgamott)

A counterargument can be easily mounted in favour of the museums' decision to show more "popular" work: as a public space, the museum should respond to the preference of people in general rather than to the tastes of an overly educated minority to whom museums have typically catered. Since these latter tastes are often seen to be disproportionately supported by state subsidy of the arts, this argument also often concerns the appropriate allocation of tax dollars and the need for the arts sector to be more market-driven. While a cultural institution can readily apply to governments for support of a show on Canada's Group of Seven, it is harder to justify showing off concept drawings of the dark Sith, Darth Maul, even if this is what the public might "really" want to see. In this case, the "popular" is evoked both as a democratic principle *and* as a judgment about who can make sense of "real" art. By including more "popular" shows, the museums invite more people inside them—but not, of course, to see the kinds of art objects they were designed to exhibit.

The second example concerns the use of the word "people" in the context of protests surrounding the 2001 Summit of the Americas, a meeting of government leaders to discuss trade liberalization (the reduction of barriers to freer trade) among countries in North and South America. To register widespread concern about the exclusivity of the meeting, which was restricted to government leaders and the chief executive officers of major corporations, and about the relatively scant attention paid to social justice issues during this meeting (and by these government leaders more generally), protestors organized a parallel "People's Summit." The aim of the People's Summit was to foreground the issues left off the agenda of the official meeting, and, in the process, to highlight the failure of the political leaders to represent the legitimate interests of their constituents. In this example, the word "people" connotes something like "democratic" or "grassroots" or "ordinary" in contrast to the powerful minority running the official summit.

However, this claim on the idea of "people" quickly becomes complicated, in this case, by the refusal of the participants of the official summit and many in the media to accept the legitimacy of the protestors' claims to embody the voice of democracy. After all, as some of the leaders pointed out, *they* were the ones who were democratically elected; the protestors represented no one but themselves. In this way, the terms get flipped around so that it is the politicians who speak for "the people" against the "special interest groups" represented by the protestors: the term "people" here becomes the symbolic linchpin of a battle to gain the moral high ground over the substantive issues under debate. As with the art museum, the word "people" and its derivative "popular" are used here to convey something roughly opposite to "elite," though the *value* of those terms means something entirely different in each context.

So, we can add a couple of new elements to our understanding of the word "popular." First, it tends to carry with it connotations of value that are implicitly contrasted with the value of what it is *not*, though those values are seen differently depending on who is talking and in what context. Second, as is particularly evident in the latter example of the People's Summit, the question of who or what constitutes the popular is tangled up with questions of power.

With this in mind, let's return to the apparently simple usage of "popular" with which we began this section, and think about it in a little more detail. Who are the people who define the "popularity" of *CSI: Miami*? Are they the unenlightened masses who lack the ability to discriminate between schlock and substance? Are they discerning viewers exercising their consumer choice? Or are they engaged in an act of political activism, employing the cultural resources of *CSI: Miami* to construct an agenda for crime prevention or progressive social change? The slightly ludicrous quality of the last possibility raises a quite serious question about how we understand the popular: what kind of *agency*—that is, possibility for self-motivated activity or action—is involved on the part of "the people" in determining or defining something to be "popular"? This question has particular significance when we start to talk about popular culture.

What Is Popular Culture?

Common uses of the term "popular culture" reflect in interesting ways our understandings of the two separate words that we discussed above. The most familiar use of the term "popular culture" identifies it with the entertainment produced through and by commercial media (television, film, the music industry, etc.) that have the economic and technological capacity to reach large, demographically diverse and geographically dispersed audiences. Popularity is measured, in this case, by patterns of **consumption**: it refers to the things we buy (or watch, or listen to, etc.). A somewhat different use of the term "popular culture" defines it in terms not of consumption, but production: popular culture is what "the people" make, or do, for themselves. This definition fits fairly closely with the anthropological definition of culture as "the practices of everyday life."

Both of these definitions differ quite clearly from the elite culture defended by those cranky art patrons who think that Leonardo da Vinci paintings should never take a back seat to *The Da Vinci Code*. Apart from this, however, their connotations are quite different and even oppositional: "do-it-yourself" popular culture is explicitly different from the culture that is produced by large corporate entities whose interest in the everyday practices of their consumers is shaped by their need to figure out how best to sell them things. Indeed, the kind of culture produced by the commercial media is often seen as threatening the culture of everyday life by diverting people's desire for fulfillment—a desire that can ultimately be satisfied only by productive activity—into habits of passive consumption.

Folk Culture and Mass Culture   To distinguish clearly between these two different forms of cultural production, critics will sometimes use the terms *folk culture* and *mass culture*. **Folk culture** refers to those cultural products and practices that have developed over time within a particular community or socially identifiable group, and that are communicated from generation to generation and amongst people who tend to be known to one another. It tends to be seen as the direct expression of the life experiences shared by its creators and their audience (Nachbar and Lause 15; Grossberg et al. 37). **Mass culture**, on the other hand, is produced for an unknown, disparate audience. While the transmission of folk culture is generally technologically simple (e.g., face-to-face, oral communication), mass culture depends on electronic (or mechanical) media to convey its message to the largest possible audience in order to secure maximum profit, which is its ultimate goal. These terms can serve to make useful distinctions between kinds of cultural production, highlighting the differences between, say, an Inuit soapstone carving and an MTV rap video. On even a superficial examination, however, the differences start to look a little fuzzy. Inuit art has become so popular among non-Inuit that it has spawned factories in the south where carvers use power tools to create an identical series of polar bears, for which they are paid by the piece (George). Rap music, now a multi-billion dollar industry, emerged relatively recently from the African-American street culture of the South Bronx. In each of these cases, it is difficult to identify the precise moment when folk culture metamorphosed into mass culture. The attempt to maintain a strict division is not just tricky in a practical sense, but also, arguably, somewhat suspect **ideologically**.

The desire to preserve a folk culture safe from the corrupting influence of commerce is often inflected by a nostalgic desire to return to a (mythical) moment of history in which cultural and social identities were secure and cultural boundaries were clear. The power of such nostalgia for homegrown, anti-commercial culture can be seen in the commercial appeal of Disney's Main Street, U.S.A, which evokes feelings toward a homey, small-town America of simple values that in reality never existed. When the desire to preserve a folk culture is extended to a socially and economically disadvantaged group, as in the two examples above, the situation becomes even more complicated. While Inuit might argue that the preservation of folk culture is a matter of community survival, the unhappiness of white collectors at the move toward mass-produced art may be motivated by concerns that have little to do with indigenous autonomy and more with how the value of their own art pieces will be affected. A less crudely **materialist** motivation for consumer nostalgia in this case might be a well-intentioned, if racist, aesthetic investment in the image of the "noble savage". This imaginary figure conjures up a purer, more natural world outside Western commercial culture while occupying a comfortable place within it.

However seemingly progressive the cause that is being (or has been) promoted in the name of "the people," *folk culture* remains a term whose peculiarly heavy ideological baggage should set off alarm bells every time we hear or read it (the same alarm bells that should go off when we hear politicians invoke the mythical category of "ordinary working Americans/Canadians/Australians." Just who are these "ordinary" people?). This is not to say that we need to abandon completely the idea of folk culture and all its troublesome derivations. Like mass culture, it retains some value as a descriptive term to designate particular kinds of cultural production, especially when referring to a time before our present capitalist moment—a moment when **authenticity** and commercial value are increasingly impossible to disentangle, when there's a sense in which, as one critic puts it, "*all* culture is mass culture" (Denning 258, emphasis added). We explore this idea a little further in Chapter 5.

Suggested Activity 1.1

Does commercialism destroy the authenticity of a cultural product or practice? Or does the authenticity of an object or practice increase its commercial value and potential? What does it mean if it is possible for us to answer both of these questions affirmatively? How does the divide between authenticity and commercial value work in the case of a practice like eco-tourism and an object like the first release of an indie band on its own label?

The Culture of Everyday Life   In order to signal this ambiguity and to avoid producing a definition of popular culture that falls too clearly on the side of celebrating the folk or denigrating the masses, we might define popular culture as something like "the communicative practices of everyday life" (where "communicative practices" comprises all those activities concerned with the production of meaning: talking, writing, social rituals such as eating, shopping, dancing, music, visual culture, sports, fashion, etc.) that are shared among many members of a society, including and especially those who aren't particularly socially, economically, or politically powerful. This somewhat clumsy definition accomplishes three things: (1) it signals the inclusion of mass media alongside, and even within, the practices of everyday life, without determining in advance what relationship it has to those practices; (2) it emphasizes the *meaningful* nature of popular culture—meaningful in the sense that it is important, as well as in the sense that it is concerned with the production of sense and social value; and (3) it highlights the issue of power that always and overtly dogs the production of culture in general, and popular culture in particular.

The Politics of Popular Culture

Why is power such a central issue for understanding popular culture? As we have already tried to suggest, culture is bound up closely with other aspects of human existence. As "the sphere of meaning which unifies the spheres of production (economics) and social relations (politics)" (O'Sullivan et al. 68), culture is concerned not just with individual tastes and desires, but also with the fundamental organization of society—with the distribution of material and symbolic power. Culture both reflects and influences social organization and the distribution of power. In the early twenty-first century, in most parts of the world, the dominant economic system is **capitalism** (for more on capitalism, see Close-Up 1.1). This means that the key characteristics of capitalism, including both its wealth-generating capacity and the patterns of inequitable distribution on which that

Capitalism

Capitalism is an economic system based on private ownership of the means of production and distribution, and geared toward the generation of profit. It is the dominant economic system in the world today. It is not the only economic system that has ever been in place, nor is it likely to be the last way in which human beings organize their economies, despite some claims to the contrary.

Loosely definable as a system of private enterprise whose primary aim is the production of profit, capitalism has been developing since at least the fifteenth century, and underwrites many of the economic and cultural institutions that we take for granted today, such as private property, individual freedom, and the imperative of economic growth. Our tendency today to see these features of capitalism as not only positive but also *natural*—the products of human nature rather than consciously worked-out ideas—makes it harder to see its less desirable aspects, such as social fragmentation, the unequal distribution of wealth, and the conversion of everything (including life itself) into something that can be bought or sold.

These brutal elements of capitalism were particularly evident during the heyday of European **colonialism** from the seventeenth to the nineteenth centuries. During this period, the exploitation of resources and enslavement of people from the non-European world helped make possible the massive accumulation of wealth enjoyed by a relatively small percentage of Europeans. This in turn fuelled the industrial revolution, in which both the productive and the destructive elements of capitalism were further intensified.

In capitalist economies, the means of creating, distributing, and exchanging wealth lie mainly in the hands of individuals and corporations (which in North America have the legal rights of individuals—see Close-Up 5.3 on page 161), rather than in public or state hands. The value of goods and labour is defined not by their social usefulness or significance, but by how much they can be exchanged for. The main goal of individuals in capitalism is to maximize the profit or the wages they receive. Proponents believe that, through the dance of supply and demand, goods and services are optimally and efficiently distributed throughout society. Detractors point to the growing gap between the wealthy and the poor, whose life activity is often organized to generate even more wealth for those at the top.

Postmodern, postindustrial, or late capitalism is distinguished by the fact that by comparison to earlier eras of capitalism there is now a far greater emphasis on the exchange of information and services (software and banking) as opposed to hard goods (steel and cars) in an economy that has become globally integrated.

capacity depends, help to determine the shape of culture. This is particularly true for popular culture.

In fact, one could argue that capitalism doesn't just inform particular *versions* of popular culture, in the sense of sustaining some dominant narratives (e.g., the story of success through hard work) and disabling others (e.g., the triumph of the group over the individual), or by enabling certain kinds of technological innovation. *Capitalism enables the production of popular culture, period.* We will go on to trace the historical evolution of the relationship between capitalism and popular culture in Chapter 2. For now, it is sufficient to note that the economic and social struggle that is intrinsic to capitalism is fought, to some extent, on the terrain of popular culture.

File-Sharing A simple example will serve to illustrate the kind of struggle we're talking about: Until the mid-1980s, the evolution of the music industry in North America was a story of skyrocketing profits. This story culminated in the introduction of the CD, which forced consumers to pay considerably more than what they had paid for vinyl LPs (with what many agreed was only a marginal improvement in sound quality), not to mention shelling out for expensive new sound systems. As promised price reductions never materialized, a quiet groundswell of annoyance with the recording industry began to grow. It seemed like a classic case of the customer getting cheated by corporations.

Enter Napster. The same digital technology that enabled the development of the CD also enabled the development of file-sharing programs that allowed people to swap music files on their computers without paying a cent. The recording industry reacted quickly, launching a series of lawsuits in a bid to recoup lost profits. Napster eventually settled with the industry, developing technology to monitor and restrict the downloading of songs, which would now be subject to a subscription fee. In the meantime, determined file-sharers—"pirates" in industry parlance—continued to find new ways to use the technology and decentralized structure of the Internet to outmanoeuvre their relatively cumbersome, slow-moving corporate opponents. For its part, the industry found its aggressive legal campaign to be increasingly ineffective, not to mention bad for public relations, as cases like the suit against an 83-year-old deceased grandmother alleged to have been swapping pop and rap music gained widespread public attention (Bangeman). Different measures, such as technologies to foil downloading and ad campaigns that described file-sharing as equivalent to theft, have met with mixed success. Meanwhile, the practice of file-sharing is no longer confined primarily to music: in the face of the rising price of popcorn, let alone the price of a seat at the megaplex, the IP BitTorrent enables movie fans to download movies for free home viewing. Unlike Napster and Kazaa, BitTorrent is a peer-to-peer network with no centralized server—in graphic contrast to the increasingly **monopolistic** movie industry that is struggling to crush it. The story of the changing dynamics of music and film distribution is a complicated one, with seemingly clear battle lines between "the people" and "corporations" blurred by such issues as the rights of musicians and filmmakers to get paid for their work, the accessibility of technology, and its implications for the construction of the community. Moreover, it isn't clear what effects the trend toward increasingly individualized, **privatized** music and film might have on our shared public culture.

Suggested Activity 1.2

What are your feelings about file-sharing? Does it constitute theft, as the film and music industries claim and the law increasingly confirms? Or is it a legitimate, even a virtuous form of genuinely popular culture? Do you see this shift in the way consumers access cultural products as empowering to producers or does it threaten their livelihoods?

"Popular culture" in this example is not simply an arena in which the disempowered fight back, defining themselves out from under corporate power. Neither does it work simply to maintain those structures by reigning in resistance back under the umbrella of the dominant ideology of consumer capitalism. Rather it is subject to a constant struggle over pleasure, profit, and, ultimately, over the distribution of social and economic power in the world.

Power Relationships   This dimension of struggle means that it is impossible to ever fix the meaning of popular culture in terms of a collection of objects or practices, or in terms of a single group who can be said to possess them. We need to understand it, as cultural theorist Stuart Hall puts it, not as "a mere descriptive inventory—which may have the negative effect of freezing popular culture into some timeless descriptive mould—but [as] the relations of power which are constantly punctuating and dividing the domain of culture into its preferred and its residual categories" ("Notes" 234). What is true for the objects and practices of popular culture is also true for those who use/participate in them. If, as another critic, John Fiske, has claimed, "popular culture is the culture of the subordinated and disempowered" (*Understanding* 4), this does not mean that it is possible to identify, by means of a simple checklist, who's "in" and who's "out." Rather than existing in a stable form as the property of a single group, power moves between and among individuals and institutions; this movement is registered with particular intensity in the domain of popular culture. In the absence of the certainty of clear categories, we are left with the less comfortable but more expansive framework of a series of open-ended questions. In evaluating the significance of popular culture, we always need to ask "Who says what, how, to whom, with what effect and for what purpose?" (Williams, qtd. in Burke 218).

Why Study Popular Culture? A Brief History of Cultural Studies

In one sense, cultural studies boils down to a bunch of theories and methodologies that help us find the answers to these straightforward questions. In order to understand why they're *good* questions—and less straightforward than they might seem—a bit of perspective is necessary. The very brief history of cultural studies that follows offers such a perspective. In the process it might also help begin to answer a question you might have asked yourself (with gentle prodding from family or friends, perhaps):

What's the point of cultural studies? Why not do something more respectable/useful/career-enhancing/*real*?

Every year, a couple of reports appear in the media about some new and outrageous course that has made it onto the curriculum of some university or college. In the 1980s it was a sprinkling of courses on Madonna and feminism; now they are more likely to be on reality television, the Paris Hilton phenomenon, or the cultural politics of fat. Less remarkable than the appearance of these courses is the fact that they still raise eyebrows. Only a few decades ago, the idea of a course on popular culture in general would have been unthinkable—the equivalent of bringing a case of beer into class and asking students to contemplate the meaning of drinking in their lives while tossing back a few. The fact that popular culture is more or less comfortably entrenched in the halls of higher learning while some aspects of it—certain celebrities, particular practices—are still excluded raises questions that are relevant for our discussion in this book: What counts as worthwhile knowledge in our culture? What is the relationship between popular culture and education? How has this relationship changed? Why has it changed?

Close-Up 1.2

Cultural Studies

Looser in its parameters than conventional disciplines such as psychology or history, cultural studies is, as one practitioner puts it, "a term of convenience for a fairly dispersed array of theoretical and political positions which, however widely divergent they might be in other respects, share a commitment to examining cultural practices from the point of view of their intrication with, and within, relations of power" (Bennett 33). It embraces a definition of culture that includes—in addition to conventional "texts" such as books—television shows, music and advertising, and ways of life (in the sense of concrete practices such as shopping, eating, drinking, fashion, etc.), as well as more abstract structures such as language, beliefs, "the contradictory forms of 'common sense' which have taken root in and helped to shape popular life," and the institutions that surround them (S. Hall "Gramsci" 26).

This broad definition of culture obviously contains a complex mix of elements—social, linguistic, political, economic; indeed, the study of popular culture might be described in one sense as the study of the interrelationships among what were once seen as discrete fields of existence. As such, cultural studies embraces a number of different disciplines, including literary studies, film studies, political science, anthropology, sociology, and communications studies, and employs a variety of methodologies: close reading, ethnography, content analysis, population surveys, and historical research.

The focus of much of this book so far is on giving you a set of tools that will help you in a practical way to make sense of your experience as a consumer, creator, or "user" of popular culture. Here we take a step back to look at some of the history and theory that lies behind these tools.

POPULAR CULTURE INVADES THE CLASSROOM

In Chapter 2, "The History of Popular Culture," we talk about the development in the mid– to late nineteenth century of a distinction between high, or capital-C, Culture and popular culture. Among the engineers of this divide were "rational recreationists"—religious and charitable groups bent on "improving" the lower classes—and education experts such as Matthew Arnold, who saw in "culture" a way to knit society together and soften the edges of the materialism infecting, in different ways, the middle and lower classes. Strangely, it was from this clearly hostile move against popular culture that the impulse to understand it—an impulse that informs this book—was first born.

Sneaking in Through the Back Door

Matthew Arnold and his followers saw mass media (understood in the form of such things as popular novels) as leading to social disintegration, through the replacement of spiritual with commercial values. They were particularly concerned with what they saw as the crass materialism of the new middle class and the degeneration of working-class morals. Behind this critique lay a powerful resistance to **industrialization** and nostalgia for an organic agrarian society in which people knew one another (and, not incidentally, knew their own place. **Class mobility** was not a feature of this society.). As people moved away from the supporting structures of church and community into the alienating and anonymous environment of the city, it was argued, they became vulnerable to all sorts of corrupting influences. Implicit in this position is a view of the masses as childlike in their ability to be easily led. The problem, as cultural conservatives saw it, was that they were being led by the wrong forces. The beneficial influences of the classic works of Culture, which discouraged the pursuits of materialism by offering more spiritual forms of sustenance, were being replaced by **commodities** that, in their form (cheap paperback novels, pop songs played on the gramophone) as in their content, seemed to celebrate values of easy pleasure and instant gratification.

These critiques grew throughout the early decades of the twentieth century, as new cultural technologies and modes of production facilitated easier distribution of forms of popular culture such as fiction, movies, music, and eventually television. Recognizing that it was impossible to shield impressionable minds from this trash, early twentieth-century educators such as F.R. and Q.D. Leavis suggested that schools should focus on training students' tastes to help them discriminate between true culture and its "multitudinous counter-influences—films, newspapers, advertising—indeed the whole world outside the class-room" (Leavis and Thompson 1). Such discrimination, they argued, was essential to the development of a sensitive moral character.

The course of study they proposed featured such inspiring study questions as "'Modern Publicity debases the currency of spiritual and emotional life generally': Discuss and illustrate." Another question lists a number of popular media clichés, such as "clean-cut executive type," "good mixer," "short-haired executive," "'regular guy' (Americanism)," and asks "Why do we wince at the mentality that uses this idiom?" (121). The target of these "discussion" questions (which don't leave a whole lot of room for discussion!) is both the products of popular media culture and the ignorant masses who consume them. Education in taste, then, is, as Pierre Bourdieu was later to point out (see Chapter 5), an education in class discrimination. That many of the students themselves came from the class they were now being taught to despise was something not taken up by the Leavises or other educators of the time.

In the Leavises' educational program, popular culture made it onto the curriculum as an example of a social problem—like alcohol, say, or bad hygiene—that could, with the proper techniques of discipline and avoidance, be successfully banished. In a way, though, these efforts were defeated by their own intentions: bringing popular culture into the classroom both acknowledged and promoted its legitimacy as a powerful social force.

The Democratization of Culture

The Leavises' approach to culture was unashamedly elitist. F.R. Leavis's 1930 work *Mass Civilization and Minority Culture* painted a picture of a society clearly divided, in which the cultured minority on the inside, the world of "*us*," fought valiantly to preserve itself from the degenerate populace on the outside—the world of "them." These certainties began to break down after the Second World War, when an increasingly diverse university student body started to challenge the boundary between "us" and "them." Particularly significant was the arrival of a large number of (mostly male) working-class students. Many of these were adults who, because of the war or for economic reasons, had deferred their education. They brought along with them a whole raft of knowledge and experiences that did not conform to elite conceptions of Culture.

Williams, Hoggart, and Thompson   From this group, three figures emerged as particularly influential in the development of the more inclusive vision of "culture" that would come to define cultural studies. Raymond Williams and Richard Hoggart, scholars of English literature, and E.P. Thompson, a historian, all began their university careers as scholarship students from working-class backgrounds. Williams' and Hoggart's later experiences working as adult-education tutors confirmed their sense that the dominant scholarly understanding of culture was far too narrow and exclusive to encompass the rich and complex fabric of their students' lives.

While the work of these three theorists is characterized by important differences of disciplinary perspective, approach, and argument, some of the central general implications of their work can be summarized here. First, all three established the legitimacy of working-class life as a subject of academic study, expanding the boundaries not just of culture but also of history to include experiences traditionally dismissed as insignificant. In the process, they also refined the definition of culture, moving away from "a literary-moral" to a more anthropological understanding of it as "the 'whole process' by means of which meanings and definitions are socially constructed and historically transformed." In this new definition, "literature and art count as only one, specially privileged, kind of social communication" (Williams, qtd. in S. Hall "Cultural Studies and the Centre" 19).

For Hoggart and Williams in particular, literature and art retained their significance as embodiments of important human values. Part of their projects recalled the efforts of F.R. Leavis in their determination to expose students to classic works of literature in order to enhance their literacy and, by extension, their understanding of the broader cultural contexts that shaped their lives. They all shared, to a certain extent, Leavis's elitist disdain for the products of the culture industry, enhanced by nostalgia for an earlier, more innocent (and partly imaginary) time when culture had yet to be totally corrupted by commerce. Hoggart and Williams extended Leavis's focus, however, in their extension of the principles of literary criticism, especially the techniques of close reading, to a wide range of popular texts—songs, magazines, newspapers—and in their emphasis on the connections between these texts and other aspects of everyday life: leisure activities, family relationships, gender roles, and so on. They also differed from Leavis in the crucial respect that, while Leavis wanted to preserve the terrain of minority culture against the threat of "mass" civilization, they sought to enhance democracy by developing the cultural literacy of ordinary people, helping them to understand the substance of their own lives.

One important area of conflict between, and even within, the works of these theorists concerns the relationship between the individual and broader institutional and social structures. While histories "from below" such as Thompson's tried to foreground working-class experience and also to highlight the agency of working-class people in shaping their own lives, his work was also characterized by a recognition of the way agency is shaped and constrained by broader economic relations. Williams and Hoggart, though equally interested in the conditions that would allow working people to become the subjects of their own history, rejected what they saw as the economic determinism of traditional **Marxism,** insisting on the substance and autonomy of culture as a shaping force. Debates about the relative power of individuals and the structures that constrain them, and about the shaping effects of economics on culture (and vice versa) became increasingly urgent in the context of a rapidly expanding culture industry.

These debates shaped the 1960 National Union of Teachers (NUT) conference, entitled "Popular Culture and Responsibility," which marked the recognition by British teachers of an increasing gap between the high culture they sought to cultivate in their students and the commercial culture those students were consuming. Rather than issuing a blanket condemnation of media culture, however, the majority of the participants in the conference agreed that it needed to be understood not as a degraded form of high culture, but as a different kind of expression that had to be approached on its own terms. While their efforts to rescue "serious" popular culture from the "pre-digested" mass culture of Hollywood still bore traces of Leavisite elitism, the conference marked a growing willingness to extend the boundaries of what counted (and what was worth studying) as "culture." It was also a recognition that the hierarchy of value that distinguished high from low culture was informed as much by ideology as by anything inherent to the cultural forms themselves. The establishment of the new Centre for Contemporary Cultural Studies at the University of Birmingham in 1964 (headed by Richard Hoggart) began to apply these insights to the study of media and youth subcultures—a diversity of subjects that marked the ambiguity of popular culture as defined simultaneously from above and below.

THE AMERICANIZATION OF POPULAR CULTURE

The changes that were occurring in Britain in the years following the Second World War were part of broader, global upheavals. One significant change resulted from Britain's shift from a dominant to a subordinate political and economic power in relation to the United States as the new leader of the "free" (i.e., non-communist) world. Combined with the position of media dominance that the U.S. had occupied since the early twentieth century, the new configuration of global power meant that, from the 1950s onward, global popular culture increasingly had an American face.

British cultural critics had a mixed reaction to these changes. In the 1950s, art critics working at the Institute of Contemporary Arts (ICA) established a working group to study contemporary trends in architecture, visual culture, and other forms of popular art. They were particularly interested in—and, generally, excited by—the growing influence of American popular culture on British culture. Their approach was different from most of the other critical responses to the culture industry, which were just that: critical.

In the U.S. itself, serious interest in popular culture was motivated by an unlikely source: the **cold war**. The contest between communism and capitalism spurred a push in American universities to study, and thereby promote, the **liberal** democratic values that represented the American way of life. American studies programs sprang up that were at first mostly committed to the teaching of American "high" culture—literature and art, along with the triumphant narrative of American history.

Soon these programs began to acknowledge the importance of the media in communicating democratic values through popular culture. The tendency to view the new media culture in a celebratory mode, as the embodiment of America's democratic spirit (as opposed to the culture of censorship and repression that was seen to exist in Russia), competed with concerns about the capacity of the commercial media to lure audiences into habits of unthinking **consumerism**. Concerns about subliminal advertising (see Chapter 5) played a large part in the move to incorporate media studies into university curricula.

While worries about the capacity of the media to weaken society's moral fibre by bombarding it with images promoting sex and shopping preoccupied many American educators, the explicit *American*-ness of the media also concerned many critics outside the United States. This vaguely defined quality was seen to shape not just the content of a popular culture that promoted values of liberalism, **individualism**, and consumerism, but also the way it was produced and distributed. Improvement in communications technology, in conjunction with American economic and cultural expansionism, granted the products of the American culture industry unprecedented access to the rest of the world. This development spawned fears about **cultural imperialism** (see Chapter 10) as well as the growth of critical media studies in Britain and elsewhere. The presence of an extremely powerful, linguistically identical culture on its southern border also led to the development of a unique form of communications theory in Canada. Major early figures in the establishment of both communications studies and Canadian studies, such as Harold Innis and Marshall McLuhan, paved the way for a wide range of contemporary work in cultural studies in Canada by scholars such as Jody Berland, Will Straw, and Arthur Kroker.

THE DECOLONIZATION OF CULTURE

Challenges to the comfortable dominance of the model of British Culture advanced by Matthew Arnold and the Leavises came not just from a shift in power away from Britain toward the United States, but also from more widely dispersed challenges to the world order associated with decolonization (see Chapter 7). The challenge was not only from the renaissance of other traditions, such as the African and South Asian cultures that had been submerged during the colonial period, but also the necessity—highlighted by anti-colonial activists such as Mohandas Gandhi and Frantz Fanon—for European culture to confront the contradictions that lay at the heart of its cherished ideals of freedom and **progress**. Around the same time, women's and labour groups, along with the civil rights movement in the United States, had begun to highlight the faultlines of **race** and gender that defined the supposedly universal norms and values of liberal democracy.

What's an Education For?

In addition to their broad consequences for society as a whole, these social justice movements, which came to a head in the massive protests launched in the U.S., France, and Mexico in 1968, had an enormous impact on higher education. Along with anti-colonial and labour rights activists, students were among the strongest participants in the protests. Their chief demand—for a greater role in determining the shape of their education—was in part an expression of anger about the detachment of the world inside the university from what was going on outside it: lectures celebrating the values of freedom, civilization, and the dignity of man did not fit with the realities of violent conflict such as the Vietnam War, human rights abuses, and environmental destruction. If academic institutions were to serve any useful role in advancing human understanding they needed to acknowledge the bankruptcy of many of their foundational principles.

The crisis of higher education sparked by the social movements of the 1960s had an intellectual as well as an institutional dimension; indeed, it highlighted the connection between those dimensions by revealing the ways in which privileged forms of knowledge were bound up with structures of power. This is one of the key insights of the cultural moment known as postmodernism (see Close-Up 6.1), which brought about what one theorist described as a "crisis of legitimation" (Lyotard): once the most fundamental beliefs of Western culture are shown to be the product not of timeless truth but of particular social arrangements, they and the structures of authority that uphold them crumble, taking with them the possibility of *any* universal, objective truth.

Feminism and Cultural Studies

Feminism played a particularly significant role in challenging the prevailing social order. It also helped to redefine the new discipline of cultural studies. In 1978, the Women's Study Group at the Birmingham Centre for Contemporary Cultural Studies published a collection of essays called *Women Take Issue*. In it, they challenged the strongly masculine bias that had characterized the field of cultural studies from the time of the "forefathers" Hoggart, Williams, and Thompson. They pointed out that Williams' account of popular culture as a "whole way of life" did not acknowledge tensions between dominant and subordinate cultures. In particular, it completely ignored the one sphere of life that women inhabited most fully, if not necessarily by choice: the sphere of home and family.

Beginning with the Women's Study Group, a succession of feminist critics throughout the 1970s and 1980s radically challenged the **mythologies** that had unconsciously underpinned the study of culture at the Birmingham Centre and elsewhere. In particular, they noted that the categories through which cultural theorists looked at life in capitalist society—"production/consumption; work/leisure; work/personal life; work/everyday life"—represented a split "which operates for *men* but which is dependent on women's patriarchal subordination—their confinement to family, home, personal and everyday life" (Winship 136–137). One of the biggest myths of cultural studies, they pointed out, was its assumption of a **binary opposition** between production and consumption, in which production was essentially seen as *good*, associated with masculine strength and creative energy, and consumption as *bad*, associated with feminine weakness and passive self-indulgence (for further discussion of the relationship between production and consumption, see Chapters 4 and 5). In a cultural context in which women were largely barred from the work force (housework and child care didn't count as work), their roles couldn't be comfortably accommodated within the categories of production and consumption; in fact, in addition to their work as (re)producers and consumers, women had also traditionally functioned as commodities, or objects of exchange. In order to speak to the experiences of women as well as men, the new field of cultural studies needed to be significantly reconfigured to take account of these conflicted identities and relationships.

Even though cultural studies might have seemed in some ways hostile, or at least indifferent, to women's experience, in other ways it offered an ideal arena for discussing issues of concern to women. Four key aspects of cultural studies fit particularly well with the principles of feminist criticism: an insistence on the relationship between culture and economics, a concern with the importance of ideology in shaping consciousness, and a rejection of a firm line between the political and the personal—or, in the case of academic work, between objective knowledge and subjective experience. Finally, the determination of cultural studies scholars to investigate not just high or capital-C Culture, but also those practices and texts that lurked in its shadows—mass media, subcultures, the practices of everyday life—echoed feminists' commitment to making visible the unacknowledged cultural lives of women. In cultural studies, Sue Thornham suggests, the primarily *political* movement of feminism found a theoretical vocabulary as well as an "academic and institutional context" that, for all its limitations, provided a place where "feminist research could explore all the complexities of women's positioning in culture" (8).

Culture Wars

The somewhat grandiose term "**culture wars**" refers to fights that took place in humanities departments of American universities in the 1980s—fights that spilled over into the arenas of media and public policy—between a traditional idea of Culture and the forces of **postcolonialism**, feminism, and postmodernism that sought to undermine it. While the move was sometimes characterized as a campaign to simply replace the Western canon—the preserve of Dead White Males—with a new and eclectic selection of texts, from works by women of colour to Hollywood films, what was actually at issue was not so much the works themselves but the structures of authority that sanctioned some forms of culture while dismissing others.

One important challenge to those structures was a shift in emphasis from "Culture" to "cultures"—a rhetorical shift that expressed more substantial changes in focus. First, and most generally, it marked a move away from the humanities/literary critical definition of culture toward a more anthropological one. This entailed both an extension of the term from its traditional focus on works of art to embrace the practices of everyday life and a recognition of the existence of multiple cultures, existing within and between societies. The idea of culture was thus transformed from something timeless and universal to a historically determined, and thus constantly changing, phenomenon with local and global dimensions. The myth of a unified *English* culture, which frequently lurked behind the "universal" label, disintegrated in the face of the recognition of the many *sub*cultures—youth culture, for example, or gay culture—on whose exclusion it was based. At the same time, the invisible lines of race (white) and gender (male) that marked traditional definitions of culture—including the more inclusivist, working-class definitions proposed by Williams and Hoggart—began to emerge through the pointed critiques of women and **minorities**, who had been stuck somewhere on its margins.

The opening-out of the idea of culture in response to the claims of its excluded others occurred in conjunction with the arrival in Britain and North America of successive waves of immigrants from the former colonies, including many who ended up working and studying in universities. Some, like the Jamaican-born Stuart Hall, who succeeded Richard Hoggart as director of the Birmingham Centre for Contemporary Cultural Studies, helped to define new directions in cultural studies by, among other things, insisting on its global dimensions, and on the necessary connectedness between intellectual work and politics.

Who won the culture wars, then? The persistence of English undergraduate programs that still require majors to take a course in Shakespeare suggests that the ideological magic of "Culture" has not entirely been exorcised. However, the enormous growth in cultural studies programs would seem to suggest that history is on the side of the culture critics. This might look like a victory for feminism and postcolonialism against conservatism—but, as should be clear by now, the relationship between culture and power is never that simple.

CULTURE AND ECONOMICS—THE POSTINDUSTRIAL REVOLUTION

As in the late eighteenth and nineteenth centuries, the social and political upheavals that marked the late twentieth century were accompanied by economic and technological changes. The growth in communications technology, and the development of a "post-industrial" economy—characterized by trade liberalization and more flexible structures of production and distribution, along with the increasing commercialization of communications itself through the entertainment and information technology industries—has made culture today a very different thing than it was a hundred or even thirty years ago. Just as industrialization brought about not just huge gains in economic productivity but also new kinds of social mobility, the new economy played a large part in facilitating the global cultural movements discussed above. As with the industrial revolution, the weakening of old regulations in conjunction with the decline in traditional structures of authority created new freedoms. However, they also eroded structures that had served to nurture and not just to suppress the development of diverse forms of popular culture.

The extension and intensification of market forces granted greater powers to private interests, but weakened the imaginary and actual power of public institutions. The university, one of the key sites for the distribution of what Pierre Bourdieu calls *cultural capital*, is affected particularly strongly by these shifts, in terms of the way its resources are allocated, as well as the role it is seen to play in society. While that role was traditionally conceived as one of nurturing future citizens—a goal facilitated by ensuring students had a solid grounding in the humanities, English (or American) literature in particular— the idea of university is now more likely to conform to the much less romantic vision of a factory for the production of workers in the global knowledge economy. Students, according to this model, are seen not as junior members of an academic community to which they are bound by an **idealized** commitment to learning or becoming "cultured," but as consumers—and, ultimately, products—to be bought up by the corporations that play an increasing role in funding, and thereby shaping, the universities' basic operations.

According to the essentially commercial logic of this model of education, resources cannot be wasted on those departments or faculties that are concerned with abstract values such as citizenship or critical thought. These departments—English, for example, or philosophy—are forced to rationalize their budgets, and to modify their course offerings to favour those that can be taught by a few faculty members to large numbers of students from a variety of different disciplines. Here, then, is one institutional explanation for why courses in popular culture are quietly popping up alongside (and sometimes in place of) more traditional courses in subjects such as, say, medieval history: they're popular in the same commercial sense that *CSI: Miami* is popular, which is to say they are profitable.

This poses a challenge for cultural studies scholars, whose aim, as we have suggested throughout this book, is not simply to affirm the value of commercial culture, nor—equally simply—to denounce it, but to map its place within a constellation of signifying practices that correspond to underlying relations of power. That constellation is constantly shifting, which means that we need to remain constantly alert to the social and political significance of *all* our cultural roles, including the roles of students and teachers of popular culture. Why—personally, institutionally—are we doing what we are doing? What other subjects *might* we be studying if we were not studying popular culture? What are the educational implications of the growing popularity of popular culture courses?

WHY THIS? WHY NOW? WHY ME? A COUPLE OF FINAL ARGUMENTS FOR THE IMPORTANCE OF STUDYING POPULAR CULTURE

To sum up the last few sections: There are lots of reasons why you are reading a textbook on popular culture instead of Chaucer's *Canterbury Tales*. First and foremost are the political and social changes that, over the course of the last century, have demanded a radical rethinking of the intellectual foundations of "culture" and its connection to other areas of life. These changes have shaped society in general and education in particular. On a more pragmatic level, schools, colleges, and universities have changed their curricula in response to economic pressures so that what is considered valuable in educational terms is increasingly determined by what is profitable. Those are large, impersonal, and, in the latter case, cynical reasons for why popular culture is suddenly a popular thing to study.

We would also encourage you to think about it in more personal terms. One compelling reason to study popular culture is that it is everywhere. To borrow an expression from T.S. Eliot, if most academic study is about helping to make the strange familiar, studying popular culture is a process of making the familiar strange. This can be a pretty uncomfortable experience, since it involves taking what feels most natural and pleasurable and subjecting it to detached inquiry. Actually *studying* popular culture helps us to move beyond a range of typical reactions to it: (a) unconscious consumption (which is only a theoretical position, since most consumers have achieved some level of critical consciousness); (b) contemptuous dismissal—"popular culture is trash, so I avoid it" (an equally mythical position, since it is virtually impossible to live entirely outside commercial culture); and (c) cynical consumption ("I *know* this is garbage, but I like it anyway"—or, stranger, "I like this *because* I know it is garbage"). Most of us probably respond to culture in a way that is something like position c. A variation on this position is the belief that, while other people are vulnerable to the messages of popular culture, *we* are smart enough to see through its manipulations.

While it might seem to make this position appear even more valid, studying popular culture usually leads to a different conclusion, revealing the culture industry to be both less and more powerful than we initially imagined. Cultural studies unmasks and to a certain extent disables the power of commercial culture by helping us to recognize the narratives, genres, myths, and discourses through which its meanings are encoded—meanings that tap into fundamental beliefs about ourselves, our relationships with others, and society at large.

But, as cultural studies also emphasizes, culture is not just about texts, about how the products of the commercial media are put together, and how certain meanings are produced, but also about how we consume those products, what we actually *do* with them. The title of this book, *Popular Culture: A User's Guide*, reflects our belief that not only is it possible for all of us to learn to *use* popular culture more effectively, in the sense of actually shaping it in productive ways, but also that it is vitally important we do so. As Stuart Hall puts it, "there is something *at stake* in Cultural Studies, in a way that I think, and hope, is not exactly true of many other very important intellectual and critical practices" (S. Hall "Cultural Studies and Its Theoretical Legacies" 278).

Many cultural studies practitioners go further, stressing a key connection between doing cultural studies and engaging in political activism—as distinct from other kinds of study, which stress mere "technocratic competence" (Freccero 5). The study of popular culture is necessarily political, in the sense of being concerned with the distribution of social and economic power in society. It's important to recognize, however—in spite of the prescriptivist tone of what we've just said about why you *should* want to do cultural studies—that each of us approaches the study of culture in different ways, and that students and teachers of popular culture are often situated quite differently in relation to the subject, based on factors such as age, class, experience, and temperament. For students, what often proves most illuminating (or, for some, simply irritating) about taking a course in cultural studies is its revelation of the connection between popular culture and power. For teachers, one of the insights that proves most strangely elusive—one that they often need to be reminded of by students—is that popular culture is about pleasure. Figuring out what happens at the intersection of those forces of power and pleasure is perhaps the principal value of studying popular culture.

As this is a particularly busy intersection, we find it helpful to access it through a few relatively straightforward paths or angles of approach. On the broadest level, these angles might be identified as *representation*, the process of making meaning from sign-systems that encompasses anything from words and images to physical structures (cars, buildings, cities) to fashion accessories; *production*, which encompasses the individual and corporate entities involved in the creation and distribution of cultural products, including the technologies through which they are produced and reproduced; and *consumption*, which involves the economic, technological, and physical processes by which different audiences derive meaning from cultural products.

Of course these categories—the subjects of Chapters 3, 4, and 5, respectively—can't help but bleed into one another. The texts and practices of culture are inseparable from the means of technological production or from what individual audiences do with them—nor can they be separated from non-cultural realms of existence such as economics and politics. Lest popular culture begin to sound like everything (or nothing), let's try to pin it down more firmly by returning to our original example of drinking coffee. An examination of this practice through the lenses of representation, production, and consumption can help us to understand how popular culture operates, drawing us in as producers and consumers and working, literally, to reshape the world.

COFFEE AS POPULAR CULTURE

Coffee is a part of culture to the extent that we can ask "What does coffee *mean*?" Coffee is not, in other words, just "a liquid brown drug" (Cohen 10), but part of a complex set of social rituals. The significance of coffee is hugely determined by context: its meaning shifts depending on whether we are drinking it at home or in a café, from a mug or a Styrofoam cup. Its significance also varies depending on whether we are alone or with friends and on what other activities we are engaged in: a social meeting, for example, or a late-night cramming session—in which case it might really be coffee's status as a "liquid brown drug" that we are seeking.

But even then, when the physical properties of coffee are arguably more important than its symbolic properties, it is *still* more than just a drug. After all, if it were just a stimulant we were after, there are obviously other, more powerful options out there. The fact that most of us are probably inclined to reach for coffee rather than, say, amphetamines speaks to more than the question of availability or a fear of being arrested for drug possession. In fact these questions (why is caffeine legal while amphetamines are controlled and pot is illegal?) are themselves tied up in the culture of coffee—what it means in a broader social context. To answer them, along with the broader question of how coffee comes to be part of culture, we need to look at coffee in the context of representation, production, and consumption.

The Representation of Coffee

To say that coffee "signifies"—that it refers to something other than its literal, physical substance—is not to say that it has some kind of intrinsic or inherent meaning. Rather, coffee acquires different, specific meanings as it is incorporated within different economic and social practices. It therefore makes sense to ask not just *what* does coffee mean, but also "*how* does it acquire meaning, and under what circumstances?"

For both Tim Hortons and Starbucks, décor is key to producing a corporate image suggestive of a particular lifestyle.

To talk about the meaning of coffee is to talk about how it operates in systems of *representation*, which translate a world of objects into one of sense, significance, and values. So, what kind of significance or value is attached to coffee?

Suggested Activity 1.3

Take a few minutes and write down some of the meanings attached to coffee in your life. What kinds of associations does it have and how do these change depending on context? Strangely, this may be easier to do if you're *not* a coffee drinker: it's easier to critically analyze a cultural practice if you're detached from it.

Something that tends to become quickly obvious when we start to come up with associations is that even something as simple as coffee signifies in multiple and different ways: for example, we might associate it with both relaxation and stimulation, both familiarity and sophistication, both social engagement and solitude. These radically different associations suggest firstly that meaning is to some extent arbitrary: there's no natural or logical meaning, only context-specific ones. It suggests secondly that meaning is qualitative or subjective, rather than objective: cultural associations fit into the category of *values* rather than *facts*. Moreover, these associations make sense only in implicit relation to a whole network of other associations to which they're connected, or from which they differ: coffee's capacity to stimulate, relax, or comfort in particular social situations derives in part from its *difference from* other liquid forms of stimulation or relaxation—beer, say, or milk—and in part through its *association with* other objects or practices—drinking containers, food, chairs, people, conversation, work, and so on. Put together, this collection of arbitrary, qualitative associations comprises what we can call a mythology of coffee: a widely understood if mostly unconscious network of meanings or narratives through which a specific culture makes sense of the world.

The Mythology of Drugs We discuss the significance of mythology in more detail in Chapter 3. A key aspect to think about for now is the ways in which cultural mythologies tap into the underlying social structures of a culture, including its relations of power. To understand how this works, we can think for a moment about the cultural or *mythological* difference between coffee and some of the other drugs we cited above. Coffee, alcohol, and marijuana are all drugs (i.e., they all have mind- or body-altering properties), but they *signify* differently. The most obvious significance concerns their legality: as legal substances, coffee and alcohol fall symbolically within the realm of things our culture accepts and condones as part of social life. Marijuana (currently) does not. This different status, as cannabis activists along with many health professionals point out, is not justifiable on the basis of each drug's physical properties: marijuana is not, in other words, inherently more harmful than beer; rather, its status is determined within broader political and social structures (see Figure 1.1).

Of course, part of the mythology associated with different drugs *is* influenced by their physiological properties: the fact that caffeine is a stimulant—conducive, at least in theory, to productivity—while alcohol and marijuana are more conducive to relaxation explains in part why coffee is tolerated in most workplaces while booze and pot (even the names connote sin!) are not. While the different physiological states induced by these different drugs, and even their social effects, might be indisputable, what is less easily explained is why our society places a higher value on productivity and stimulation than on relaxation. Thinking about this question puts us in the realm not of nutrition or health, but of culture and representation.

Figure 1.1 Effects of Caffeine and Marijuana

| Normal | Caffeine | Marijuana |

When researchers in the U.S. experimented with giving drugs to spiders, they found that caffeine had a more severe effect than marijuana, resulting in much more sparse, haphazard webs.

The Production of Coffee

Clearly, the mythologies surrounding coffee, alcohol, and marijuana—mythologies that influence, as they are influenced by, their legal status—do not exist in a vacuum. Rather, they are generated out of real, material processes: social, political, and economic. This becomes clear when we think about the differences in how coffee operates symbolically (i.e., what it represents) in the cultures of the North, where coffee is consumed in such large volumes, in comparison to the cultures of the South, where it is produced.

In North America, coffee is entangled in the lifestyle of postindustrial society: it is fuel, pleasure, instant gratification, relaxation. In many parts of the South, coffee is an equally integral part of life, associated not (or not only) with pleasure, but more substantially with labour and the basic conditions of life. Those social rituals that *do* exist in the South surrounding coffee are shaped by an awareness of its economic as well as its cultural significance. For example, among some coffee-growing cultures in Tanzania, coffee has an almost religious significance, associated with the *amagdala,* or the "life force" of the coffee grower, such that the death of a coffee tree was traditionally taken as an omen of its owner's death (Hyden, qtd. in Weiss 96).

The History of Coffee in Western Culture   In the North, by contrast, coffee's role in the global economy is something that most of us, unless we're involved in the stock market or even more directly in coffee sales, are only dimly aware of. And yet its popular cultural significance is profoundly shaped by the history of its production, in conjunction with European colonialism in the seventeenth century as well as with more contemporary processes of **globalization** (see Chapter 10). A brief discussion of this history helps to illuminate some of the ways that coffee signifies today.

The story of coffee's arrival in the West from the Middle East in the seventeenth century is part of the history of European colonialism. The importation of coffee was part of the much bigger process by which European nations sought to fuel their economies by finding new resources to develop, satisfying and promoting the desires of European consumers, and creating new markets for European manufactured goods. Coffee entered European popular culture via the eighteenth-century institution of the coffeehouse, a new meeting place described by one historian as "*the* site for the public life of the eighteenth-century middle class, a place where the bourgeoisie developed new forms of commerce and culture" (Schivelbusch 49–51). Patronized mostly by commercial agents such as merchants and insurance brokers, coffeehouses were places for both socialization and the transaction of business. Both functions came together in the establishment of a connection between coffeehouses and newspapers. Coffeehouses such as the famous Lloyd's of London, established at the end of the seventeenth century (now more familiar as the financial institution it eventually became), often became centres of journalism, thus linking cornerstones of eighteenth-century public life—industry and print capitalism.

Coffeehouses became sites for the development of capitalist society in more direct ways, as Brad Weiss points out, through the drinking of coffee itself. As both a consumer good and a drink that promoted sobriety, coffee could be enlisted in the encouragement of good middle-class values—values such as "clear-headed rationality, alertness and restraint"—values not associated with the "rude" pleasures of ale. In short, coffee, "through the short, sudden burst of energy and concentration it supplies . . . is the original therapy for the micro-management of bourgeois personality" (Weiss 101). Coffee was thus enlisted in the reconstruction of the working day associated with the industrial revolution (see Chapter 2), as "coffee breaks" became a means of both marking and *making* time that is now routine in labour practices. Coffee fulfills nicely the goal of defining a break from work that is taken in order to make work more effective—a direct conversion of leisure into productivity.

Coffee and Colonialism   If it is no exaggeration to say that coffee contributed to the growth of European and North American economies over the last two hundred years, it can also be connected to the *under*development of many Southern nations. While colonialism has now formally ended (in most places, in the middle of the twentieth century), trade regulations preferential to the economies of dominant nations force developing countries to adopt agricultural practices that consign them to continued poverty. Coffee is a good example of a cash crop whose growth is encouraged in places like Central America to satisfy North American consumers. Coffee has replaced the traditional crops that once allowed the region to feed its own people, forcing them instead to import food produced and/or processed elsewhere and, in many cases, causing severe environmental degradation. While growing coffee once offered a relatively decent living to many farmers, its falling price on the world market due to overproduction means that farmers in places like Haiti are struggling to survive.

The effects of fluctuating coffee prices, so critical for producers, are barely felt at the retail end. A 2004 report states that

> for every pound of coffee that sells in the U.S. for between US$2.69–8.49 (depending on quality) a Guatemalan farmer receives less than 35 cents and the coffee picker less than 14 cents. Put another way, an entire crop of Guatemalan coffee earned one producer US$8,500 which sold (notionally) for three quarters of a million dollars retail in the U.S. (Simons 85–86)

The principal reason for the growing discrepancy between the wealth of primary producers and retailers is the growing concentration of power in the coffee industry, which is now dominated by just four companies—Nestlé, Kraft (owned by tobacco company Philip Morris, which has been newly rechristened as Altira Group, Inc.), Sara Lee, and Procter & Gamble—who are able to exercise disproportionate control over the wages received by growers and the prices paid by consumers.

These economic circumstances, which have a big impact on the day-to-day existence of coffee farmers, are remote from the experience, or at least the consciousness, of the average North American coffee drinker. While we might feel a momentary twinge as we fork over the price of a sandwich or a beer for a Styrofoam cup full of burnt beans and water, our unease is quickly forgotten as we sink into the comfy chairs of our favourite coffee bar, dimly but pleasantly aware of the hum of activity around us as we enjoy moments—or hours—of leisure away from the demands of work, home, or school. That enjoyment might be diminished by a too-acute awareness of the economic context in which we are drinking our coffee: part of the magic of the experience of consumption—a magic that is invoked, with variations, whether we are trying on a new dress, drinking a steaming latte, or driving a new car—is its ability to bury the crude facts of the economic transaction we have engaged in beneath the mythology surrounding the item we have just bought.

The Consumption of Coffee

We use the term "magic" deliberately to describe the experience of consumption. Karl Marx employed the phrase *commodity fetishism* to describe what happens under a capitalist system in which material objects are bought and sold: commodities come to stand in for relationships between people as symbols of meaning and value, while people and social relationships themselves become objectified (they are turned symbolically into objects). A "fetish" in premodern culture is an object that is believed to have magical powers or that excites erotic feeling. Commodity fetishism, then, is literally the attribution of a magical or sexual power to a commodity, assigning it a value that has no logical connection either to the human labour that produced it or to the usefulness of the object itself, but that is derived from the abstract system of exchange which determines that such-and-such an object is worth so-many dollars.

Commodities don't acquire these "magical" properties by accident, of course; rather, they are generated by sophisticated marketing campaigns that tap into prevailing social mythologies. In fact, in a commerce-driven society, the language of marketing increasingly works to *shape* mythologies, thereby defining and creating new values and desires as much as it tries to appeal to already existing ones.

We can get a sense of how this process works by looking very briefly at the mythologies evoked by two different coffee chains: Starbucks and Tim Hortons. Each works through systems of *representation* that conceal relations of economic *production* in order to enhance the consumer experience. The significant differences between the "magic" of Starbucks and Tim Hortons reflect a contemporary consumer culture that differs from earlier forms of mass culture in the way it draws on, and indeed seeks to promote, individualized **identities** (see Chapters 6 and 7) defined largely by lifestyle. The concept of lifestyle, discussed in more detail in Chapter 4, is most easily associated with Starbucks, which indeed deserves some credit for promoting it. The secret of lifestyle marketing is in the way the product falls into the background of a mythology, a mythology centred on the consumer's attitudes and practices and the identities they imply. While the attitudes or practices may have ethical or **aesthetic** overtones—for example, concern about the environment, a love of art—the overriding premise is one of individualism, expressed through consumer choice.

Starbucks For a company like Starbucks, the mythological value of individualism is paramount, and it is represented not just through the diversity of blends available, but also through the careful structuring of the whole consumer experience. While it's difficult to generalize across outlets, some of the signal features of Starbucks outlets are dim, natural-looking (as opposed to fluorescent) lighting; moveable furniture, often mismatched but clearly designed with an eye not just to comfort or utility but also to style; serve-yourself cream, milk, sugar, and so on; and an aura of creativity, whether signalled by the presence of large murals featuring art or poetry or by individual paintings available for sale. The presence of other sale or display items—designer mugs, dishes, even books or CDs—emphasizes that the Starbucks experience is not about just having a cup of coffee but an act of self-expression, entry into a privileged and sophisticated world.

Launched in Seattle in 1987, Starbucks is now a truly global corporation—global in terms of its expansion throughout Western Europe and the Asian Pacific, but also in terms of the image it projects of the urbane, cosmopolitan consumer. Located mostly in large cities, in areas patronized mainly by middle- and upper-class, educated consumers (e.g., Starbucks outlets are often near, if not affiliated with, university campuses), Starbucks aligns itself with the values of style, mobility, and progressive thinking. These values emerge all the more strikingly when we compare Starbucks with Tim Hortons, a chain started in Hamilton, Ontario, in 1964 and named after the late hockey player who founded it.

Tim Hortons   If the "magic" of Starbucks is associated with globalization and progress, Tim Hortons is strongly nationalist in its flavour even though it was bought by the U.S. chain Wendy's in 1995 and spun off to shareholders in 2006. (In fact, *Globe and Mail* reporter John Stackhouse titled his 2003 account of hitchhiking across Canada *Timbit Nation*, signalling the centrality of Tim Hortons to the Canadian experience.) This mythology is intensified by a long association between Tim Hortons and the Canadian Armed Forces, an association emphasized in marketing campaigns such as the 1999 television ad featuring Canadian soldiers on a ship somewhere in the Persian Gulf, gratefully receiving a massive shipment of Tim Hortons coffee. In contrast to the foreign, slightly scary location of the Middle East (signalled in the ad by jerky camera footage of a chaotic market scene, accompanied by vaguely Arabian sounding music) Tim Hortons is a piece of home, something which presumably (like the Canadian military) "you can always count on." The soldiers in the ad are almost all men, and the servers who appear briefly to pay tribute to "our boys" overseas are all women, dressed in the familiar brown of the Tim Hortons uniform.

The world represented in the Tim Hortons ad is strikingly different from the ambience of Starbucks, evoking traditional values of the nation defended by a strong military, traditional gender roles, and clear boundaries between the familiar and comfortable and the foreign. This atmosphere is replicated in Tim Hortons restaurants, in which the comfortably padded but immovable benches, functional (and easy to clean) Formica tables, and fluorescent lighting convey an atmosphere of order and uniformity. The institutional flavour of the décor is softened somewhat by the service dynamic, in which the largely female staff deliver your coffee just the way you want it (at least within the parameters of "black," "regular," or "double-double"). Though the chain has expanded its selection of both food and beverages in recent years, the emphasis here is not on choice, and certainly

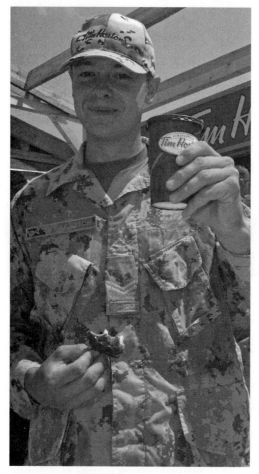

The image of Tim Hortons as an emblem of Canada persists in media coverage of its arrival on a military base in Kandahar, Afghanistan, in July 2006, in response to intense lobbying by troops.

not on style, so much as on comfort, embodied in the familiar combination of coffee and doughnuts. In fact, the mythology of Tim Hortons is arguably defined in obvious, even self-conscious, opposition to the snazzy ambience of Starbucks, revelling in its preservation of old-fashioned, working-class family values against the tide of globalization, speed, and the blurring of traditional identities.

Of course *both* of these mythologies are constructions—imaginary replications of the world rather than accurate reflections of it. Nevertheless, they *work*, through the dynamics of consumption—a dynamic increasingly central to the formation of popular culture—not just to sell coffee or doughnuts but also to create compelling pictures of everyday life and of human relationships that are increasingly indistinguishable from "the real thing." What's interesting about our comparison of Tim Hortons and Starbucks is not as much their differences as the similarities that are concealed beneath those differences: both are large **multinational** corporations that capitalize on cheap labour and resource costs in the South to generate significant profits in the North; both derive the bulk of their profits by selling coffee and sugary baked goods—products that might not do a lot for anyone's health, but which are staples in a traditional North American diet; and both are major parts of the popular cultural landscape.

SUMMARY: AND IT ALL BOILS DOWN TO . . . WHAT *IS* IN A CUP OF COFFEE?

Using coffee as an example, we might come up with a fairly depressing reading of popular culture. Dominated by practices of consumption, much of our experience of popular culture is tangled up in relations of economic exploitation—relations that are concealed by the mythologies and ideologies of capitalism, to which we are helpless, caffeine-addicted victims. Of course this is a partial picture, and one that is contradicted by the practice of coffee drinking itself.

While there is no escaping the consumerist aspect of coffee drinking, this practice—more, perhaps, than many other aspects of commercial culture—highlights the possibilities for different kinds of consumption. For example, at a time when people are increasingly diverted by home entertainment, cafés can, at least in theory, serve as public spaces for the promotion of community, much as they did in the eighteenth century. It's easy to exaggerate this function: with its comfy chairs, free newspapers, and generally artsy aura, the image of the contemporary coffeehouse is as much a product of slick marketing as genuine community. However, it *is* possible to recall some of the positive aspects of public culture in private space, not by "seeing through" the lifestyle concept of places like Starbucks, but by taking it at its word. In other words, it's possible to sit in a Starbucks reading for hours with an empty cup in front of you, and the culture of the café (a culture Starbucks itself has actively nurtured) is such that no one's likely to ask you to leave. "Going for a coffee" need not mean actually going for a coffee—a concept places like Starbucks have successfully promoted, sometimes at the cost of their own profits.

Coffee's evolution into a highly charged commodity brings it within the realm of popular **discourse**, thus creating new channels of meaning and knowledge and new forms of "anti-consumerist" consumerism. The success in recent years of the Fair Trade Federation and other cooperative ventures that seek to preserve the natural environment while ensuring that coffee producers receive a fair price for their products has been motivated by activists in conjunction with consumers themselves. The overwhelming commercial power of corporations such as Starbucks, while contributing to some extent to the growing gaps in wealth that characterize the coffee industry, has also shed a strong and sometimes harsh light on the industry, forcing it to change in productive ways. The excessive (and, some argued, unfair) focus on Starbucks as the target of protests at the 1999 World Trade Organization meeting in Seattle spoke less to the corporate sins of Starbucks per se than to its *representative* status as a model of globalization.

Mythology, then, works not just to contain, but also to spark and activate new forms of resistance, not all of which are constrained by the harness of corporate culture. Popular culture isn't just would-be poets sipping mocha lattes or commuters grabbing a box of Timbits at the drive-through; it's also the bricks through the window at Starbucks and Niketown, the creators of ads raising consumer awareness about the "real" price of coffee, and the bunches of guys who happily imbibe the "lifestyle" of the café, sitting around in animated conversation for hours without actually buying anything. The relationship between these different faces of popular culture is part of what this book will examine.

Our study of popular culture occurs at a historical moment in which there is no human activity that is free from capitalism, commodification, and the profit motive. No space in people's everyday life remains outside these economic processes. This is most apparent in the case of culture and communication, which have become totally commercialized. By the same token, culture and communication have come to dominate the economy, with the result that, as Fredric Jameson observes, "no society has ever been saturated with signs and messages like this one" (Grossberg et al. 53).

Many contemporary cultural critics see this shift as a wholly depressing situation, representing the end of collective culture and its replacement with a society of atomized individuals who are consumed by the drive toward self-gratification at the same time as they are entirely colonized by consumerist ideology. They despair over what they see as the erosion of people's ability to think critically, to produce and create things for themselves in a context where everything is supplied for them, subject to their ability to pay for it. A less bleak view, and one that we share, is that while commercial culture's grand promise to provide fulfillment and liberate individual and social potential is essentially an empty one, there are, within its intricate networks of power, all kinds of opportunities for creativity and even resistance. Through a series of concrete examples, the remainder of this book develops an idea of popular culture as a process defined by the often contradictory but sometimes collaborative interests of private and public interest, of commerce and creativity, of capitalism and community. Its ultimate goal is to provide tools that will help you to think about your own place in this compelling and sometimes invisible matrix of possibilities.

SUGGESTIONS FOR FURTHER READING

During, Simon. *The Cultural Studies Reader.* London: Routledge, 1999.

Edgar, Andrew, and Peter Sedgwick, eds. *Key Concepts in Cultural Theory.* London: Routledge, 1999.

Fiske, John. *Understanding Popular Culture.* London: Routledge, 1989.

Grossberg, Lawrence, Cary Nelson, and Paula Treichler. *Cultural Studies.* London: Routledge, 1992.

Jenkins, Henry, Tara McPherson, and Jane Shattuc, eds. *Hop on Pop: The Politics and Pleasures of Popular Culture.* Durham, NC: Duke University Press, 2003.

Miller, Toby. *A Companion to Cultural Studies.* Oxford: Blackwell, 2006.

Mookerjea, Sourayan, Imre Szeman and Gail Faurschou, eds. *Canadian Cultural Studies: A Reader.* Durham, NC: Duke University Press, 2009.

Naremore, James, and Patrick Brantlinger, eds. *Modernity and Mass Culture.* Bloomington, IN: Indiana University Press, 1991.

O'Sullivan, Tim, John Hartley, Danny Saunders, Martin Montgomery, and John Fiske. *Key Concepts in Communication and Cultural Studies.* London: Routledge, 1994.

Storey, John, ed. *Cultural Theory and Popular Culture: A Reader.* Athens, GA: University of Georgia Press, 2006.

Thornham, Sue. *Feminist Theory and Cultural Studies: Stories of Unsettled Relations.* London: Arnold, 2000.

Chapter 2

The History of Popular Culture

INTRODUCTION: TAKING IT FROM THE STREETS

On January 7, 2002, a Hamilton, Ontario, man and his 10-year-old son appeared in court to defend themselves against charges of playing touch football and hockey on the street. Responding to the complaints of a neighbour who had become tired of retrieving balls from her garden, police charged the father with violating a municipal bylaw banning the playing of games on city streets. The case became a *cause célèbre* across Canada, as hockey fans and defenders of the right to play in public places called in to radio talk shows and wrote letters to the editor expressing their outrage. The neighbour had a different perspective, maintaining, "It is not about hockey, it is about property rights. It's about trampling my family's garden" ("Fighting"). The case was eventually thrown out because the judge determined that the Crown couldn't prove its case that the man and his son had been playing a game on city property. City councillors promised to look into revising the bylaw.

This case relates to our study of popular culture in a number of ways: first, it's about an aspect of popular culture—informal recreation—that tends to get ignored in favour of an emphasis on the commercial products of mass media; second, it features sport, whose relationship to "culture" of any kind is often questioned; finally, it concerns the critical issue of public space: Who gets to use it and how? How are rights concerning the recreational use of public space balanced against laws protecting private property? These questions and issues lie at the heart of contemporary popular culture. They are, in a sense, what makes it distinct from earlier cultural forms.

We begin this chapter with the story about road hockey as a way of entering an exploration of how popular culture evolved into the form we recognize today. Beginning with

Recalling traditional "grassroots" forms of recreation, a game like street hockey exists in complicated relationship with contemporary commercial sport.

a look at traditional (pre-1830) recreation, we trace some of the broad cultural changes that led to a rupture between communal enjoyments, such as "street" games, and commercial entertainment. We also look at the development of the institution of "culture" as a refined and exclusive preserve, remote from the "low," physical entertainment of the streets. And finally, in relation to the previous two developments, we look at the struggles that, beginning in the early nineteenth century, determined the shape of popular culture—struggles over work and leisure, over the emerging class structure, and over public space.

Among the questions we will be asking in this chapter are: How is contemporary popular culture different from what came before? What factors—economic, social, and political—contributed to the development of popular culture as we know it today? How is the development of popular culture tied to the broader history of the disappearance of public space? How are relationships of power, particularly class and gender, mediated through culture? Returning at the end of the chapter to the example of street hockey, we suggest that while the answers to these questions may have changed over time, the issues they touch on remain critical to an understanding of popular culture from the nineteenth century to the present day.

MAKING THE STREETS SAFE FOR COMMERCE

In 1835, a small item was added to the English Highways Act, imposing a fine of up to 40 shillings for playing "at Football or any other Game on any Part of the said Highways, to the Annoyance of any Passenger" (qtd. in Malcomson). The amendment to the act was part of a bigger movement toward the limitation and management of public space, a movement that had a major impact on the organization and practice of popular culture. As we suggested in Chapter 1, the tension between democratic or popular will and corporate control—the question, in other words, of who owns/produces the space in which we live our lives—continues to be the primary force defining popular culture today. The prohibition of street football reflects a small but significant moment in that conflict.

The reallocation of public space, which was strongly contested at every turn, occurred in conjunction with a whole series of other changes—economic, spatial, and social—that came about during the period from about 1830 to 1900, the period of the industrial revolution. In order to understand the magnitude of those changes, we'll take a brief look at what life looked like before. Much of our discussion in this chapter focuses on the U.K., where the effects of these tumultuous changes were experienced first and most intensely.

POPULAR RECREATION BEFORE 1830

Beginning around 1830 in Britain (though it is hard to pin down an exact date), popular recreation underwent some fairly rapid and dramatic changes from the forms that had existed, with few variations, since the Middle Ages. In a primarily farming economy, recreation was closely tied to work in the form of holidays and festivals associated with particular times in the agricultural calendar, and everyday social interactions that occurred as part of farm labour. Games, dances, and entertainments were largely public, in the sense that anyone could participate, and they took place on lands customarily shared (at least to some extent) by the community as a whole. Together with work, recreation tied the community together through activities whose form and meaning had been established through long tradition. Perhaps the most notable difference from popular culture today is that traditional recreation was mostly homemade, consisting of sports, games, and dancing that required little in the way of organization and equipment. Life in the towns may have involved more diverse and complex entertainment, but in general, urban forms of leisure were not all that different from rural forms, with social activity strongly tied to work and both work and leisure still strongly influenced by the traditions and rhythms of the agricultural economy.

There's a tendency to view this early form of popular culture through the rosy haze of nostalgia, to represent it as somehow purer (since less commercialized) and more wholesome and community-minded than, say, television or video games. It is undeniably true that preindustrial recreation was in many ways more active than contemporary forms of entertainment, in terms of both the creativity and the physical effort demanded of its participants. It also served an important role in maintaining strong community relations, uniting workers of both sexes and all ages.

Harder to romanticize from a contemporary perspective are the brutally violent elements of "blood" sports involving animals, such as bullbaiting and cockfighting, and the high level of social conformity recreation demanded. While holiday practices such as decorating and dancing around the Maypole were condemned by Protestant reformers of the time as incitements to "lasciviousness" and "ribauldrie" (qtd. in Malcomson 9), they ultimately served the conservative cause of courtship. While unsupervised trips to the woods to gather May flowers may have offered lots of opportunities for sexual activity, these did not translate into sexual *freedom*: when these encounters led to pregnancy, as they often did, the outcome was shame for the woman—marriage if she was lucky, but in any case a confirmation of traditional gender roles.

The Bonds of Community

The communal and strongly ritualized form of traditional popular culture reflected a highly stratified society in which leisure, like work, expressed clear distinctions between the ranks of labourers and landowners, with virtually no possibility for social mobility. However, what was in one sense a bigger gulf between socioeconomic categories than exists today was partly bridged by a tradition of patronage, in which the ruling class recognized a duty of care toward those on whose labour they depended. This meant that, among other things, wealthy landowners tolerated and in some cases actively facilitated the recreational activities of their workers (by granting time off, for example, or allowing the use of their land for sports and festivals). This occasional relaxation of social discipline served the landowners as well as the workers, partly because both groups inhabited the same small communities and also because giving workers an outlet for play made it much less likely that they would challenge the ruling class's authority.

In sum, romantic images of entertainment in preindustrial society are in some senses accurate: fun was mostly free, even when closely bound up with the economic activities of the community; it reflected a strong attachment to the natural world, and recreation fostered connections between people. On the negative side, the conservative and traditional nature of recreational activities allowed only occasional ritual challenges to social authority and tended to emphasize social solidarity over individual pleasure or inclination. For example, among the entertainments surrounding courtship, there were no alternatives for men or women who weren't interested in heterosexual coupling. Finally, traditional recreation, with its strong emphasis on blood sports, reflected the hardship and brutality of farm labourers' lives—brutality enacted most violently on animals.

CAPITALISM AND THE INDUSTRIAL REVOLUTION

The industrial revolution brought with it a new culture—new pleasures and identities, but also new kinds of brutality. One of the key preconditions for the development of popular culture in its contemporary form is the economic system of **capitalism**, which, throughout the eighteenth and nineteenth centuries, was dramatically altered and intensified by a series of events that came to be described as the industrial revolution. (For more on the development of capitalism, see Close-Up 1.1 on page 11.) Of the many social and cultural consequences of the industrial revolution, the banning of street football might look pretty trivial. However, this example offers one illustration of the effects of industrialism on the organization of physical space and social relations. We will look at some of these effects in more extensive detail in the section that follows.

Redefining Cultural Spaces

The 1835 ban against football in the streets was one minor event in a succession of restrictions of communal space by state or private interests happening in conjunction with changes associated with the developing capitalist economy. Among the most far-reaching of these changes were the series of Enclosure Acts that converted common grazing land to much smaller, private holdings in order to make the land more economically productive. This practice, which as its name suggests involved enclosing formerly open spaces with fences, affected popular culture in very direct ways by placing physical constraints on certain kinds of activity. It also influenced popular culture more generally, changing the relationship between work and play and reconfiguring people's sense of community.

First and most obviously, enclosure placed an obvious restriction on the kinds of recreation that could take place. No longer was it possible, for example, to engage in the vast games of football that used to take place with unlimited players (and few rules) between villages located up to five kilometres apart. Even more modest recreations, for example, the dances and wrestling matches that tended to be organized around particular times of the agricultural year such as mowing or harvesting, were gradually discontinued as the fields they were once performed or played on were closed off to the public. Beyond the significance of the loss of these specific activities was the severing of a vital link between agricultural work and recreation. As landowners fenced off property with the aim of increasing its economic productivity, a vital connection was lost between the creative realms of work and play. More generally, the reorganization of space that resulted from enclosure changed the way people related to one another. Not only did it accentuate divisions between the landholding and labouring classes, but it also made it harder in general for people to connect with one another, resulting in the fragmentation of traditional forms of community.

Urbanization   In addition to the privatization of mostly rural land represented by enclosure, the process of **urbanization** contributed significantly to the reduction of open spaces available for recreation as land was expropriated for the building of industrial infrastructure. As fields disappeared with no new playgrounds to replace them, it became harder to find places to hold outdoor sports, festivals, and other forms of public gathering. Urbanization also affected the production of popular culture in more indirect ways. One of the most obvious changes people experienced as they moved from the country to the city was a change in their living spaces. For poor working people in particular, life in the city meant coping with crowded and unsanitary conditions. An 1844 newspaper report describes a typical slum in which

> there are whole streets . . . which are neither flagged, paved, sewered, nor drained; where garbage and filth of every description are left on the surface to ferment and rot; where pools of stagnant water are almost constant; where the dwellings adjoining are thus necessarily caused to be of an inferior and even filthy description; thus where disease is engendered, and the health of the whole town perilled. (qtd. in Engels 49–50)

The huge influx of workers to the city meant that housing had to be built quickly and cheaply. At the same time, wealthy industrialists wanted to be spared the sights and smells of crowded working-class slums; thus, factory workers—in their small identical houses, crammed together on tiny lots—lived in more or less segregated neighbourhoods interspersed with upper- and middle-class enclaves.

But the marginalization of the poor wasn't only physical. In the complex middle-class values of the day (values that still hold sway, if you believe the ads for household cleansers), physical dirt corresponded symbolically to spiritual impurity and immorality. As convictions about the inherent character deficiencies of the poor became institutionalized, backed up by new sciences of hygiene and public health, the poor suffered from simultaneous moves to banish them from sight and to subject their behaviour to increasingly vigorous policing. These social constraints, combined with actual space constraints, powerfully reduced people's freedom and mobility.

However, the crowded conditions of working-class slums also fostered new forms of social and political solidarity. Courtyards, which functioned as sort of communal backyards, became gathering places in which people could find some respite from the isolation and loneliness that are the paradoxical byproducts of life in a crowded city. For some, "allotments" (rented gardens) provided space to grow flowers or food and recall, in however modest a way, the pleasure of outdoor life. As cities grew, however, and the demand for space increased, most of these allotments were swallowed up by development. The one other obvious location for outdoor recreation was the street, which had the advantage of more space and light than the courtyards but the disadvantage of the presence of the police, who were charged with putting a stop to recreational activities that threatened to disrupt more "legitimate" commercial activities.

The Pub as Community Space   The lack of public space, combined with the excess of official **surveillance** in what little space there was, contributed to the growth of what became the centre of urban community—the pub. In addition to camaraderie and beer (which, besides being cheap and satisfying, was generally safer than the drinking water), the pub supplied comforts such as heat, light, and toilets that were frequently superior to what people had at home. Indeed, the density of pubs was greatest in the poorest areas (Best 220). Pubs were often associated with particular professions, as shown in names such as "The Weaver's Arms" or "The Sailor's Dickey." In general, however, they can be seen as part of the trend in urbanization toward the separation of places of work and places of recreation.

Along with the class segregation and crowding that characterized urban life, this fragmentation of a formerly more organic existence undermined familiar forms of **identity**, community, and popular recreation. At the same time, it fostered new forms of sociality, as well as new forms of social freedom. The positive flipside of the anonymity that went along with life in the big city was increasing privacy—i.e., if you kissed a stranger in a pub, your Great Aunt Ethel, neighbours, and minister wouldn't necessarily all be there to see it and tell your parents. Moreover, the layout of the city, in which people's homes tended to be some distance from their places of work, commerce, and leisure, helped to create a new kind of mobility, both literal and symbolic. Of course, the expansion of opportunity was often more abstract than actual, particularly for women and the poor, who were prevented by a lack of economic power and an excess of social discipline from enjoying the liberation from custom and greater freedom of movement enabled by life in the city. In general, however, the process of urbanization contributed to the trend of expanding individual freedom that was to shape social life over the course of the nineteenth and twentieth centuries.

Industrialism

The term "industrial revolution," generally used to refer to the period in British history from approximately the mid–eighteenth to the mid–nineteenth century, describes the transition from an agricultural/small-scale commercial society to one based on organized mechanical production. While the term "industry" is often used to refer specifically to factory production as distinct from other kinds of organized work, it is also sometimes used to describe the increasing capitalization, organization, and mechanization of what were formerly thought of as non-industrial kinds of work: farming, for example, or—more significant for our purposes—culture. (We will discuss the implications of this shift in more detail in Chapter 4.) In contrast to the relative stability of earlier modes of production, industrial enterprises require major investments of capital in order to generate growth. They also require a large and disciplined work force, trained in the performance of repetitive, specialized tasks. The industrial revolution thus marked a significant change not only in the *mode* of production—the physical process used to generate the necessities of life—but also in the *relations* of production, or division of labour.

In the preindustrial economy, work was not only closely integrated with other aspects of life; workers also had a strong sense of connectedness to their labour and its products. In preindustrial agriculture, for example, workers were involved in every stage of production, from planting to harvest, and, crucially, they had at least some degree of ownership of the process, including small holdings of land. The same is true now of craftspeople, who own and/or have direct control over their workshops, as well as every aspect of the production of their finished crafts. The critical difference for workers in industrial society is that their labour is detached (or, in Karl Marx's terms, alienated) from the larger process of production: rather than having any direct economic stake in the products of their labour, they receive only a small hourly wage and their activity is focused on one single fragment of the final product.

New Modes of Production   This style of work was a key part of the new production process known as **Fordism** (after Henry Ford, who pioneered it), a form of assembly-line labour that proved to be extremely efficient at churning out products, from cars to household furnishings. However, the factors that contributed to the high quantity and uniform quality of products had a much more negative effect on the human participants in the process. Fordism worked on the principle of *mechanization,* a process that aimed to turn every facet of the economy, including human society itself, into the equivalent of an efficiently run machine. The consequences of this restructuring of labour reverberated far beyond the factory walls. Fordism is now widely understood to refer not just to a particular mode of production but also to a form of social organization based on discipline, uniformity, and atomization ("atomization" describes a social structure defined by separate individuals rather than by a vision of the community as a whole).

The mechanization of society was accompanied by what we might term the "mathematicization" of human life. As historian Eric Hobsbawm puts it, "arithmetic was the fundamental tool of the Industrial Revolution. Its makers saw it as a series of sums of addition and subtraction: the difference in cost between buying in the cheapest market and selling in the dearest, between cost of production and sale price, between investment and return" (*Industry* 61). As with the mechanical innovations of Fordism, the mathematic precision of the new economy extended to social relations as a whole, with relationships between employer and employee, individual and community, increasingly determined less by custom or the incalculable interactions of character and circumstance than by relations of money, or what is often called the "cash nexus."

The ideal of an economy in which human labour is enmeshed obediently and productively with machines is not so easily accomplished in reality. In order to ensure a compliant work force, employers and legislators collaborated in the drafting of a series of new regulations and other disciplinary innovations, both in and outside the workplace, to ensure worker obedience. Perhaps the most effective form of regulation was the extremely low wages workers were paid, which meant that they had to work long hours just to earn enough to feed themselves. Workplace discipline was reinforced by such technological innovations as the punch clock, which secured the cooperation of workers in policing their own attendance at work. In instituting such forms of on-the-job discipline, employers were motivated by the (reasonable) belief that, given a choice, most people would prefer to spend their time at play rather than work. A raft of social measures sought to correct this attitude, including *master and servant laws,* which prescribed jail time for workers who violated the terms of their contracts, and *poor laws,* which "took care of" the unemployed by incarcerating them in workhouses. Poverty, once seen as a consequence of unfortunate circumstances to be remedied by the assistance of the community, came to be read as a sign of personal failure or moral weakness.

The Production of the Working Class

A more abstract but farther-reaching goal of the new laws was the radical alteration of culture, with the aim of creating a society devoted not to the goal of working hard enough to live, to put food on the table, but of feeding itself in order to work harder, to produce profits. One of the dominant **mythologies** in contemporary society is the idea that individual effort is always ultimately rewarded with economic and social success. (For a discussion of mythology, see Chapter 3.) This mythology developed in conjunction with the industrial economy. However, it was hard to sustain during the early days of the industrial revolution, when the fundamental inequality on which capitalism depends was so starkly evident: by definition, an economic system designed to produce a surplus requires that the majority of labourers are paid less than what their labour is actually worth, and in the early stages of industrialism this amounted to less than the barest living wage for many workers. While preindustrial society had also been characterized by inequality, bonds of custom connected the rich and the poor—sometimes through patronage and sometimes through force, but the two groups were always in close relation with one another. Industrial society effectively broke these bonds, producing a new kind of class-consciousness.

According to E.P. Thompson, one of the foremost historians of English working-class history, "class" comes about when a group of people

> as a result of common experiences (inherited or shared), feel and articulate the identity of their interests as between themselves, and as against [others] whose interests are different from (and usually opposed to) theirs. The class experience is largely determined by the productive relations into which men are born—or enter involuntarily. Class-consciousness is the way in which these experiences are handled in cultural terms: embodied in traditions, value-systems, ideas, and institutional forms. (10)

It's worth pausing on this definition in order to grasp elements of class that are often overlooked in contemporary uses of the word that either equate class simply with wealth—"low class" equals "poor"—or link it to a quality of morality or style, as in "that lady may be rich, but she's got no class." Thompson's definition is important in emphasizing that: (1) class describes a material relationship to the wealth-generating structures of society; specifically, it distinguishes capital's owners from its labourers; and (2) one's class position has a determining influence on one's identity and social orientation. To be class-conscious is to recognize the role of class in determining those

Ideology

Ideology is a term that we will make use of throughout this book. It is a concept with many shadings, but with a relatively simple idea at its core. At the most general level, ideology refers to the process by which the set of values and beliefs that bind individuals together in a society becomes "naturalized." The belief and value systems of any given society are the outcome of *history*; that is, of collective human activity that gives shape (in large and small ways) to the characteristic features of a society. Ideology names those social and political processes that directly and indirectly mask or hide this historical process by making everyday life seem natural, inevitable, and unchangeable. The claim that capitalism is the only rational form of economic organization is often ideological in this way, especially when what this claim suggests is that history was inevitably moving toward a worldwide capitalist system anyway: people did nothing to bring it about and can do nothing to stop it. This is false, and ideology is often at work in attempts to make false statements sound not only like the truth, but also like common sense.

A more restricted meaning of ideology that is related to this one has to do with the difference between how things appear to be and what they are really like. Ideology names the processes through which the real conditions in which people live are obscured by other ideas and beliefs, usually for the sake of maintaining political and social power.

aspects of one's existence—a recognition that goes against the dominant **ideology** (see Close-Up 2.1).

Working-Class Consciousness The industrial revolution coincided with the expansion of working-class consciousness, which expressed itself, among other ways, in distinct cultural forms. These consist of songs, sketches, and poetry—some that were preserved in written form and many that weren't—as well as a richly interwoven set of practices (well documented in Thompson's *The Making of the English Working Class*) including sports, games, conversation, eating, and drinking that took place both in private homes and in working men's clubs. While women were included in some of these activities, on the whole, working-class leisure activities, like other aspects of English culture, were strongly masculinist in character, an element that was often glossed over by early work in cultural studies that tended to cast working-class culture in overly romantic terms.

Drawing on your personal experience and general knowledge, try to answer the following questions: Is class-consciousness a significant force in the world today? Where and how is it manifested? How, if at all, is politics shaped by class concerns? (How) are hopes for radical social transformation expressed today? What role does popular culture play in promoting or subduing these hopes?

Even though it displayed the sexism of its time, one of the distinctive aspects of nineteenth-century working-class culture was its highly developed political consciousness, a sense of the urgency and possibility of radical political and economic transformation. Attempts to effect such a transformation took many forms, from the Luddite rebellions of 1811–13, in which workers smashed the machines that were replacing their labour, to the Chartist movement in the 1830s and 1840s that was concerned primarily with political reform, to the less formally organized trade union movement. What most of these movements had in common was a strong sense of *collectivism,* or worker solidarity, and a demand for expanded democratic rights.

Workplace Reform   In the latter half of the century, slowly and often through an uneasy alliance with employers' own desires for change, these movements achieved some important workplace reforms, including laws restricting working hours and the establishment of Saturday half-holidays. (In the first half of the century, many factory workers worked a 72-hour week, with only Sundays off. Even this brief respite often meant nothing to working women, for whom Sunday was the only day available to do washing and other domestic tasks.) These, in combination with Bank Holidays, gradually extended to other professions and came to replace traditional holidays, resulting in a clearer, more generally shared division between work and leisure, if not exactly less time at work.

The one other significant change in the latter half of the nineteenth century that created new possibilities for popular culture was a gradual increase in wages. As with the other changes, this reform came about both because workers agitated for it and because the system demanded it: as capitalism became more efficient at producing goods, more consumers were required; hence, higher wages (see Chapter 5). The social impact of these changes—improvements, really—to working conditions was far-reaching and complex. Besides providing an obvious outlet for enjoyment and relaxation, the formalization of "free" time outside of work also influenced in subtler ways how people understood themselves and related to one another. The new distinction between spheres of work and home played a big part in establishing the almost sacred significance of the nuclear family, a development that had a particular impact on women. While she in all likelihood was still required to contribute to the household economically, the woman of the house assumed a new and arguably more difficult role as symbolic guardian of the family's moral and spiritual health. This expectation, expressed as part of a more general middle-class ideology of moral discipline, functioned in odd concert with the limited expansion of workers' freedoms: with the expansion of leisure time (and buying power) came new ideological pressures toward social conformity.

Perhaps more significantly, the extension to the poor of some limited forms of relief from the systemic deprivation they suffered arguably worked to mute demands for more substantial forms of social justice. Once arrived at, working-class consciousness remained precarious, never achieving the revolutionary expression that Marx projected. One common explanation of the decline in working-class political culture attributes it to the hegemonic success of commercial culture, a development we discuss further below. It's important not to discount the role of class solidarity, though, both as a catalyst for subsequent forms of political consciousness (discussed in more detail in Chapter 7) and as a critical dynamic in the production of popular culture as an ongoing process of social struggle.

POPULAR RECREATION AND RESISTANCE

So, by the end of the nineteenth century, in fulfillment of one of the clichés of capitalism, some of the fruits of the industrial revolution had begun to "trickle down" to the working classes. The benefits were hard-won, though, and had to be struggled for against the efforts of the ruling class to rein in the pleasures of their social inferiors. While the ruling classes had long been concerned with how the poor enjoyed their off-work time, these concerns took on a new urgency in the industrial revolution. The charge against frivolity was led by the middle classes (small factory and shop owners and other capitalists whose wealth derived from their business activities and investments and not from inherited wealth and property, as was the case for the traditional ruling class). This group, whose economic interests and ideology of productivity came increasingly to dominate society, directed their stern disapproval at both the "parasitic ruling class" *and* the "reckless carousing of an irrational working class" (Bailey 76). That this disapproval was qualified by a contradictory desire among many middle-class people to *join* the leisure activities of the "parasitic ruling class" didn't make things any better for the working classes, whose own recreation became the target of stringent surveillance and discipline. These efforts at control, which ranged from outright prohibition to more subtle forms of persuasion and direction, were never entirely successful, but were met at every turn by working-class resistance to interference in their way of life.

Rational Recreation

In a bid to keep the behaviour of the "unruly masses" in check, many towns established new or enlarged police forces, charged with strictly enforcing new regulations against blood sports and street games and arresting people for such vague offences as vagrancy, trespass, and desecration of the Sabbath. While strong middle-class support existed for the establishment of "a good police" and "set of laws," many of the most dedicated moral reformers also believed that "if possible, the effects of such laws should be produced, almost insensibly, and without the appearance of force: for force will hardly ever answer the end proposed in this land of liberty" (qtd. in Malcomson 97).

The move toward subtler, less overtly coercive means of social control reflected a new cultural complexity that was developing in the shadow of the industrial revolution. One paradoxical element of a society that in many instances produced new forms of servitude for working people was a strong emphasis on individual liberty. This critical element of capitalist ideology took on a slightly different—and, from a ruling-class perspective, less desirable—flavour in growing democracy movements. The call for individual freedom had been an important part of the middle class's rise to power, against the pillars of tradition and inheritance that had worked to sustain the dominance of the aristocracy. However, the prospect of extending the privilege to the lower classes and thus risking powerful challenges to a social order built around their own dominance was a source of much middle-class anxiety. Though they were committed in principle to the goal of general social freedom, particularly in the domain of leisure, they were not willing to leave the working classes to determine their own forms of recreation, which might challenge the prevailing moral standards or social hierarchy.

With a primary aim, then, of keeping the lower classes out of the pub—or, worse, the trade union or Chartist halls—significant groups of concerned middle-class citizens got together to promote what they called "rational recreation." Some groups, such as the Society for the Suppression of Vice and the Lord's Day Observance Society, had a strongly Christian bent. Others—many of which were dominated by women—were more loosely organized around the aims of providing forms of public recreation in which people of different classes could mingle, with the poor benefiting from the good influence of their betters. In all cases there was a strong impulse toward diversion—that is, the sponsorship of sports and activities that would draw interest away from undesirable pastimes: drinking, traditional games, blood sports, and so on. Thus, part of the rational recreationist mandate was the promotion of so-called "counter-attractions," including trips and exhibitions scheduled to conflict with the old, discredited forms of pleasure.

The inspiration for this project was not entirely cynical; some middle-class people may have been moved by a genuine desire to alleviate the severe restrictions that had been imposed on workers and also to heal the fractured class relations brought about by industrialism. It was hoped—naively, maybe, and with a mix of motivations both compassionate and self-serving—that the inequalities that marked the workplace could be temporarily forgotten in forms of recreation designed to be inclusive. The main goal was not inclusivity, however, but "improvement" in the form of intellectual, moral, and spiritual development. In all the activities and organizations promoted by the rational recreationists—concerts, educational institutes, and (increasingly toward the end of the century) libraries and museums, there was a strong emphasis on encouraging intellectual as opposed to physical pursuits, the latter being regarded as base and uncivilized.

Matthew Arnold   The efforts of the rational recreationists were accompanied by an elevation of capital-C Culture as a powerful, almost mystical stimulant of moral and spiritual growth. Poet and critic Matthew Arnold (1822–1888) was one of the foremost proponents of a program of education that would instill civilized virtues in the masses by exposing them to "the best that has been thought and known in the world" (*Culture* 70). Culture, which up until this time described a general process of cultivation, now encompassed a set of objects—artifacts of supposedly timeless and universal value, exposure to which would encourage the student to transcend his petty and narrow **materialist** (we might read "class") interests to recognize his place in the universal—or at least the national—order. The title of Arnold's most famous work of cultural criticism, *Culture and Anarchy*, gives a clear sense of the social chaos he foresaw if the guardians of culture failed in their aims. The power of Arnold's definition of Culture lies partly in its emptiness: its value can't be measured by any precise criteria, but those of discriminating tastes—like Arnold himself, presumably—know it when they see it. It worked as a powerful social ideology, one that influenced literary education until well into the twentieth century, through its contradictory gestures toward universality and hierarchy: Culture was precisely that which united everybody, but its *value* rested in its being understood by only the educated few.

Ambivalence, Appropriation, Resistance   The contradictions that characterized Arnold's definition of culture informed the project of rational recreation as a whole, a project that was only partly successful. To the extent that rational recreation was meant to bring classes together with the aim of cultivating a community defined by middle-class tastes and morals, it was an almost total failure. In part, the failure stemmed from middle-class ambivalence about what they were attempting to do. The impulse to smooth relations between the classes was always complicated by the desire of the middle class to forget their own working-class origins and confirm their alliance with aristocracy.

This was achieved partly by the promotion of sports and leisure activities from which working classes were excluded. In the case of some sports, such as golf, cost alone was an impediment to participation. For others such as rowing—once a popular working-class activity—amateur associations drew up rules prohibiting participation from "artisans, mechanics or labourers" on the pretext that the physical nature of their labour would give them an unfair advantage (Bailey 140). Moves toward the democratization of other cultural activities such as the theatre were countered by the physical segregation of audiences through prohibitive prices at certain events or through restrictive conditions of attendance. Museums, for example, were initially closed on Sundays, which was the only day most working-class people had free. The move to extend opening hours was opposed by some on the grounds that the lower classes were not yet ready for capital-C Culture, and so could not be trusted to appreciate it in the right spirit. When museums finally did open on Sundays, to an enormously enthusiastic public, the *New York Times* warned that canes and umbrellas would have to be checked at the door "so that no chance should be given for anyone to prod a hole through a valuable painting, or to knock off any portion of a cast" (qtd. in Levine 183).

Suggested Activity 2.2

Consider the following questions: Are cultural activities still segregated today? If so, how is participation formally (or informally) restricted? To whom do restrictive conditions apply?

Middle-class nervousness about the encroachment of the lower classes on their newly won exclusive cultural terrain ironically confirmed that, in some ways, the rational recreationists were more successful than they could have hoped: working-class people not only subscribed enthusiastically to programs of self-improvement, but also, not surprisingly, showed a strong desire to run the programs themselves. A general appetite for knowledge, along with huge improvements in literacy associated with the move toward compulsory primary education, helped to blur boundaries between workers and their middle-class benefactors in ways most of the benefactors never anticipated. From the mid-1880s onward, many social clubs and mechanics' institutes (popular educational organizations) were independently run by their working-class members. Some had quite politically

Fight between John Jackson and Daniel Mendoza, 1795. Sports such as prizefighting flourished in part because of—rather than in spite of—middle-class moralists' attempts to ban them.

radical aims; many ended up focusing far more on recreation than education, in clear opposition to the vision of their founders. While the continuing need for financial sponsorship ensured that the wealthy continued to have some hand in running things, historical research suggests that the lower classes took what they wanted from the activities and societies offered them, making over rational recreation for their own purposes in ways that were often quite different from what their sponsors intended. Accepting middle-class sponsorship, in other words, did not necessarily mean accepting middle-class values (Cunningham 128).

Booze and Blood Sports While many aspects of the rational recreationist program were **appropriated** by the working classes, people in general strongly resisted attempts to reform and regulate traditional forms of leisure. Drinking was notoriously hard to curb—even on the job—and blood sports and street games survived in spite of official prohibition and the promotion of alternatives. Prizefighting, or bare-knuckle boxing, is an example of one sport that flourished in spite of attempts to curb it, which ranged from fining publicans who promoted it to charging fighters themselves with assault (and occasionally homicide). The lengths to which its participants would go to maintain the sport were demonstrated in the famous international match between Sayers and Heenan in 1860, in which fighters were taken, in disguise, to a secret location outside the reach of mounted police, followed by supporters who left London via a special early-morning train (Bailey 37). While this and other blood sports eventually did decline, there is a lot of evidence to suggest that they persisted throughout the nineteenth century *because of*, rather than in spite of, attempts to outlaw them. (While we like to think we've come a long way since the nineteenth century, the popularity of YouTube videos of Ultimate Fighting or amateur locker-boxing suggest that perhaps we have not come so far.)

As one historian puts it, by the beginning of the twentieth century "the great majority of London workers were not Christian, provident, chaste or temperate" (Jones 471), and the favoured institutions were "not the school, the evening class, the library, the friendly society, the church or the chapel, but the pub, the sporting paper, the race course and the music hall" (Jones 479). The mass demonstrations that greeted attempts to close pubs and shops on Sunday in the 1860s offer evidence of the extent to which popular recreation had come to be regarded as a right to be defended, by force if necessary.

Popular Culture and Politics

This passionate defence of popular entertainment was a source of concern not just to the middle-class reformers, but also to two distinct groups of working-class activists—political radicals and evangelical Christians. Though their aims were very different, what these two groups had in common was a clearly defined vision of a strong and disciplined working-class society whose integrity was undermined by the corrupting influence of mass entertainment.

Pub culture was particularly suspect because of the intoxicating effect of drinking. The opportunities to get drunk increased substantially with the lifting of duty on spirits in 1825, and the deregulation of beer sales shortly afterward. Like other moves toward freer trade, this liberalization of alcohol sales had ambiguous consequences for working-class people's autonomy. For the radicals in particular, this and other aspects of popular culture were threatening not just because they were often produced through the patronage of the ruling classes, but also because they consumed energies that might otherwise be directed toward more directly self-improving activities, such as education or the struggle for democracy.

The growth of popular recreation, then, was by no means a uniform or uncontroversial process. Not simply a battleground on which people sought to free themselves from the physical or ideological constraints of industrial society, popular culture was also a critical ground for struggle over exactly how that freedom could or should be pursued. The goal of working-class reformers, whose vision of freedom included the extension of democratic privilege, granting to all people the right to determine the shape of the society they lived in, never quite jibed with the more conservative view of popular culture as a necessary, if temporary, escape from the demands of working life. This conservative view (which finds echoes in the contemporary perception of popular culture as an arena in which to pursue the freedom to "be oneself") didn't challenge so much as reflect the entrepreneurial ideology of industrialism. As the most intense suffering associated with the industrial revolution passed, and the poor began to glimpse at least the possibility of beginning to share in its benefits, the more conservative view prevailed, assigning popular culture the role of escapist complement rather than radical antagonist to dominant social structures. The increasing commercialization of popular culture played a major role in hastening that trend.

THE PRODUCTION OF COMMERCIAL MASS CULTURE—THE BIRTH OF THE CULTURE INDUSTRY

When we talk about popular culture today, it's generally assumed to refer to the products of the mass media—television, film, music, Internet culture, and so on. An important goal of this chapter has been to illuminate some of the currents that swirled around the birth of media culture, shaping it even as they were shaped by it. Thus, even though traditional recreation, working-class culture, and the earnest efforts of the rational recreationists were all largely eclipsed by the power of media culture, the *popularity* of media culture cannot be understood without them. Popularity, you should recall from Chapter 1, is *not*, as the makers of commercial media would have it, simply a measure of how many people buy stuff; rather, it is a shifting and contested arena of power. Commercial culture was an in-your-face challenge to the Arnoldian guardians of "Culture" at the same time as it eroded the tradition and politics of the working class; however, it is in the context of the *persistence* of those alternative cultural strains—elitist attempts to defend their definition of "high" culture, and the efforts of ordinary people to shape the meaning of their own experience—that the significance of the commercial media, the most far-reaching cultural development of the last two centuries, must be measured. The concept of **hegemony** (see Close-Up 2.2) has proved most useful to cultural theorists attempting to measure the significance, in political terms, of the explosive growth of commercial culture.

It is tempting to see media culture as truly *popular* in its satisfaction of the desire and will of the people. Nineteenth- and early-twentieth-century critics (both working-class activists and middle-class reformers) along with more recent theorists such as Stuart Hall ("Deconstructing the Popular") challenge this assumption, pointing out that the pleasures offered by what came to be known as the *culture industry* (see Chapter 4) are glossy substitutes for the satisfying kind of empowerment that would result from, say, better working conditions, stronger communities, or expanded democratic rights. This does not mean that commercial culture succeeds purely by virtue of trickery, by exploiting people's stupidity; rather, it works hegemonically, through engagement and negotiation with their real desires, which it transforms into shiny novelties—magazines, musical entertainment, films—that can be sold for profit. We will explore the concept of hegemony more fully in subsequent chapters. For now, it is important to keep it in mind as a key element in the successful development of early commercial culture.

A key assumption of this chapter has been that modern popular culture—and specifically commercial culture—emerged in the wake of the industrial revolution. This is something of an exaggeration: commercial forms of entertainment long predated the nineteenth century—cultural producers such as publishers of pamphlets and ballads, travelling musicians, and other performers did earn a modest living from their work. The major shift in the nineteenth century concerned the forms and scale by which culture was turned into a profitable **commodity**. Products of the culture industry differed from earlier forms of culture in at least two crucial ways: first, they relied on relatively sophisticated and expensive forms of media technology in order to reach a mass audience; second, mass media was produced by a **vertically integrated** factory system, supervised by committees or boards of executives and assembled according to complex divisions of labour. This contrasts sharply with traditional cultural forms that tend to be strongly rooted in the working-class community, with performers and their material reflecting the everyday lives of their audiences. Rather than reflecting the actual experiences of any social group, mass media are designed to appeal to as many social classes or class fractions as possible in order to generate maximum profits for their producers (Naremore and Brantlinger 13).

Several factors combined to make possible the development of a mass entertainment industry. First, a large and concentrated urban population, which by the late nineteenth century enjoyed rising income levels and an increase in leisure time, ensured a captive audience for new forms of popular culture. Second, developments in technology made it possible to produce and deliver entertainment on a vast scale.

Technology

For the Canadian media theorist Marshall McLuhan, whose complex insights often get reduced to the single aphorism "the medium is the message," technology—the form, or "medium" of culture—has greater material significance than the content, or "message."

Hegemony

Developed by the Italian **Marxist** Antonio Gramsci in the 1930s, the concept of hegemony refers to the ability of dominant groups in society to exercise control over weaker groups not by means of force or domination, but by gaining their consent, so that the unequal distribution of power appears to be both legitimate and natural. In other words, hegemony operates not by forcing people against their better judgment to submit to more powerful interests, but rather by actively seeking the spontaneous cooperation of subordinate classes in maintaining social relationships that continue their subordination. Hegemony, significantly, is never total, but operates in constant struggle with newly emerging forms of oppositional consciousness. It works not by crushing those forces, but by a constant process of negotiation.

So how is popular media culture hegemonic? First, it operates in conjunction (and sometimes in tension) with institutions like the state, the law, education, and the family to legitimate the values of capitalist society—**individualism**, **consumerism**, the priority of private versus public interests, and so on. But unlike these other institutions, which sometimes resort to force, commercial culture works almost entirely through the promise, if not the fulfillment, of pleasure. That the pleasures of commercial culture are often opposed by more official institutions—the church, education, and so on—makes them that much more seductive.

This is a fairly radical proposition that few cultural theorists accept in its totality today. However it offers a useful way into understanding the impact of media technology in shaping our consciousness. Its radicality lies in its suggestion that new media technologies don't just function as the means to create new forms of entertainment or communication; they also literally change us as societies and as individuals, rewiring our perception of and means of engaging with the world.

The Printing Press—Template for the Industrial Revolution A brief flashback—way back to the fifteenth century—offers a glimpse of the critical role of technology in shaping the nineteenth-century popular imagination. The printing press, invented by Johannes Gutenberg in 1450, was one of the earliest mass-production technologies. By mechanically reproducing texts that would once have been copied out by hand, the printing press radically altered the possibilities for the distribution of knowledge. It decentralized the production of written information, making it accessible to a much broader segment of the population, and also made possible the creation of a vast print industry, starting with the Bible but quickly expanding to encompass a variety of publications on different subjects, to satisfy the appetite for information (and titillation!) of an increasingly literate population. Print technology offered new opportunities for social control in the form of education and propaganda, as well as democratic empowerment, as people were exposed to ideas and knowledge from different perspectives.

It also affected people's understanding of their place in the world in more indirect ways. By removing the necessity for face-to-face contact in communication, mass-printed texts such as newspapers enable the creation of imaginary connections between people geographically removed from one another, linked only through their consciousness of being part of a broader audience (see Chapter 7 for a discussion of the nation as an "imagined community"). McLuhan goes further to suggest that the invention of the printing press and associated growth of literacy reconfigures human consciousness in a way that favours linearity, a mode of thinking that is implicated in the Enlightenment ideologies of scientific rationalism and **progress**. The printing press, in a sense, put the machinery in place for the production of the industrial revolution, both materially (the book was one of the first mass-produced objects), and metaphorically, in that the mode of interacting with the world associated with print—linear, forward-looking, rational, mechanical—came to define a whole culture, one that is only now starting to shift.

Suggested Activity 2.3

According to Marshall McLuhan, innovations in media technology—photography, radio, film, television—have all influenced culture and consciousness in profound ways, some, paradoxically, taking us back to preliterate tribal ways of conceiving the world, enabling the creation of the so-called "global village." Based on your own and others' uses of contemporary media, how (if at all) do you think the technology enhances or limits different forms of perception, mental or social engagement?

The Engines (and Wires, Cameras, Projectors, Screens) of Change

The last half of the nineteenth century saw massive changes in the technological landscape of popular culture. By the 1870s, the telephone and phonograph joined a raft of recent inventions including photography, telegraphy, and the railroad, which all worked in different ways toward what one writer termed with no exaggeration "the annihilation of time and space" (Solnit 4).

In both the U.K. and the U.S., the development of a national railway system—not the first thing that usually comes to mind when we think of popular culture—was hugely influential in extending people's physical and imaginative horizons. The most obvious impact of trains was to make travel much easier and more accessible for ordinary people. By the mid–nineteenth century, even working-class families were able to escape the city to spend a few days at the lake or the beach, where they stayed at resorts that offered them all kinds of commercial entertainment. Within the urban environment itself, improvements in public transit made it possible for people to travel between the suburbs and the city at night to attend the theatre and, by century's end, the cinema. Besides creating mobile audiences, better transportation fuelled the development of popular culture in other more obvious ways, by facilitating the faster, larger, and more extensive distribution of goods and services. The train, in other words, isn't just a mode of transportation; it's also a technology of delivery for products of the industrial economy.

In conjunction with technologies of production, technologies of delivery play a critical role in the development of popular culture. The telegraph, invented in the mid–nineteenth century, revolutionized the delivery of information by enabling the almost instantaneous transmission of information over wires in the form of electric signals. James Carey describes its significance in an interesting way, suggesting that the telegraph

> marked the decisive separation of "transportation" and "communication." These words had always been synonymous, until, that is, it became possible to communicate information immediately from one side of the country to the other. The telegraph revolutionized communication by allowing symbols to move independently of geography and independently of and faster than transport." (213)

It also turned those symbols into viable objects of exchange and, in conjunction with visual technologies such as the camera and film projector, helped to create a culture industry founded on mass media. The evolution of that industry, with particular focus on the development of cinema, is taken up in Chapter 4.

These brief examples show us how industrial technology affected the domain of popular culture by changing the physical processes of production, the kinds of objects that could be produced, and the ways they were consumed. It also changed and improved means of distributing cultural goods to a vast audience. In sum, it played a key role in the **commodification** of culture, or its transformation into a collection of products that could be bought and sold.

Regulation, Innovation, Consolidation

Technological development doesn't take place in a vacuum. The nature of new cultural technologies, the uses to which they are put, who uses them, and who profits by them are questions that are all determined by broader political, economic, and social factors. Critical among these factors are the kinds of regulations—laws, trade agreements, unwritten social rules—that determine the circumstances in which forms of popular culture are produced and consumed. The increasingly liberal trade regulations that characterized British industrial society (developments that were not always matched by a loosening of moral and social restrictions) helped to create a climate of entrepreneurial innovation that fuelled the development of new forms of popular culture. The period is characterized by genuine rags-to-riches stories of itinerant actors, songwriters, and musicians who emerged from humble beginnings to control small-scale entertainment empires. The same environment that made their enrichment possible, however, also paved the way for the consolidation of ever-larger entertainment conglomerates, effectively shutting the door on the emergence of new independent cultural producers.

The Expansion of Mass Media   The development of print mass media offers a glimpse into how this process worked. A number of factors contributed to a growing market for printed materials over the course of the eighteenth and nineteenth centuries. Growing literacy rates—enhanced by laws such as the Education Act of 1870, which made public education compulsory—in combination with developments mentioned above, such as increased leisure time, created a vast audience for cheap reading matter such as political pamphlets, chapbooks, and broadsheets (collections of poems or ballad lyrics). While the profit margins on these types of literature were small, there was enough demand to ensure a modest living for their publishers. Their success was guaranteed in part by their intimate familiarity with the audiences to whom they catered.

Throughout the nineteenth century, growing opportunities for print production on a much larger scale helped to create a thriving newspaper and magazine industry that effectively destroyed the livelihood of these small-scale, independent operations. Specific regulatory changes such as the abolition of taxes on ads (1853), newspapers (1855), and paper (1861) made it increasingly feasible to sell newspapers and periodicals cheaply, while earning huge profits through advertising. Typical among these was the *Daily Mail*, established in London in 1896 and achieving an average weekly circulation of more than 200,000 in its first year. To satisfy such a large and diverse audience, the *Daily Mail*, like many other mass-produced papers, relied on sensationalism, balancing political coverage with a strong focus on sports and crime. Capitalizing on the success of the *Daily Mail*, its publisher, Edward Harmsworth (later Lord Northcliffe), quickly established *The Daily Mirror*, a tabloid initially targeted to a mostly female audience, whose stories of crime and romance were enhanced by lots of pictures. While the two papers were widely criticized—the *Mail* as "the paper for people who could not think" and the *Mirror* as "the paper for people who could not read" (Briggs 9)—they were both massively successful, with the *Mirror* becoming for a time the paper with the largest circulation in the world.

The establishment of media empires in the late nineteenth century anticipates the much more significant kinds of media convergence that are in evidence today, linking not only forms of media (say, print with television) but also form with content (for example, television networks and sports teams; see Chapter 4). Among the costs of achieving such vast economies of scale, which can (though does not always) mean greater efficiency of delivery and higher production values, are a reduction of the diversity of opinion and a dilution of content to satisfy as vast an audience as possible. This latter issue points to one of the most significant consequences of media consolidation in the nineteenth century: the production of a new kind of cultural literacy, based not on an intimately shared knowledge of one's own familiar surroundings but on a more general social outlook made up of ideas, beliefs, tastes, and opinions shared with a vast group of strangers. The consequences—both positive and negative—of that move toward national and, eventually, global **mass culture** are taken up in detail in Chapter 10.

Pub Culture and the Music Hall   The expansion of the media industry did not diminish people's appetites for more sensual kinds of entertainment. The pub remained a cornerstone of popular recreation, forming a basis for new entertainment enterprises such as the music hall. While the deregulation of alcohol sales, mentioned above, was a welcome development for pub owners in some ways, it remained difficult to make much money in an increasingly competitive environment through the sales of food and drink alone. Pub owners thus had to resort to other innovations in order to turn their establishments into profitable commercial enterprises. While many early nineteenth-century pubs were "little more than parlours of private houses," as one historian describes them (Bailey 28), starting around the 1830s, changing building regulations led to the establishment of bigger, more commercial pubs—so-called "gin palaces." Among the structural elements incorporated into these establishments were bar counters separating customers from liquor and dispensers, thus safeguarding the product and allegedly adding to an atmosphere of professionalism. A more blatantly commercial innovation was the elimination of seats, which encouraged a high volume and rapid turnover of customers. Gas lamps hung outside as well as inside helped draw in customers by extending the territory of the pub into the street (Bailey).

The commercial activity of the pub also extended beyond the immediate business of the sale of food and alcohol. As has already been mentioned, pub owners sponsored all kinds of recreational activities, from sports to musical events. Perhaps the most substantial move to transform the institution of the pub into a form of mass culture came with the advent of music hall, in which musical and dramatic performances formed the central component of a comprehensive entertainment package. The experience was enhanced by food and drink, and enjoyed—as pub culture had not been previously—by women as well as men (the wholesome family image was no doubt complicated by the thriving trade in prostitution that its critics maintained was a key sideline of music hall). Like many early forms of mass entertainment, music hall resists easy categorization. While its commercial aspects and the presence of professional performers distinguish it from more traditional forms of do-it-yourself popular culture, it was not yet purely corporate— at least not at first.

Developed out of the more loosely organized "free and easy," in which pub patrons watched—and, more significantly, participated actively in—songs

Music hall represented a transitional moment in the evolution of "homemade" popular culture into mass culture.

and sketches, music hall represented a bridge between those earlier forms of participatory entertainment and the kinds of mass culture we are more familiar with today, in which audiences tend to be reduced to passive spectators. (A similar cultural transition can be traced in the U.S. during this period, in the development of vaudeville, a slightly **higher brow** form of musical variety show entertainment usually served up alcohol-free.) In this transformation, producers of commercial entertainment found allies in a middle-class notion of culture that discouraged audience participation in public art as part of a more general campaign against the public airing of "private" feeling—along with a whole range of other activities, such as eating, spitting, nose-blowing, scratching, and farting. While certain forms of mass culture—in particular, sport—still sanctioned (as they continue to do today) some degree of public participation, thus confirming their relegation to a "lower" category of entertainment, the rules of middle-class etiquette proved to be far-reaching in their influence on a general trend to transform audiences from collective participants into passive, individual spectators (Levine 198–199). Music hall nevertheless retained many of the features of earlier forms of participatory entertainment, with audiences joining in choruses and loudly registering their approval and disapproval of performances.

Significantly, though, music hall has been linked by historians with a moment of decline in working-class democratic movements. Unlike earlier forms of pub culture, in which recreation and politics were often closely bound together with songs and skits blatantly critical of the prevailing class structure, the tone of music hall entertainment tended toward a more conservative acceptance of the dominant ideology of capitalism. Like successive forms of mass entertainment, music hall was not geared toward changing the social order; it offered, rather, a temporary escape from its constraints, a culture not of protest but of "consolation" (Jones 499).

The imbrication of music hall with prevailing economic structures was reflected not just in the transformation of its audiences, but also in the professionalization and organization of its production. In some significant ways, music hall remained rooted in the mostly working-class community that it served, with most of its performers, as well as the songs and skits they performed, coming directly out of that experience. In its ownership, however, music hall came to resemble later forms of corporate entertainment. From the opening of Charles Morton's music hall in 1851, the industry developed quickly, with the first music hall agency established in London in 1858 and others soon following. In 1860, owners of the larger halls formed the London Music Hall Proprietors' Protection Association, which helped establish standards, including common (low) wages for performers. This association, along with the tightening of building regulations, led to the closing of smaller halls and the consolidation of bigger ones. As the larger halls grew more successful, other industries grew up around them, including a thriving music hall press featuring magazines including *Era, Magnet,* and *London Entr'acte.* Music hall also forged connections with other forms of entertainment, as proprietors began to invest in multiple ventures including sport, drama, and (later) the circus, economizing through the construction of ever-larger entertainment complexes that could accommodate multiple activities.

In an irony characteristic of the evolution of popular culture, music halls also offered ideal venues for the screening of films—a form of entertainment that eventually came to supplant them. Only a very few entertainers, such as Charlie Chaplin, successfully made the transition from vaudeville to cinema.

CONTINUITIES AND CHANGES

We have looked at a number of developments occurring in the domain of popular culture that were strongly influenced by **industrialization**. The fragmentation—spatial, economic, and social—of an earlier way of life changed the way people related to one another and pursued work and recreation. The struggle of working-class people to define their lives, including labour and recreation, on their own terms met powerful resistance in the form of middle-class reformers and the rise of commercial culture. In general, the growth of mass media involved the intensification of commercialization and concentration of corporate control.

This movement was neither steady nor uniform, however: moves toward consolidation of corporate power were routinely challenged by competition and the flourishing of independent operators, as well as by the unionization of performers, technicians, and other employers (these tensions are discussed in more detail in Chapter 4). They were also challenged by those outside the industry—audiences and consumers whose willingness to be passively entertained existed in tension with a powerful impulse to make and do things for themselves. These tensions continue to inform the terrain of popular culture today.

The Organization and Commercialization of Sports

We began our history of popular culture by looking at street football as an apparent casualty to the movement to privatize space, and with it, popular recreation. In many ways football offers a perfect example of the operation of forces of corporatization. Proceeding in tandem with the moves to ban football from the public streets were efforts to organize it into a successful commercial venture. The sponsorship of "soccer clubs" led to the establishment of organized leagues, and the eventual founding of the Football Association in 1863. Considerable effort went into the task of regularizing the rules of the game, though this was not totally successful, as demonstrated by the evolution of two games: rugby, and Association football, or soccer. (The two games differ widely both in rules of play and in culture, with the former maintaining a fairly elitist flavour in keeping with its roots in the British public school system, and the latter enjoying a strong working-class following—at least until recently, when commercial success has arguably all but severed the sport from its roots.) Professionalism—that is, the introduction of salaries for players—was legalized in 1855, and clubs began charging admission in 1870, gradually incorporating other commercial enticements such as food, drink, and other entertainment for spectators. As with music hall, a sports media industry soon developed, with

A hardy and determined band of players resisted the general trend toward the organization and institutionalization of football.

Routledge's 1867 *Handbook of Football* helping to foster fan solidarity around a sport that was rapidly becoming institutionalized.

The commercialization of sports followed a similar pattern in the colonies. In Canada, as in England, industrialization (which occurred more than 50 years later in Canada) played a large role in the transformation of sports from a casual, spontaneous, and relatively inclusive activity into a regulated, formalized, and, eventually, commercial enterprise. Most obviously, urbanization placed restrictions on space as it had in England, moving sports out of fields and other open spaces into specialized athletic facilities. The introduction of fixed spatial boundaries served to transform, and eventually to formalize, rules of play. Industrialization also influenced the temporal organization of sports in at least two ways: first, the institution of long and regular working days made it necessary to establish rules limiting the duration of play (a significant development in sports such as lacrosse, in which games might once have lasted anywhere from a few minutes to several hours). Second, the marking of time into distinct periods of work and leisure made it possible to establish formal schedules of play, based on the assumption that players and spectators had regularly scheduled time off (Metcalfe 50).

Specialization, Professionalization, Commercialization Historian Alan Metcalfe also identifies another indirect consequence of the importance of time as part of a general emphasis on quantification: the meaning of sports shifted "from the process, the contest itself, to the product, the record" (51). As a consequence, the nature of competition changed, with less emphasis on its social aspects and a greater and greater focus on winning. As in other areas of the industrial economy, sports was increasingly shaped by specialization: from a chaotic, collective endeavour in which the different tasks of the game were shared by everyone, players gradually assumed positions in accordance with their specific talents—offence, defence, goalkeeping, and so on (Guttman, qtd. in A. Hall et al. 50).

The incorporation of football into schools as part of an ideology of masculine character development was an important step in its institutionalization.

Metcalfe identifies a number of other changes associated with industrialization that contributed to the organization of sports in Canada, including the development of transportation and communications technology—the train, the telegraph, and radio and print media—that made it possible not only to arrange contests between far-flung teams, but also to broadcast schedules and results, creating a national audience for sport (52). (From the expansion of national and, eventually, international leagues, we arrive at the contemporary situation in which virtually none of the players on "local" professional teams come from the city—or even the country—in which the team is based. This development, a logical outgrowth of the forces of global capital, changes not only the organization of players, but also the relationship between players and fans, whose relationship to "their" team is an oddly contrived one, connected only arbitrarily to place.)

The evolution of "fans" is another major development in the organization and commercialization of sports. By the late 1800s, football—played according to a still unfixed set of "Canadian rules" that drew something from British rugby and something from the American game—had become a spectator sport. Ice hockey—a game that, according to at least one account, was established by Montreal football players as a form of winter training (Wise and Fisher 44)—quickly followed. Commercialization and professionalization

The celebrity status and colossal salaries accorded to professional athletes, such as soccer player David Beckham, are among the most visible signs of the commercialization of soccer.

went hand in hand, as the involvement of highly skilled, salaried players made games more exciting to watch. With ice hockey in particular, the expense involved—equipment, rink rental and maintenance—gave the game a strongly middle-class flavour, in terms of ownership if not participation or interest. Again, as with the geographical expansion of sports, its commercial intensification has even more dramatic consequences today, among them the pricing of tickets far out of the range of the average fan.

Commercialization alone was not responsible for the wresting of sports such as hockey and football from the people to the elites; in fact, much in the same way as commercial media were challenged by the rational recreationists, professional sports faced strong challenges from amateur associations, connected in particular with private schools and universities. The leagues that were established by the universities especially maintained a strong policy against professionalism, a policy motivated as much by an elitist desire to maintain class privilege as it was by a concern for the purity of the sport. Some clubs defined their codes of amateurism according to the exclusion of particular professions and even ethnic groups (see Table 2.1). An 1873 regulation, for example, banned "labourers" and "Indians" from membership in the Montreal Pedestrian Club on the same grounds that mechanics and labourers had once been barred from rowing clubs: they were seen to enjoy a physical advantage over their more refined middle-class counterparts (A. Hall et al. 59).

In general, nineteenth-century football and hockey amateurists (as distinct from contemporary promoters of amateur sport) were, if anything, more bound up with economic status than professionals, since a strict ban on professionals meant that participation was restricted to those with plenty of time and money. Between them, however, both middle-class amateur associations and corporate owners of professional teams contributed to the creation of a culture of organized sports, a culture of spectatorship rather than participation. Indirectly, but most significantly, the propertied interests represented by both the professionals and the "gentleman amateurs" contributed to the decline of public space available for community athletic activity—a development that foreshadows the conflict over street hockey today.

As the above discussion suggests, we can read into the histories of football and ice hockey a fairly straightforward movement from the loss of public recreation space and the banning of street games to the creation of professional sports, and the conversion of players into fans. More recently, the intensification of the commercial imperative in sports has begun to wrest enjoyment of the game away from players and fans alike, as players (in exchange for hugely lucrative salaries, depending on the sport) are subject to being traded (or dropped) at the whim of owners, and attendance at games is (economically) restricted to corporate executives entertaining clients. The only real winners in professional sport today, arguably, are commercial sponsors, who depend on a still-enthusiastic television audience. And yet . . . when we look back to the original English battle over street football, and then forward to the road hockey case in Hamilton, the answer to the question of who controls popular culture is more complicated, and more encouraging.

Table 2.1 Early Definitions of "Amateur"

The Amateur Athletic Association of Canada and its successors established the following definitions of an amateur:

1884: An amateur is one who has never competed for a money prize or staked bet with or against any professional for any prize, or assisted in the practice of athletic exercises as a means of obtaining a livelihood.

1896 (add): Or who has entered any competition under a name other than his own.

1902 (add): private or public gate receipts . . . who has never, directly or indirectly, received any bonus or a payment in lieu of loss of time while playing as a member of any club, or any money considerations whatever for any services as an athlete except his actual traveling and of selling or pledging his prizes.

1909 (add): promoted an athletic competition for personal gain.

Back to the Streets

Street games might, in theory, have been banned in 1835 in Britain, but players were not put off that easily. In Derby in 1845, footballers responded to attempts to stop the annual Shrovetide match by throwing things at the police, including a "brick bat and bludgeon" (one or both of which hit the mayor). Pursued by police, special constables, and dragoons, players ran away to the next village—where, after a vigorous skirmish, they finally surrendered the ball (Malcomson 142). While the footballers eventually lost that contest—with greater police reinforcement in subsequent years ensuring that the tradition was eventually quashed—in other places public protests against the prohibition resulted in the setting aside of public playing fields where the game could continue without interfering with other (commercial) activities.

The Hamilton street hockey story didn't end quite so violently, and its implications are a little more complicated. Like the English footballers, Ryan Kotar and his father enjoyed a partial victory. Their case was dismissed not because the judge deemed that road hockey was *not* a crime, but because of contradictions in witnesses' testimony. The bylaw prohibiting street games still stands, in spite of a motion to Hamilton city council to rescind it. Similar bylaws exist in most Canadian municipalities, though they are rarely enforced. The tenor of the neighbour's attack on hockey as "totally uncivilized and dangerous" (Clairmont "Road Hockey") echoes some of the rational recreationists' charges against street football as leading not only to "moral degradation" among its players, but also to "injury to health, fractured limbs and (not infrequently) loss of life" (qtd. in Cunningham 78). However, the nationwide rallying of community support behind the hockey players, along with their exoneration from charges, would seem to demonstrate a popular determination to keep alive people's rights to enjoy themselves in public spaces. The defence of the hockey players—even by government officials in Hamilton, who promised to try to have the ban struck down—would seem to confirm the survival of grassroots, popular entertainment in spite of both attacks from moralists and the expansion of private property rights, including the conversion of sports into a corporate activity.

There are other ways of reading the story, however, that point to both its continuity with the British street football incident and its important differences from that event. First of all, although this story tended to be represented as a victory for grassroots sports—street hockey as opposed to league hockey, or the overly commercialized professional game—the distinctions between the two aren't all that clear-cut. Following the Hamilton incident, NHL players rallied in support of street hockey—as much, no doubt, out of a recognition that street hockey nurtures professional hockey fans as out of pure-hearted devotion to the game. In an article calling for the preservation of outdoor hockey rinks, columnist Roy MacGregor touted the value of "being left alone to play the game the way it is played in the imagination," in part because that kind of play nurtures the talent that goes on to win junior world championships and Olympic gold medals.

National Mythology   Victory in such international contests is substantial fodder for the **national** mythology of Canada—which points to another wrinkle in the story: there is no question that one of the reasons the Hamilton incident received so much press was because the sport in question was hockey—not baseball, not Frisbee, not soccer, but a sport whose restriction, according to one Hamilton city councillor, would be positively "un-Canadian" ("Game On!"). As one supporter put it, "hockey is Canada's national pastime. . . . When I stumble across kids playing hockey in the street, it brings a smile to my face" (qtd. in Wente "It's Okay"). That hockey occupies a significant place in the official mythology of Canada is indisputable. However, as we discuss in more detail in subsequent chapters (see Chapters 3 and 7 in particular), national mythologies are not spontaneous expressions of citizenly love. They are, rather, contrived and partial stories whose collective rhetoric conceals the stakes of *power*—both economic and social—involved in their dissemination.

It's in the interests of professional sports and its sponsors that the dream of "the game" be kept alive by powerful images such as the 1998 Labatt beer television commercial in which Toronto commuters spontaneously join in a giant game of street hockey, and the 2002 Tim Hortons calendar that features an image of kids playing shinny. These heart-warming images are at odds with the sacrifice of public space and resources to the forces of commercialism. Corporate team owners' and sponsors' demands for tax breaks for their teams contribute to this problem by taking funds away from public facilities such as parks and outdoor rinks. Some corporations, including Tim Hortons, *do* make financial contributions to amateur sport, part of a growing trend necessitated in part by the erosion of public support due to commercialization! The underfunding of Canadian amateur hockey, particular women's hockey, in relation to the vast and increasingly U.S.-dominated entertainment complex of the NHL offers yet another contradiction in the mythology of Canada's "national game." These facts complicate the widely asserted notion that hockey is "a big part of what makes us *us*" (sportswriter Stephen Brunt, qtd. in Wente "It's Okay").

Gender in Sports As the street-hockey story attests, distinctions between grassroots and governmentality, populism and commercialism, are less clear-cut in Canada today than they were in Victorian England. The politics of the popular have also become more complicated: while it's easy to read the 1845 contest over street football in Derby as a contest between "the people" and their political and economic rulers, the question of who constitutes "us"—the people—today is not so simple. We have already mentioned some of the gender implications of the hockey story, in relation to the underfunding of women's sport. Sports columnist Laura Robinson goes further to note an unspoken assumption of many of the defenders of street hockey players: when they say "kids," they mean "boys." She goes on to note,

> I can't recall seeing a group of girls commandeering a public street at any time to play any team sport. Boys have always understood that public space is the right space for their physical performance. The theatre of masculinity is public because we have constructed masculinity in a way that demands of men and boys constant physical proof of "who the man is," to use a basketball term. ("Girls")

Nowhere, arguably, is the ideology of masculinity more evident than in hockey, whose increasing violence at the professional and amateur levels has been cause for public concern. Such concern was not, significantly, voiced in relation to the street-hockey case, except by the players' neighbour, Nadia Ciuriak—a woman and an immigrant, who was demonized for, among other sins, being "un-Canadian." When she lost her case, columnist Margaret Wente notes, "the neighbourhood boys were directed to wave their hockey sticks triumphantly for the approving cameras" ("It's Okay").

The question of what, or whose, culture triumphed here is ambiguous.

SUGGESTIONS FOR FURTHER READING

Ashby, Leroy. *With Amusement for All: A History of American Popular Culture Since 1830.* Lexington, KY: University of Kentucky Press, 2006.

Cullen, Jim. *Popular Culture in American History.* New York: Blackwell, 2000.

Cunningham, Hugh. *Leisure in the Industrial Revolution.* London: Croom Helm, 1980.

Hobsbawm, Eric. *Industry and Empire: An Economic History of Britain Since 1750.* London: Weidenfeld and Nicolson, 1968.

Levine, Lawrence W. *Highbrow/Lowbrow: The Emergence of Cultural Hierarchy in America.* Cambridge, MA: Harvard University Press, 1988.

Malcomson, Robert W. *Popular Recreations in English Society 1700–1850.* Cambridge, UK: Cambridge University Press, 1973.

Thompson, E.P. *The Making of the English Working Class.* Harmondsworth, UK: Penguin, 1963.

Chapter 3

Representation and the Construction of Social Reality

INTRODUCTION: TRUTH2POWER

As of September 2008, the website www.urbandictionary.com had 16 definitions for the word "represent." Lodged between "represemble" and "representative democracy," "represent" is best defined by the contributor Truth2Power. With 139 thumbs-up to 36 thumbs-down from other contributors and readers, Truth2Power defines "represent" in the following way:

1. Lend physical presence or voice on behalf of a constituency defined by geography or purpose, when such manifestation of presence or voice by the whole of that constituency would be logistically impractical or impossible.
2. Stand in for a person, organization, or principle in a manner prescribed by law or formal custom where knowledge of protocols is specific and germaine [*sic*] to a particular forum of [*sic*] jurisdiction.

From a popular cultural perspective, we think that Truth2Power has done a pretty good job of defining the term "represent." We are also pleased with Truth2Power's definition because it offers a window into the way that cultural theorists understand the conceptual background and framework of one of the key terms to understanding popular culture: *representation*. While some of the actual usages of the word "represent" provided by other contributors to www.urbandictionary.com do not exactly meet with our approval, it is more than clear to us that contained within them are the intellectual threads that reach back to the early decades of the twentieth century. For example, while we would not encourage you to go home at the end of the semester to tell your relatives that your professors quoted material like this:

> Dad: Your Mom wants you to square up this joint, yo.
> Kid: So you want me to clean my room?
> Dad: Dat would be da hizzy.
> Kid: O.K.
> Dad: Represent.

Or this:

> Represent yo clique mother fucka.

we would be pleased if you could see within statements like these, uttered in a vast range of contexts, a discursive, ideological, and political import that has a historical dimension rooted in the way that language and power are always intertwined in any cultural expression you encounter.

We start this chapter by departing a little from www.urbandictionary.com's focus on real-world relations to look at the codes or **sign** systems—the **language**—that makes representation possible. We look at both the mechanics of sign systems—*how* meaning is generated—and the values or **ideologies** that determine *what* meanings circulate in particular historical contexts, and with what effects. This process of **representation**, what may loosely be described as the social production of meaning through sign systems, underpins the fuzzy but firm cultural rules that determine who gets to speak, for whom, and under what circumstances; that is to say, that the words, images, and other signs that we use to define our world both *reflect* and *shape* the relations of togetherness and opposition, love and power, that are possible within it.

CONSTRUCTING A CRISIS—THE DISCOURSE OF VIOLENT YOUTH

> Victoria is Canada's garden playground. Golfers are still on the links in January and flowers bloom all year. Its image is of a prim and proper government and tourist town. At first glance, the city is scenic, safe, and secure, but this is a tale of two cities.
>
> It may be hard to believe but there is a dangerous and violent side to Victoria, especially at night. It's when roving gangs of young people are out looking for trouble and someone to hurt. . . . In the last five years in Victoria, there has been victim after victim of violent teenagers who hang out, drink and assault. All the publicity and public outrage hasn't stopped it.
>
> —"Victoria's Secret"

In March 2002, as part of a week's programming schedule that included no less than three specials on teen violence, CTV's *W5* aired a documentary called "Victoria's Secret" that examined the phenomenon of teenage violence in Victoria, British Columbia. In documenting the "youth gang problem," the two-part show assembled a picture of an emerging social crisis that had thus far remained hidden because of victims' fear of talking and civic boosters' reluctance to tarnish the image of the city. Together with a host of other print and television stories that began appearing in the early 2000s, "Victoria's Secret" contributed to a developing public discourse on youth violence in Canada. As in "Victoria's Secret," other stories point to a long-simmering problem that has only recently begun to receive sustained attention.

In seeming contrast to the emphasis on the invisibility of the problem and to the "numbing indifference" of teens (Wong A30), many stories also testify to a growing atmosphere of fear. Following a shooting episode in a Toronto high school, one article—citing comments by the former vice principal who heads the Canadian Safe Schools Network—noted that "principals lived in constant fear that their schools could be next . . . try as they might to keep students safe with video-surveillance cameras, zero-tolerance policies, hall monitors and—increasingly—uniforms or dress codes that make it easier to spot intruders" (Galt A30). School board officials acknowledge that some security measures such as lockdown drills, which simulate emergencies involving armed intruders, may actually serve to heighten fears, particular among very young children. However they defend such drills (compulsory in many urban school boards across Canada since 2006) as necessary, in conjunction with ongoing efforts to "[identify] possible threats such as troubled students" ("From the Front Door"). Along with new school security measures, a number of new and changed policies and laws—the creation of boot camps, the Youth Criminal Justice Act that came into effect in 2003, the Safe Streets Act, and so on—testify to growing public and official determination to combat the problem.

Statistics tell a somewhat different story. Youth crime in general shows a steady rise from 1985 that peaks in 1991 then falls off through most of the 1990s. In 1999 a brief increase occurs, only to recede again in 2003. Indeed, in 2005, the youth crime rate, calculated by the number of youths charged plus youths cleared by means other than the laying of formal charges, dropped 6 percent to end near a 10-year low. Likewise, violent youth crime dropped 2 percent in 2005 and youth property crime was down by 12 percent (Gannon 1) (see Figure 3.1). Countering perceptions that violent youth crime is increasing out of proportion to adult crime, the number of homicides committed by youth expressed as a percentage does not indicate a dramatic increase in the past few years. In 1995 the percentage of homicides committed by youths was 11.6 percent; in 2005, the percentage was up a fraction to 10.9 percent from the 9.3 percent average registered in the years from 1995 to 2004 (Dauvergne and Li 24). The all-too-familiar refrain that youth in society have lost touch with fundamental human values is easily contradicted by the simple fact that homicide in general (as expressed through national figures in Canada) peaked in the mid-1970s at 3.0 homicides per 100,000 people. It has been dropping since then, reaching a low of 1.7 in 2003, and bouncing back to 2.0 homicides per 100,000 in 2005 (Statistics Canada 2).

So what's going on? Statistics would appear to refute media claims of an unprecedented crisis of youth violence. Then again, statistics themselves, which *seem* to offer the

Figure 3.1 Youth Crime Rate Decreased in 2005

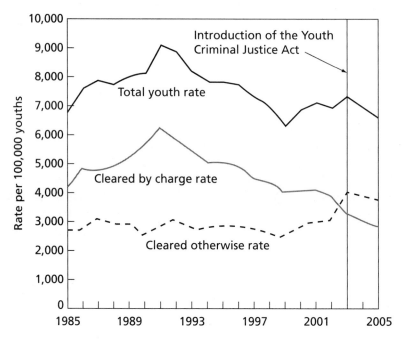

Source: Maire Gannon. Statistics Canada. *Juristat*. Figure 15: Youth Crime Rate Decreased in 2005. Catalogue no. 85-002-XIE. Vol. 26, No. 4, Pg. 13.

irrefutable proof of numbers, need to be understood in context. According to critics, among the factors shaping what looks like a large escalation of youth crime between 1986 and 1992 are a significant increase in the size of the youth population; the introduction of the Young Offenders Act in 1984, which reclassified 16- and 17-year-olds (typically the age group most likely to commit crime) within the category of youth; changes in policing practices, including a tendency for police to charge a greater number of suspects for each crime; and, finally, increased reporting of incidents such as "minor schoolyard scuffles" that formerly would have been dealt with by schools and/or parents (John Howard Society).

We present these different accounts of youth violence, which are also different ways of representing the issue, not simply to contrast media hype with the "real" picture presented by statistics, or to illustrate the inadequacy of statistics to comprehend the complexity of the truth. Rather, we want to use the "story" of youth violence as a way into talking about representation and the role it plays in the construction of social reality. Questions this chapter seeks to address are: How do language and other sign systems work to signify, or to create, social meaning? How does representation map or produce relations of power? How do different media genres (advertising, news, entertainment) and different types of media (television, print) help shape the production of meaning? How have processes of representation shifted historically? What is the nature and extent of media representation in contemporary global culture? And, finally, how does representation work (or fail) as a means of granting **agency** to groups and individuals?

SIGNIFICATION—THE PRODUCTION OF SOCIAL SENSE

We have introduced the story of youth violence—a story we return to later in the chapter—in a way that we hope will encourage you to think *counter-intuitively* about representation. That is, rather than reading the stories and statistics as we ordinarily would—as a transparent window on the phenomenon of youth crime—we want to muddy the window, to suggest that the way these stories are represented has an important role in how the "facts" of our social life are created. Before proceeding to some more examples of how this process works, let's step back and try to get a handle on it from a theoretical perspective.

Broadly speaking, representation involves the social production of meaning through sign systems. Signs are the fundamental units of communication. A sign can be a word, a gesture, a facial expression, an image, a musical note, even an item of clothing—anything that refers to something else, and is recognized as doing so by users of the sign system. Conventional wisdom has it that sign systems, or languages, evolve to communicate pre-existing realities. But even a superficial examination of different languages tells us that "reality"—at least, the way reality is organized and understood—differs from culture to culture. For example, verbs in the Native American Hopi language have no past, present, or future tenses, reflecting the fact that Hopi culture doesn't measure time in a linear sequence the way most Western cultures do. While it might be supposed that the Hopi language and culture are less evolved than European cultures, linguist Benjamin Lee Whorf advanced the controversial argument that contemporary scientific theories such as quantum physics resonate naturally with a Hopi world-view. European language and culture, by contrast, remain wedded to a binary mode of thought that is incapable of imagining something existing in two states at once—past and present, or wave and particle. Language by itself isn't the determining factor here; rather, it is that language, as the central medium of culture, influences the way we perceive the world around us and our place in it.

Structuralist Theories of Representation

The suggestion that language does not simply *reflect* but actually *constructs our understanding of* reality emerges from a shift that occurred in the 1960s in cultural and linguistic theory. The principles underlying that shift are clustered under the general heading of **structuralism**. Structuralist theories are concerned not with *what* words or cultural practices mean, but rather with *how* they mean, according to the structure and rules of the system from which they are generated. One of the first structuralist theorists was Swiss linguist Ferdinand de Saussure, whose **semiotic** theory has had a significant impact on the study of culture (see Close-Up 3.1).

One of the important aspects of Saussurean linguistics is the distinction it draws between *langue,* or the whole system as it exists on an abstract level, including all possible signs and conventions, and *parole,* the individual utterance or the things we do with language. Subsequent critics point out the artificiality of that separation: languages can't really be said to exist apart from their specific usage. The distinction between *langue* and *parole* is useful, however, in showing that language, in the form of *parole,* embodies all kinds of possibilities for making meaning, but that those possibilities ultimately exist with a frame—the *langue*—that places a limit on what we can intelligibly say. An obvious example of this limitation is the rules of grammar, which dictate the possibilities for word combination in a sentence.

Rules of Representation   We can build from these basic linguistic principles much broader, less clear-cut rules that determine possibilities for putting together whole narratives: for example, a convention in the Western novel that has come to shape other forms of expression is the movement from chaos to order, conflict to resolution. While it is obviously possible to challenge these conventions, to depart from them entirely risks not making sense. Jim Jarmusch's 2005 movie *Broken Flowers* is a good illustration of the fine line between cleverly breaking the rules of storytelling and ignoring them entirely. While a portion of the movie is structured along a relatively stable plot axis, Don Johnston (Bill Murray) travels from one ex-lover to another, trying to discover the identity of his child's mother and forge a relationship with a son he never knew existed. *Broken Flowers* mischievously toys with the viewer's expectations that the final scene will ultimately reveal the identity of Johnston's son and former lover and thereby vindicate Murray's tribulations and appease the viewer's interest in the story. Instead, *Broken Flowers* ends with a disconcerted Murray in a frantic state, haunted by the possibility that every teenager he encounters in a track suit *could be* his son wandering the country in search of a father. The lack of narrative cohesion and ambiguous ending made many viewers cranky, including the critic who observed

> I suppose, if you are hugely turned on by director Jim Jarmusch's fragmented directorial style, you might not be as bugged by *Broken Flowers* as I was. I'm a big fan of little things like narrative arc and interesting character development in the films I watch, and this film didn't have either. The film played like a series of loosely connected pieces, but the end result was like trying to put a puzzle together when the pieces don't quite fit, and you're missing about half the pieces you need to make a complete picture at the end. (Voynar)

What is interesting here is the level of emotional discomfort viewers displayed. Partly, they might have been mad simply because it wasn't a typical Bill Murray film. The extremity of people's reaction to narratives that don't make sense, however, also suggests that there is something more at stake here that has to do with representation

Semiotics

Ferdinand de Saussure (1857–1913) was a key figure in launching a move in linguistic theory away from understanding how languages developed historically, or *diachronically*, to looking at them as structures at a single moment in time, or *synchronically*. Saussure was interested in how the individual elements of language—*signs*—worked together, according to rules of selection and combination, to produce meaning. A fundamental principle of Saussure's theory was the premise that the relationship between the two "parts" of a sign—a word (or *signifier*) and the concept it refers to (the *signified*) is not natural but arbitrary, determined by convention. Meaning is produced not by correspondence between word and world, but by differences within the system. Thus, just as the letters c-a-t are meaningless except in relation to other possible selections and combinations of letters (c-a-r, for example, or r-a-t), the word "cat" derives its meaning—an association with a particular furry animal that says "meow"—by virtue of its *difference* from a series of related words—"dog," "mouse," "lemur," "fish." Meaning here is produced by selecting particular elements from a whole *paradigm* of possibilities, and combining them in a particular order, or *syntagm*, according to rules of spelling, grammar, and sense that are specific to each language.

In formulating this theory of language (similar versions of which were being developed simultaneously by the American psychologist C.S. Peirce), Saussure argued for the necessity of a new "science" that would study "the life of signs within a society." This approach, which he termed *semiotics*, has been taken up by theorists of popular culture to read not just spoken language, but also television, film, music, fashion, and architecture.

more broadly. It is ultimately the "rules" of representation—the ways in which they are upheld or broken—that shapes the stories we tell, in films and other forms of entertainment as well as in our everyday conversations; stories that allow us to figure out our place in the world.

As the example of *Broken Flowers* suggests, the "rules" pertain not just to basic linguistic functions, but also to broader cultural processes of sense making. Language functions not as an isolated structure within those processes, but as part of a complex social fabric that cultural theorists have sought to illuminate using structuralist principles. Anthropologist Claude Lévi-Strauss (1908–), for example, worked to uncover the general cultural structures underlying specific myths in primitive societies. A critical part of his theory derived from Saussure's argument that the process of signification, or meaning making, works according to principles of *difference*, with a particular emphasis on **binary opposition**. In other words, things and concepts acquire meaning through what they are not, through their relation to terms that are more or less opposite and mutually exclusive. The far-reaching cultural consequences of this structuring principle become evident when we look at culturally loaded concepts—culture–nature, say, or man–woman— concepts that crucially define the values not just of "primitive" myths but of our own contemporary culture.

Mythologies

French cultural theorist Roland Barthes (1915–1980) uses the word **mythology** in a much more generalized sense, to talk about how sign systems work ideologically to reproduce and legitimate particular social relationships. Barthes elaborates Saussure's theory of how meaning is encoded in signs to take account of the fact that, in addition to their *denotative*, or literal, meanings, signs also assume *connotative*, or mythological, significance. That is, they take on additional associations that are more clearly subjective, charged with a culture's dominant, often unspoken, beliefs or values. In his book *Mythologies*, Barthes examines a collection of texts, images, and practices from French mass culture with the aim of exposing the myths that underpin their seemingly natural symbolic significance. Myth, in Barthes's sense, is a form of representation that works to express and, more or less invisibly, to justify the dominant values of a culture in a particular historical moment.

Unlike the relatively simple level of denotation, in which a word or image often corresponds to a single, obvious definition, myth generally brings into play a whole chain of associated concepts (for example: tree–nature–goodness) by which members of a culture understand certain topics and that help to shape their collective identity. Mythological meanings are generated by the juxtaposition of images and words in particular texts, produced in particular cultural contexts. In one essay, for example, Barthes analyzes a photographic exhibit touring France in the 1960s called "The Great Family of Man." On a denotative level, the exhibit consisted of images of people of different **races**, wearing clothes that signal different cultural backgrounds, all engaged in simple everyday activities— eating, singing, laughing, and so on. The denotative sign, or literal image, of people laughing in turn becomes the signifier for the **humanist** *myth* of universal human nature—a myth that erases historical conditions of inequality in which actual human beings live. The text uses superficial signs of difference—skin colour, dress—which it then brings together into a harmonious, seemingly *natural* whole. This process covers over the actual material and *historical* contradictions that underlie its simple message (Barthes 101). Myth works, Barthes's analysis suggests, to the extent that we read it "straight," accepting unquestioningly its naturalness. The principal goal of his critical reading is to reveal the mechanism behind the myth, "to track down, in the decorative display of *what-goes-without-saying*, the ideological abuse which . . . is hidden there" (11)—to show how myths are not natural but historical, the product of particular relations of power.

Reading the Headlines

A key focus of Barthes's work is the way in which particular representational technologies—colour film, for example—work to create specific ideological effects. Before we move on to talk about visual culture, however, let's try to apply some of the principles of semiotic analysis to some simpler texts: newspaper headlines. The following headline appeared in the *Hamilton Spectator* as part of a story about the introduction of computer software programs written in Inuit languages (Akin B1).

FROM IGLOO TO INTERNET: FIRST NATIONS GAIN ENTRÉE TO THE ELECTRONIC AGE

These programs, the story suggested, would help facilitate government operations and education in the Canadian North. On a denotative level, the signs in this headline are easily legible, though we might struggle with the metaphor in the last half—what does it mean to "gain entry" to an age? On the connotative, mythological level the headline is more complex, and its seemingly straightforward message more open to question. Meaning, as we noted above, is produced by the selection and combination of signs. Thus, "igloo" and "Internet," the main signs in the beginning part of the headline, derive their meaning in part from their juxtaposition with one another, and in part by the grammar of the phrase in which they appear. What sorts of associations do these terms have in relation to one another?

"Igloo" and "Internet" both come out of distinct cultural and historical contexts that inform their mythological associations. Rather than evoking their specific historic origins, however, these associations tend to be much more vague, subjective perceptions of the cultures they carry: "igloo" is associated with "Inuit"—or perhaps more precisely "Eskimo," since igloos belong to a world that for the most part no longer exists, and a time when Southerners' ignorance about the cultures of the North led to the use of the generic term "Eskimo" for all Northern indigenous peoples. While there's nothing obviously pejorative about "igloo," as there is about "Eskimo" (generally thought to be derived from an Algonquin word meaning "eater of raw flesh"), the word does carry connotations that come from the same Southern perspective of the North: it is remote; it is cold; it is barren; it is primitive.

Contrast this with the associations summoned up by the word "Internet": connectedness, speed, modernity, globalization. The sense of the headline, which is reinforced grammatically by the use of the prepositions "from" and "to," is not only one of *opposition* and *contrast* between the two terms, but also of a hierarchical relation in which the movement from one to the other constitutes a progression, a move in the right direction. The positive connotations of the move are also signalled by the phrase "gain entrée," which implies induction into a privileged space, with the suggestion (if we want to really use our imaginations) that the Inuit have finally been brought in out of the cold and into the modern world, after waiting breathlessly on the doorstep of the frozen wasteland of the tundra through much of the twentieth century.

It might be argued that there's actually nothing ideological about the headline at all: it simply describes what happened—Internet connection arrived in the Arctic—and that it does so using the catchy alliterative words "igloo" and "Internet" to draw in readers. There's no question that headlines work partly through verbal cleverness (rhyming, alliteration, puns, etc.) that has little to do with the sense of what's being conveyed (although we might argue that the compulsion to *be* punchy, to reduce complex stories to simple tags, is itself ideological, reinforcing the primary imperative of the media, which is not so much to inform the public as to sell papers). Word choice has other implications, however, for the ideological frame of the story.

The choice of the word "igloo" as a shorthand for the North, for Inuit society, characterizes that society in a way that, besides carrying certain value-laden assumptions, happens to be false: the igloo, and the hunter–gatherer lifestyle that goes with it, hardly exists anymore, a fact that can be celebrated or lamented but that contradicts the picture of the Inuit as a primitive people being catapulted into the twentieth century. Beyond announcing the introduction into the Arctic of what the sources cited in the story agree will be a useful technology, the headline places the story in a wider frame shaped by mythological assumptions about cultural difference, civilization, and the inevitable and desirable course of **globalization** and human **progress**. The issue is not whether these myths are valid or useful; it is that they are *myths*, not naturally given truths—a status that is exposed only by subjecting them to the kind of critical reading that media representations, indeed most conventional uses of language, work against.

Discourse and Power

A semiotic reading like the one we just did focuses on the way in which meaning is generated through the relationships between signs in a text. Of course, the sense of that meaning and its substance—the kind of weight it carries in the world—are determined by the broader cultural context. This includes a community of readers who share a broad collection of cultural references, and the broader system of social relations that determines not only what has meaning in a culture, but also who gets to say what, under what circumstances, and with what social effects.

French philosopher and social critic Michel Foucault (1926–1984) uses the word *discourse* to describe the way speech and writing work in conjunction with specific structures and institutions to shape social reality. **Discourse**, in Foucault's specialized sense of the word, describes a distinct area of social knowledge and the linguistic practices associated with it. Along with particular subjects and ways of talking about them, discourse also defines broad rules about the context of speech or writing, including who is officially permitted to speak on particular subjects and what kind of authority particular kinds of speech (and speakers) carry. Knowledge, according to this concept of discourse, is constituted through relations of power, which determine what is true, what value is accorded particular kinds of knowledge, and, by extension, what material effects that knowledge will have in the world. Knowledge, in other words, *is* power: it comes into being through the operations of power and it *exercises* power by making things happen.

Science, medicine, and law are all examples of specific discourses that emerge in the context of specific historical conditions and in connection with particular institutions.

They are all broadly connected with social power, defining ways not only of talking about but also of managing human subjects, through study, treatment, incarceration, and so on. We will talk more about discourses in Chapter 6, in relation to the construction of identity. For now, the two key points to keep in mind about discourse are (1) its emphasis on the connection between knowledge and power, which legitimates forms of social control over particular groups in society—those deemed unwell, unfit, socially maladjusted, criminal, and so on, and (2) its incorporation of forms of *representation* with forms of social *practice*, which work in reciprocal relation with one another.

REPRESENTING THE YOUTH CRISIS

Bearing in mind the concept of discourse along with Barthes's theory of mythology, we are ready to return to the example that began this chapter—the phenomenon of the youth "crisis" and its representation in the media. To understand the dynamics of that representation, we need first to look at the discourses through which the concepts of youth and criminality are defined, and then to look more specifically at how they are reproduced in specific media.

The Construction of Youth

Media representations of the youth problem are shaped by a variety of separate but overlapping discourses through which we have come to understand not just crime, but also the phenomenon of youth itself. As debates about shifting age thresholds for things such as sexual consent, drivers' licences, paid employment, and subjection to the *Criminal Code* only begin to suggest, the concept of "youth" is a slippery one, with no clear biological or cultural grounding in an objective distinction between childhood and adulthood.

Historical research shows that the idea of childhood is a relatively recent one, emerging in the eighteenth century in conjunction with new ideas about education and psychological development. Almost concurrently with the Romantic idea of childhood innocence there arose a concern about juvenile delinquency, a new social problem whose identification was closely tied to the dominant class's determination to educate, reform, and discipline the urban working class (see Chapter 2). Police, health officials, and the newly emerging fields of psychology and sociology collaborated to record, monitor, evaluate, and "treat" wayward youth with the aim of turning them into obedient, productive members of bourgeois society.

The category "youth" emerges more clearly in sociology around the late 1920s, in conjunction with American theories of urban development—and, more specifically, urban breakdown. The commonly identified problems of urban life—alienation, rootlessness, social deprivation—get projected onto youth, a demographic category that is itself thought to be characterized by confusion and social alienation. This urban theory then becomes the model for studies of youth crime and the formation of youth gangs and subcultures (Hebdige 27). While the perspective of most social investigators tended toward sympathy with their subjects, the discipline of sociology collaborated with institutions of education and the police to construct youth as a new target for **surveillance**, management, and reform.

The dominant perception of youth has changed over the last half-century, largely in response to the growth of teenagers and, increasingly, children as a huge consumer market. Whether this development has contributed to the empowerment of young people is open to question (see Chapter 5 for a general discussion of consumer culture). In any case, alongside an increasingly youth-centred discourse of marketing, the representation of youth continues to be shaped by sociological and legal discourses that emerged in the 1950s. The major contemporary discursive development can be seen in the identification of the "new" phenomenon of girl violence, which is a kind of spinoff from the more general category identified below.

The Kids Are Not All Right

The contemporary fascination with youth crime covers up the history of the idea of youth, specifically the timing of its emergence in conjunction with initiatives to tighten social control. It would seem that youth and crime have been linked together from the beginning. One of the critical elements of the current stories about violent youth, though, is an emphasis on the *newness* of the phenomenon—not just that youth are more dangerous than they were before, but also that we are seeing the development of new and terrifying forms of violent crime. To understand the construction of the "new" youth problem, it's useful to look at an earlier "new" crisis of violence that occurred in 1970s Britain and which has been extensively analyzed by Stuart Hall, Chas Critcher, Tony Jefferson, John Clarke, and Brian Roberts.

In their book *Policing the Crisis: Mugging, the State, and Law and Order,* these writers document the emergence in 1970s Britain of a "new" category of crime—mugging. The word definitively entered British consciousness for the first time following the stabbing death of an elderly man by three men in their early 20s, an event described by a police officer and subsequently in the press as a "mugging gone wrong" (qtd. in S. Hall et al. 3). While the term *mugging* had never before been used to describe crime in Britain, it was familiar from its more widespread use in the United States, where it was associated not just with a particular kind of crime—violent robbery—but also with a whole range of broader themes connected to general social breakdown. Following the 1972 incident in Britain, "mugging" quickly came into routine use, appearing in media stories about crimes that actually didn't differ all that much from earlier forms of violent crime except by virtue of the new and ominous name. Fuelling new statistical surveys (that inevitably demonstrated that "mugging" was on the rise), it became part of a broad law-and-order discourse that eventually gave rise to new and tougher criminal penalties and other forms of social control.

The story Hall et al. tell about mugging in their book is an important one—not, they acknowledge, because it tells us why muggings happen or what should be done about them, but because it places the whole issue in a broader context, looking at mugging as a social phenomenon defined not only by the crime itself, but also by society's *reaction* to that crime and the way it is represented. Hall et al. thus begin their study by looking at the emergence of "mugging" as a label that drags along with it a whole referential context, a whole narrative network overlaid with particular assumptions and values. "Mugging" picked up its symbolic baggage from the history of its usage in the United States, where it "not only dominated the whole public discussion of crime and public disorder—it had become a central *symbol* for the many tensions and problems besetting American social and political life in general" (Hall et al. 19). "Mugging" acquired this significance, they go on to say,

> because of its ability to *connote* a whole complex of social themes in which the "crisis of American society" was reflected. These themes included: the involvement of blacks and drug addicts in crime; the expansion of the black ghettoes, coupled with the growth of black social and political militancy; the threatened crisis and collapse of the cities; the crime panic and the appeal to "law and order". . . . These topics and themes were not as clearly separated as these headings imply. They tended, in public discussion, to come together into a general scenario of conflict and crisis. In an important sense the image of "mugging" came ultimately to contain and express them all. (20)

The term entered the British public vocabulary in this broad, general sense *before* it gained widespread use to describe specific crimes. In other words, "mugging" acquired significance in a *mythological* sense before being applied literally to describe concrete events. And it was in its mythological sense that mugging inspired what sociologists refer to as a "moral panic" (see Close-Up 3.2).

New Categories of Crime   In a situation that echoes the mugging crisis of 1970s Britain, the period since the mid-1990s in North America has produced what amounts to a **moral panic** about crime, particularly violent youth crime. A key sign and instigator of that panic is the emergence of apparently "new" categories of crime, each of which carries with it a host of anxieties about general and specific social problems. As with mugging, many of these "new" crimes really amount to the redefinition of old categories: thus, "common assault" became "swarming," "break and enter" became "home invasion," "car theft" became "carjacking," "drive-by shootings" appeared, "serial" rapes and murders became common, and the term "road rage" appeared—all justifying a push for tougher interventions (Page).

Suggested Activity 3.1

Can you think of other words or phrases that have entered (or reentered) public discourse recently to describe "new" social phenomena? In what contexts—in relation to what issues or debates—are they employed? What kinds of symbolic baggage do these words and phrases carry? What ideological assumptions do they rest on? What sorts of social practices do they condemn or legitimate?

These interventions extend beyond harsher penalties for crime to more general policies aimed at youth: dress and conduct codes in schools, extension and intensification of the use of identity cards, curfews (in some places), video cameras in downtown streets, and new regulations designed to prevent youth from hanging out or loitering in public and private spaces such as malls.

The *National Post* ran a headline in its May 8, 2002, edition that read, "Pierced girls are bad girls: study." The caption of the accompanying photo stated that "A U.S. researcher says parents, teachers and doctors should view an adolescent's desire to obtain a body piercing as a warning sign, prompting a closer inspection of the teenager's friends and pastimes."

Close-Up 3.2

Moral Panic

In his book on cultural responses to the 1970s subculture of mods and rockers, *Folk Devils and Moral Panics*, Stan Cohen defines moral panic this way:

> Societies appear to be subject, every now and then, to periods of moral panic. A condition, episode, person or group of persons emerges to become defined as a threat to societal values and interests; its nature is presented in a stylized and stereotypical fashion by the mass media; the moral barricades are manned by editors, bishops, politicians and other right-thinking people; socially accredited experts pronounce their diagnoses and solutions; ways of coping are evolved or (more often) resorted to; the condition then disappears, submerges or deteriorates and becomes more visible. (28)

At its height, moral panic spreads a wide blanket over social experience, interpreting diverse and random behaviours or practices as signs of a danger. Regardless of its generally mythological origins, moral panic has real measurable effects in the form of individual behaviour, social behaviour, and governmental policy. These reactions to the perceived threat come to play an integral role in (retrospectively) defining its meaning.

Making the News

Before we turn to some specific examples of media representations of youth violence, let's take a general look at the role of the media—specifically the news—in producing social knowledge. Looking at the news media as a whole helps to illuminate the conditions in which individual stories are produced, as well as by showing how particular meanings (particular stories) get favoured over others, and how they come to assume material significance.

Critical to an analysis of the presentation of events in the news is a recognition that the news is not a transparent window on the world; rather, it is an account assembled from a mass of chaotic data according to particular principles of selection and ordering, framed by internal, organizational constraints and broader social codes. It reflects not a single set of interests, but a limited range of interests that tend to support the preservation of existing relations of power—that is, the position of dominant social groups. This tendency should not be understood in terms of a crude conspiracy theory, which sees the news media as always serving the agenda of "the state" or "big business" (though the reliance of the news, like all mainstream media, on advertising and the tendency for news production to be concentrated in the hands of fewer and fewer large corporate owners leads inevitably to a corporate capitalist bias). Even when media empires rest in the hands of outspoken defenders of the political right wing (e.g., Rupert Murdoch), the relationship of news media to forces of social and economic conservatism is generally more subtle, and more mundane, than theories of direct and overt manipulation would suggest.

News-Gathering Structures News organizations are not monolithic ideological forces; they are complex organizations in which editors and journalists generally exercise a great degree of control over the subject matter and perspective of their stories. Writers do not enjoy absolute freedom (particularly since 9/11, when heightened security measures are cited in support of incidents curtailing press freedom, such as a 2004 RCMP raid on the house of an *Ottawa Citizen* reporter in order to uncover her sources in a story relating to a botched terrorism investigation). In general, however, the media's reproduction of dominant ideology stems not from coercion, or even conscious cooperation; rather, it is built into established structures of news-gathering. Faced by time and resource pressures, the media rely on a steady supply of stories from reliable, accredited sources: these sources, not surprisingly, usually turn out to be dominant institutions (government, police, the courts) as well as accredited "experts" (academics, think tanks, leaders of interest groups) (Hall et al. 58). As well as being, by virtue of their size and influence, the biggest news-*makers* of the day, these sources also set the terms by which stories are *interpreted*, constructing them within frameworks whose dominance conceals their partiality or bias. Thus, even though the media will often consult alternative voices in order to satisfy the imperative of impartiality (generally defined in terms of showing "both sides" of a story—as though there are ever only two sides to a story!), the overall framework of the story is set by the dominant institution: its perspective determines how the issues are framed, what questions can be asked, and what *doesn't* get included in the discussion.

In reportage of the Gulf crisis that led to the war of 1990–91, for example, the late cultural critic Edward Said notes that discussion in the United States tended to be framed around two options: should the U.S. attack Iraq immediately following Iraq's invasion of Kuwait, or wait to see if sanctions worked? These two positions crystallized into the official boundaries of discussion when they were erected as the poles of debate between journalists Karen Elliott House and Anthony Lewis on the news/discussion show the *MacNeil/Lehrer NewsHour*. As intelligent and reasoned voices of the respected papers the *Wall Street Journal* and *The New York Times*, respectively, House and Lewis could be trusted between them to give viewers the "whole" picture, a balanced and fair assessment of the possibilities it entailed. Left unexamined in their discussion was the assumption that America *should* intervene somehow, that it "ought *to be* in the Gulf, regulating the behavior of states armies, and peoples several thousand miles away" (Said *Culture and Imperialism* 293). Consistent with the unquestioned emphasis on the United States, there was virtually no mention of the Arabs "as having something to do with the war, as its victims, for instance, or (equally convincingly) its instigators" (293). The event, rather, was circumscribed, framed in a limited way that was perceived to speak to the interests of its American audience, an audience whose character was not merely reflected, but *constituted* through the debate. That is, rather than speaking to a group whose interests were already defined around common goals and values, this news broadcast, in conjunction with ongoing CNN coverage, played a significant role in helping to *define* a consensus around which all American viewers could gather.

Consensus   The process of assuming and building consensus is, according to Hall et al., a key aspect of news production. " 'Consensual' views of society," they go on to explain, "represent society as if there are no major cultural or economic breaks, no major conflicts of interests between classes and groups. Whatever disagreements exist, it is said, there are legitimate and institutionalised means for expressing and reconciling them" (55). The ideological imperatives of consensus-building, along with the practical imperatives of news-gathering, mean that non-central, or marginalized, voices rarely get to contribute to the debate. Thus, the educated "expert"/journalist, with privileged access to government sources, becomes the voice of "all of us"—including, presumably, expatriate Iraqi-Americans and Canadians whose own "expert" views might be very different. The same rules of consensus-building apply to forms of media such as talk radio, in which broadcasters assume a populist, common-sense persona that functions to unite an "us" against "them" (with "them" in this case often caricatured as the "elite" media, "special interest groups," or simply "intellectuals").

Suggested Activity 3.2

Over the last decade, satirical news programs such as *The Daily Show* and *The Colbert Report* have come to dominate the news media landscape, serving as the principle view on current events for many people. One of the chief appeals of these shows is the way they lampoon traditional ways of creating consensus (e.g., by offering a tongue-in-cheek defence of "conservative values"). Even as they reject simplistic or obvious forms of conformity, these shows clearly speak to different models of belonging. How do these models work? Comparing coverage of major news events by satirical and "straight" newscasts, try to identify similarities and differences in the strategies they use to create consensus, and the values they reflect and/or try to instill in viewers.

Echoes of the representation of the 1990–91 Gulf War resounded in the 2002 buildup to the war against Iraq. Once more the terms of the debate are set by dominant interests: "the honest choices now are to give up and give in, or to remove Mr. Hussein before he gets his bomb," as an editorial in *The Economist* put it ("The Case For War" 9). Once again, the news media engage in the work of consensus-building, with headlines in Canadian newspapers reading "Today We Are *All* Americans" (Wente A6; emphasis added), or, after the bombing of a nightclub in Bali in which most of the victims were Australians, "We Are *All* Australians Now" (Wente A23; emphasis added). Of course, the delineation of an inside—"we"—also entails the construction of an outside ("they," i.e., terrorists and their alleged sympathizers) without whom there would be no story. During the 2003 U.S.–led war on Iraq, the Pentagon-sanctioned practice of "embedding," in which selected reporters were attached to military units, helped to generate sympathetic coverage of the American soldiers, and thus to shore up consensus within the news audience about the justness of the war.

Suggested Activity 3.3

While the goal of consensus-building characterizes news media in general, the *terms* and *extent* of that consensus differ depending on which media outlet we look at (local vs. national television news, for example; public vs. commercial; print vs. television). Take a look at different news media and try to analyze how consensus is assumed or actively enlisted in each case: Around what common beliefs is consensus defined? Who's included, and who's left out? Does the boundary of the community shift depending on the news item?

Media and Youth Crime

Nowhere, perhaps, is the consensus-building function of news more evident than in stories about crime. Crime is a dominant feature in news in part because it so nicely fits the general ideological criteria for what Hall et al. term "news value": it is out of the ordinary; it is dramatic in a tragic way; it is easily personalized; and it can be incorporated into a broader pattern of stories. As with all events deemed newsworthy, the media make crime stories meaningful by identifying them and placing them in a context familiar to the audience—that is, locating them "within a range of known social and cultural identifications" (Hall et al. 54). The assumption of consensus is obviously an important part of this process: the news is intelligible only to the extent that its audience shares common ideas about how society is defined and how it operates. Consensus assumes the more specific, ideologically charged significance discussed above, depending on the kind of news story being reported. Crime stories are particularly successful consensus-builders because, besides being out of the realm of the ordinary, they also fall outside the bounds of community; in fact, they play a key role in defining those boundaries. On the one side is the respectable, law-abiding community—"us"—for whom the victim becomes an innocent and sympathetic embodiment. On the other side is "them"—the accused criminals who, for reasons both ideological and pragmatic (most people charged with crimes aren't affiliated with journalists' regular "trusted sources"), don't have a voice in their story. Their lack of symbolic representation translates into a more concrete lack of power in the court system where, as a result of diminishing government funding for legal aid, many people accused of crimes are appearing in court without a lawyer. Under these circumstances it has been shown that "they may also be more likely to plead guilty, get convicted and receive stricter sentences" (Tsoukalas and Roberts 87).

Picturing Crime

In its construction of social reality, the news gains its substance through the power of myth. The operation of myth is evident in the photo and caption below, from a story in the *National Post* about the Ontario provincial government's proposed Safe Streets Act

This photo appeared in the *National Post* with the headline "Harris vows to rid streets of pushy beggars, squeegees." The caption below the photo provided further information: "The Tories would amend the Highway Traffic Act to keep 'Martin' from his post at the corner of Spadina Avenue and Queen Street West."

that came into effect in 2000 (Ibbitson A1). Before we analyze the text itself, we need to make a few observations about the significance of photographic representation. Unlike words, the images in photography do not translate what they signify into an arbitrary code; they are a precise *analogue*, or copy, of the objects they reproduce. This purity of reproduction encourages us to think of photographs as offering a truer, more authentic representation of the world than language is capable of doing; indeed, it is photography's capacity for **realism** that makes it such a valued part of print media.

Our inclination to trust the evidence of our eyes, for which the photographer functions as a kind of proxy, makes it hard to remember that realism, which describes a mode of representation that is taken to provide a faithful and objective picture of the world, is itself a kind of code or convention, and one with a very recent history (see Close-Up 3.3).

Close-Up 3.3

Realism

The history of realism is closely tied up with the development of **capitalism** (and popular culture) in at least three important ways. First, the emphasis in realism is on an objective reality, a world of material things, which it is the job of representation, whether textual or photographic, to capture. Connected explicitly with the discriminating power of vision, realism is part of a broader ideology of *enlightenment*, defined by rational scientific knowledge and economic **liberalism**. This ideology powerfully challenged traditional forms of perception, in which the seen and the unseen, the physical and spiritual, were taken to exist in conjunction with one another.

Second, the birth of realism, which critic John Berger connects with techniques of sixteenth-century oil painting, can be seen as part of a new **materialist** ideology. In its convention of rendering objects in almost three-dimensional substance, "oil painting," Berger suggests, "did to appearances what capital did to social relations. It reduced everything to the equality of objects. . . . All reality was mechanically measured by its materiality" (87). The growth of art collection, not surprisingly, coincides with the rise of **consumerism** in general: oil painting depicts a world of objects whose visual consumption becomes an emblem of material ownership.

Finally, realism flourished in part because of the advent of the technologies of photography and film. Besides their direct commercial significance, these technologies also contributed to the development of modern capitalist society more generally, by providing tools of information-gathering to scientists, government, and corporate bodies and by providing the public with forms of mass entertainment—including and especially advertising (see Chapter 5)—that stimulate them to engage in ever higher levels of **consumption**.

Representation and the Construction of Social Reality

What makes photographic realism so powerful—and so deceptive—as a reproduction of reality is its capacity to capture the constant movement of things and freeze it in a single instant. In that instant, the images captured weirdly stand out as more vivid, more intense than our actual experience can ever be. This vividness contributes to photography's seeming ability to convey a world more substantial than that represented by language. The pitfalls of this vividness are twofold: first, it works by tearing objects out of their place in space and time (essentially robbing them of their historical context); second, its apparent naturalness conceals the mediating role of culture in its construction.

"Culture" here refers to the practices that make the photo make sense. First, it includes the decisions made by the photographer—what to include or exclude, how to frame the subject, what kind of lighting or other technical codes to use, and so on. The increasing ability of photographers to manipulate images digitally (even many compact cameras now boast a "slimming" feature) is only an extension of these cruder **aesthetic** technologies. Second—and harder to identify—are the multiple cultural resources viewers bring to bear in interpreting the photograph. With these cautions in mind, we are now ready to look at the photo and caption from the *National Post*.

Those "Pushy Squeegees"

On a denotative level, the photo depicts the view from inside a car, its windshield being washed by a young man in a torn T-shirt. Through the haze of the wiper fluid, a city street is visible. Separately, and even together, the images in the photo could evoke a number of different associations: they are, in semiotic terms, "polysemous." Their meaning is fixed, however, or *anchored*, by the story headline, which reads: "Harris vows to rid streets of pushy beggars, squeegees." It is the headline that gives the story its connotative significance and makes it intelligible in a particular cultural context.

Both conventional codes of reading and knowledge of the specific context make it clear that the youth cleaning the windscreen is not "Harris" (whom *National Post* readers would recognize as Mike Harris, the then-premier of Ontario), but a "pushy squeegee." If the image alone isn't enough to convey menace and the threat of violence, the word "pushy" makes it clear that the youth in question is not providing a service, but committing an aggressive act (the squeegee being a metaphor for . . . a switchblade? a club?), while the phrase "rid the streets of . . . " confirms his place in the category of socially useless, even dangerous things. The caption below the photo reads, "The Tories would amend the Highway Traffic Act to keep 'Martin' from his post at the corner of Spadina Avenue and Queen Street West"; "Martin" is thus not only identified as one of the targets of the legislation, but also made representative of *all* the beggars and squeegees: men, women, and children living on—and allegedly terrorizing—the streets. The arrangement of the photo works nicely with the grammar of the sentence so that the reader identifies both with the perspective of the camera, which is inside the car, under siege along with the car's driver, *and* with Harris, who embodies the force of law and order with his reassuring vow to make the streets safe again.

We are thus made to feel both vulnerable and reassured: the threat (which is made real in the representation of this story, even if we didn't feel it before) will be taken care of. The meaning of the story and photo are further anchored through their presence in the *National Post*, a paper whose general political slant favours law-and-order policies such as the criminalization of squeegees. The same photo and caption in a different paper—a different frame—might produce a slightly different interpretation.

In its actual context, a story like this one works to elicit public support for political programs like the Safe Streets Act, as well as more generally to reinforce a vision of social order in which "we" are on the inside, protected morally and legally from the onslaughts of those pushy street people. The photo reinforces the division, with the frame of the car window defining a material and ideological fortress between the driver and "Martin," a shadowy figure whose marginality is confirmed by the quotation marks surrounding his name.

Crime on Television

While the newspaper article about the Safe Streets Act uses image and text to turn "Martin" into the poster boy for urban disorder, the television special "Victoria's Secret" cited at the beginning of this chapter employs the more expansive codes of television to weave representations of specific instances of violent youth crime into an elaborate narrative defining a major social issue. While photos promise to deliver a more accurate representation of the world than words, television claims a more privileged place still in its capacity to make connections between images, in a simulation of real-life change and movement. As with photography, however, we need to resist the urge to read television representations naturalistically, and instead think about *how* they are simulated.

With television even more than photography, this means paying attention to the way its status as a form of commercial media structures its content. While the function of television clearly changes depending on whether the program being broadcast is a game show, a sitcom, or the news, a common feature of all television programming is the need to produce meaningful information out of an inherently erratic stream of programming: that is, individual television shows need to convey self-contained narratives that mark them off from the general flow of programming, and construct meaningful bridges over commercial interruptions. At the same time, the structure of commercial breaks requires that programs be broken down into manageable segments or "packages" that fit comfortably between the commercials (and it's worth remembering that, from the television industry's point of view, it's the commercials that are the meat and potatoes of the programming: the shows merely provide the hooks to bring in viewers/consumers). The tidy-package imperative, according to which information has to be marshalled into compact (i.e., 10-minute), easily digestible bits, contradicts one of television's key selling points, which is its ability to tell stories—to place images, events, and people into a broader context. These structural imperatives have begun to shift with the increasingly seamless blending of commercials and programming, a manipulation of "reality" that further blurs our perception of crime.

Victoria's Not-So-Nice Secret

This is the mandate of a show like "Victoria's Secret," which seeks not just to document, but also to make sense of, the phenomenon of youth violence in Canada. The show opens *in medias res*, or "in the middle of things," with a shot of a plane landing and a stretcher being unloaded. The sense of crisis conveyed by the opening sequence is heightened by the darkness and even blurriness of the scene, which is filmed in the rain, and by a rapid series of jump-cuts from plane to ambulance to stretcher. The images are knitted together by the voiceover, which identifies the scene as the conclusion of a "mercy flight" from Victoria to Toronto. The unconscious patient on the stretcher, a teenaged boy, is "home for Christmas, but not the way he left." The dramatic events of the story are personalized in the next shot, in which the boy's mother, facing a battery of microphones, explains that her son, who is in a coma, "was very badly beaten up by three guys for no rhyme or reason; he just happened to be in the wrong place at the wrong time." The "wrong place," the voiceover resumes to tell us, is Victoria, B.C., "Canada's garden playground."

And the story, as the title suggests, is as much about this place as it is about the terrible plight of Nicholas Johnson. Specifically, it's about Victoria's "dark side," as a city besieged by roving teenaged gangs. The threatening quality of these gangs is established by words and images that from the opening shots of the program work to establish clear contrasts between safety and danger, the familiar and the unknown, light and darkness. The world of humane, civilized community and family, summoned up by phrases like "mercy" and "home for Christmas," is contrasted with—and shown to be threatened by—a chaotic underworld, in which anonymous groups of guys—gangs—roam around looking for violence. The theme of contrasts is set up by initial shots of a tourist's Victoria—a sailboat leaving a marina, golfers playing in the middle of winter, flowers, people drinking tea at the Empress Hotel—accompanied by the voiceover warning ominously that, while the city is "at first glance, scenic, safe and secure . . . this is a tale of two cities. It may be hard to believe, but there is a dark side to this city. A violent and dangerous one."

Here the image changes dramatically to a scene of the reporter talking to the camera as she walks along what appears to be a dark alley, flanked by walls covered with graffiti. If the mother functions to bring us into the story, presenting a suffering human face with which the viewer is asked to identify, the reporter serves as the controlling perspective of objectivity. In the mode of a correspondent sending dispatches from a war zone, she brings alarming news of a situation that, while barely visible until now, constitutes a pervasive social problem rendered all the more threatening by its manifestation in apparently "random" and "senseless" acts of violence.

Inciting panic in its viewers, the revelation that there is "a youth gang problem in the midst of Canada's Shangri-la" also offers a kind of comfort, conveyed in the rational, authoritative voice of the reporter, that the problem has been identified, given a label. "These are legitimate gangs," a police officer confirms. "They have a hierarchy; they're wearing colours." The use of the word "legitimate" is interesting, signalling not, clearly, that the gangs are on the side of law and order, but that they fit a template, they are classifiable—and hence manageable. No longer random and unintelligible, the problem has assumed a handle we can grasp. And we are persuaded that, though we might not have been conscious of it, this is a problem whose presence we somehow recognized all along: "For too many years, gangs of young people have been allowed to terrorize the streets." This is a cause for outrage that translates into relief that "citizens are now standing up at community meetings demanding action, searching for solutions"—solutions that are forthcoming in the form of police task forces, tougher laws, and pressure on young people to inform authorities about violence, or threats of violence, committed by their peers.

The "Inside versus Outside" Perspective   As well as being a story of contrasts, this is also, like the squeegee article, a story of insides and outsides. "Inside" represents the community, concerned citizens, the media, and us as viewers, threatened by an "outside" inhabited by dark and unruly forces, nameless young people who commit acts of violence with "no rhyme or reason." The story also invokes other "insides" and "outsides" in its characterization of Victoria as a place where things like this are not "supposed" to happen. Even the working-class suburb of Esquimault, where two of the assaults occurred, "is a far cry from the mean streets, urban decay and inner-city ghettoes normally associated with street gangs."

At the same time, then, that "Victoria's Secret" might be working to shake its urban or suburban viewers out of their complacency, suggesting that there really aren't "two cities"—we all inhabit the same big, dangerous world—it also serves to shore up boundaries, to reassure us that, unlike in the "mean streets" (of Toronto? South Central L.A.?), we *do* still live in a community where civilized values prevail. Problems such as poverty and racial tension, summoned up by the word "ghetto," remain "outside," not part of this story or part of Canada's garden playground, though they might hover dangerously nearby, threatening to spill over if we don't monitor the borders vigilantly enough. Because the story of youth violence is perhaps above all a cautionary tale about the dangers of complacency, of not attending to signs of social disorder and not treating them seriously enough when we find them.

In looking at "Victoria's Secret" as an example of how representation constructs social reality, we are not trying to suggest that the instances of violence it documents are somehow fabricated, or that their effects are negligible. Rather, we want you to think about the process by which the media frames those instances in a particular way, incorporating them within a narrative that draws on and in turn helps to consolidate specific beliefs, emotions, and assumptions. Extending far beyond the specific crimes the show documents, these beliefs, emotions, and values inform—often unconsciously—our ideas about community, youth, law, and the society we live in. Similarly, a show like "Victoria's Secret" doesn't just inform us about events that are going on in our society; it *re-presents* those events as part of a broad vision of what society should look like. The "facts" of the story are inseparable from—indeed, they are largely manufactured by—values and politics. As an authoritative force in society that holds a near-monopoly on social knowledge (in more than one sense, as control over media falls into fewer and fewer hands), the news, particularly in the area of crime, plays an effective role in constructing and delimiting public opinion. In order to recognize, and to critically challenge, the ideologies that underpin dominant constructions of the social order, it is necessary to ask, as Hall et al. do in their book on mugging, a series of questions about the news stories we watch, hear, and read: "'What, other than what has been said about this topic, *could* be said?' 'What questions are omitted?' 'Why do the questions—which always presuppose answers of a particular kind—so often recur in this form? Why do certain other questions never appear?'" (65). In the case of the representation of youth violence, some of the missing questions might be: What kinds of relationships exist between trends in youth crime and trends in adult crime? How does youth crime fit into an overall pattern of youth culture? How does society function (or not) to address the needs of youth in relation to areas such as education, job opportunities, public space, social programs, and so on? How have social views of youth changed? If you think about it, you can probably come up with other questions, other ways of framing the "youth problem."

TRUTH2POWER: THE POLITICS OF REPRESENTATION

As the analysis above suggests, representation has a lot to do with power—with what gets spoken about in what way, and with who gets to speak, on whose behalf. In both the organization of media and the ideological structure of language and other sign systems, representation tends to reproduce and to naturalize existing relations of social power. The example of media representation of youth violence demonstrates the function of discourse in the maintenance of social order: the simultaneous classification and marginalization of relatively powerless members of society—in this case, youth—works to keep them in their place, through discourse and, more concretely, in the form of laws and social policies.

Representing the Other: Gender and Race

The connection between symbolic and material power relations also emerges clearly with respect to political categories such as gender, sexuality, and race. Gender is one of the most basic, if not *the* most basic, binary oppositions that underlies the process of signification. The critical thing about binary opposition, from a cultural and/or political perspective, is that its significance is rarely neutral: rather, it involves not just a differential but also a *hierarchical* relationship between the two terms. Thus, the associative chain that links the sign "man" with culture, reason, and consciousness and "woman" with nature, passion, and physical being doesn't just assert an absolute distinction between the opposing sets of terms; it also establishes a relation of dominance in which the first term is read as *normative* or natural, and the second is characterized by difference or lack—a quality of "not-quite-ness."

This relation is not only expressed through language and culture generally; it is also reinforced by the technologies of visual culture. **Psychoanalytic** theory suggests that identity formation, the process of defining a "self" in relation to "others," is powerfully shaped by different kinds of looking, and that these forms of looking are gendered. It is the visual perception of others that enables both *identification*—the narcissistic projection of oneself into the place of another, based on perceived similarity—and *objectification*, the imaginary possession of another based on perceived difference. "In a world ordered by sexual imbalance," film critic Laura Mulvey suggests, "pleasure in looking has been split between active/male and passive/female" (326). Traditional Hollywood cinema perpetuates these roles, she suggests, through the production of films that enable the audience to simultaneously identify with an active (male) hero and objectify the passive heroine. This is a simplification of Mulvey's complex (and controversial) argument; the main point of her article for our purposes is that the *activity* of looking, in its contradictory narcissistic and voyeuristic aspects, is coded male, while woman, connoting "*to-be-looked-at-ness*," is consigned to the role of object of the gaze (326).

In practice, as we note in Chapter 6, the business of identity formation is a messy one, as the fantasy of mastering the other always threatens to tip over into the nightmare of *becoming* the other, of losing the power of selfhood—a power, in psychoanalytic theory, that is tied to possession of masculine agency, symbolized by the phallus. Traditional Hollywood film resolves that anxiety, offering through the combination of narrative and spectacle the simultaneous pleasures of identification and objectification: one can "be" the hero while enjoying the spectacle of the objectified heroine, with all potential contradictions or tensions miraculously resolved through the fantasy-world of the screen. The consequence for the male viewer is not just pleasure, but also a consolidation of his sense of self and power in the world; the female viewer's pleasure is more ambivalent, as she is excluded from the fantasy of complete identity and confirmed in a role of passivity and powerlessness.

Popular visual culture, then, has traditionally worked to reinforce and accentuate the cultural code of masculine dominance and female subjection by spectacularizing difference and inequality. Much the same thing occurs in the representation of minorities, whose visible embodiment of difference has served, like the category of femininity, to shore up the dominant—white, masculine—code of identity. Like the female body, the non-white body, both male and female, has historically served the function of spectacle, a site for the projection of fear and desire in the form of **stereotypes** (see Chapter 7).

Suggested Activity 3.4

Many critics have challenged Mulvey's thesis of narrative pleasure in cinema by looking, for example, at the role of women as active viewers of film images. Her thesis is also challenged by the increasingly complex ways women are represented on film and television. Film and video game heroine Lara Croft and television detective Veronica Mars (Kristen Bell) are both sexy and powerful, passive objects and active, aggressive agents. Can you think of other examples of women in film that disrupt the simple binary code described by Mulvey?

"Powerful female roles like television detective Veronica Mars complicate Laura Mulvey's theory of active masculinity and passive femininity in visual culture"

Challenging Negative Representation

As the preceding discussion on media representation of youth crime suggests, negative or stereotypical representation has political consequences: it reflects and reinforces the marginality of **minority** groups. Thus it follows that the political empowerment of subordinate groups in society—women, youth, racial minorities, gays and lesbians, the disabled, the poor, the elderly—depends in part on changing the way they are represented. General acceptance of this principle is evident in the process by which our culture self-consciously changes the words it uses, often at the instigation of educators or activist groups, to replace pejorative terms with more inclusive ones. The word "coloured," for example, has long been abandoned as a description of racial minorities, while the more recent phrase "people of colour" (which emphasizes personhood first, and race only secondarily) reflects—but also works to bring about—general acceptance of the principle of racial equality.

Representational Strategies   We can track similar shifts in popular visual culture toward more inclusive representation. In the case of racial minorities (and there are clear historical parallels in the representation of women and gays and lesbians), it is possible to identify a number of different strategies that attempt to work against dominant codes of racial representation. *Integrationist* or *assimilationist* strategies, embodied in films such as *Guess Who's Coming to Dinner* (1967), serve metaphorically to invite blacks into mainstream white society on the strength of the reassuring message that "they" are "just like" us. *Affirmationist* messages work in a contrary way to emphasize **essentialist** black identities, but in a way that challenges the mainstream. So-called "blaxploitation" films from the 1970s (discussed in more detail in Chapter 7) fulfill this function. Many popular films and television shows use a combination of these strategies. For example, the 1980s television series *The Cosby Show* represents blacks succeeding in white society through their own efforts, but in a way that plays down the history and ongoing reality of discrimination, as well as politics of resistance. A related genre is the "black-and-white friendship" film (examples include *Pulp Fiction, Die Hard with a Vengeance, Lethal Weapon 1, 2, 3,* and *4, Men in Black 1* and *2, The Shawshank Redemption, The Fast and the Furious,* and *Remember the Titans*), which highlights the possibility of overcoming the barriers of race through individual tolerance and understanding.

All of these strategies—which can be plotted more or less historically, though remnants of earlier forms persist—aim toward more positive representations of blacks in the popular media. While it is tempting to frame them in terms of an evolutionary narrative toward greater equality, there are problems with each of these counter-narratives. First, as we discuss in more detail in Chapter 7, the attempt to counter negative stereotypes with more positive ones reverses the hierarchy while leaving the codes of essential identity–difference intact. The black–white friendship movie, which avoids the stereotype altogether by constructing highly individualized relationships, is problematic in a different way. By suggesting that the problem of racial discrimination is a matter of individual morality, these films ignore the broader social and material context of race relations: it means that, while overt acts of individual **racism** can be universally condemned, "the more subtle, deeper forms of discursively and institutionally structured racism remain unrecognized" (Shohat and Stam 201). In more explicit social terms:

> The good news at the movies obscures the bad news in the streets and confirms the [U.S.] Supreme Court's recent decisions on busing, affirmative action and redistricting. . . . Because black–white friendship is now understood to be the rule, there is no need for integrated schools or . . . affirmative action. The Congress and state governors can guiltlessly cut welfare, food assistance, fuel assistance . . . housing money, fellowship money, vaccine money. (DeMott 33)

The obvious criticism to make of these films, then, is that their "realistic" representation of black–white friendship glosses over the real social conditions of black people living in the United States, including disproportionate rates of mortality, poverty, and imprisonment. Serving as an emblem of already-achieved equality, these films help to legitimate neoliberal social policies that contribute to the further marginalization of minority groups. A number of recent films, such as *Monster's Ball* and the Spike Lee documentary *When the Levees Broke*, counter the upbeat message presented by these films with a more *social realist* perspective, one that emphasizes the economic and social relations of *in*equality that are concealed by the myth of tolerant individualism. Rather than focusing on exemplary characters who rise above their social circumstances (characters who always manage to be a bit richer/smarter/better-looking than everyone around them), these films offer a more complex view, one that acknowledges the role of culture and economics in shaping individual lives.

By now it should be impossible for you to read the words "real" and "realism" without warning bells going off. However praiseworthy the efforts to create an accurate, rather than a simply positive, picture of a group or situation, such efforts remain troubled by the shaky "reality" of representation itself, according to which myth and ideology are not simply everywhere present, but inescapable. Under these conditions, one could argue that the only way seriously to undermine the politics of representation is to highlight the hidden conventions and codes on which they're based—much as we did in our semiotic readings of newspaper and television news reports. As Laura Mulvey puts it,

> the magic of Hollywood style at its best . . . arose . . . in one important aspect, from its skilled and satisfying manipulation of visual pleasure. Unchallenged, mainstream film coded the erotic into the language of the dominant **patriarchal** order. In the highly developed Hollywood cinema it was only through these codes that the alienated subject . . . came near to finding a glimpse of satisfaction: through its formal beauty and its play on his own formative obsession. . . . It is said that analysing pleasure, or beauty, destroys it. (323)

That, Mulvey announces, is the intention of her article. It is also the intention of avant-garde cinema—those films, such as *Paris Is Burning* or *Boys Don't Cry*, for example, that deconstruct, as they represent, dominant codes of representation. Satire is another powerful way to highlight through humorous exaggeration the construction of stereotypes. The 2005 film *Borat* is a good example of this genre. The film features British comedian Sacha Baron Cohen, who travels through the U.S. posing as "Borat," a journalist from Kazakhstan who holds outrageously ignorant views about women, Jews, and other minorities. By expressing these views, Baron Cohen (himself an orthodox Jew) gets unwitting Americans to reveal their own strongly held prejudices. One danger of such satirical critiques is that the distinction between laughing at and laughing with offensive humour is sometimes murky. The repetition of powerful myths, even if it is done with the aim of critique, always carries the risk of merely reinforcing them.

Satire, when it works to critical effect, is another illustration of Mulvey's argument about destroying or demystifying the images that seduce us, reminding us that negative representations can't be undone without attending to their underlying politics, including the contexts from which they're produced.

Beyond Representation: Who's the Boss?

This points to another issue in media representation: namely, its production. In 2007, minority groups would appear to have made huge strides in television and film, with shows such as *Grey's Anatomy*, *Heroes*, and *Ugly Betty* featuring black, Asian, and Hispanic characters in lead roles, and non-white actors claiming a healthy share of Oscar nominations. However, for many media critics, the way minority groups are represented is secondary to who controls the production, distribution, and exhibition of those representations. Reports on Hollywood employment practices released by the NAACP (National Association for the Advancement of Colored People) reveal that African-Americans are underrepresented in every aspect of the entertainment industry; where they participate at all, it's as performers rather than as producers. The consequences of this underrepresentation (using "representation" in a more directly political sense) are not just cultural, in the sense of determining whose stories get told and in what way, but also economic, since it is in production that—celebrity salaries notwithstanding—the real profit in the entertainment industry lies. Thus the 2001 Academy Awards, in which black actors took away an unprecedented share of prizes, could fairly be described as "progress but no net gain" (Kweisi Mfume, qtd. in Lyman). In the words of actor/director Mario Van Peebles, "We have to be in there not just as actors, but as writers and directors—and as development executives and programmers, that's the next goal. Playing basketball's not enough any more, we've got to own our teams. Without economic power, you have no power" (qtd. in Schnellner R3).

As the preceding discussion suggests, representation has political consequences. In discussing the politics of representation, however, we need to go beyond the dynamics of representation itself in order to understand the contexts in which representation occurs. The next section examines some of the ways we might go beyond the simple analysis of texts to understand representation as part of a larger process of creating popular culture.

CONTEXTS OF REPRESENTATION

We have talked a lot so far about the power of representation, particularly media representation, to construct social reality—literally, to create the world we live in, shaping our beliefs and behaviour, fears and desires. It has become commonplace to recognize the role these representations play in our lives, for good or, from the perspective of many commentators, for ill. In the words of one media critic,

The American industrial-entertainment complex has pretty much replaced the church as the maker and enforcer of values on this continent. . . . We hit 18 having spent more time in front of the TV than at school. We can summon the face of Bruce Willis, the stubble and the crooked smile, more readily and vividly than our own father's. Our heads resound with the voices of strangers. (Grierson 24)

Grierson makes these observations in an article that begins by recalling the death of Reena Virk, a Victoria, B.C., teenager beaten unconscious, then drowned by a group of other teens after a party one night. Speaking at a memorial service for Reena, Budgie Basi-Reed, a family friend, drew a direct connection between what happened to Reena and the kinds of images children and teens get bombarded with in television and video games. "Violence," she notes, "has become an acceptable form of entertainment" (qtd. in Grierson 24). In the article that follows, Grierson advances what has become a familiar argument, that brutal media imagery is largely responsible for the creation of an increasingly violent society.

In the introductory section to this chapter we began by talking about the role of media in promoting the *idea* that not just violence, but youth violence, is a growing social problem. We talked about the role of representation—and, in particular, mass media representation—in creating a climate of social fear in which dominant myths about community, morality, race, gender, and age harden into "facts" about youth violence. A critical premise of our argument is that representation plays a determining role in shaping the world we live in. We need now to take a step back from that argument, and to recognize the perils in taking it too far. Just as we need to wriggle our way out of the belief that we all like to cling to—that we as individuals possess an independent mind that somehow exists prior to language and other cultural forms—we also need to reject the equally common assumption that words and images are all-powerful, that their effects are clear and easily measurable. Interestingly, most of us are able to hold onto both these beliefs at once by maintaining a dodgy distinction between our *own* ability to see through the snares of advertising and other forms of representation, and the infinite impressionability of *others*, particularly children, to what they see, hear, and read. We have already tried to show, both in this chapter and the previous one, some of the weaknesses in the assumption that it's possible simply to see around or through ideology. Now we need to tackle the converse theory of mass media manipulation.

The Myth of Mass Media Manipulation

This theory is familiar to all of us in the form of arguments such as Grierson's about the social effects of certain kinds of representation—particularly sex and violence. Gary Bauer, former head of the U.S. Family Research Council and one-time Republican presidential candidate, puts the argument more crudely: "If you expose children to uplifting and noble material, you're more likely to have noble citizens. If children are wallowing in sexual images and violence, that is bound to have an impact on those who are most vulnerable" (qtd. in Lacayo). While this observation seems, on first appearance, to make a certain kind of sense—the images and ideas we are exposed to *do* shape who we are—there are also some obvious problems with it.

Locating Meaning First, the concept of "uplifting and noble material" assumes first that we all agree on what is uplifting and noble and, second, that nobility and uplifting-ness are somehow inherent, present in some representations and absent from others. The difficulty of making that assessment is shown in the clearly arbitrary criteria by which would-be censors evaluate controversial images, particularly those that feature violence. For example, when the Republican presidential candidate Bob Dole issued his famous 1995 rant against Hollywood's "destructive messages of casual violence and even more casual sex," included among his list of good "family" fare was the Arnold Schwarzenegger film *True Lies*. Along with its spectacular violence, the movie gained notoriety from a scene in which CIA agent Harry Tasker (Schwarzenegger), having encouraged his wife (Jamie Lee Curtis) to become a spy-posing-as-a-prostitute, poses himself as a client, then has her perform a lengthy striptease before revealing his real identity. "Uplifting and noble" this isn't! However, leaving aside perhaps the most likely reason for Dole's endorse-ment (at the time a major supporter of the party, Schwarzenegger is now the [Republican] Governor of California), we can surmise that the sex and violence pass the test here because the former occurs in defence of family values (Tasker puts his wife through the humiliating ordeal of the striptease as a kind of punishment or test in response to his sus-picion that she is cheating on him), and the latter is committed against obvious "bad guys"—their badness signalled, as many commentators noted, by their Middle Eastern appearance. More recent examples of violence in visual culture that presumably would pass the Dole test are television shows such as *24* or video games such as *America's Army* that depict extreme violence whose use is justified as necessary to the task of keeping good (American) people safe in increasingly dangerous times. While a chorus of voices contin-ues loudly to decry the problem of "antisocial violence," the years since 9/11 have seen an increased tolerance in politics and entertainment (realms that are often confusingly blurred) of what's represented as "pro-social violence," including government-sanctioned torture.

The point here is not to suggest that *True Lies* and *24* belong in the *bad* representa-tions bin, not the good one. Rather, these examples reveal that the value and meaning of cultural texts are not qualities that reside objectively within them; they are instead deter-mined in part by the audiences that watch and respond to them. Thus the representation of *True Lies* has a different meaning for Bob Dole than it does for some feminist viewers (including Jamie Lee Curtis herself, who in a 2002 interview included it among roles that she now regretted taking on [Wallace]). Similarly, viewers might cringe at the depictions of violence in a show for any number of reasons, including opposition to the cause in whose name its enacted or an objection to violence in general, but continue to watch out of enjoyment of other elements: the comedy, for example, or the brilliant dialogue or sus-penseful plot. The meaning of texts is complicated not just by the complex interplay of signs within them, but by the complex—and often unpredictable—responses of readers and viewers.

Representation and Social Consequences   A second problem with media theories such as Bauer's is his assumption, echoing beliefs of early twentieth-century critics such as F.R. Leavis (see Chapter 1), of a direct relationship between the consumption of particular images and particular social effects. Leaving aside for a moment the undefined (and undefinable) question of what constitutes noble citizenship, the assumption that viewing "good" images will lead to "good" behaviour rests on a simplistic understanding of how pedagogy, or the process of teaching and learning, operates. The meanings we take from cultural texts come from a combination of convention—ways of interpreting particular signs that are shared widely among members of a society—and individual subjectivity and experience. What we *do* with these interpretations is also influenced by those diverse factors.

Some studies do draw conclusive links between the consumption of violent media images and aggressive behaviour. One of the most compelling of these studies is the work done on violent video games by David Grossman, a U.S. army lieutenant and former psychologist. In his book *On Killing: The Psychological Cost of Learning to Kill in War and Society,* Grossman draws some disturbing parallels between the effects of media, particularly television and video games, on youth, and the techniques the military uses to train its soldiers to kill. In particular, Grossman points to two kinds of conditioning that work to desensitize subjects to killing. In the first form of what is called "classical" conditioning, the military trains its soldiers to find killing acceptable, and even pleasurable, by associating it with rewards. The same process is at work as "children watch vivid pictures of human suffering and death, and they learn to associate it with their favorite soft drink and candy bar, or their girlfriend's perfume or their boyfriend's touch" (Grossman 26).

The second form of conditioning, what psychologists term "operant" conditioning, works by teaching subjects to perform acts habitually, without thinking. Military technology such as flight simulators and moving-target practice help to teach this kind of behaviour by offering a rapid series of stimuli that require immediate—violent—response. The same process is at work in point-and-shoot video games, Grossman notes, in which targets pop up randomly and success depends on the ability to shoot quickly and accurately—without, needless to say, imagining the consequences for the simulated victims. As evidence of the translatability of those skills to real life, Grossman presents the chilling example of the 14-year-old boy in Paducah, Kentucky, who shot up a school prayer group, firing eight shots from a .22-calibre pistol and hitting eight victims, five of them in the head. (The average U.S. law enforcement officer, shooting at a distance of seven yards, has a less than one-in-five rate of actual hits.) When questioned, the killer, who had never fired a real gun before, admitted to being an avid player of video games. While this is an extreme example of the effects of simulated violence, Grossman argues for a host of more subtle and pervasive effects on children who, if they don't grow up to become killers themselves, become more or less desensitized to the effects of violence, thus creating an atmosphere of bystander tolerance for events like the beating death of Reena Virk.

Grossman's thesis is a compelling one, which seems to suggest that specific kinds of representational *content*—that is, violence—conveyed in a specific *form*—electronic media, and interactive video games in particular—produce undesirable social effects. However, in its reliance on relatively simple "behaviourist" psychological theories, his argument seriously underrates the complexity of the processes by which human beings read and respond to the world around them. Moreover, by placing the burden of proof on the representations themselves, on what they are saying and/or asking users to do, arguments such as Grossman's neglect the broader question of how and under what circumstances people consume this media—on what they *do* with it.

Representation and Imagination   This is not to say that imagination and reality are utterly distinct from one another: they aren't, which is why the realm of the imagination is such a potent place. As well as providing a storehouse of images that interpret and mediate the world for us, the imagination—culture, in general—also offers resources that help us to cope with painful aspects of reality in ways that can be both harmful and productive for individuals and society but are rarely simply one or the other. Representations of violence, which have been around since the beginning of human civilization—though admittedly not in so graphic a form as today—offer a site for particularly complex workings-out of fear, aggression, anger, and desire. While it is frequently pointed out that youth who commit violent crimes tend to be avid consumers of violent media, what is not so frequently pointed out—and what is more difficult to measure—is the role such media might play in helping many others to work through feelings of frustration or anger, thus avoiding their explosion into actual acts of violence. As media critic Henry Jenkins puts it:

> the key issue isn't what the media are doing to our children but rather what our children are doing with the media. Eric Harris and Dylan Klebold [the Columbine murderers] weren't victims of video games. They had a complex relationship to many forms of popular culture. All of us move nomadically across the media landscape, cobbling together a personal mythology of symbols and stories, and investing those appropriated materials with various personal and subcultural meanings. Harris and Klebold happened to be drawn toward dark and brutal images, which they invested with their personal demons, their antisocial impulses, their maladjustment, their desires to hurt those who had hurt them. (23)

Jenkins goes on to describe a website constructed by a 16-year-old girl who invited submissions from across the U.S. of poems and stories based on characters from popular culture. The submissions drew on many of the same media products that had been cited in the Columbine case, particularly the film *The Basketball Diaries*, reading them not as incitements to violence, but as complicated explorations of themes such as love, friendship, and community (23).

Even when popular culture becomes the site of darker imaginings, the connection between fantasy and violence is far from clear-cut. In the atmosphere of fear following the Columbine shooting, however, social authorities were quick to establish a link, establishing "zero tolerance" policies against "violent" forms of cultural expression, ranging from making verbal threats to wearing trench coats. In one notorious case, a Grade 11 student in Cornwall, Ontario, was jailed for more than a month in 2000 after reading aloud in class a story he had written called "Twisted" in which a bullied student plots to blow up his school. The student claimed that the piece was a work of fiction, inspired in part by the work of Stephen King. Many writers, including King himself, leapt to the student's defence, organizing a special forum/fundraiser to draw attention to the student's plight. Protesting what was clearly a violation of the boy's freedom of speech, many of his defenders were careful to distance themselves from the claim that art has no bearing on reality: a victim of bullying himself (seven of his classmates were subsequently arrested for assault), the student was clearly expressing, in the form of creative fiction, many of his own frustrations and fantasies. To draw a straight line from that expression backward to Stephen King and forward to some future act of violence is, however, to grossly oversimplify the effects of representation on individuals and society.

What Do We *Do* with Texts? The Role of the Audience in Constructing Meaning

As examples such as this suggest, we should think of representation not simply in terms of a collection of texts or images that promote irresistible messages, leading to specific kinds of desirable or undesirable behaviour. This is the assumption underlying Gary Bauer's vision, cited above, of children "*wallowing* in sexual images and violence" (authors' emphasis). This phrase paints a picture of glassy-eyed teens flaked out on the couch, washing down their Doritos with Red Bull, with images of the Pussycat Dolls writhing around on MTV. Besides assuming that this (hypothetical) audience's viewing practices are completely uncritical or reflective, the term "wallowing" also suggests that the *pleasure* they derive from the texts they're consuming is decadent and lazy, and should be viewed with suspicion.

The problem with that idea is demonstrated not just in the website Jenkins describes, which showcases the creative uses to which some popular culture fans put the texts they consume (and we can all probably think of countless other examples of such creativity, in particular the fan groups for programs such as *Star Trek* that construct elaborate new, and often subversive, narratives based on the characters), but also in the documented responses of ordinary viewers, who may characterize themselves as neither hardcore fans nor creative artists. Studies on the use of cultural products, from the 1980s television series *Dallas* to romance novels to video games, suggest that audiences *read*—rather than passively consume—cultural texts in complex ways, finding in them—often within a single text—sources of fantasy, consolation, irony, and humour.

Janice Radway explores this idea in her 1987 book *Reading the Romance: Women, Patriarchy and Popular Literature*. Countering what was then a standard feminist critique of romance fiction as reproducing the worst aspects of traditional patriarchy—passive heroines pining after dark, mysterious bad-boy heroes who abuse, then "save" them—Radway's book, which is based on an ethnographic study of actual romance readers, offers a much more complex view of the romance than a simple semiotic reading can provide. Among the elements Radway notes are a strong level of discrimination among romance readers, who articulate a clear sense of the difference between romances that "work" for them and those that don't. Among the most popular heroines tended to be those described by readers as "intelligent," "spunky," and "independent," even if that independence were eventually sacrificed to some extent to the conventions of the romance. Contrary to what we might expect would be the principal appeal of romance reading, some women also cited their interest in reading the books, many of which are set in remote places or times, in order to learn about history and about other cultures. Some admitted that they used the information gleaned from their reading in order to impress their husbands, who otherwise disapproved of their habit. In general, the activity of reading romances turned out to be a highly ambivalent one.

For many of the readers, married women conditioned to perform uncomplainingly the traditional wifely roles of housekeeping, cooking, and child-rearing, the romances provided a kind of escape that was both pleasurable and guilty. In Radway's words, the women's reading was both "combative" and "compensatory":

> It is combative in the sense that it enables them to refuse the other-directed social role prescribed for them by their position within the institution of marriage. In picking up a book . . . they refuse temporarily their families' otherwise constant demand that they attend to the wants of others even as they act deliberately to do something for their own private pleasure. Their activity is compensatory in that it permits them to focus on themselves and to carve out a solitary space within an arena where their self-interest is usually identified with the interests of others. (211)

The line between combat, or rebellion, and compensation, or comfort, is not a clear-cut one. Critics of the romance genre could credibly argue that, by providing temporary solace from drudgery, it merely encourages women to accept the constraints of their current lives. It serves, in other words, like the standard products of the culture industry described by Horkheimer and Adorno (see Chapter 4), to induce passivity and unthinking acceptance of the status quo. However, the desire and longing that the novels address and enhance might also help to make women aware that their needs are not being satisfied in their current situations, thereby leading them to struggle to change them. While this reading might seem overly **idealistic**, it successfully avoids the simplistic assumption of media effects by acknowledging that representation is not a message but a *process*, controlled in part by readers who are not just readers but also *producers* of meaning.

Encoding and Decoding

Stuart Hall describes this process of meaning-making in terms of two key operations, *encoding* and *decoding*, which are divided into multiple stages (see Figure 3.2). Focusing on television representations in particular, this model recognizes that meaning does not exist in the heads of creators, or the show itself, in a clear form that then gets distorted, either by technological constraints (a lousy satellite signal, say) or by viewer misinterpretation. Rather, meaning is created and altered at every step along the way, from the way in which producers construct a visual text, using signs and narrative forms supplied by the surrounding culture and their own position within that culture, to the way in which those encoded meanings are transmitted, via particular technologies, and then received and decoded by viewers—once again, based on the technologies of the medium as well as on their own individual and cultural storehouse of meanings.

Representation and the Construction of Social Reality

Figure 3.2 Encoding/Decoding

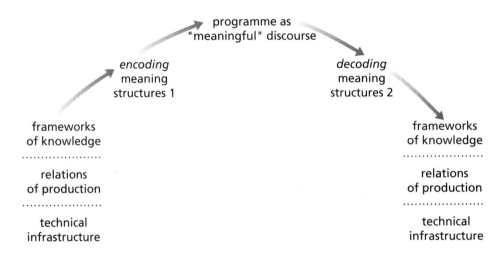

Source: Stuart Hall, "Encoding, Decoding," extracted from *Culture, Media, Language* (London: Unwin Hyman 1990).
© 1990 Stuart Hall. Reproduced by permission of Stuart Hall.

A critical point to note in Hall's theory is that, while it acknowledges a level of agency on the part of viewers, it does not suggest that audiences are free to take whatever meaning they wish from texts. Because the stages at which meaning is produced work interdependently with one another, the way in which messages are encoded places limitations on the way in which they are decoded. Hall identifies a continuum of possible reading positions, ranging from the *dominant–hegemonic*, in which the audience's interpretation of the text is consistent with the ideological codes in which it is produced (in other words, they subscribe to the "preferred reading"), to a *negotiated* position, in which the audience accepts the legitimacy of the **preferred reading** on a general level but modifies it in light of personal interests or circumstances, and finally to an *oppositional or counter-hegemonic* reading position, in which the audience understands but rejects the text's code and reads it in light of an alternative code.

Reading a Television Scene   An informal experiment, conducted in one of our introductory Popular Culture classes, highlighted the operation of these different kinds of readings. In the class, we watched a scene from the popular 1990s television show *NYPD Blue*, in which two of the detectives were interviewing a suspect in a murder/drug case (if you're not familiar with *NYPD Blue*, think *Law and Order* or *CSI*, in which scenes like this one occur pretty frequently). Employing the familiar "good cop–bad cop" television formula in which one detective acts sympathetically toward the suspect, appearing to offer refuge from his more aggressive colleague (and, thereby, hopefully eliciting a confession), the two detectives were alternately coaxing the suspect and yelling at him. Eventually, Andy Sipowicz, playing the "bad cop," loses his temper and starts beating the suspect, a young Latino man, who falls to the floor, shielding his face with his hands. Our understanding of the scene is aided by our knowledge of Sipowicz as a talented cop, plagued with problems with alcohol and a generally bad temper. When asked to read the scene, focusing in particular on the issues of conflict and morality (Is there a "right" and "wrong" being depicted here? Whom do we as audience members identify with and why?), students came up with a variety of different answers.

A dominant–**hegemonic** reading—one that many students subscribed to—agreed that the morality of the scene was murky, but that it should be read in the context of "standard" police procedure: that is, Sipowicz may have gotten a bit carried away, but a certain amount of force is justified in extracting a confession from a criminal. The assumption that the audience identifies with the police, and not with the criminal, is primary in a dominant–hegemonic reading of the show. Other students read the scene according to what they identified as a more negotiated position. While not questioning the fundamental rightness of the police's position, they were uncomfortable with the violence depicted (both within the context of the story in terms of Sipowicz's apparent loss of control, and at the level of the show in terms of the representation of violence in general).

A few other students took up a counter-hegemonic or resistant reading position, which understood but rejected the premise of the unquestioned legitimacy of the police. These students focused on the status of the suspect as a member of a racial minority, and therefore as someone in particular danger of being subject to arbitrary arrest and detention. The presumption of innocence—a presumption that, they pointed out, the criminal justice system was meant to rest on in any case—becomes more highly charged in a context in which race is sometimes read as a sign of likely guilt. This reading is oppositional because it refuses the underlying principle of the show, that the police are self-evidently the "good guys," there to protect the citizens (read: "us") against the "bad guys." Rejecting the more or less black-and-white moral code of the show and replacing it with one based on various shades of grey (or, in the case of a few viewers, reversing the code altogether and rooting for the underdogs—the so-called "bad" guys) represents not a misreading but an aberrant, or atypical, form of decoding, one that may signal an explicit mode of oppositional politics.

While this example highlights the practical operation of these different kinds of readings, Hall's model can't be applied wholesale to every cultural text. Some texts are more susceptible or "open" to negotiated or oppositional readings than others, depending on such factors as the extent to which they conform to or depart from formula, and the range of audience to which they're targeted. We also need to be careful not to try and read Hall's model of encoding/decoding as offering a clear map of distinctive kinds of readings or readers. In practice, the distinction between different kinds of reading, particularly "negotiated" and "oppositional," is often murky, and readers or viewers rarely react in a uniform way to what they consume. In other words, it's possible to object to the representation of women in James Bond movies from a feminist perspective while appreciating the plots as perfect examples of the action formula.

Generally our reactions to popular culture—even of those of us who study it for a living!—are less self-conscious than that, or they are a mix of self-conscious critique and pleasure, even the wallowing kind condemned by Bauer. In addition to being shaped by our experiences and beliefs, our responses to cultural texts are powerfully influenced by the situation in which we watch them. Depending on the mood we're in, our motive for watching (distraction/stimulation/intellectual engagement), the people we're watching with, and even the other kinds of texts we've consumed recently, our response to a given text will be different in different circumstances.

Suggested Activity 3.5

Try to identify the patterns in your own responses to different forms of popular culture. How, and to what extent, is pleasure moderated by critical consciousness and vice versa? How do your responses to popular cultural texts change depending on the nature of the text, the circumstances in which you are watching/reading/ listening to it, or the people you are with?

REPRESENTATION IN CONTEMPORARY CULTURE

The fact that the process of making meaning is complex, individualized, and even arbitrary (based, for example, on something as trivial as whether you happen to be watching *Entourage* with your mother or your girlfriend) does not mean that it does not have effects. As Stuart Hall's model suggests, material practice is a critical part of the "circuit of meaning," one that determines, as it is in turn determined by, representation. As a broad indication of the connection between reading and social practice, Hall suggests that an increased instance of counter-hegemonic or oppositional readings can be taken as both symptomatic and predictive of radical shifts in the political and social landscape. The wide availability of digital video technology has also contributed to a diversity of images. In the past few years, a number of widely publicized stories about police brutality and racism (including the 1987 Rodney King beating in California, and more recently, in Toronto, the publication of a series of articles suggesting police treat blacks more harshly than whites [Shears; Rankin]) have prompted general questioning of the relationship between ideology and the administration of justice. That kind of questioning, Hall suggests, can lead not only to a shift in popular culture but also to significant political change.

Political and Ideological Context   In contrast to the trend of interrogating traditional patterns of social authority, following the events of September 11, 2001, we have also witnessed a move in the opposite direction, toward more unambiguous representations of good and evil/innocence and guilt (think, for example, of how the CIA, until recently represented as beset by corruption, has been rehabilitated, along with the military, in television shows such as *Alias, 24,* and *NCIS*). These shifts mirror a more general ideological move toward increased support for practices such as racial profiling—practices that had, until recently, fallen into general disfavour because of their theoretical grounding in crude stereotyping and their practical effect of infringing the civil liberties of minority groups. Changes in political circumstances determine changes in dominant ideology, which in turn consolidate the new political order.

But the relationship between representation and reality that this example highlights goes beyond a comment on the causes and/or effects of particular kinds of representation. The new tolerance of the once-discredited practice of racial profiling, a practice that represents an uncritical embrace of the most simplistic form of representation, suggests that the material effects of representation are not consistent over time—that is, the power of representation to influence reality changes, depending on broader circumstances.

To take a concrete, and perhaps overly simplistic, example, representation in the crude form of political propaganda is most powerful in times of economic, political, and social anxiety. It is no accident that Horkheimer and Adorno (see Chapter 4) formulated their culture industry thesis in the context of the buildup of fascism in 1940s Germany. A large part of their horror at the potential for mass media to lull people into an acceptance of brutal social regimes stemmed from the fact that audiences of Nazi propaganda *were* being lulled into such a state—to the point of accepting the slaughter of thousands of innocent people. What makes Horkheimer and Adorno's thesis particularly provocative is their argument that that media power extended to the United States, where the ideologies of **industrialism** and progress helped to create a mass media machine and an audience particularly receptive to its products.

Many theorists suggest that contemporary North American culture, which some see simply as the fruition of Horkheimer and Adorno's worst predictions, is characterized by the triumph of representation. That is to say, we should not be focusing concern on the content of this representation or that representation, but on the dominance of representation itself as a social, political, and economic force. French theorist Jean Baudrillard puts it this way: "Abstraction today is no longer that of the map, the double, the mirror or the concept. Simulation is . . . the generation by models of a real without origin or reality: a hyperreal" (166). The phenomenon of hyperreality, of total mediatization, that characterizes contemporary culture goes beyond the paranoid fantasy of the James Bond movie *Tomorrow Never Dies*, in which one media conglomerate tries to seize control of all the world's communications industry. It resembles something more like the vision in *The Matrix*, in which people's experience of reality—even their sense of themselves—turns out to be merely a computer simulation.

Like a lot of good movies, the vision of *The Matrix* is both more and less extreme than the real-life situation it alludes to. While it would be hard to identify a real-world counterpart of the sinister conspiracy that created the matrix and enslaved people within it, *The Matrix* offered the possibility of escape, which in practice proves more difficult. One of the characteristics of the "instantaneity of communication" that characterizes **postmodern** popular culture is "the incursion of imagery and communication into those spaces that once were private—where the psyche previously had the chance at least to explore the 'other'; to explore, for example, alienation" (McRobbie 16). The disappearance of the mental space from which to experience a tension between the world as it is and the world as one would like it to be explains what many people who recall the sixties lament as a lack of political idealism in contemporary generations.

Virtual Culture   The disappearance of this space also has more immediately dangerous effects. For theorists such as Thomas de Zengotita, the media are absolutely central to events such as the Columbine killings—not because the killers were fans of violent movies or video games, but because they and the surrounding culture were so steeped in the culture of virtuality that the difference between the video "rehearsal" of their murder that they prepared for a class and the actual event was in some significant way immaterial. The air of unreality was not confined to the action of the shooting itself but extended to the coverage of the event, in which, de Zengotita observes, events had a generic quality, indistinguishable from coverage of hundreds of other depictions of "violence in the heartland" right down to the stock characterization of "correspondents . . . in moved-to-the breaking-point-but-professional mode"; anchors in "grave-demeanor-reserved-for-inexplicable-evil mode," and so on (56). As for the mourners themselves, de Zengotita asks, "Can anyone doubt that [they], no matter how authentic their feelings, respond at some level to implicit expectations when the cameras roll? Especially since they have seen this show on TV before; now, suddenly, they are in it" (56).

The idea that representation, and the representational power of the media in particular, is all-pervasive—that we are all, somehow, watching it or "in it" (think: *The Truman Show*)—raises important questions about our ability ever to critically assess the material conditions of our existence, let alone do anything to alter them. How, and to what extent, is it possible to challenge, or at least creatively intervene in, our symbol- and image-saturated culture? The strategies of **deconstruction** advocated by Laura Mulvey, and taken up in different ways by avant-garde artists, filmmakers, and culture jammers, work to critique not just individual texts or ideologies, but also the codes that underwrite them, thereby robbing visual culture of some of its magic. Many critics have pointed out, however, that the ironic awareness with which we all tend to read images now has outlived its usefulness as a strategy of critique: there is no outside in postmodern culture.

The Trouble with "Truthiness"

We have spoken at length in this chapter about the power of representation—of language and discourse—to define what we accept as truth. It is important at the same time not to fall prey to the view that there is nothing outside of discourse—nothing, that is, that eludes the scope of power/ideology. Truth, by this reckoning, has disappeared, surrendering authority not to critique but to "truthiness," a buzzword popularized by the comedian Stephen Colbert to describe U.S. President George W. Bush's habit of appealing not to evidence or logic but to instinct or gut-feeling. Taken to its cynical extreme, the dismissal of the traditional concept of truth enables the exercise of power that is totally resistant to the kind of cultural critique that we take up in this chapter—a kind of power that does not deny but actually revels in its use of ideology. Under Bush's presidency, the White

House has come to exemplify this postmodern style of domination. As one of President Bush's aides put it to *New York Times* reporter Ron Suskind:

> [People like you are] "in what we call the reality-based community . . ." [i.e.] people who "believe that solutions emerge from your judicious study of discernible reality. . . . That's not the way the world really works anymore. . . . We're an empire now, and when we act, we create our own reality. And while you're studying that reality—judiciously, as you will—we'll act again, creating other new realities, which you can study too, and that's how things will sort out. We're history's actors . . . and you, all of you, will be left to just study what we do." (51)

These words are chilling; they're also somewhat absurd in their claim to have closed the circuit of discourse/reality. That circuit can never be closed, not just because the world exceeds our ability to represent it, but also because the field of representation is fluid and always subject to contestation and struggle.

Keeping these limits in mind, we argue for the necessity of paying critical attention to the words and images that mediate our social lives. As our analysis of a diverse array of media texts in this chapter demonstrates, these elements of representation—the "signs" of our times—might not point to the truth, but they do tell us, figuratively, where to go (and perhaps more importantly who can go where). Symbolic representation is in other words a crucial aspect of *political* representation, a subject that, as www.urbandictionary.com reminds us, informs practically every aspect of our social lives. In analyzing representation, the important issue is not finally whether popular culture offers us truth, but whether it allows us to imagine and enact a more democratic, a more truly *representative* society.

SUGGESTIONS FOR FURTHER READING

Barthes, Roland. *Mythologies.* Trans. Annette Lavers. London: Granada, 1973.

Berger, John. *About Looking.* New York: Pantheon, 1980.

Hall, Stuart. *Representation: Cultural Representation and Signifying Practices.* London: Sage and Open University Press, 1997.

Mirzoeff, Nicholas, ed. *The Visual Culture Reader.* London: Routledge, 1999.

Radway, Janice. *Reading the Romance: Women, Patriarchy and Popular Literature.* Chapel Hill, NC: University of North Carolina Press, 1984.

Said, Edward. *Culture and Imperialism.* London: Chatto and Windus, 1993.

Shohat, Ella, and Robert Stam. *Unthinking Eurocentrism: Multiculturalism and the Media.* London: Routledge, 1994.

Sturken, Marita, and Lisa Cartwright. *Practices of Looking: An Introduction to Visual Culture.* Oxford: Oxford University Press, 2001.

Chapter 4

The Production of Popular Culture

INTRODUCTION: THE BUSINESS OF CULTURE

Popular culture is big business. Each and every year, trillions of dollars are spent on the production of popular culture, and trillions more on purchasing popular cultural objects (music CDs, DVDs, fashion, video games), services (cable and satellite television, Internet providers, personal trainers), and experiences (cinema-going, musicals, tourism, restaurants, etc.). With the exception of a few recessionary dips, each year also brings an increase in the size of the contribution of popular culture to the overall economy. As just one example, video game sales in the United States totalled $9.9 billion in 2004, $500 million greater than movie ticket sales during the same period.

While it is difficult to determine with precision the amount that the production and **consumption** of popular culture contributes to standard measurements of economic performance, such as **gross domestic product (GDP)**, what is certain is that the production of culture has an unprecedented significance for today's economies. For instance, the stock market boom of the 1990s was fuelled to a very large degree by a popular cultural phenomenon: the promise of new services, experiences, and consumer objects (primarily consumer electronics) associated with and generated by the rise of the Internet—new services that investors believed could result in new profits. Many of the companies whose stock valuation rose highest during the 1990s (and correspondingly fell hardest by the end of the decade) were involved in producing the equipment that allows the Internet to function: routing and switching hardware, fibre optics and other kinds of telecommunications infrastructures, and computer hardware itself. But many more were rushing to produce what can only be described as new kinds of cultural experience: new ways of dealing with personal finance, interacting with the government (as immortalized in the documentary *StartUp.com*), communicating with others (MUDs, weblogs, chat rooms), and shopping (for books, groceries, plane tickets, and even, in the case of eBay.com, the ephemera that one usually finds at garage sales). These kinds of cultural experiences wouldn't be possible without the technological infrastructure provided by companies such as Oracle, IBM, and others; at the same time, there would be no need for this infrastructure without public interest (however short lived or, in the end, limited) in the experiences and services that this infrastructure enables. Depending on how one chooses to look at it, one could say that the *entire* economy is now dependent in surprising ways on popular culture. As we will discuss in more detail in Chapter 5, the performance of the overall economy has become dependent to an unprecedented degree on consumer spending, especially spending on supposedly "nonessential" items—the kinds of discretionary purchases that often include forms of popular cultural entertainment and other cultural experiences. But this is equally true of economic *production* itself. As a number of recent writers have pointed out, "processes of production and systems of organization can be seen . . . [as] assemblages of meaningful practices that construct certain ways for people to conceive of and conduct themselves at work" (du Gay 4). It would be a mistake to see production as outside of or exempt from the historical development of popular culture over the past 150 years. The "culture of production"—that is, the guiding production philosophy of the factory or office—has become increasingly important to CEOs and management consultants intent on increasing productivity and profits through the creation of an effective work culture. The ideas that are championed in attempts to reframe work culture—for instance, the airy loft spaces and game rooms that were associated with the workspaces of the "new" Internet economy—often find their origins in popular culture; even if the links cannot be located directly in popular culture, supposedly "scientific" ideas of business management circulate in and through **mass culture**, and books on office management have themselves become a part of popular cultural consumption, with new fad management ideas emerging as frequently as shifts in fashion. The prevalence of these ideas is reflected in the popularity of television shows such as *The Office, 30 Rock,* and *Mad Men.* They are funny to the extent that many, many people are conversant with management-speak and the hypocrisies of business and office dynamics.

There is no simple way to separate the production of popular culture from the processes through which it is consumed. The aim of this chapter and the one that follows is not to suggest that production and consumption have to be treated separately; nor is it to suggest that the values and meanings generated in one don't spill over into the other in a perpetual process of osmosis across a very thin and permeable boundary. Rather, we are separating production and consumption only in order to stress the ways in which each contributes in its own way to the creation of individual and social meaning in popular culture.

Surprisingly, in the history of the academic study of culture, *neither* production nor consumption has been taken seriously enough. For the most part, cultural critics (for example, literary and art critics) have focused their interpretive and critical energies on the completed objects of culture—novels, poems, artworks, films, songs, and so on— while paying scant attention to the processes that brought these cultural forms into existence (printing presses, the invention of the film camera, recording devices, the factory production of DVDs, etc.) as well as to the multiple uses that consumers make of culture.

This has changed dramatically over the past 40 years. Far more attention is now paid to the historical, social, and political contexts in which culture emerges and is read, watched, and heard. Due to the influence of various sociologies of culture, there has been relatively more attention paid to production—to the large array of processes by which culture is fashioned—than to consumption or the experience of culture. Even so, production has been considered for the most part both too generally and too abstractly: the production of culture has been seen as a small segment of economic production in general, and the culture that is produced has been treated as secondary to more primary economic and material forms and forces. To put it perhaps too simplistically, the production of steel and cars has been treated as the "real" economy, whereas the production of films and television shows has been seen as a marginal economic practice.

This chapter looks at the role of production in shaping culture in less abstract terms. While we will consider the big question of how culture is shaped by economics, we will also explore the specific economics of cultural production today in order to think through the ways in which it shapes the experience and meaning of popular culture.

"MONEY CHANGES EVERYTHING": THE PITFALLS OF THINKING ABOUT PRODUCTION

We are *all* familiar with discussing popular culture in reference to production. The entertainment section of our daily newspaper contains movie reviews, interviews with television personalities and rock stars, reports on the legal troubles of the rich and famous (e.g., Paul and Heather McCartney's divorce, Michael Richard's (*Seinfeld*'s Kramer) racist tirade, and Paris Hilton's, Nicole Ritchie's, and Shia LeBouef's arrests for impaired driving), and, perhaps, reviews of local theatrical performances and art exhibitions. Just as important, however, are stories that directly describe the economics of popular culture. Each Monday's newspaper reports the previous weekend's box-office grosses in full detail (e.g., for the last week of May 2008, the top grossing movies were *Indiana Jones and the Kingdom of the Crystal Skull*, $126.9 million; *Chronicles of Narnia: Prince Caspian*, $29.8 million; and *Iron Man*, $26.1 million) and long newspaper and magazine articles on (among other things) the impact of illegal music and movie downloading on each of these industries are regular fare. Indeed, it is often the case that we know *more* about the economics of pop culture than the "content" of pop culture itself: we might know which movies were big hits, and even know some elements of their plots, without ever having set eyes on them.

For example, the releases of the video games *Grand Theft Auto: Vice City* (2002) and *Grand Theft Auto IV* (2008) (and all the ones in between) were widely reported, both as a financial story about their unprecedented successes and as a (rather typical) story about the degree to which contemporary culture has continued to degenerate, reaching new lows of violence and amorality. Regardless of how popular the game will become, far fewer people will ever play it than will have heard it reported as a pop-culture phenomenon. A similar point can be made about top-ten lists of movie ticket and album sales:

while even dedicated movie fans will not be able to take in all the films that circulate in and out of a top-ten list from week to week, one of the functions of the list is to inform audiences about the (financial) importance of cultural objects that they might not see immediately, but which are perhaps worthy of their attention at some point given the attention that other members of the public have bestowed on them.

Economic versus Artistic Success

Reports on contracts, financing deals, and profits and losses in the film, book, and music industry highlight the intimate connection that exists between popular culture and money. The "success" of stars, movies, pop albums, and so on—and not merely their financial success—is very often measured by the number of units sold. Directors who make movies that generate huge profits are more likely to be given the opportunity to direct future movies: one huge financial success early in a career can lead to literally dozens of chances to make future stinkers, all in the hope that the director might recapture the "magic" that led people to empty their wallets in the first place.

Just as commonly, however, financial success is taken by many consumers of popular culture as the inverse of "quality": in other words, the more *financially* successful a product might be, the less *artistically* successful it must be. The band REM's later CDs sold many more copies than their earlier ones; for early fans, the band's move from obscure club band in Athens, Georgia, to heavy rotation on MuchMusic and MTV is seen as a clear sign of a decline in the quality of REM's music. Examples of this formula abound and have been applied to every aspect of popular cultural experience: the beaches of Negril, Jamaica, were more interesting before resorts arrived; Queen Street West in Toronto was hip until the Gap showed up; the Haight-Ashbury district in San Francisco was a site of **authentic** popular culture, but is now simply a tourist trap of the first order; the writer William S. Burroughs was cool until he became a shill for Nike. This formula, which places economic success and artistic or **aesthetic** value in an inverse relationship, offers one common way of theorizing the impact of production on popular culture. Unfortunately, its real utility for serious cultural analysis is limited for a whole number of reasons, not least of which is that it closes off any real attention to the role played by production, by deciding on the relationship between production and popular culture in advance.

What is wrong with assuming, for example, that because a film is made in Hollywood it must necessarily be "bad" or uninteresting? After all, isn't this generally true (as anyone who saw *Harold and Kumar Escape from Guantanamo Bay*, *The Love Guru*, and *Bangkok Dangerous* must surely admit)? There are a number of different claims or assumptions being made in a statement such as this one that need to be carefully separated out. First, one of the central assumptions lying behind this connection between money and popular culture is that if the great, unwashed masses like something, then it's impossible for it to be good. Put bluntly, such claims continue a tradition of class elitism and snobbery (discussed in Chapter 2) that presumes the intrinsic value of its own opinions while dismissing the crowds lined up for *Drillbit Taylor* as little more than crude, uncultured people without any form of aesthetic or artistic discrimination. To take popular culture

*"I like his earlier work better, particularly the
ones I said I didn't like at the time."*

seriously means to also take seriously the whole range of reactions, interests, and values placed on the products of popular culture.

Second, such claims simply aren't true. "Hollywood" cinema—already a far too general term that applies to a vast range of products and production techniques—*has* produced films that are admired worldwide. Films that have been both critical *and* popular successes have been produced throughout the history of American cinema, including those that emerge in many ways from the belly of the beast. "Classic" Hollywood films, which were much admired, for instance, by French film critics after the Second World War, were produced on a kind of filmic factory-line whose goal was to produce as many films as cheaply as possible in order to obtain the maximum profit. The profitability of these films (from the classic Westerns of director John Ford to *film noir*), or of, say, the *Godfather* trilogy or *Jaws*, seems to belie any easy equation between value or sophistication and money.

Third, even what is sometimes considered to be "high" art, from painting to the nineteenth-century novel, was produced in conditions in which money played an important role. Though we continue to have a romantic idea of the artist in which he or she is motivated by considerations other than money (which is why bio-pics of artists, such as *Frida* or *Pollock*, always focus on the suffering and poverty that artists endure), this is largely just that: a romantic fable that tells us more about our own discomfort with the links between money and art than with the real conditions of cultural production during our own or past centuries.

Walter Benjamin

We could go on dissecting the problems of the art–money equation. The main point that we want to articulate, however, is the problem that reliance on this equation introduces into an examination of the role of production in popular culture. As the German philosopher Walter Benjamin (1892–1940) understood clearly in 1936, our discussion of cultural products continues to make use of what for him were already "a number of outmoded concepts, such as creativity and genius, eternal value and mystery" (*Illuminations* 218]).

These concepts don't seem to be appropriate for describing a situation in which culture is produced in a new and very different sense than how we might imagine a nineteenth-century painter "producing" a painting (by standing in front of a canvas) or a classical composer "producing" a symphony (angrily stabbing at a piano as his long, curly white locks flip up and over his shoulders). As much as we might confer the status of "genius" on a film director and clap a screenwriter on the back for her great "creativity," a film is produced in a far different way and under far different circumstances than a painting or a musical composition (even in the examples we give above, we are indulging in a romantic vision of artistic creativity perpetuated by the movies). The filmic equivalent of the painter's scrawl in the bottom corner of a painting are the credits that run for minutes on end at the conclusion of a film, detailing all of the personnel required to create the finished product—set designers, sound engineers, lighting experts, assistant directors, continuity editors, technicians, accountants, and so on. The **myth** of the intrinsic value of "independent" films, which generally have lower budgets and are made with fewer personnel, seems to derive from the fact that in these cases it is easier to assert the filmmakers' unique voice or "genius": there are fewer intermediaries to deflect from the director's true vision. In understanding the role of production processes in the creation of contemporary popular culture, it seems essential to move away from these "outmoded concepts" that are addressed to the critical evaluation of popular culture—not because contemporary popular culture is valueless, but because a focus on value tends to obscure the complex ways in which cultural products are produced, which in turn leads us to misunderstand how production contributes to their form, shape, and broader social significance.

To summarize: we need to avoid the common connection that is made between production and value. Concentrating on how something is produced helps us to better understand the object or experience under examination. The fact that popular culture is produced for profit, and, in general, by large groups of people instead of single creative individuals, should tell us right away that understanding popular culture means to understand the process through which it is made. It doesn't tell us anything on its own, however, about how "good" or "bad" these things are. This is in some ways the wrong question to ask. The right questions would lead us to consider things such as the standard length of pop songs, the temporal structure of television programming (in which a half-hour television program means 22 minutes of "real" content), and the reasons why there is a disconnection between the collective labour required to produce a film, television program, or video game and the credit bestowed on those involved, which generally goes only to stars and directors. As just one example of this, the individuals who have taken credit for the *Grand Theft Auto* games that we discussed above don't even know how to program! In what sense, then, is this game an expression of *their* creativity and genius?

THE CULTURE INDUSTRY THESIS

When we think of "culture" as the kind of thing that one might experience while visiting a museum of fine art or going to the opera (while wearing a dapper white suit and sporting a pencil-thin moustache and a monocle, of course), it seems hard to make a connection to "industry"—to the factory, work, and labour. Indeed, as we have touched on before, one of the most powerful definitions of culture that has been passed down to us positions culture as the refined, genteel *opposite* of the crude, utilitarian world of industry. One of Matthew Arnold's worries when he was writing *Culture and Anarchy* (1869) was that the Victorian faith in technological **progress** and the wealth created by industry was displacing culture from the centre of British society. The pursuit of human perfection through encounters with "the best that has been thought and known" was for Arnold of paramount importance; industry was a secondary, less important feature of social life. In Arnold's time, this "natural" arrangement had become (in his view) dangerously inverted: "the idea of perfection as an *inward* condition of the mind and spirit is at variance with the mechanical and material civilization in esteem with us" (23). Arnold's famous description of the "pursuit of perfection" as the "pursuit of sweetness and light" (31) is made in deliberate opposition to both the real and symbolic heaviness and dirtiness of nineteenth-century industry. The pristine, white space of art galleries, with their untouchable objects and church-like quiet, is just one of the areas where we can see the continuation of this vision of culture—even in those cases where new galleries have occupied abandoned nineteenth-century factories to take advantage of their exposed brick and massive open spaces, such as the Power Plant Gallery in Toronto, the Tate Modern in London, or the Massachusetts Museum of Contemporary Art in North Adams.

While it is easier to see popular culture as something that is necessarily produced in a way that the fine arts are not (which is part of the fascination audiences have with the television show *Canadian Idol*) the link between *culture* and *industry* still remains mainly a figure of speech. The common use of the terms "film industry" and "record industry" points to the large productive and administrative apparatus that helps to get the band Apocalyptica's funereal heavy-metal dirges to the record stores and Steven Spielberg's latest films to the cineplex. Typically, however, these terms do not evoke images of factory workers piecing together jewel cases and etching code into CDs along an assembly line (which isn't how it's done in any case), but only, perhaps, a gentler, kinder form of production—one that takes place in office buildings and studios, and that is anchored in the productivity and creativity of the "talent." While we all understand that popular culture is mixed up with business, it nevertheless is only by stressing the connection between culture and industry that we can truly get a sense of the impact of production on popular culture.

The Frankfurt School

The social theorists Max Horkheimer (1895–1973) and Theodor Adorno (1903–1969) were the first people to use the term "culture industry" to describe the conditions in which contemporary popular culture was produced (see Close-Up 4.1). In *Dialectic of Enlightenment*, published in 1947, Horkheimer and Adorno pushed "culture" and "industry" together in an effort to create a new consciousness about the changed conditions of cultural production in contemporary societies. It was, at the time, a revolutionary new way of thinking about culture. Over the past half-century, the *cultural industry thesis* that Horkheimer and Adorno advocated has generated an enormous range of debates and discussions. It remains central to explorations of the production of culture, whether as an articulation of an idea that remains important to understanding popular culture today, or as an extreme view about the limits of popular culture that contrary theories and viewpoints have had to contend with.

Close-Up 4.1

The Frankfurt School

The Frankfurt School is the name given to a group of innovative social theorists whose ideas remain important decades after the School was formally dissolved. Though there is no "Frankfurt School" approach to popular culture *per se* (the individual members agreed on no fixed set of ideas or concepts, and often disagreed with one another), the School's name is used to describe approaches that emphasize the production of popular culture and insist on its **ideological** constraints. Though not affiliated with the School, many contemporary critics of popular culture—especially critics that look at the influence of television on society, including Thomas Frank, Todd Gitlin, and Mark Crispin Miller—draw heavily on the general arguments made by the school.

Established in 1923 at the University of Frankfurt as an independent research centre, the goal of members of the Institute for Social Research was the elaboration of a "critical theory" of society. Critical theory has since become the name for a diverse set of practices in social and cultural theory, philosophy, and literary studies. For the Frankfurt School, critical theory was meant to preserve critical reflection on the possibilities and problems of contemporary society as a way of continuing the political work of achieving human freedom.

Members of the Frankfurt School included Horkheimer, Adorno, philosopher Herbert Marcuse, psychologist Erich Fromm, and sociologist Leo Lowenthal. Some of the key texts produced by members of the school include Theodor Adorno's *Negative Dialectics* and Herbert Marcuse's *One-Dimensional Man*.

What Is the Culture Industry?

What is the culture industry? And perhaps more importantly, what kind of culture does the culture industry create?

The British communications scholar Nicholas Garnham has described the cultural industries as "institutions in our society which employ the characteristic modes of production and organization of industrial corporations to produce and disseminate symbols in the form of cultural goods and services, generally, though not exclusively, as **commodities**" (25). To put it in a somewhat circular fashion, the cultural industries are the industries of culture—those institutions (generally, corporations) whose product is culture. At one level, it is easy to locate such industries in contemporary society: the institutions that create films, television programs, popular music, and video games, for example, can all be seen as cultural industries.

But why stop there? While films, television programs, and CDs may be concrete cultural products, there are numerous other institutions that "produce and disseminate symbols in the form of cultural goods and services." For example, the merchandising of sports equipment and clothing is "cultural" in this sense, as are the products of the fashion industry more generally (at all levels, from H & M to Hollister to Harry Rosen) and all the activities and products associated with tourism. But we can even go further, and make the claim that the marketing and advertising of *all* consumer products has transformed consumer production in general into cultural industries (we will discuss this process in more detail below in the section entitled "How Is Culture Shaped by Economics?"). "Basic" foodstuffs such as eggs, milk, beef, chicken, and cheese are carefully marketed to consumers as part of a healthy lifestyle. The great cliché of automobile advertising is the link made between vehicles and nature: when you buy an Audi Quattro or Subaru Outback, you aren't buying an environmentally damaging mode of transportation, but the adventure of the outdoors, and an outdoors that you wouldn't be able to access *except* with these vehicles. Ads for banks and mutual funds commonly feature images of cottages, beaches, or family settings: dealing with these institutions, the images suggest, will secure you the freedom that your life otherwise so clearly lacks. The products of these industries may not be directly "cultural" in the same way as the film industry. What these examples should suggest, however, is that today the borders between cultural industries and other industries have become difficult to draw, due in part to the expansion of the field of cultural experience (such that even buying cheese has become culture in some strange way), as well as to the creation of new forms of production, such as marketing and advertising.

Garnham's definition applies to cultural *industries*; Horkheimer and Adorno spoke of a singular "culture industry," a single system that explains the function of culture in contemporary society, both those forms and kinds of culture produced by cultural industries and those that are not. There is little dispute over the fact that culture today is produced (at least in part) through an industrial process. What *is* in dispute is Horkheimer's and Adorno's assertion of a single, dominant system of cultural production, and the social, political, and cultural significance that they attribute to this system. Before we can ascertain how

My son used to have his own hopes and aspirations. Now he has mine.

Thanks, Obay™!

From the makers of WhyBecauseISaidSo.™

The 2008 "tease and reveal" ad campaign by Ontario Colleges drew attention to common attitudes toward community colleges as a second choice to university programs. The ad above was later covered a few weeks later with a sticker saying "Luckily, Obay Isn't Real . . . Explore all the options at ontariocolleges.ca." What makes this ad especially effective is that it plays on common assumptions about the function of advertising, especially as it relates to teens and young adults. The subtext is that parents would need a drug such as Obay just to get teens to listen to them instead of to ads like this one!

successful this thesis is in describing the production of popular culture, we need first to explore Horkheimer's and Adorno's theories in greater detail.

Culture, Experience, and the Culture Industry

In order to fully grasp Horkheimer's and Adorno's worries about the culture industry, it is necessary to have some sense of the larger issues explored in the *Dialectic of Enlightenment*. It is a notoriously dense and difficult book, so a brief overview cannot help but miss many of the its nuances, especially as a good deal of the energy and effect of the book comes out of the authors' highly stylized and rhetorical mode of writing. In the introduction to *Dialectic of Enlightenment*, Horkheimer and Adorno describe their task as "nothing less than the discovery of why mankind, instead of entering into a truly human condition, is sinking into a new kind of barbarism" (xi). The legacy of Enlightenment thought that we still (to a large degree) live with sees history as a process of continual improvement and development—in a word, history is marked by **progress**.

The narratives of history that we encounter in classrooms, newspapers, in government documents, and on the History Channel suggest that things are constantly getting "better": once women couldn't vote, now they can; once humanity could move around the earth only slowly, now there are jet planes; once there was only semaphore, now there's the Internet. The political part of this narrative makes the claim that humanity in general is slowly increasing its degree of freedom. Horkheimer and Adorno object strongly to this "myth" of progress and to the belief in human reason that lies at its core. Far from leading to greater freedom, they see people's lives today as more restricted than ever. Humanity's faith in progress has created an inescapable system of **instrumental rationality** that limits what we understand and experience to a considerable degree, and a domination of nature that threatens the continued existence of the world (see Close-Up 4.2). The historical events that the narrative of

Instrumental Rationality

Instrumental rationality is a complex concept that has a simple idea at its core. In essence, the use of rationality or reason in an instrumental fashion suggests the use of the most efficient means to achieve the desired end. Analysis of instrumental rationality is usually associated with the German sociologist Max Weber (1864–1920), whose work had an impact on the Frankfurt School (see Close-Up 4.1) and on the shape of *Dialectic of Enlightenment* in particular. For Weber, the rise of **capitalism** introduces instrumental rationality into all spheres of life—not just in economics, but also in politics, culture, and other parts of society as well. It might seem as if it is a good idea to achieve efficiency in all areas of life. However, there are drawbacks to instrumental rationality, especially when it becomes applied generally. The concept of efficiency isn't a neutral one; that is, it implies a certain set of values about the goals of human activity and human life that may in fact contradict other values that people hold dear. The Frankfurt School was critical of instrumental rationality because it eliminated the critical use of reason. Perhaps most dangerously, instrumental rationality can turn into an autonomous force. Even though human beings invented this use of rationality (indeed, they invented the concept of rationality itself), it has come to be treated as an irresistible, unchallengeable fact of nature.

Many conflicts today concern the problems of instrumental rationality. For instance, the "efficient" pursuit of profits and technological development has resulted in considerable damage to the environment. The difficulty that environmentalists have faced in changing the politics of governments and businesses has to do in part with how deeply instrumental rationality is embedded in the structure of these organizations. Similarly, the global push to **privatize** public services (e.g., in Canada, electricity utilities in Alberta and Ontario and, more controversially, health-care services, already privatized throughout much of the world) has been justified in terms of greater efficiency. Those opposed to the privatization of public services oppose instrumental rationality with a different set of values, which emphasize the need to provide collective goods to everyone in society at a reasonable cost.

progress would see as exceptions to the rule (in particular, the rise of fascism in Europe), Horkheimer and Adorno see as a direct outcome of this narrative. To paraphrase Walter Benjamin, for them every document of civilization is also a document of barbarism.

The culture industry plays an important part in perpetuating the domination of human beings and nature under the guise of increasing their freedom. The subtitle of the chapter on the culture industry in the *Dialectic of Enlightenment* says it all: "Enlightenment as Mass Deception." The culture industry produces culture that is designed to deceive and mislead those engaged in it. What the culture industry creates—what we now describe as mass or popular culture—has for Horkheimer and Adorno only one real function: to reproduce incessantly the values of capitalist culture. A century earlier, Karl Marx had analyzed the exploitation of workers by capitalists in the factory system. The existence of the culture industry is one of the main reasons why over the course of a hundred years little had been done about the exploitation of labour. The culture industry deceives by making it difficult, if not impossible, to see the social limits of a life that appears to be filled with an endless degree of consumer choice, and in which one can at least engage in amusements of various kinds after the work day is done. For Horkheimer and Adorno, these choices and pleasures are false ones, and the function of amusement is little more than "the prolongation of work" (137).

Three Points about the Production of Popular Culture   In their discussion of the culture industry in *Dialectic of Enlightenment*, as well as in related work by Adorno on popular music, three main points emerge about the production of popular culture in the twentieth century.

First, what characterizes popular culture for Horkheimer and Adorno is the **standardization** of cultural production *and* of audience reaction to contemporary culture. In the age of the culture industry, culture comes packaged in a small number of predictable forms and genres and is produced by an increasingly limited number of giant corporations for consumption by a global audience. The small number of genres into which CDs are categorized at record shops (country, rock, alternative, jazz, etc.) and the similarly limited number of film genres and plots (horror, teen films, thrillers, action films, romantic comedies, etc.) are broad examples of what Horkheimer and Adorno seem to have in mind; the fact that today, just as in the 1940s, a small number of major **transnational** companies make the majority of films *and* music available for global consumption suggests that standardization remains a problem for contemporary cultural production (see the discussion of transnational media corporations in Chapter 10). Standardization of cultural production is necessitated by the mass **commodification** of culture: there are only so many films that can be made (the number of films produced each year by Hollywood is still surprisingly low) and so many CDs that can be pressed, and the available "prime time" space on major television networks is constrained by the temporal limits imposed by the workday. We are all familiar with the effects of standardization. Indeed, one of the great complaints of cultural consumers is that there is so little that is "truly" new being produced for us to listen to, watch, and experience. Even with access to two hundred television channels, it is not an uncommon experience to flip through them over and over and still find "nothing" to watch.

This might seem paradoxical or contradictory, since one of the key features of contemporary popular culture is the importance of the "new." Spin a new disc for a few weeks and its novelty has been used up: we grow bored of it and long for something new to spend our money on. The creation of newness is linked to the perpetuation of profit: as long as the cultural industries have something "new" to offer us, the money will continue to flow in. But the creation of "newness" also presents a problem: how can any cultural producer or industry create genuinely "new" objects for culture consumers? Standardization offers a paradoxical solution to this problem by allowing producers to continue to pass off apparently new objects in old shells: the endless stream of pop love songs, which contain not only the same sentiments but often the same chord progressions and melodies; Britney Spears, Rhianna, and Miley Cyrus; all *11* films dealing with the hockey-masked horror assassin, Jason (if one includes *Freddy vs. Jason*); and iPods in different colours.

Standardization is closely connected with what Adorno describes as **pseudo-individualization**. In his essay "On Popular Music," Adorno suggests that in the case of the popular music of his day, "the composition hears for the listener" (215). This is not meant to be taken literally, of course. The claim being made is that popular music (and popular culture more generally) is so standardized that not only is the audience's response predictable, but also it is in a sense "built in" to the cultural product itself. To get a sense of what Adorno has in mind, we need only think of the times when we can feel ourselves being very directly manipulated by cultural objects. The "tearjerker," a movie that leans heavily on sentimentality to hook its viewers, can bring tears to our eyes no matter how trite or predictable its plot might be; a good deal of Top 40 music at any one time seems to rely on recycling licks, hooks, and themes that we like despite ourselves (in the world of the standard pop song, humanity is engaged in the trials and tribulations of dating to the exclusion of virtually every other experience). If pop culture is so effective today at capturing our emotions and desires, it is in part because those emotions and desires have themselves been coded, created, produced, and reproduced by our experiences with popular culture to begin with.

Pseudo-individualization implies the production of a false identity: the experience of a sense of individuality and selfhood that doesn't match up to the experiential depths that these terms usually suggest. To be an "individual," as both philosophers *and* advertisers tell us, is to be separated from the crowd and in control of one's decisions and actions. Everyone is supposedly an individual in this sense—though if that's the case, then it begs the question of who exactly forms the mass or the crowd that an individual distinguishes him- or herself against. A belief in this strong sense of individuality runs deep in contemporary culture, even if almost everyone also believes that popular culture has taken away people's individuality, causing them to pursue one fad and fashion after another, year after year. For Adorno, it is precisely this belief in one's own "real" individuality that constitutes pseudo-individualization. He writes that the "standardization of song hits keeps the customer in line by doing their listening for them, as it were. Pseudo-individualization, for its part, keeps them in line by making them forget that what they listen to is already listened to for them, or 'pre-digested'" (217). Pseudo-individualization is what enables standardization to function. For instead of seeing contemporary popular culture as a landscape in which the directions we can travel are circumscribed and limited, we see (for ourselves, at least, if not for all others) a world of nearly infinite choice that emerges out of our individuality. Pseudo-individualization is the ideological screen that makes a standardized culture seem like a culture of genuine artistic expressions that we interact with in our own supposedly unique way. Standardization and pseudo-individualization pose a problem for Horkheimer and Adorno because of their political implications: they suggest we are free, when the reality is very different.

This leads into the second point they make about the production of popular culture, one that we have already anticipated. In their view, popular culture is produced only in order to reinforce and maintain the power of the status quo. Not only are the products of the cultural industries uniform and without real artistic merit, but also their aim isn't to engage the public, but to distract them from reality by drawing attention away from the contradictions and problems of contemporary society. In the case of popular music, Adorno writes that "listeners are distracted from the demands of reality by entertainment which does not demand attention either" (219). The ubiquity of standardized, mass-produced culture, the pseudo-individuation it both produces and invites, and the distraction it creates make it difficult for human beings to confront fully the enormous social and political challenges that face them. To put it bluntly, it's hard to stay focused on the problems of the environment and on the increasing corporate influence of government decision making when there's so much good television to watch.

As the political process itself becomes more and more beholden to the structures and systems of popular culture (the sound bite, political advertising, the carefully staged press conference, opinion polling, etc.), it is not surprising to find that people are tuning politics out and exercising their choice in the one arena that appears to allow it: the consumption of popular culture. For Horkheimer and Adorno, the rise of popular culture seems to signal the death of the project of human emancipation. "The idea of 'fully exploiting' available technical resources and the facilities for aesthetic mass consumption is part of the economic system which refuses to exploit resources to abolish hunger" (139); this is, for them, one of the great obscenities of the production of popular culture. There is something genuinely obscene about an economic system that devotes billions of dollars to beer commercials and wrestling spectacles but that seems unwilling to intervene in the increasing polarization of wealth throughout the world, and the lack of resources to treat AIDS in those African nations that have been ravaged by the disease.

Finally, a third related point concerns the possibilities and prospects of oppositional art and culture. The vision of popular culture that emerges in Horkheimer's and Adorno's work is one in which artistic and cultural resistance has all but evaporated. But how can this be? On the contrary: contemporary culture seems to be characterized by all manner of *opposition* to the standardization of popular culture. The limits and problems of standardized culture form a prominent theme in contemporary art, from Andy Warhol's soup cans to Roy Lichtenstein's pop art drawings, from the photos of Roy Arden to the sculptures of Jeff Koons. The same can be said of contemporary fiction and drama as well. Even within popular culture, it is possible to find criticisms of contemporary culture on television (in *The Simpsons*, *Family Guy*, or *South Park*, for example) and in popular music (from Radiohead to Wolf Parade). Contemporary culture is also home to numerous subcultural groups that oppose "the way things are." These include pop-culture **subcultures** (e.g., the rave scene and skateboarders—see Chapter 8 for a more detailed discussion of subcultures), but also span the range of activist and extremist groups. There seems to be an awful lot of dissent and opposition going on in a world that is supposedly dominated and controlled through the medium of popular culture. Indeed, for all its popularity, it seems that even the biggest fans of pop culture are frequently disappointed that the things they watch or listen to aren't always as good or interesting as they'd like.

Be that as it may, it is worth noting that all of this oppositional activity seems to have left the basic structures of capitalism and popular culture production in place—no matter how much they might wish to do away with it. Horkheimer and Adorno are well aware of the fact that dissidence and dissatisfaction still exist within the system of amusement and distraction that they outline. Indeed, this is to be expected by the very fact that this system limits human possibilities and expression. The amusements of popular culture might put salve on the wound of human exploitation under capitalism, but they can't heal it: the pain is still there, even if we don't always feel it.

Though the dissatisfactions that are expressed at all of the different sites suggested above are real enough, Horkheimer and Adorno believe that there is a way in which such resistance is already factored into the larger system. "Whenever Orson Welles offends against the tricks of the trade," they write, "he is forgiven because his departures from the norm are regarded as calculated mutations which serve more strongly to confirm the validity of the system" (129). Dissidence isn't a problem; indeed, it helps to offset the need to introduce "newness" into the system of standardization. Rebellion keeps the system going. "Real" art, which requires the kind of serious attention that popular culture generally doesn't, might be able to knock us out of our stupor. That this hasn't happened and seems unlikely to happen suggests that such art no longer exists: "high art," the kind that appears in museums and galleries, has also succumbed to the effects of the culture industry, becoming little more than wall decorations for rich people. In the words of Horkheimer and Adorno, "something is provided for all so that none may escape" (123).

Ashley Bickerton's *Tormented Self-Portrait (Susie at Arles)* (1987–88) is part of a growing body of contemporary art that draws attention to the visual power of commodity culture and the continuities between the art world and the world of commerce.

Summarizing Horkheimer and Adorno   If we were to summarize Horkheimer's and Adorno's position on popular culture, it would be that its meaning and function is determined primarily at the level of production. By understanding the ways in which popular culture is produced, in this view, we also seem to be able to understand virtually *everything* there is to know about how popular culture works—not just its production, but how it is consumed, what it means socially, and so on. From this perspective, analyzing or understanding the meaning of specific cultural objects is pointless. While you might learn that *The Simpsons* is a different kind of cartoon than the old Disney cartoons that Horkheimer and Adorno discuss in *Dialectic of Enlightenment* (134–38), you would have to conclude that their general social function is, in the end, the same: the amusements that they generate impede reflection on the realities of our social and political situation. Put bluntly, what popular culture does is distract us from seeing the way things really are.

On one level, this is a powerful point: it lends credence to the central role that popular culture plays in contemporary life. Far from being "mere" amusement, popular culture is at the heart of the production and management of social order. At the same time, Adorno's and Horkheimer's view of popular culture is decidedly one-sided (it's all bad). Quality aside, the most superficial comparison of *The Simpsons* and, say, *Bambi* would suggest that this mode of interpretation leaves out a big part of the story of popular culture. While the culture industry thesis offers a systemic analysis of popular culture in contemporary society and draws attention to production as an important site of investigation, there are ways in which it closes off continued critical reflection and exploration—the opposite of what its formulators intended.

Some Problems with the Culture Industry Thesis

As influential as the culture industry thesis has been (and it has exerted a considerable influence, both implicitly and explicitly), Horkheimer's and Adorno's analysis of popular culture has been attacked from a number of different positions. Indeed, much of what constitutes the field of cultural studies can be seen as a reaction to the limits of this thesis. The insistence within cultural studies on the need to consider the consumption of popular culture emerges in part as a reaction to a view that imagines what audiences and individuals do with popular culture can be determined in advance at the level of production. Taking popular culture seriously means to take seriously the ability of diverse individuals and communities to interact with popular culture in their own creative ways—within, of course, specific social, cultural, and political limits.

Criticisms of the culture industry thesis can be grouped into three main categories. It is worth reviewing these criticisms (if briefly) in order to get a sense of how we might move beyond the limits of the culture industry thesis in our explorations of the production of popular culture.

First, and most commonly, Horkheimer's and Adorno's cultural industry thesis has been criticized as elitist. As Keith Negus puts it,

Adorno and Horkheimer's view of cultural production has, with some justification, often been portrayed as the pessimistic lament of cultural elitists who were dismayed at what they perceived to be the homogeneity and vulgarity of "mass" taste, and who were concerned that the potential for artistic creativity in music, literature and painting had been co-opted and corrupted by the production methods and administrative regimes of industrial capitalism. (70)

The ubiquity of these criticisms alone suggests that there is something to this point. But criticisms of the elitism of the culture industry thesis actually confuse or conflate a number of points. As we suggested above, it is true that the culture industry thesis does not account for the creativity (or at least the potential creativity) of consumers of popular culture. But this does not mean that, on the contrary, Horkheimer and Adorno leave room open for connoisseurs of "difficult" novels or abstract art. Rather, they are equally critical of the political limits of "serious" or "elite" art as well. In "The Culture Industry Reconsidered," Adorno makes a case for the "seriousness" of *both* high and low art. The problem with the culture industry for Adorno is that it attacks high *and* low culture, forcing them together in a way that strips both of their potentials to resist total social control.

What Adorno identifies as an element of certain forms of avant-garde literature and art he thus sees as residing in the "rebellious resistance" of low culture as well. In other words, it is simply *not* the case that Adorno sees only "high" art as having political potential. The problem with contemporary culture is not that it is "low," but that its political and social effectiveness has declined. If the culture industry thesis is elitist, it is because it prioritizes production to the total exclusion of consumption and not because it suggests that *Masterpiece Theatre* taken with brandy is superior to *Hockey Night in Canada* enjoyed with beer.

A second criticism is that the culture industry thesis is historically limited. Like everything else, it is a product of its times and the circumstances in which it was produced. In his introduction to an excerpt from Horkheimer's and Adorno's book, Simon During points out that

> it is worth emphasizing that when this essay was written the culture industry was less variegated than it was to become, during the 1960s in particular. Hollywood, for instance, was still "vertically integrated" [in the mid-40s] so that the five major studios owned the production, distribution, and exhibition arms of the film business between them; television was still in its infancy; the LP and the single were unknown; the cultural market had not been broken into various demographic sectors—of which, in the 1950s, the youth segment was to become the most energetic. (29–30)

Some of the features characterizing the culture industry in the 1940s have returned: there are once again highly integrated forms of cultural production, **vertical** in some cases, **horizontal** in others (see the discussion of media convergence in Chapter 10). Nevertheless, the fundamental point that During makes is one worth considering. The cultural industry thesis was one of the first attempts to analyze the new form of **mass-produced** culture that emerged by mid-century in the United States, Canada, and Europe.

As Bernie Gendron points out, while Horkheimer and Adorno have been criticized for denigrating popular music in the 1940s, the songs produced in the song mills of Tin Pan

Alley *did* make use of an extremely limited melodic and lyrical palette. In the intervening years, the production of popular music has changed significantly and in complex ways in reaction to cultural and social shifts, and in accordance with the development of new technologies (in ways that we will discuss later in this chapter). No general theory of the culture industry such as the one set out by Horkheimer and Adorno could sustain the wild shifts that have taken place in popular cultural production. Even if we use the cultural industry model as a rough framework for an analysis of the production of popular culture, we need to be attentive to changes in the conditions in and under which pop culture is and was produced.

Finally, critics have suggested that Horkheimer's and Adorno's vision of contemporary social life is far too "totalizing." What this means is that their sense of the extent of influence of the culture industry is too widespread: like the Borg in *Star Trek: The Next Generation*, they seem to insist that all "resistance is futile." Indeed, as we saw above, Horkheimer and Adorno suggest that even resistance to the system of the culture industry is part of the system, too. The truth, however, is that popular culture is a messy and unwieldy object that can't be explained by reference to a single explanatory model.

The Relevance of the Culture Industry Thesis   In many respects, the culture industry thesis extends Karl Marx's assertion that the dominant culture at any given time is the culture of the dominant class: popular culture, then, reflects and supports the power and dominance of that class. But, as Raymond Williams has argued,

> the body of intellectual and imaginative work which each generation receives as its traditional culture is always, and necessarily, something more than the product of a single class. It is not only that a considerable part of it will have survived from much earlier periods than the immediately pre-existing form of society. . . . It is also that, even within a society in which a particular class is dominant, it is evidently possible both for members of other classes to contribute to the common stock, and for such contributions to be unaffected by or in opposition to the ideas and values of the dominant class. (320)

While the culture industry thesis may account for a significant degree of the production of standardized culture in contemporary society, it would be a mistake to forget the considerable remnants of "older" forms of culture (opera, classical music, art, **"folk" cultures** and practices, etc.) and to minimize the anarchic energies of subcultures and countercultures: dominant culture is never so dominant as to form the single face of culture at any given historical moment, despite how easy it can be to envision total control by big business.

None of this is to minimize the contribution of Horkheimer and Adorno to the study of popular culture, whose general points and the issues that they raise remain central to our imagining of contemporary culture. What we can conclude from our lengthy analysis of the problems and possibilities that the culture industry thesis introduces is that, while it is important to consider the role of standardized production, no general theory of production describes the full experience of contemporary pop culture. One of the things that we need to realize is that contemporary cultural production is complex and often contradictory. As the film scholar Gill Branston puts it, "capitalist products have both an exchange value for their owners and shareholders, and a use value for their audiences, and sometime the two can be fairly far apart" (19). Popular culture is produced in part to make money, but this doesn't completely determine what it means for its users—nor, for that matter, does it completely determine *why* popular culture is made. The two sections that follow will provide some sense of the multiple, complex reason on both sides of the equation. The first section ("How Is Culture Shaped by Economics?") will explore the development of a single consumer product, while the second ("Shifting Modes of Cultural Production") will show historical shifts in production in a single segment of the culture industry: Hollywood films. The final section of this chapter ("Cultural Production Today") will deal with some recent developments in the production of popular culture (a discussion expanded further in Chapter 10).

HOW IS CULTURE SHAPED BY ECONOMICS? THE STORY OF THE WALKMAN

How is culture shaped by economics? This is far from an easy question to answer, especially if we break away from the "natural" assumptions about the ways in which art and economics are related. Though this may seem frustrating, the answer is that while culture *is* shaped by economics, this shaping occurs in indirect rather than (or perhaps, in addition to) direct ways. The shaping effect of economics on culture is best seen in the changes that culture undergoes over time: looking at our present circumstances will tend to lead us only to a first-level analysis of the kind we described above, in which art and money are imagined as related inversely. We also need to remember that the relationship between economics and culture is a reciprocal one: just as economics shapes culture, so culture effects and shapes the economy. The constant back-and-forth flow of force between culture and economics means that if we stop the process in midstream in order to dissect it, we get only part of the overall picture. Then again, if we look only at the larger historical frame, we tend to miss the dynamics of this interchange. The solution, of course, is to do both things simultaneously, as is done in the book *Doing Cultural Studies*, which offers an overview of the field through a thorough examination of the making and marketing of a single consumer object: the Walkman.

Though it was first introduced to the market just over 25 years ago (in Japan in 1979), the pace at which the consumer electronics revolution has changed the ways in which we interact with one another and amuse ourselves (changes explored in detail in Chapter 10) has meant that this little marvel of technology already seems antiquated. Cassette tapes? Foam-padded metal headphones? A rewind button? AA batteries for power? In an age when digital downloads to miniature hard-drives powered by new forms of rechargeable batteries are the norm, a device that produces sound by dragging audio tape over a metal head seems to belong to the annals of once-popular devices that no one needs to concern themselves with any longer.

In many respects, however, the production and marketing of the Walkman offers an object lesson in the complex process by which an object makes it to market—a system of production, design, and marketing that in many respects establishes a precedent for the production of *all* of the consumer electronics that have followed in its wake: MP3 players and iPods, cell phones and PDAs, portable video games, laptop computers, and so on. With the production of the Walkman, Sony not only connected with pre-existing social practices connecting music and mobility (as in the transistor radio or car stereo), but helped to create new social practices that we now accept as normal features of everyday life. Though it may now be the tell-tale white wires of the iPod that snake down from ears everywhere, the practice of listening to music while travelling by subway, bus or plane, while jogging or gardening, or while just drifting around college and university campuses was in large part made possible by the development of the Walkman. How did it come to be? And what does its birth tell us about the production of contemporary culture?

The Birth of the Walkman

In her account of the creation of the U.S. mass market, sociologist Susan Strasser has argued that

> the corporations that made and distributed mass-produced goods did not neces-
> sarily set out to create needs, nor did they do so in any straightforward way. . . . The
> process that makes people into consumers amalgamates changing ideas, habits,
> technology, demographic trends, and many other facets of culture, few of which
> are controlled even by the most powerful marketers, who concentrate their efforts
> on perceiving and taking advantage of those changes. (17)

This certainly holds true of the Sony Corporation in its development of the Walkman. The Walkman emerged into a world in which the massive expansion of pop music from the 1950s on—which was made possible in part by cheap LPs, record players, and transistor radios—had not only made the purchase of recorded music a common practice, but had also provided the fuel for a new phenomenon of "youth culture," "with its supporting industries in entertainment, fashion, sport and leisure activities, magazines and the image-creation, publishing and public relations industries" (du Gay et al. 19). The possibility of a new consumer device that would enable youth to listen to music "on the go" began to be discussed within Sony in the mid- to late 1970s. The precise origins of the idea have been the subject of considerable debate, with both the unique corporate and engineering structure of Sony—collective and relatively non-hierarchical—and specific executives and designers claiming credit for the burst of inspiration that led to the open salvo in the ear of private, mobile music (42–51).

Like many consumer products, the Walkman is not something that anyone "needs" (in the sense of food, clothing or water). As a company whose main products are broadly in the field of entertainment, the challenge for Sony is to capture at least a portion of the budget that different groups spend each year on entertainment. At roughly the same time as the company was developing the Walkman, it was also creating a number of other products that have played a role in reshaping contemporary culture, including the Betamax videocassette-recorder (eventually abandoned due to the popularity of the alternative format VHS), the next generation Trinitron colour television, and with Philips, the compact disc and CD player (76). The Walkman was created with a very specific audience in mind: young consumers already addicted to popular music, who hopefully would see the Walkman as a perfect device with which to enjoy their music anywhere without bothering anyone.

An immediate consequence of the development of a consumer item for the youth market was the need to create an object that was affordable. To keep costs down, Sony decided initially to develop all of the Walkman components (integrated circuits, headphones, etc.) on-site, thereby eliminating the need to negotiate with external producers over cost and delivery schedules. Despite the popularity of the Walkman and its retail success, the high cost of research and development, and the speed with which others companies produced competing models, meant that Sony profits actually *fell* in the four years (1980–83) following its introduction. Once the quirks and flaws of initial Walkman models had been worked out, Sony followed many of its competitors and sought production sites in countries with low wages in an effort to reduce costs and increase profits. This process, in which research and development and production (among other elements of the overall production process) are divided geographically in order to minimize costs and maximize profit, is one of the defining features of what has come to be called **globalization** (see Chapter 10).

Marketing, Design, and Lifestyle

The production of a consumer item such as the Walkman goes well beyond the physical assembly of the component parts in a factory. Design and marketing are also key elements of the overall production process. In both of these areas of production, Sony relied heavily on feedback from users of the Walkman to shape and rework the Walkman in order to maximize its fit with its intended youth market, as well as with markets that it couldn't have anticipated prior to launching the product: by the end of its life, more than seven hundred versions of the Walkman had been produced for use by different age groups (including a "My First Sony" for children), in specific national markets, and in conjunction with specific activities (such as the yellow waterproof Walkman for swimming or diving). The Walkman model that many remember as the original, the WM2, followed the introduction of the first and represented an extensive redesign based on feedback from initial consumer use. In the case of the WM2, the design came first: it was then left up to the engineers to produce a device that could function within the ideal design-size of two AA batteries plus a cassette tape, and which could work with the switches located on the front as opposed to the sides.

The initial Walkman came equipped with two headphone jacks, a feature that was emphasized in the first television advertising campaign in Japan, which showed "'a very tall American woman and an old Japanese gentleman' who were both wearing headphones connected to the same Walkman from which they were sharing the music" (du Gay et al. 59). It was consumer feedback that led Sony to recognize that users weren't using the Walkman in the way they had expected: listening privately even in public wasn't seen by consumers as rude, but as offering them (among other things) new ways to encounter public spaces and situations. As the authors of *Doing Cultural Studies* point out, in the case of the Walkman—and indeed, this is the case today with all consumer items—"the technology was not simply produced as a finished artifact which then had an impact on consumption. Consumer activities were crucial to the introduction, modification and subsequent redevelopment and marketing of this product" (59).

The invention and marketing of the Walkman highlight the complex cultural and social contexts within which popular culture is produced. In trying to assess the contribution that production makes to popular culture—not just the limits it imposes, but also the possibilities that it opens up—we want to make sure to attend to this complexity rather than resorting to simple narratives about the role that money plays in culture.

Suggested Activity 4.1

Can you think of other cultural products whose invention has created, rather than fulfilled, an existing need? What products have you acquired recently that you might once have had no need for, but that now seem essential? What would your life be like without these cultural products?

SHIFTING MODES OF CULTURAL PRODUCTION

In the last section we looked at the production of a single consumer object (in a broad sense that includes marketing, advertising, and distribution). This section will highlight the changes in the production and distribution of one cultural form—Hollywood film—over the course of its relatively brief history. It should be obvious enough that forms and modes of production change over time. For one thing, there are technological reasons for these shifts and changes: as new technologies are introduced, the systems of production and distribution of existing forms undergo significant changes.

In the history of recorded music, numerous formats have come and gone, including record albums (of various speeds and formats), 8-tracks, and cassette tapes. The heated formal and informal discussions about the superiority of albums versus CDs (the "warm" sounds produced by albums contrasted to the tinny-ness of CDs, etc.) seem, 15 years later, to have been a quaint debate between audio-Luddites and technophiles that was settled in advance by the relentless march of new technological formats. In the case of film, too, the introduction of sound and colour had implications for the way in which films were produced, and the possibilities of widespread digital distribution (foreshadowed by recently introduced video-on-demand technologies and the online swapping of films through high-speed digital access) promise to change the ways in which films are both shot and screened.

Changes in production result not only from technological developments, but also from social and economic ones. Film became a popular cultural phenomenon in part because it arose at just the right time. By the end of the nineteenth century, leisure time had become a reality for more and more people. Prior to the invention of film, a system of public entertainments in which audience members exchanged money for cultural experiences had also become well developed. Such public entertainments included travelling orchestras, music hall, vaudeville and burlesque shows, magic shows, and amusement parks (see Chapter 2). Film arrived in a social situation in Canada and the United States, in which there were both venues in which films can be screened (e.g., vaudeville theatres) and an audience accustomed to seeing spectacles "performed" for their pleasure.

The Evolution of Hollywood

The history of Hollywood filmmaking can be divided into roughly five main eras: (1) early cinema (1895–1920), which is the period between the invention of film and its organization into an industrial system of routinized production; (2) the studio system (1920–1960), the era of "classical" Hollywood film production; (3) the so-called "Hollywood Renaissance" period (1965–1975), which describes the period of innovative and edgy film production that occurred between the end of the studio system and its reorganization; (4) the blockbuster era initiated by Steven Spielberg's *Jaws* (1975), which has continued (for the most part) up to the present; and (5) the digital era that is just beginning to take shape at the present. Each of these eras is characterized by a different relationship among the three main elements of the film industry: *production, distribution,* and *exhibition.* The history that we offer in this section has to be understood as merely a sketch of a very complex story of a single national cinema. At different times during this history, the national cinemas of other countries have been powerfully active as well (for example, the Indian film industry today produces as many feature-length films as all the major Hollywood studios combined). However, our aim is not to offer an overview of film history in general, but to provide an example of shifting conditions and circuits of cultural production through a single, relatively well-known example.

Early Cinema   The first public film screening took place in Paris on December 28, 1895. It was organized by Auguste and Louis Lumière, who adapted Thomas Edison's Kinetoscope viewing machine, which could be viewed only by single patrons in peep-show fashion in specially designed parlours. Over the next few years the Lumière brothers screened their films around the world, in various parts of Europe and also in South Africa, Russia, India, Brazil, Mexico, Australia, and Japan. The content of early cinema has been described as "a scatter of inventions" (Williams "British" 14), which ranged from the recording of everyday events and activities (the Lumières' *actualités,* the most famous of which shows a train coming into a station from background to foreground), to early forms of short narrative films, such as Georges Méliès's *A Trip to the Moon.* The visual vocabulary of filmmaking developed as quickly as the technology of filmmaking itself. By 1916, the director D.W. Griffith had released two full-length features—*The Birth of a Nation* (1915) and *Intolerance* (1916)—which contained many of the visual elements that would come to comprise the classical Hollywood style.

In terms of cultural production, the period of early cinema was a troubled one. As with the development of any new medium, numerous players entered into various parts of the production process only to be driven out by the ferocious competition over the potential spoils. For the first few years of film exhibition, the greatest degree of control in the cinema business lay with the exhibitors. Since early films were very short, exhibitors chose films offered by numerous producers and assembled longer custom-made film programs out of the bits and pieces they had purchased. The period from 1905–07 witnessed a boom in the United States in the construction of small theatres (nickelodeons) in urban centres where a wide cross-section of the public would congregate to watch films. In order to sustain interest and keep people coming, exhibitors would change films often—sometimes on a daily basis—which produced a boom in film production as well.

As films became longer, control began to shift to film producers. In order to generate profits from longer (and, so, more expensive to make) films, producers began to evolve forms of studio production that allowed for more precise control over the contexts of production (lighting and, later, sound) and over costs. Studio production worked like a factory for films: all of the fixed elements needed to create a film (cameras, lighting, etc.) were located in one place, at which the actors, directors, and staff involved in the film would assemble. Studio production also enabled advance planning of the production process. By 1904, films were no longer sold to exhibitors but rented to them, which allowed producers to retain control over their films and to further extend their profits by reducing the physical amount of film stock they had to produce. By the time of Griffith's films the era of "factory filmmaking," in which there were clearly defined roles for directors, cinematographers, script supervisors, and so on, was in full swing. Scripts became elaborate blueprints for the production of films, and advances in editing allowed for films to be shot in the cheapest and most efficient manner and then assembled in the correct order for exhibition.

Some of the major studios still in existence today began as chains of nickelodeons (e.g., Warner Brothers, Universal, Paramount, and Fox). These exhibitors quickly saw the advantages of producing their own films in order to ensure a steady supply for their theatres and to bypass the system of competitive bidding for films that drove profits up for producers (who would sell their films to the highest bidder) at the expense of exhibitors. Thus was born the studio system: a system in which a small number of companies became vertically integrated, controlling the production and distribution of films that they would then exhibit in their own theatres.

In 1908, the 10 most powerful U.S. production companies tried to establish a **monopoly** on the industry by setting up the Motion Picture Patents Company, which demanded licensing fees from all film producers, distributors, and exhibitors. A group of rivals who called themselves the "Independents" fought against the Company's dominance. Their strategies included using illegal equipment and imported film stock, and moving as far away as possible from the film industry's home in New York to the then-village of Hollywood, California. When the Motion Picture Patents Company was finally forced to shut down in 1915, in response to the finding that it constituted an unfair monopoly, the Independents were in a position to do what so many industry outsiders and renegades have done since, and assumed a position of dominance (think Bill Gates in the computer industry). Thus, led by Adolph Zukor, the Independents (which eventually became Famous Players Lasky

Corporation) quickly came to dominate the industry, integrating production, distribution, and exhibition, raising capital through the stock market, and establishing the Hollywood star system in the process. By 1921, Famous Players Lasky controlled more than three hundred cinemas and was itself being accused of monopolistic practices (Briggs 51–52). While the film industry was to change dramatically over the course of the twentieth century, this early struggle between independents and conglomerates, entrepreneurs and monopolistic organizations, established a dominant pattern that was to characterize not just cinema, but also the entertainment industry as a whole.

There is one other issue we need to raise with respect to film production in its early years. In early, pre-sound cinema, film technology *and* films themselves were often imported from Europe to North America. In the first years of film, France, England, and Germany were sites of film production that rivalled the United States. By 1920, the United States had established itself as the global centre of film production. There are a number of reasons for the sudden dominance of U.S. filmmaking. Most significant was the impact of the First World War (1914–18) on film production in Europe. While film production on the continent was shut down, U.S. companies rushed to fill the continued global demand for film products. For example, by 1916, 60 percent of the films shown in Argentina and 95 percent of the films exhibited in Australia originated in the United States. The establishment of the U.S. film industry in California helped to solidify the U.S. position through the availability of cheap land and nonunionized labour in a perfect climate for year-round production. Finally, the gains that the U.S. film industry made during the war allowed it to spend far more money on production values than its European counterparts even after the war. This continues to be the case today: the most expensive European–financed film to date was Jean-Jacques Annaud's *Enemy at the Gates* (2001), which was made for US$70 million. This is well below the Motion Picture Association of America's figures for the *average* cost of a U.S. feature film, which in 2005 was US$ 90.2 million.

The Studio System   The 1920s were a period of enormous growth in the U.S. film industry. Between 1922 and 1930 investment in the film industry rose from US$78 million to $850 million, and average film attendance doubled between 1922 and 1928 from 40 million to 80 million people per week. The studio system marks the fullest expression of the factory film system. The five major studios and the "little three" (see Table 4.1) kept all of the staff required to make a film, from actors and directors to cinematographers and stagehands, under exclusive contract to a specific studio. Films were assembled based on the available in-house elements: scripts were assigned to the available directors, cast with those actors who were under contract but not working on other films being made by the studio, and so on. Humphrey Bogart was cast in the lead role of the film *The Maltese Falcon* only because bigger stars were busy doing other projects; such stories of fame by accident in studio-era Hollywood are legion.

The studio era is also characterized by an unprecedented degree of economic and corporate integration in the film industry. Studios owned all aspects of the industry, from production to distribution to exhibition. For example, by the 1930s Paramount owned

Table 4.1 The Studio System

The Five "Majors"	• Paramount
	• MGM (Metro-Goldwyn-Mayer)
	• Fox
	• Warner Bros.
	• RKO (Radio-Keith-Orpheum)
The Little Three	• Universal
	• Columbia
	• United Artists
Independents	• Samuel Goldwyn
	• David O. Selznick
	• Hebert Biberman
"B" Movie Producers	• Roger Corman, Ed Wood, Russ Meyer

1,210 theatres in North America, which would, of course, exhibit Paramount films exclusively. The studio era is also the period in which the major companies, in a bid to outdo one another, built opulent theatres to capture the attention of audiences. As a result of their control over the industry, independent film production in the United States dried up, with the exception of films put together by a few major producers. Independents found it challenging to get their films financed, mainly because of the difficulty in finding locations to screen their films once completed. Foreign films more or less faded from the U.S. cultural landscape. The themes of movies also narrowed considerably in comparison to cinema's early years, with the fictional drama becoming *the* genre of Hollywood filmmaking.

In 1946, Hollywood recorded its highest box office and attendance figures of all time at a figure of 98 million tickets sold per week. From this point on, however, the studio system entered a precipitous decline that was to endure for the better part of three decades. The film industry encountered two major challenges. First, in 1948 the U.S. Supreme Court ruled that the eight largest studios were guilty of violating antitrust laws enacted at the turn of the century in order to prevent the creation of monopolies or oligopolies in American business. The studios were forced to sell off major parts of their assets, in particular their theatre chains, which opened the way for independent, non-studio productions. Second, the mid-1940s to the mid-1960s saw a shift in American movie-going habits. In part, this was the result of the movement of the middle classes after the Second World War from the cities to the suburbs, which left many large theatres devoid of the audiences needed to sustain them. In combination with the growth in television ownership (90 percent of U.S. homes owned a television by the end of the 1950s), the film industry was badly damaged: profits declined by a shocking 74 percent between 1947 and 1957. The film industry responded to these changes in ways that would begin to bear fruit only from the mid-1970s onward. Films began to be made and marketed for specific segments of the audience: children's films, movies aimed at teens, more serious dramas for adults, and so on. Foreign and "art" films, imported for distribution from abroad, were once again shown, though seldom outside of major urban centres.

Hollywood Renaissance   Before these responses to the decline of cinema-going could take hold, the decade between 1967 and 1976 saw a remarkable flowering of U.S. cinema. Eschewing the limits and standard narratives that characterized classic Hollywood cinema, a number of young directors redefined the parameters of film form and content. Often dealing with edgy narratives on contemporary themes, the films of directors such as Robert Altman, Arthur Penn, Martin Scorsese, and Francis Ford Coppola (all graduates of recently established film school programs) captured the imaginations of a society that was undergoing significant changes as a result of the sixties **counterculture** and the social movements associated with this period.

This era of filmmaking is now often lamented as a lost or squandered opportunity for the creation of serious American cinema. The lingering belief in the inherent connection between independent production and quality filmmaking (a connection that has been revived in the recent use of the term "independent" as a term of approbation) originates with the films of this era. While filmmakers were able to exercise a degree of control over their films that harkened back to the days of early cinema, films such as *Bonnie and Clyde*, *The Godfather I* and *II*, *Nashville*, and *Taxi Driver* were nevertheless still produced and distributed under the auspices of major production companies. Whatever their aesthetic successes, the remnants of the studio system continued to assert their influence on these films and their directors. Indeed, there is a way in which this era functions as a kind of laboratory in which different models for the reorganization of the film industry could be tested out. The kind of independent production that took place during this period, which brought together all of the personnel necessary to create a film on a film-by-film basis, did create the conditions for more idiosyncratic filmmaking than the old studio-based production system. At the same time, it also created a model for the mode of production that would take place in the blockbuster era that followed.

The Blockbuster Era   During the past 30 years, there have been numerous shifts and developments in Hollywood filmmaking—so much so that to claim that one could describe all the shifts and changes in one general category misses some important nuances. Nevertheless, the dominant idea and ideal of Hollywood film since the breakout success of *Jaws* and *Star Wars* is captured in the idea of the "blockbuster": films that shatter the barriers between market segments and draw crowds who line up around the block. Blockbuster films are crafted as events or spectacles—they are highly anticipated and carefully controlled. In order to maximize profits, distributors plan the release dates of different films to coincide with periods of high attendance (the Christmas season, early summer, etc.) *or* low attendance (which is when serious or "mature" films are released), and to minimize competition with other blockbuster movies (*Spider-Man* and *Attack of the Clones* were released on separate weekends in order to avoid impacting on each other's profits, as were *Harry Potter and the Philosopher's Stone* and *The Fellowship of the Ring*). Though no longer organized into oligopolies, as they were during the studio system, during the blockbuster era the majors have once again come to dominate: from 1970 to 1987, films produced by the big studios generated 84 percent of box office revenues in Canada and the United States. In the first six months of 2005 alone, the major studies— Paramount, Warner Bros., 20th Century Fox, Disney, Universal and Sony—took in US$3.2 billion at the box office alone.

The production process has changed considerably from earlier eras. The big companies, such as Paramount, Warner Bros., and 20th Century Fox, are now primarily finance and distribution companies. Like much of the rest of the global economy, the production of films has been reorganized into a more flexible system. Production has become the responsibility of individual producers, financed by the old studios, who rent production space, equipment, and personnel on a short-term, film-by-film basis. There are very few stars and directors under "exclusive" contracts to production companies; everything is done on the spur of the moment during available windows of opportunity for directors, stars, and production crew.

The exhibition of films has also changed in ways that have impacted the film industry in general. Beginning with the creation of spaces such as the (now defunct) 18-screen Cineplex theatre in Toronto's Eaton Centre, new exhibition spaces have been designed with multiple screens on which a range of movies appealing to different market segments can be screened. Distributors wield enormous power over exhibitors. Especially for popular films, distributors can dictate the number of screens that an exhibition company must run its films on and the minimum length of time that the films have to be screened. Independent exhibitors have once again faced difficulties in competing for films against large exhibition companies, such as Cineplex Odeon and Famous Players in Canada—one of the reasons that Canadian films get so little screen time at home.

Actual film screenings currently make up only one small part of the overall revenue generated through the production and distribution of films. Companies can now recoup costs in numerous ways: through the licensing of secondary screening opportunities (after the opening period but before video distribution); through distribution in the form of DVDs, cable and broadcast television rights, and online digital sales; through various forms of merchandising, especially in the case of children's films; and, finally, even through such mechanisms as the sale of advertising space within movies themselves in the form of product placements (Reese's Pieces in *E.T.*, FedEx and Wilson in *Castaway*, Omega Watches and Ford in *Casino Royale*).

Production and Meaning

This brief history of Hollywood filmmaking highlights the huge number of changes that the industry has undergone over the past century. A more detailed history would introduce further divisions and differences in the production process. One of the first things that this history should tell us is that although we might be able to watch *The Birth of a Nation* and *The Fellowship of the Ring* at home on DVD on the same evening, they are *not* the same kind of cultural object. We refer to both as *movies* or *films*, but we should not forget that they were created under very different conditions. If we obscure this fact (which we all too often do), we risk forgetting the ways in which different systems of production create different forms of popular culture. For instance, the difference in dominant film themes and styles in each era is not simply an accident of history; nor can it be accounted for as shifts that occur on their own (that is, without influence by the productive process). At the same time, we need to be cautious about drawing direct lines of influence between style and production. Our aim in this chapter is not to argue for the reduction of theme to the logic of production practice, but to insist that we consider production when we explore the social meanings and significance of popular cultural objects.

A summary of our discussion in this section is provided in Table 4.2.

Suggested Activity 4.2

In what ways might this production history differ in the case of popular music or other major areas of popular culture (books, tourism, eating out, etc.)? Unlike film, popular music combines a form of craft labour—that is, the labour of a small number of individuals practising a craft that is in some sense preindustrial—with mass, standardized production. In addressing the question, make sure to keep this point in mind.

CULTURAL PRODUCTION TODAY

Just as production techniques and systems have changed over time in Hollywood film, they continue to evolve in significant ways in other parts of popular culture. The final section of this chapter looks at recent developments in cultural production that have an impact on the ways we examine popular culture today. As you will see right away, these developments constitute an extension of aspects of the culture industries thesis and offer important challenges to it. For example, the expansion of the Internet as a means of cultural communication and the growth of the digital production of sound and images offers cultural producers the chance to circumvent the typical channels of cultural production and distribution. But before we celebrate the birth of a new cyber-utopia, we need to be conscious of the fact that these alternative productive practices exist in a world of popular culture production that continues to be dominated by a relatively small number of major corporations. While bands with limited resources can now make their music available to people around the world through the Internet, it remains true that even a considerably weakened music industry has far greater distribution and marketing powers (and so, also, the ability to generate massive profits) than any independent band that relies

Table 4.2 Production Modes and Film Styles

Period	Production System	Theme/Style	Representative Films
Early Cinema (1895–1920s)	• Independent • International • Power divided between production and distribution	• Actualités • Varied styles • Experimental	*A Trip to the Moon* (1902); *The Birth of a Nation* (1915)
Studio System (1920s–1960s)	• Oligopolistic • Vertical integration • American narrative (social conflict/ love stories)	• Fictional drama • Classical Hollywood	*City Lights* (1931); *Stagecoach* (1939); *Strangers on a Train* (1951); *From Here to Eternity* (1953)
"Hollywood Renaissance" (1965–1975)	• Independent/ corporate • "Return" of foreign film • Production	• Experimental and critical • *Cinema verité* • Documentary	*Bonnie and Clyde* (1967); *McCabe and Mrs. Miller* (1971); *Mean Streets* (1973); *The Conversation* (1974)
Blockbuster Era (1975–present)	• American • High budget • Synergy • Distribution/ cross-production • Video/TV	• Classical narrative • Special effects • Spectacle	*Jaws* (1975); *Terminator 2* (1991); *Jurassic Park* (1993); *Lord of the Rings* (*Trilogy:* 2001–2003)
Digital Era (2000–?)	• International • High and low budget • Internet distribution	• Mixed genre • New documentaries • Remastered classic/ foreign films • Digital animation • Digital effects	• *Monsters Inc.* (2001); • *Bubble* (2005); • *An Inconvenient Truth* (2006); • *Singin' in the Rain* (1952; digitally remastered);

on getting the word out through their MySpace page. David Bowie, Prince, Public Enemy, and other major musical acts have attempted to distribute their music solely online with considerably less success than distribution through record stores.

Lifestyle Marketing and Market Segmentation

A recent full-page newspaper ad for Cadillac mimics the time lines that one often finds in art history books. The line begins in the dark recesses of history with an image of the Lascaux cave-paintings, which are among the earliest examples of human artistic expression. Next in line is the paradigmatic expression of Ancient Greek sculpture, the Venus de Milo, followed by Leonardo da Vinci's *Mona Lisa* and, closer to the present, a painting by Picasso. Bringing us up to date, at the end of the time line are photos of three vehicles—the new Cadillac XLR, the CTS, and the Escalade EXT (a truck). The caption to this ad reads: "It seems to be humanity's destiny to find new ways to express beauty. Presenting the latest installment."

It is tempting to dismiss the artistic pretensions of this advertisement: surely a Cadillac is not a work of art in the same sense as the paintings by da Vinci and Picasso. But this would be to miss the real insight the ad offers into the character of contemporary popular cultural production. To an ever-increasing degree, as Celia Lury has argued in *Consumer Culture*, the production of all consumer goods has been subjected to a process of stylization. Consumer objects have become increasingly aestheticized: like art objects, it is as often as not how something "looks" that guarantees that it will sell, *not* what the object actually does or is used for. This stylization of contemporary production, Lury suggests, was achieved via a long process "through the introduction of the principles of fashion to an ever-wider range of products, often following the model developed for the product category of clothing" (61).

Product Packaging   The most common place in which this stylization or aestheticization is encountered on a day-to-day basis remains product packaging, whether we think of this in terms of the enticing photographs on cereal boxes or of the first great form of aesthetic packaging, album-cover art. But the link between the stylization of production and fashion goes deeper than this. Mimicking the fashion seasons, new models of automobiles and consumer electronics, such as stereo equipment, computers, and cell phones, are "released" annually or biannually. Bending the supposedly immutable laws of time, the resplendent curves and shiny surfaces of *next* year's car models are available in the summer of the preceding year. Most brands of cell phones and MP3 players are designed with removable faceplates that can be changed and adapted by consumers to coordinate with their clothing or to express their artistic sensibilities. The fashion sense at work in these product lines is exemplified by the success of Motorola's RAZR ("one of the slimmest phones on the market") and the rainbow hues of Apple's iPods or LG's Chocolate MP3 phones. The availability at any one time of numerous models of Nike running shoes, of sleek modernist household appliances designed by architect Michael Graves for Target stores, and of trendy clothing created by designer Mossimo for Zellers, all point to ways in which style and design have become essential elements of the production process, if not *the* essential element in the design of products for end-users. And no one knows this better than the shops connected to art museums, which have used the general stylization of popular culture to boost their profits through the sale of all manner of knick-knacks whose main appeal is not found in their utility, but in their artistic style.

Lifestyle   The increasing prominence and importance of style in popular culture production goes hand-in-hand with a redefinition of consumption as an aesthetic or artistic exercise. This shift is captured perfectly by the term "lifestyle." The idea that each of us has a lifestyle—a way of living, consuming, and being that uniquely defines us—has come to prominence only over the past several decades. Though lifestyle can be used to refer broadly to the way one lives—in the city or the country, a laid-back personality as opposed to a "work hard, play hard" mentality—the element of style emerges mainly out of what and how one consumes, and especially how one consumes popular culture (see Chapter 5 for an extended discussion of this point). The idea of life being akin to a work of art has a longer heritage, with origins in the mid-nineteenth-century idea of the urban *flâneur* and the figure of the dandy explored by, among others, the writer Oscar Wilde in *The Picture of Dorian Gray*. What has changed is that the expansion of consumption in the twentieth century has generalized the belief in lifestyle.

This has had some significant social consequences. For instance, the critic John Seabrook has suggested that as a result of lifestyle consumption the divisions between high and low culture, between "**highbrow**" and "**lowbrow**," have broken down into what he refers to as "nobrow." In perfect synchrony with lifestyle consumption, Seabrook argues that, in nobrow, "commercial culture is a source of status and currency rather than the thing that the elite define themselves against" (106). The question is no longer whether one participates in popular culture; rather, it is *how* one participates in it—and, through the consumer choices that one makes or refuses to make, the kind of lifestyle that one carves out of popular culture.

At one level, we can see the relentless production and consumption of style as a perfect embodiment of the idea of pseudo-individualization that Horkheimer and Adorno describe. The idea that increasingly stylized forms of production have transformed standardized popular culture into a situation in which everyone can assume the role of the "modernist notion of artist as hero, as the advocate of radical values, challenging the consensus of public life and disturbing the complacency of domestic life" (Lury 75) seems to confirm the Frankfurt School's worries about popular culture. But things aren't quite so simple. The stylization of cultural production has extended and enhanced the power and role that popular culture plays in everyday life and in the economy. But it has also introduced surprising challenges and problems for the producers of contemporary popular culture. As Simon During suggested in his criticisms of Horkheimer and Adorno, contemporary popular culture has becoming increasingly variegated, diverse, and unruly.

In the 1950s, cultural production was, in general, geared toward the mass market as a whole. Since then, there have been greater and greater degrees of **market segmentation**, with the result being that cultural producers have to gear their products to increasingly small and specialized segments of the overall group of consumers. This trend has perhaps been most evident in television programming. In the United States, the three major networks have tried to combat declining overall audiences by adopting the techniques of their competitors: cable networks defined around specific lifestyle interests (Outdoor Life Network, Food Network, etc.) or programming to specific demographic groups (e.g., the WB network targets audiences under 35). The segmentation of the consumer market has affected producers of clothing, food, and consumer electronics as well.

As just one example, in an effort to boost its stagnant sales the Coca-Cola Corporation has unveiled an ambitious strategy to design specific beverages for up to five hundred clearly defined segments of the market (e.g., children under three whose parents will allow them to drink only milk products, teens interested in skateboarding, adults who work long hours but eat healthy foods, etc.), which will be further adapted to account for national and regional differences (Stevenson).

Of course, the segmentation of the market presents producers with possibilities in addition to problems. There is the potential to tap into new markets and so to expand profits. However, the problems are significant, and go beyond, for instance, the energy and coordination required to produce thirty models of athletic shoes instead of one or two. The idea of life as style may in some sense be a false one. But inasmuch as people take it seriously, there is some evidence that they have grown more suspicious of certain forms of advertising and marketing and are resistant to being categorized even in micro-market segments. The more producers need to concentrate on style and the more (and more different) styles they have to produce, the more likely it has become that they will miss the mark when it comes to targeting their intended audiences.

In a recent interview, the heads of three of the major U.S. networks admitted that they had no idea that television programs such as *Survivor* and *The Sopranos* would be hits (Hirschberg 67). Their grasp on what the public "wants" is tenuous at best, and their ability as producers to dictate to audiences seems equally limited, which is attested to by the number of cancelled "sure-fire hits" that litter the television landscape each season. One of the reactions to this situation has been an increase in more invasive forms of marketing and advertising that try to grasp the moods and preferences of consumers and audiences in advance of their full cultural expression (for more on this, see our discussion of "cool hunters" in Chapter 5).

Suggested Activity 4.3

How does the reintroduction of "retro" fashions and styles contribute to lifestyle consumption? In *The Conquest of Cool*, cultural critic Thomas Frank suggests that "retro's vision of the past as a floating style catalog from which we can choose quaint wardrobes but from which we are otherwise disconnected is, in many respects, hip consumerism's proudest achievement: it simultaneously reinforces contemporary capitalism's curious ahistorical vision and its feverish cycling of obsolescence" (227). How does this reinforce, challenge, or expand our discussion in this section?

Copyleft: Challenging Copyright

> It is vain for painters or poets to endeavour to invent without materials on which the mind may work, and from which invention must originate. Nothing can come of nothing.
>
> —Joshua Reynolds

Though it has remained a central idea of Western culture since Romanticism, artists and writers do not create authentically only when they do so autonomously—that is, when they are off on their own, away from people and the influence of the society in which they live. Such ideas of artistic autonomy might help to reinforce our belief in creative "genius"; what they fail to do is capture the complex ways in which cultural productions are always an expression of the broader social and cultural contexts out of which they originate.

This is a long way of saying that there is no such thing as absolute innovation in cultural production. Rather, as Joshua Reynolds suggested in 1797, cultural production depends on creative borrowing and adaptation; whether this is consciously done or not, it is out of such adaptation that "new" culture is produced and through such borrowing that cultures remain vibrant and alive.

Sampling   One of the clearest examples of such creative and productive "borrowing" today is in rap and hip-hop music, which often samples previously recorded songs in interesting and provocative ways. For instance, Jay-Z's anthemic "Hard Knock Life" employs the chorus of "It's the Hard-Knock Life" from the musical *Annie*; P.Diddy produced an album with samples of popular eighties songs, including "Been Around the World," which borrows from David Bowie's "Let's Dance"; Maestro's "Stick to Yo' Vision" uses The Guess Who's "These Eyes" in a memorable fashion; and, in the case of "mash-ups," the complimentary interweaving of two generically different tracks to create something new, there is a sense in which the entire product is sampled, as in DJ Danger Mouse's infamous *The Grey Album*, a fusion of The Beatles' *White Album* and Jay-Z's *The Black Album*. There are similar examples of reusing or borrowing in film remakes (e.g., Gus Van Sant's attempt to produce a scene-by-scene remake of Alfred Hitchcock's *Psycho*), in literary adaptations, and in the visual arts (Douglas Gordon's "Twenty-Four Hour Psycho" stretches the Hitchcock original to a full day by projecting it slowly frame by frame).

Legal Issues   Over the past decade in particular, the use of borrowed materials has begun to run into legal roadblocks. As Sven Lütticken writes, even though "some sort of appropriation of pre-existing material is ... integral to many forms of contemporary cultural practice ... these are increasingly under pressure from armies of lawyers" (89). One of the major issues in contemporary cultural production concerns the use and abuse of **copyright** legislation to limit and control free expression. Disputes over copyright form just one of the many disputes over **intellectual property** today, a category that includes not just copyright, but also trademarks and patents. For producers of popular culture, there is a great deal to be gained by asserting and maintaining one's copyright privileges. As cultural production has become increasingly susceptible to copying and illegal redistribution (something that might have been difficult with a painting is easy with music in the digital era), corporations and cultural producers alike have ever more stridently asserted their copyright in order to control all the profits generated by their products. In many cases, however, it seems that the original intent of copyright has been subverted and that the eagerness with which copyright claims have been pursued have reduced culture to mere profit-making and have made free, unfettered cultural borrowing all but impossible. Only recently (in November 2006), for instance, were film professors in the United States given the right to put together clips of films for classroom instructional use.

The Evolution of Copyright   The history of copyright differs from country to country. In the English-speaking world, it first developed alongside book printing as a form of state control or censorship. The Crown granted publishers the right to produce a specific book over a certain period of time, less to guarantee publishers a profit than to get access to and approve its contents. The first violations of copyright were attempts to circumvent state censorship, as in the "forbidden best-sellers" of pre-revolutionary France that the historian Robert Darnton has explored. Copyright in its contemporary sense "was stimulated by the wish to enable authors to make a decent living and hence be able to create new works" (Lütticken 94). By 1831, copyright legislation in the United States covered books, maps, engravings and etchings, and musical compositions. By limiting the reproduction of these works to the original producer, the goal was to boost the indigenous cultural production of the young republic and to create a self-sustaining cultural sphere.

While copyright legislation may have been developed in order to protect cultural producers, in the context of contemporary cultural production copyright seems to have become a tool of those corporations most directly involved in the culture industry. There are two kinds of copyright infringements that need to be separated in our discussion: the first involves direct infringement of existing copyright standards, while the second concerns increasingly suspect challenges to cultural **appropriation**, parody, and the artistic use of popular culture. The continuing debate over file-sharing services, such as Napster and Kazaa (not to mention their over-charging quasi-legal and legal imitators), and the illegal pirating of videos, DVDs, music CDs, and computer software occurring worldwide are examples of the first kind of dispute (see Chapter 1). There's little question that sharing music files without copyright permission (for example) constitutes copyright violation.

What these forms of copyright violation have highlighted, however, is the degree to which copyright works in favour of corporations rather than cultural producers and audiences. In terms of the latter, the popularity of Napster (discussed in Chapter 1) constituted a public rejection of a kind of standardized production described by Horkheimer and Adorno: tired of being sold overpriced CDs with a few songs that they desired and a bunch of "filler" material, audiences could now access only the songs that they wanted.

Napster also presented consumers with a chance to sample music outside of the limited frame of popular music imposed by the marketing and distribution practices of major record labels in an effort to maximize profits. File sharing also brought to light the dirty half-secret of the contemporary music industry, which is that the artists who create the music see very little profit. While the band Metallica sued Napster in a heavily publicized case, other artists saw file sharing as an opportunity to provide their music directly to their audiences, thereby circumventing the music industry altogether.

The second form of dispute over copyright has become more prominent as of late. These are disputes over cultural appropriation of various kinds, and have come to the fore as the idea of what constitutes copyright is stretched farther and farther. Copyright has now been applied to thematic *similarities*, to original music compositions that supposedly *sound like* something else (as in the case of John Fogerty, former lead singer of Creedence Clearwater Revival, sued by his former record company for songs on his solo album that sounded too much like CCR), and even to bits of lyrics. It now seems as if copyright covers the general *idea* of a product as much as the product itself. Mattel, which jealously guards its major product, Barbie, has been one of the companies to press its claim over its product the farthest. On different occasions, Mattel has: sued rival producers of female toy figures on the basis that they "own" the general proportions of Barbie's surreal measurements (bust-waist-hip); blocked distribution of director Todd Haynes' film *Superstar: The Karen Carpenter Story*, which uses Barbie action figures to tell the life of the pop star who succumbed to anorexia; ended artist Mark Napier's *Distorted Barbie* project through a threatened suit; and even (though unsuccessfully) took on the band Aqua over its song "Barbie Girl."

Mattel is hardly the only corporation to engage in such practices. The Disney corporation has also sued artists for making use of its iconic images in artworks and has even effectively blocked publication of a critical biography of Walt Disney himself, on the basis that it would hurt corporate profits by damaging the image of wholesome fun that the company has built up around its **brand**. It seems today that almost every successful pop-culture object has been subjected to litigation. The author of the *Harry Potter* series, J.K. Rowling, has been sued (unsuccessfully) for supposedly stealing the term "Muggle," and she and her publisher have in turn pursued attempts to cash in on the Potter name, as in the case of the parodic Russian novels by Dimitri Yemetz, author of *Tanya Grotter and the Magic Double Bass.*

Who Is Popular Culture For?   The suits over the artistic reuse of popular cultural images and the use of materials for the purposes of parody or criticism raise a more general question about cultural production today: Just who and what is popular culture for? Audiences and artists seem to believe that popular culture, even if produced by large corporations, forms part of the commonly held stock of images, sounds, experiences, and ideas that make up contemporary experience, standing alongside great works of literature and masterpieces of artistic expression. Corporations seem to believe otherwise. For them, cultural production represents profits to be made—or lost, if copyright isn't enforced. The bending of copyright in the direction of corporate interests threatens the

The copyleft symbol invites users of a product to make new creative and original uses of it.

cultural commons that Reynolds describes in the quotation that begins this section. A great deal of the art made in this century, for example, has made creative use of popular culture, from Marcel Duchamp's "readymades" (the transformation of everyday objects into art) to the surrealists through to rap and contemporary art. These possibilities now seem threatened, as does our more general access to the images of art history, which have been slowly but surely assembled into image data banks by corporations such as Microsoft, which now holds access to copyright of many artworks. The extension and expansion of copyright benefits few at the expense of many; it constitutes one of the major sites of control over popular culture in the world today.

Computer Software Copyright   One of the most successful responses to the extension of corporate control through copyright has been in the field of computer software, where the stakes over intellectual property have been perhaps the highest. The "product" created by computer software companies is in many respects immaterial: the product as such isn't the CD the program comes on but rather the program itself, which doesn't exist physically in the same way that even a film does. Software is also uniquely susceptible to being copied easily and exactly. As such, the software industry has ferociously defended the intellectual property that it has created in order to safeguard its investment both in the products and in the profits they generate. Protecting intellectual property in software has meant that companies have closed off access to the source code of their programs. No one can access this code except other companies who have paid a licensing fee in order to create programs that work in conjunction (for example) with the various incarnations of the Microsoft Windows operating system.

In response to this closed system, programmers such as Richard Stallman and Linus Torvalds have created forms of free, open-source software such as GNU and Linux. Open-source software can be used by anyone free of charge. Because the software source code is "open"—that is, accessible by everyone—not only can new programs be created to work with Linux by programmers anywhere in the world, but also the bugs (or errors) that plague most complex software programs can be pointed out and repaired in the basic code itself. With free software, the often high cost of software programs is mitigated entirely. "Copylefting" is Stallman's innovative way of using copyright against itself. Free software that is made available under a general public license legally requires all software derived from it—"even those that carry only a tiny fragment of the original code" (Stallabrass 144)—to be copylefted; that is, made public and accessible to all.

As cultural production becomes increasingly important to the economy at large, struggles over the ownership of popular culture are likely to become more important. The de facto assertion of U.S. copyright regulations as the global standard through the auspices of the World Intellectual Property Organization is certain to have an impact on the ways in which popular culture is produced and distributed in the future.

Digital Production

For much of the past century, the forms of production of popular culture have effectively ruled out mass participation in many kinds of mainstream popular cultural production. Producing a film, television program, or record album "independently"—that is, outside of major production systems—was difficult, if not impossible; as we have seen above, the creation of a standard 35-mm film narrative requires the use of enormously expensive equipment, the use of equally expensive fixed capital (in the form of sound studios, sets, etc.), and, finally, a considerable investment in production personnel for the creation of even a modest film. This was true of television programming and music production as well, and was a general rule for most forms of popular cultural production. And production was just one part of the problem; even if one could make an independent film, the ability to distribute and market it to a wide audience was severely circumscribed by the degree of access one had to the "official" or standard systems of popular cultural production.

One of the major developments in popular culture over the past decade has been the introduction of new forms of production and distribution that have challenged and circumvented older modes of popular cultural production. The digital revolution in image and sound production, recording, and distribution promises to change the shape of popular culture in ways that we are only beginning to see at the present time. There have been a variety of formats that have allowed cultural producers to take control of the production and distribution of their own products, from Super 8 movie cameras to four-track recorders that allowed "garage bands" to produce their own audio tapes. Forms of digital production not only permit more effective distribution of these products—whether via sound and image files shared over the Internet or through the pressing of CDs and DVDs that retain sound and image quality—but also increasingly place "small" or independent producers on par with major producers, at least in terms of the quality of sounds and images produced.

There is effectively no important difference between popular music produced within and that produced outside of the music industry (at least not in terms of sound quality), which is why the challenge of digital production has been felt most acutely to date in music. In terms of film production, however, a gap remains, due in part to the extreme visual density of 35-mm film in comparison to the highest quality digital video (though this, too, may change) and in part to the cinematic spectacle of special effects in mainstream Hollywood cinema.

The Impact of New Technologies on Popular Culture   Even so, digital production has had a decisive impact on the production of popular culture, both inside and outside the dominant forms of production. On television, "reality" television shows make use of lightweight digital cameras to record perspectives that more traditional production techniques would be unable to capture (e.g., the "helmet cam" used during some segments on *Fear Factor*). Since the popularity of *The Blair Witch Project* (1999), major studios have released a number of films shot entirely on digital video, such as Richard Linklater's *Tape* (2001) and numerous others that have incorporated digital video into standard 35-mm filmmaking (e.g., Steven Soderbergh's *Traffic* [2000]). For some film-makers, digital video has presented an opportunity to rethink the medium of film in a wholesale way by rejecting the limits imposed by standard production practices. Eschewing artificial lighting, sound stages, sets, and so on, filmmakers who have adopted the Dogme 95 manifesto, which calls for a return to single-camera filmmaking with an absolute minimal use of non-natural lighting and sound (it actually calls for none at all, but this has been difficult to achieve in practice), have produced a series of films celebrated for their innovation and freshness. In this way the increasing accessibility of sophisticated production technologies creates vibrant niches for the revitalization (using those same sophisticated technologies!) of earlier, low-tech production methods and styles.

These uses of digital video are hardly revolutionary—that is, we have not yet seen the creation of new genres of completely original narrative modes as an outcome of the new format. But there are spaces and places in which digital video has already played an important new role. The low cost and high quality of digital video has produced an explosion in the production of documentary film, in two different senses of this term. First, digital video has revived the flagging fate of feature-length documentary productions, as has (for that matter) the ability of independent companies to distribute documentaries in DVD and VHS formats in place of film stock. Recent feature-length documentaries that have been enabled by digital video include *Who Killed the Electric Car?* (2006) and *An Inconvenient Truth* (2006).

Second, digital video has been used by groups and individuals around the world to document social and political realities that mainstream media miss or deliberately avoid reporting. Video has played an important role in documenting the abuse of state power during anti-globalization demonstrations. Mainstream media outlets, including the Canadian Broadcasting Corporation, covered the demonstrations against the Free Trade Agreement of the Americas (FTAA) in Quebec City in 2001 largely from the perspective of the government officials who were meeting behind the chainlink fence separating most of Old Quebec from the rest of the city. From this perspective, the use of pepper spray, water cannons, and plastic bullets against the demonstrators was justified by the perceived threat that demonstrators posed to these officials. The tens of thousands of hours of footage shot by the demonstrators with digital video cameras offered a very different view of the demonstrations. Not only did these images highlight the numerous unprovoked attacks on peaceful demonstrators by police, but by allowing the demonstrators to articulate their own views on the FTAA, they challenged the repeated assertions by the mainstream media that the protestors knew almost nothing about what they were demonstrating against.

Through its ability to bypass the systems that have defined the production of popular culture for much of the twentieth century, digital production promises to shake up the production of popular culture. Though it is unlikely to re-democratize popular culture to the extent that its most optimistic supporters suggest, it offers at least the potential for new forms of and relationships to popular culture.

SUGGESTIONS FOR FURTHER READING

Dorland, Michael, ed. *The Canadian Culture Industries: Problems, Perspectives, and Policies.* Toronto: Lorimer, 1996.

Ellis, Jack C. *A History of Film.* Fourth Edition. Needham Heights, MA: Allyn & Bacon, 1995.

Hesmondhalgh, David. *The Cultural Industries.* London: Sage, 2002.

Nealon, Jeffrey T., and Caren Irr, eds. *Rethinking the Frankfurt School: Alternative Legacies of Cultural Critique.* Albany, NY: State University of New York Press, 2002.

Negus, Keith. *Producing Pop: Culture and Conflict in the Popular Music Industry.* London: Edward Arnold, 1993.

Rosenbaum, Jonathan. *Movie Wars: How Hollywood and the Media Limit What Movies We Can See.* Chicago: A Capella Books, 2000.

Chapter **5**

The Consuming Life

INTRODUCTION: BACK TO "NORMAL"

In the immediate aftermath of the events of September 11, 2001, a large number of discourses started to circulate in both political circles and among members of the general public. Most of these were concerned directly with the events and their political and economic consequences. In order to better understand "9/11," discussions began on the concept of terrorism, the responsibility of the West to the rest of the world (especially the degree to which it had evaded this responsibility), the "clash of civilizations" (Islam vs. the West), the role of the United States as the world's policeman (and the problems with the role), the problems and benefits of military action, the implications of the new security measures adopted in a number of countries, and so on.

Perhaps more surprisingly, what also emerged was a debate on the underlying values of Western societies and the appropriateness of these values. In the days and weeks following 9/11, political and business leaders encouraged Americans and Canadians in particular to continue to shop, travel, and spend money (see Close-Up 5.1). New Mexico Senator Pete Domenici, for instance, stated "I'm hopeful the American people will . . . buy the car they planned to buy, not wait around. The terrorists will have won if consumers wait around because they're fearful." Many leaders expressed the conviction that to go out and shop was important as a means not only of sustaining the economy, but also of defending "our" fundamental cultural values.

Even if statements such as Domenici's captured something real about the economic and social practices important to the contemporary Western way of life, there was for many people something disturbing about this frank admission of the central role played in our lives by **consumption** and consumerism. In the immediate wake of 9/11, the

Consumption and 9/11

If our airline [industry] goes down, the terrorists will have won.

—Texas senator Kay Bailey Hutchison, on the need for industry-wide bailouts, in the *Dallas Morning News* (September 18, 2001)

As trivial as it may seem, every time we don't freely enjoy our recreational activities, that's a win for the terrorists.

—Sports editor Alan Hunt, writing in the *Lompoc (California) Record* (September 30, 2001)

We cannot allow terrorism to get a victory . . . by changing our way of life. That way the terrorists will have won.

—John Fund, *Wall Street Journal* editorial page editor, on CNN's *TalkBack Live* (October 11, 2001)

I understand why some parents are worried, but we can't let the terrorists win. . . . More than ever, people need the kind of escapism bands like ours provide.

—Christopher Read, saxophonist for the Frank Scott Bunnell High School Marching Band and Guard of Stratford, Connecticut, arguing in favour of his band's appearance in the Tournament of Roses Parade in Pasadena, California, on New Year's Day, in the *New York Times* (November 4, 2001)

To me, the terrorists have certainly succeeded if so few of you participate in a companywide effort to get together.

—Martha Stewart, in an e-mail to staffers at *Martha Stewart Living Omnimedia* urging them to host staff holiday parties in their own homes following her cancellation of the company's annual Christmas bash, reported in the *New York Post* (November 18, 2001)

I want women in evening gowns. I want to see men in tuxedos. I want elegance and class. I will not let terror win.

—Dagmar Dunlevy, president of the Hollywood Foreign Press Association, which stages the Golden Globes, on his vision for the 2002 event, reported in *Variety* (November 29, 2001)

If you don't want to let the terrorists defeat us, have that extra piece of cake and third drink.

—Gucci designer Tom Ford in the *New York Times Magazine* (December 2, 2001)

Compiled by Christi Schuermer

public stopped spending in an apparent attempt (or so the media told us) to recapture more "wholesome" values, whether this was expressed through a reaffirmation of familial relationships or connection to friends, or through a deliberate attempt to "slow down" and appreciate more greatly the days and weeks that we usually race through. Predictably, this decline in consumption caused a slowdown in the U.S. economy (something experienced to a lesser degree in Canada after 9/11). A few years later, however, things were definitely "back to normal": the streets and malls were full of shoppers snapping up, among other things, memorabilia related to 9/11 (T-shirts, postcards, designer clothing, etc.), which appeared quickly in the stores of New York in the days and weeks after the tragedy.

Consumption Patterns

9/11 offers an example of the importance of consumption to contemporary culture, as well as the profound ambivalence that attends all forms of consumption. We consume endlessly and in multiple ways and forms, and not just when we slide money across a store counter and walk away with a bag of goodies. Consumer spending patterns are carefully monitored by both businesses and governments, since they have a direct impact on the overall state of the economy (see Close-Up 5.2). A tremor in the consumer confidence index, a measurement that tries to anticipate future consumer desires, can produce very

---

Close-Up 5.2

The Consumer Confidence Index

In the United States, consumer confidence is measured monthly through a survey of 5,000 representative households. The overall score is measured against a baseline of 100 established in 1985 (in September 2002, the index was 93.3). The index is based on responses to five survey questions: (1) an appraisal of the current business environment and (2) expectations about the business environment six months from the survey date; (3) appraisal of current employment conditions and (4) employment conditions six months down the road; and, finally, expectations about family income six months from the survey date.

This is a survey of subjective feelings about the economic environment. For economists and business leaders, it is important because it is such subjective reactions to economic circumstances that guide consumer behaviour, much more than objective data. This is why there is often a disconnection between economic reports that pronounce the fundamental or underlying strengths of the economy (productivity levels, capital investment, etc.) and consumer behaviour that suggests otherwise (decline in stock investments, downturn in consumer spending, etc.).

---

real effects, including layoffs, business bankruptcies, and cutbacks to government programs in anticipation of declines in tax revenues.

Critiques of Consumerism   Consumption is a normal, everyday social practice around the globe in our increasingly complicated world, no one can produce everything they need (if they ever could), so the exchange of goods and services by individuals and institutions is a necessity. At the same time, consumption and **consumerism** are often treated as social ills. Consumerism has been associated by many critics with the rapid decline of the quality and character of social life, the result being a crass, utilitarian culture dominated by the ultimately empty pursuit of money and goods. Some of the social complexity of consumerism is captured by the fact that this uneasiness with it has become an occasion for further consumption, whether in the form of practices of consumption that express a desire for more "**authentic**" forms of consumption (organic food, Fair Trade coffees, holistic medicines, massages, "get away" weekends, adventure travel, etc.) or through the purchase of cultural goods that criticize consumerism implicitly or explicitly (in films such as *Fight Club* and *American Beauty,* the music of bands such as Radiohead, NOFX, and Rage Against the Machine, books such as Michael Moore's *Stupid White Men,* Naomi Klein's *No Logo,* Eric Schlosser's *Fast Food Nation,* and so on).

It is common enough to discount these criticisms by pointing out the simple contradiction produced by the sale of goods that criticize consumption (tracts against consumerism that activate further consumerism). Some critics argue that what we might think of as anti-consumerist forms of consumption (buying vintage clothing, for example, or listening only to music by obscure local bands) are not so much critiques of consumerism as they are rebellions against conformity—or what we perceive as the conformity of "the masses" or society in general. The "rebel consumer," as Joseph Heath and Andrew Potter term the person whose buying habits fit this model (108), is really just seeking a pure, extreme form of social distinction (we discuss this aspect of consumerism in more detail below). Heath and Potter do not denounce consumption as a social evil; however, they do dismiss it as an essentially empty practice, one that (unlike politics for example) is incapable of producing social meaning or change. Like the more straightforward anti-consumerist positions they critique, Heath's and Potter's argument fails to capture adequately the full complexity of contemporary consumption. Nor do such criticisms manage to locate the ambivalence over consumption within definite geographic and social circumstances. According to the United Nations, in the year 2000 more than two and a half billion people spent less than US$2.00 per day, a figure that should act as a constant reminder of the limits of the discussions of consumption and popular culture both in this chapter and in cultural studies more generally. Around the world, the main problem that people experience with consumption is not that it has come to make their lives empty; that is, not that there is too much consumption, but that there is too little—both of the necessities of life and of a wide range of other goods.

Whether we love or loathe it, consumption has become a key aspect of social life. If we are to make sense of its social significance and its key role in contemporary popular culture, we need to begin by understanding consumption as more than exchange.

Economic measurements of consumption tend to focus narrowly on the instant of exchange, the moment that money and goods change hands. However, the cultural and social dynamics of consumption extend well beyond the moment of exchange. A study of consumption has to consider what takes place before and after exchange. Why do people engage in the forms of consumption that they do? What do people do with the objects and services that they consume? What symbolic meanings are contained in consumption? How is consumption connected to our deepest emotions, desires, and fantasies? And what are the consequences of the ways we consume? These are the questions that will be explored in this chapter.

Suggested Activity 5.1

When do you shop? Do you ever find yourself deciding to "go shopping" in order to reward yourself, to alleviate stress, to buy gifts for others, and so on? What does it mean when consumption becomes an end in itself—that is, when the point of shopping is not necessarily to purchase any specific item or service, but mostly to engage in the act of consumption?

A BRIEF HISTORY OF CONSUMER CULTURE

In our introduction to this section, we have used a number of terms more or less inter-changeably: consumption, **consumerism,** and consumer culture or society. In practice, the meanings of these terms overlap considerably; however, exploring contemporary consumption necessitates that we draw some distinction between these terms. As we saw in Chapter 4, in social theory consumption has long been opposed to production. Until relatively recently, scholars have paid far more attention to the processes of production than consumption: consumption has been understood as little more than the completion of the process of production, with production privileged as the site at which the most significant social processes take place. As Karl Marx expressed famously in his preface to *A Contribution to a Critique of Political Economy* (1859), it was the "relations of production"—that is, "the economic structure of society" (45)—that for him formed the real foundation of society. How human beings organized themselves productively deter-mined to a large degree the social experiences and cultural possibilities of their society.

Even among sociologists and other social scientists unsympathetic to Marx's view of society, the idea that the form in which human beings organize production (i.e., how they organize their economy) is the most important determining characteristic of society has been central to social theory throughout most of the twentieth century. The outcome of this has been that the study of consumption has only slowly emerged from the shadow of production in the analysis of popular culture.

Commodities and Desire

Consumption—all of the practices commonly associated with what happens at the end of production—came to the fore of social studies only when it became clear that a new kind of society was emerging in the twentieth century: a consumer society, a historically unique form of society in which consumption plays not only an important, but even a central, role. As a general concept describing a particular form of human interaction and kind of social relationship, practices of consumption predate the twentieth century. It is possible, of course, to apply the concept of consumption to exchanges dating back millennia—all the way back to at least the early development of money and even possibly before that if the most common meanings of consumption are evoked.

Nevertheless, it does appear that a significant social shift takes place around the end of the nineteenth century as a result of a new focus on the consumption of commodities. **Commodities** are objects and services produced for consumption or exchange by someone other than their producers. Almost everything produced for consumption today is a commodity: we work at a specific job producing specific goods and services, whether this involves selling insurance or producing automobiles in a factory, or, in the case of professors, "producing" educated students in a university. Through the exchange of our labour for salary or wages, we are then able to purchase all of the other goods and services that we require (food, clothing, utilities, entertainment, etc.)—including, it should be added, those things that we work at producing (insurance salespeople aren't given free insurance, nor are auto workers invited to take home some of the automobiles that they produce).

Human beings have long exchanged goods that they produce for other goods: it has always been difficult to produce everything that one needs (and, certainly, everything that one wants). What has changed, then, is less the fact of exchange than the range of commodities that have become available, the ability of more and more people to engage in wider and wider forms of consumption, and the creation of new wants and desires through advertising and display. The conjunction of these and other factors has produced **consumerism**, the name for the dominant values and practices arising from, and providing fuel for, life in a consumer society.

The Creation of Consumer Society: Advertising, Credit, Debt

How and when did this new kind of society come into being? While the rise of consumer society is generally associated with the industrial revolution, it actually wasn't until relatively late in the game—the late nineteenth and early twentieth century—that people started to consume in earnest. The obvious reason behind the intensification and exten-sification of consumption was that the expansion of industry resulted in a massively increased amount of goods produced. Factories became bigger and more efficient, and so could produce more items more cheaply than before, which made widespread consumption possible. But, as the most elementary economic theory should tell us, the relationship between supply and demand doesn't work this simply or easily.

As Richard Robbins notes in *Global Problems and the Culture of Capitalism*, the rise of consumerism can best be understood, not as the natural and inevitable consequence of a burgeoning economy, but rather as a largely *manufactured* response to a specific (and continuing) crisis in the **capitalist** system of production. To put it simply, industry had by the end of the nineteenth century reached a level of efficiency that threatened to topple the whole economy through overproduction. The production of goods for which there are an inadequate number of buyers is clearly unsustainable and is one of the causes of economic recessions and depressions. In order to stimulate demand and so avoid a total crisis, it was necessary not just to increase, but also to fundamentally change patterns of consumption in order to make buying things a more central part of everyday life. Consumerism is the answer to the inevitability of capitalist overproduction. This change in the way we consume was as much *cultural* as it was economic. That is, it wasn't enough simply to increase wages so that people could buy more with the money they earned. Rather, according to the logic advanced by Henry **Ford**, one of the most important products of the factory line was the consumers who were produced out of the wages that he paid his workers. In addition to automobiles, Ford created not only the kind of people that could afford to purchase them, but also the kind of people that increasingly understood their lives in reference to possibilities of consumption.

Shifting Values in Western Society   For consumerism to function correctly, what was needed was a revolution in the underlying values of Western society—a shift from thrift and the virtues of parsimony to the come-what-may carpe diem philosophy of the consumer. This shift is often described—particularly by critics of consumerism—as representing a decided decline in spirituality, accompanied if not actually caused by a rise in **materialism**. In fact, the relationship between spirituality or religion and materialism is not that simple: they cannot be considered as simply and clearly opposites, the "good" of the spiritual standing above the "bad" of materialism.

At the beginning of the twentieth century, the sociologist Max Weber argued that the materialist "spirit of capitalism" could be located (apparently paradoxically) in Protestant asceticism. While asceticism involves the rejection of worldly temptations, over time the ceaseless labour carried out to increase the glory of God became disassociated from its religious roots, leading to a situation in which "material goods . . . gained an increasing and finally an inexorable power over the lives of men as at no previous period in history" (181). The growth of materialism represented not so much an abandonment of religion as a shift in its orientation, away from guilt and self-denial toward values of self-enhancement and emancipation. This shift was enabled in part by the Enlightenment belief in **progress**, as well as by the actual alterations in people's material circumstances associated with the industrial revolution (see Chapter 2). While traditional religious doctrines, combined with the sheer difficulty of life, tended to rule out the prospect of happiness on earth in favour of an emphasis on the glories of heaven, the **ideology** of industrialism made secular comfort seem not only possible, but also morally good. As James Twitchell puts it, at this point "the culture of consumption . . . replaced the culture of contrition" (230). The "spiritual" redemption of materialism was accompanied by a shift away from the ideas of humility and the subordination of the self to a higher power to an emphasis on the possibility of changing and enhancing one's life through individual will. And if self-enhancement required a new stove or pair of shoes—well, so much the better, both for the individual and for the economic well-being of society as a whole.

Still, the conversion of a society organized around thrift and self-sacrifice to one committed to shopping did not come about easily. The birth of consumer society required more concerted and more creative action on the part of manufacturers and government. Richard Robbins identifies a number of key developments that together fuelled what was seen as this necessary change. The first of these were developments in retail sales, in particular the invention of the department store. Beginning in Paris, with the Au Bon Marché (1852), followed in 1902 by Marshall Field's in Chicago, the department store offered a whole new shopping experience: in fact, it was the department store that, more than any other development, turned shopping into an *experience* rather than simply a routine, generally boring duty. Featuring such novel attractions as coatrooms and restrooms, the department store was committed to the enhancement of consumer pleasure and comfort, inviting its mostly female patrons to leisurely browse the aisles while enjoying musical performers or drinking tea. Complementing the structural appeals of the department store was a new emphasis on service, in which sales assistants would welcome customers (the precursor to Wal-Mart greeters), offer advice, and administer general

Growing from a small shop founded in 1838, Au Bon Marché in Paris is often considered to be the oldest department store in the world. This 1928 ad is for a sale on handbags, dresses, and umbrellas.

pampering. The emphasis on friendliness, however contrived, played an important role in turning an essentially economic transaction into a personal one—an important function, in an age in which the relationship between primary producers and consumers was growing ever more distant.

Advertising and Marketing Perhaps the most significant factors in boosting consumerism were innovations in advertising and marketing. Until the mid–eighteenth century, ads were mainly informational, announcing new products and providing more or less straightforward accounts of their qualities, sometimes complete with testimonials from satisfied customers or accredited experts—doctors or pharmacists, for example (this kind of advertising finds echoes today, in those ads in which a serious, white-coated commentator, whose credentials appear in print at the bottom of the screen or page, points to simple graphs or other scientific-looking data to show how this particular brand of antacid or painkiller or diaper outperforms the competitors). With the flourishing of competition among manufacturers, the emphasis in advertising changed from informing customers about new products to encouraging them to discriminate between a host of virtually identical brands of the same product. Part of this was achieved by innovations in packaging, beginning with the production of prepackaged goods with labels—Ivory Soap and Quaker Oats were among the earliest such brands, promoted as early as the 1870s.

Quaker Oats is an early example of a brand name that has become synonymous with its product. This ad for the product is from 1920.

Over the course of the twentieth century both packaging and advertising quickly became more sophisticated, as marketers realized that the way goods were displayed and promoted was at least as important in getting people to buy them as their actual substance. Starting around the time of the First World War, marketers began to marshal the forces of psychology to help them develop more subtle and unconscious forms of persuasion. The most well-known instance of early marketing psychology was the use of so-called **subliminal advertising**, in which, for example, the ice cubes in a glass of Coke were engineered to look like the body of a naked woman, or the word "sex" flashed up on the screen in the middle of an ad for, say, dental floss, disappearing too quickly to be registered on anything other than an unconscious level. While advertisers have dabbled in subliminal messages, the attention paid to this kind of trickery tends to overstate its significance, ignoring the much simpler and arguably more effective use of straightforward images with complex emotional resonances—in other words, Barthes's **mythology** (discussed in Chapter 2). The need to use mythology in advertising is obvious: the actual objects being sold are not valuable enough in and of themselves to persuade us that we actually *need* them; they therefore need to be associated with something deeper, more intangible in order to evoke our desire—what Raymond Williams in "Advertising: The Magic System" terms, simply, "magic."

Over the last 50 years or so, advertising has come to occupy a position of unparalleled dominance, reflecting both the intensification of consumerism and the growth of the information economy—a development we explore in more detail in the last section of this chapter. Advertising is, as Williams puts it, "the official art of modern capitalist society: it is what 'we' put up in 'our' streets and use to fill up to half of 'our' newspapers and magazines: and it commands the services of perhaps the largest organized body of writers and artists, with their attendant managers and advisers, in the whole society" ("Advertising" 336). As such, advertising is both a barometer and a key producer of dominant social values, chief among which is, of course, the value of consumerism itself. Underpinning the myths invoked by the specific **signs** in any given ad that are meant to compel an attachment to this brand over that brand is another *über* myth, that our deepest needs and desires—for love, autonomy, security, freedom, self-development, friendship— can be met by buying something. The pervasiveness of this myth, which we oddly cling to even as we recognize it *as* myth, accounts for the second major development in advertising in the last few decades: the "magic" of advertising has been kicked up to a new level so that it is simultaneously more transparent, and more powerful, than it was before.

Branding   If advertising was once about cloaking a product in a sparkly glow, disguising its mundane qualities in shimmery illusion, now it achieves its most dramatic effects by eliminating the product altogether—even to the point of announcing the product's redundancy (as in ethical ads by companies like Patagonia that actually plead with us to "buy less"). This is the hallmark of the contemporary art of **branding**, in which companies vie to sell us not individual products but lifestyles that are defined by broad patterns of selective consumption. The disappearance of the actual commodity in advertising weirdly confirms the triumph of consumerism, such that "goods"—including entertainment, vacation packages, and services—are thoroughly and inextricably "knitted into the fabric of social life and cultural significance" (Jhally 80).

But the expansion and intensification of consumer society has not been stimulated by the efforts of retailers alone. As Richard Robbins notes, government policy, encouraged by corporate lobbyists, has worked in conjunction with other broad institutional changes to create a cultural climate hospitable to consumption. The introduction of MBA programs and design institutes in the early 1900s marked both the recognition and encouragement of the possibilities for the professionalization of marketing. This in turn led to the formalization of what had once been an informal, vaguely disreputable sector of the contemporary economy into a specialized profession that young people could yearn to one day join: those major advertising firms such as J. Walter Thompson, Young & Rubicam, and Ogilvy & Mather that established Madison Avenue as a fixture in the collective unconscious.

Credit and Debt   Around the same time, changing government policies in the United States placed increasing focus on commerce, including the eventual creation of government ministries devoted to researching and promoting its expansion. One major campaign in the U.S. and Canada was the drive to get people to buy houses. A 1920s government-issued pamphlet touted the "family values" of owning a single-detached home, backed by psychological research highlighting the importance of separate bedrooms for each child (R. Robbins 16). Of course the boost in home ownership could not be achieved without another major initiative—the expansion of credit. By putting limits on interest payments, making it easier to take out a mortgage or get a car loan, governments and banks have played a crucial role in fuelling consumer spending. They had the added benefit, Robbins notes, of bolstering the discipline of the work force, which was kept in line by the fear of being unable to make credit payments.

The major cultural effect of policies making credit both easier to get and also more accept-able socially is that being in debt—a situation that was once an occasion for embarrass-ment—has become a way of life, such that according to one estimate the average household debt-to-income ratio in Canada in 2006 hovered around 125 percent (Certified General Accountants). Of course, the dark side of this good-news picture, which was exposed by the economic meltdown of 2008, is that an alarming number of individuals and families live just a hair's breadth away from bankruptcy. The ideology of consumerism, by creating not just an unquestioned right but a moral imperative out of the ownership of stuff, works to conceal, without overturning, huge discrepancies in wealth between the rich and the poor. And in the global economy, this formula applies not just to individuals, but to nations as well.

Consumerism is a value system that has rapidly (though unevenly) spread around the entire world. It is most developed in North America, Europe, Japan, and Australia (those areas commonly referred to as "the West"), but it is difficult not to see that aspects of consumerism are present globally. As discussed previously in this chapter, consumerism refers to a complex set of values and practices. What is central to consumerism is the belief that the organization of life around the purchase of commodities is in fact, for all its other problems, the optimal way to address the needs and wants of individuals, and even the best way to allocate social goods. This "belief" is often more implicit than explicit. Explicitly, people often express worries about consumption and its social, political, and environmental effects. But through the *practices* that individuals engage in—constrained as these are by the structures and institutions of consumer society—faith in the optimal efficiency of the market is restated day after day around the world. And it is not just the efficiency of market forces that is valorized in consumer society, but the underlying goals of such an economic system, too. The consumer lives what Ernest Gellner has described as a "society of perpetual growth" (Gellner 24); the consumer's central goal is to accumulate money so that he or she may purchase and consume ever-increasing quantities of goods and services.

Consumer Culture and Mass Culture

The history of consumer society closely mirrors the history of popular culture offered in Chapter 2. The two histories are intertwined: to a large degree, contemporary popular culture *is* consumer culture. The description of contemporary popular culture as a form of **mass culture** is one way of capturing the historical novelty of contemporary forms of consumption and its links to the popular. At the beginning of his book *Selling Culture*, the cultural critic Richard Ohmann offers a definition of mass culture that can help us to identify the distinctive features of mass and consumer culture and to see the ways in which our ideas and practices of consumption differ from those prior to the end of the nineteenth century. Ohmann describes mass culture as a system characterized by

> voluntary experiences, produced by a relatively small number of specialists, for millions across the nation to share, in similar or identical form, either simultaneously or nearly so; with dependable frequency; mass culture shapes habitual audiences, around common needs or interests; and it is made for profit. (14)

What does this definition tell us about popular culture and consumerism? There are forms of consumption that are socially or physically necessary: food, clothing, shelter, and so on. In his discussion of mass culture, Ohmann wants to omit these in order to concentrate on forms of voluntary consumption, specifically on what we have come to refer to as "entertainment."

As we will see below, the meanings that circulate around consumption cannot be limited in quite this way. We all require shelter; this requirement, though involuntary in comparison to our choices of entertainment, is explicitly connected to contemporary forms and practices of consumption through the kinds of shelter that we strive for: a big house in the suburbs, a sleek condo in a downtown high-rise, a farmhouse in the country, and so on. One of the interesting things about consumer culture, at least in those countries with relatively high standards of living, is that there is no longer anything "basic" about the necessities of life: we require clothing to keep us warm or shelter us from the sun, but, as we all know, the kinds of clothing that we choose to consume have significant social meanings and implications.

Even though Ohmann's definition is geared toward a characterization of mass cultural entertainment, it still helps us to grasp just what is unique about consumer culture. In general, we purchase the objects or services that we consume from the specialists that produce them: for the most part, we don't make our own clothing (we certainly don't make the cloth), grow our own food, or manufacture electronics in our basement. Consumption is dependent on a vast specialization of labour and industry, and on the development of an enormous set of institutions that are geared toward the production and distribution of consumable objects and services: it is no coincidence that the history of the modern corporation parallels the rise of consumer culture (see Close-Up 5.3). There continues to exist a wide range of hand-made goods, home-baked foods, and so on, but these exceptions merely prove the rule of specialized production.

Further, the things we consume, from T-shirts to soft drinks to televisions, are consumed by millions of others around the world in virtually the same form, with only slight variations from country to country. McDonald's, for instance, has famously modified parts of its standard fast-food menu to account for local tastes or prohibitions against certain

Corporations

Though it might seem as if corporations have been with us forever, they are relatively recent inventions; it is more recently still that they assumed the legal status they hold in most Western countries today.

Corporations first emerged in the seventeenth century through the establishment of chartered corporations, which were given specific missions outlined by an act of government. Such chartered corporations were granted the exclusive right to engage in colonial ventures over a specifically defined geographic space. The economic logic of these corporate bodies was to allow for huge pools of capital to be accumulated in order to carry out ventures that would have been impossible for small groups to carry out independently. The United States was initially settled by a corporation, the Massachusetts Bay Company, as was a large part of Canada under the auspices of the Hudson's Bay Company.

Early corporations were chartered to fulfil some form of public mission. In the United States after independence, corporations were involved in building bridges, in constructing roads, and in other activities that now fall to governments. Once corporations began to be involved in raising capital for the creation of private wealth, it became necessary to define their status more formally in legal terms. In a landmark case in 1886, corporations in the United States were defined as "persons" as a result of the application of the 14th amendment to the U.S. Constitution, which was originally designed to protect recently emancipated slaves, to a case involving a dispute over differences in tax rates for individuals and corporations. The 14th amendment states that "no state shall deprive any person of life, liberty or property": once defined as "persons," corporations gained the same rights and protections as individuals. Though corporations have slightly different status in different countries, the trend globally has been toward the U.S. model of corporate rights. This nineteenth-century quirk in legal jurisprudence has bolstered the strength of corporations immeasurably: corporations have repeatedly appealed to their rights as individuals to strike down laws that attempt to limit or regulate their activities.

food items. On the whole, though, one of the appeals of McDonald's is in fact the almost global **standardization** of its menu: consumers can expect a Big Mac to taste the same in St. John's as it does in Santa Cruz, Munich, or Osaka. Contemporary consumption is premised on such uniformity. It makes little sense to prefer to buy Nikes in one store over another on the assumption that the shoes that one can purchase in one location are "better made" than in the other (though they may of course be priced differently).

Simultaneity, dependable frequency and the creation of habitual audiences are important for understanding the ways in which most forms of popular entertainment are offered up to us for consumption. Television schedules are standardized across nations (*Lost* or *Canadian Idol* don't appear on different nights in Toronto than in Edmonton), NFL football games and *Hockey Night in Canada* take place at predictable (and scheduled) times, and new videos and DVDs miraculously appear on video store shelves across North America at midnight each and every Monday (or, in the worst-case scenario, Tuesday morning). Finally, what links everything together is profit. Today, consumption almost always involves the exchange of money and almost always occurs in a situation in which it contributes to the creation of profit.

Identifying these general features of consumer society does not mean that it is impossible to find contrary examples or situations. It is not to suggest, as theorists of consumer culture sometimes have, that there are no forms of exchange, social relationships, or cultural experiences that are not part of consumerism. Education, religious participation, and forms of "self-produced" entertainment (playing your guitar for your friends) are just some examples of experiences that fall somewhat outside the guiding values of consumer society, even if they are informed by those values (as when education becomes merely a way to secure a high-paying job so that one can buy a big-screen LCD TV). Rather, what we want to draw attention to is that our particular forms of consumption are a recent historical "invention." Only recently did we turn to others to the extent to which we do today to feed, clothe, and entertain us.

It is this fundamental shift in the character of consumption that in turn produces a need to explore the new and complex social and cultural meanings generated by consumer society. We will do this by turning now to look at three important ways in which consumption produces the cultural meanings that are an important part of contemporary culture: consumption as a means of producing and reinforcing social and cultural distinctions and differences; the connections between consumption and individual **identity** and agency; and the political meaning of contemporary forms of consumption, which includes the impact of consumption on social spaces that we now inhabit. Many of the issues raised in this chapter overlap with the explorations of identity (Chapter 6) and **representation** (Chapter 3).

CONSUMPTION AS DISTINCTION

As we've already noted, the practice of consumption is not exhausted in the moment of exchange; nor is what is exchanged "used up" or destroyed through consumption, even if this is one of the typical meanings associated with "consuming." To consume food means that the food gets "used up" and broken down. But in its social and cultural meanings, exchange is only one part of a larger system of meaning produced in and through consumption. *What* we choose to consume and *how* we consume are already pregnant with social significance. The ability or lack of ability to consume certain objects and services, or even to consume at all (in the case of extreme poverty or social and geographic isolation), has profound consequences that most of us implicitly understand. For example, we might choose to purchase an automobile that is more expensive than we can really afford because of what we imagine that it enables us to do (climb effortlessly over boulders to the top of a butte where we can survey the endless desert stretching in front of us, as suggested by ads), and what that particular make and model symbolizes. Automobiles offer mobility and convenience; they can symbolize youthfulness or hipness, comfort or a concern with safety, economic status or thrift. In the end, however, all automobiles perform the same function—moving people around. The existence of a vast number of brands and models, colours and option packages, and so on suggests that other forces of meaning are at work in an individual's choice of vehicle—forces that may seem more important than (in this example) fiscal responsibility or concern over the environment (in which case the best option would be not to purchase a car at all). *What* we choose to consume in this case highlights certain values (mobility, convenience) at the expense of others (a habitable planet); *how* we do so—what kind of vehicle, what colour, what features we add or subtract—immediately brings to light other values or symbolic associations (for example, the importance of youthfulness in our culture) that are involved in all forms of consumption.

Consumption and Agency

There is one important category in this scenario that needs to be addressed in further detail before we proceed. It is perhaps the central concept at issue in contemporary analyses of consumer culture, and indeed it is essential to consumerism itself. This is the category of **agency**, the ability of individuals to act as self-conscious, willful social "agents" or actors and to exert their will through involvement in social practices, relationships, and decision making. This concept is discussed in more detail in Chapter 6. Certainly, debates over the ultimate social significance of consumer culture often revolve around questions about the degree to which individuals are able to express their free will or agency in their day-to-day decision making as opposed to their actions and decisions being relatively determined, decided on in advance as a result of the structures and institutions within which they live.

Analyses of consumerism and consumer practices will differ depending on the degree of real choice that we imagine individuals have in contemporary society. For instance, we are free to vote for whom we want; on the other hand, that freedom is limited by the degree to which political parties in North America tend to express small variations on the same political theme. We can see this same "non-choice" in our automobile example. You are able to choose the colour and make of your car. What is more difficult to "choose" in most North American cities and towns is to go without an automobile: mass transit systems are underfunded, and low-density development has made it difficult to go (for instance) from a suburban home to work at a light industrial park, and from there back home, or to shop for food at a supermarket located on a retail strip.

Going beyond these examples, what feels to each of us like free choices is also heavily determined by our social and cultural backgrounds. Our choices define and are defined by the social categories within which we *want* to situate ourselves and in which we are already situated. There are certain ways in which we have to act and dress in order to "belong" or participate in certain social or career circles. We might in some sense "choose" to belong to these groups; nevertheless, it is important to put aside the idea that there is some kind of *absolute*, unconstrained agency or free choice in consumer society (or any society, for that matter). There is a reason that demographical studies of consumer choice capture patterns of consumption linked to income levels, geographic region, and so on. All of the consumers in an area may be freely choosing to buy one brand of clothing over another, one brand of beer over another. And yet, when grouped together, these individual "free" choices point to similarities in consumer choices that cannot be written off as mere coincidence. There is also a reason why television programs are developed in order to "deliver" certain target audiences to advertisers interested in selling their products to (say) 19- to 25-year-olds. No one is twisting the arms of young adults to tune in to these shows, but hopefully they do anyway, so satisfying both the hopes of television executives and of advertisers.

Understanding the meanings of contemporary consumption involves a comprehension of both the structures and institutions of consumption that define and shape our choices *and* the way in which these choices in turn shape and define these structures and institutions. It is common to understand social structures and institutions as necessarily imposing constraints or limits on behaviour. Attending high school, for example, places limits on what you do and where you can go during the day on weekdays. But if schooling limits some behaviours and choices, it also enables a whole range of others (through education, exposure to peers and extracurricular activities, etc.) and does so in ways that cannot be easily controlled or predicted. The structures of consumption both enable individual consumption and provide restrictions on it in a continuously shifting way: our choices are structured, but this does not mean that they are determined in advance. While realizing that agency and structure always go together, we will look first at some of the structures that consumption produces and reproduces, and then will consider in the next section the individual and collective meanings that we make through our use of the things that we consume.

Taste and Distinction

It is obvious to most of us that the things we own have a meaning above and beyond the simple possession of them. Few if any of us have a sense of the monetary value of all of the things around us taken together. But what we do know is that many of the objects we surround ourselves with mean something to us: they may remind us of the person who gave it to us, or they in some way express our individuality—who we are and what we like. The furniture we own, the objects that we place on our walls, the music we collect and listen to, the books that we display on our shelves, the way our apartments or houses look—all of these objects externalize our own sense of ourselves, whether explicitly or implicitly. What they also do, however, is connect us with others through the subtle forms of **distinction** they produce. For example, if we like the music of Belle and Sebastian and Broken Social Scene, seeing these CDs in other people's homes will indicate a connection between them and us; conversely, seeing a rack comprised only of Céline Dion and Michael Bublé CDs will suggest something very different.

Sociocultural Differentiation　One of the most important ways in which contemporary consumption functions is that it produces systems of sociocultural differentiation. To put this more plainly, what we "choose" to consume *includes* us in some groups and *excludes* us from others. Once again, to a certain degree, what we can consume (or not consume) has always functioned as a form of social distinction. At an earlier point in European history, only the nobility could afford to consume large quantities of meat flavoured with exotic spices from abroad; peasants, craftspeople, and city dwellers had to make do with bread and beer.

In comparison to contemporary forms and modes of social distinction through consumption, even up to the end of the nineteenth century there was a relatively minimal degree of social differentiation signalled by the consumption of different kinds of commodities. Shops in the late nineteenth century had a limited number of consumer items, few of which were readily identifiable by brand name: coffee, sugar, and other food items came out of barrels rather than in the clearly distinguished packages of a specific brand. To a considerable degree distinction through consumption is a relatively recent phenomenon, first described by the sociologist Thorstein Veblen in 1899 and more fully theorized and systemized by the French sociologist Pierre Bourdieu in the 1970s and 1980s.

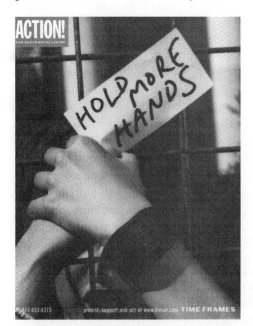

In contrast to earlier print ads, contemporary ads, such as this magazine ad for Diesel clothing, rely more on abstract visual signs—to the point where it's sometimes difficult to tell what product is being advertised!

Thorstein Veblen　Veblen's famous analysis of **conspicuous consumption** explored the uses to which "excess" consumption was already being put by the end of the nineteenth century. "Wasted" or excess consumption was the result of a widespread increase in incomes and consequent expansion of consumption that occurred at the end of that century. For Veblen, "wasted" consumption wasn't illegitimate, useless, or purposeless. What he was trying to capture by using this term were forms of consumption beyond those that "serve human life or human well-being on the whole" (203). Consumption at the turn of the century was becoming "conspicuous"—obvious, noticeable, visible—in order to signal or symbolize class differences and distinctions. As Veblen points out, there are a number of possible categories that could be used to symbolize social differences: moral and intellectual qualities, physical or **aesthetic** differences, and so on. In the United States and Canada, all of these categories were being subsumed by displays of money. But one needn't be rich to be able to render one's forms of consumption visible to other classes. Veblen insisted that there existed conspicuous forms of consumption all the way down to the very poorest groups. A difference between the very rich and the poor and middle class rested in the creation of the category of "taste." Veblen writes that

> the growth of punctilious [precise or demanding] discrimination as to qualitative excellence in eating, drinking, etc., presently affects not only the manner of life, but also the training and intellectual activity of the gentleman of leisure. He is no longer the successful, aggressive male. . . . In order to avoid stultification he must also cultivate his tastes, for it now becomes incumbent on him to discriminate with some nicety between the noble and ignoble in consumable goods. (190)

Pierre Bourdieu   In many ways, Pierre Bourdieu's research and writing takes up the same themes as Veblen. Bourdieu, too, is interested in the social uses of consumption as a form of class or group distinction or discrimination. For Bourdieu, whenever we consume—be it images, types of food, music, or art—we are engaging in complex forms of social differentiation, discrimination, and display, whether we realize it or not. We may be aware of being involved in this social "game of distinction," as we most definitely are when we dress up for a job interview (for instance). But for Bourdieu, we participate in this game of social distinction even when we make decisions that seem to express personal or individual choices. The sum meaning of consumption for Bourdieu *is* this game of distinction. "Taste," the faculty that Veblen believed the rich had to cultivate in order to be able to make accurate distinctions between better and worse forms of consumables, is now something that we all exercise.

But even in our expressions of our likes and dislikes through consumption, Bourdieu believes there is a form of social meaning at work. He writes: "Taste is the basis of all that one has—people and things—and all that one is for others, whereby one classifies oneself and is classified by others" (45). Taste appears to us as something that is individual; however, it is not only social, but also a site at which social power is produced and maintained.

Suggested Activity 5.2

Reflect on your own consumption and the purchases that your peer group makes. What forms of distinction can you see yourself engaged in? How is social distinction represented in popular culture? Think, for example, of the importance of forms of display in music video and in contemporary Pygmalion narratives, such as in films like *Pretty Woman, Maid in Manhattan, Sweet Home Alabama,* and *Real Women Have Curves*, or the television show *Ugly Betty*. What do such narratives tell us is required in addition to money in order to move from the lower to the upper classes?

Consumption and Power

In his exhaustively researched book *Distinction* (1979), Bourdieu and his research associates perform a number of experiments in which they ask respondents from different economic levels of society (expressed through their job titles) to rank and identify films, pieces of classical music, and photographs based on their likes or dislikes. Astonishingly, there was a remarkably strong correspondence between the choices individuals made and the socioeconomic groups to which they belonged. There was, for example, a link between supposedly "difficult" music and art and members of higher income groups, while blue-collar workers "liked" more melodic forms of classical music, narrative films versus more experimental films, and so on. The grounds of this difference in taste between socioeconomic groups have most often been thought to be based on either education or innate ability. Bourdieu saw things differently. He argued that differences in consumption express *only* the way in which consumption has been used to create and reinforce pre-existing class divisions. There is no "taste" that is more correct or accurate than any other. Rather, by virtue of their socioeconomic status, groups in power have been able to transform *their* tastes into the legitimate ones by which others are measured. In this way, consumption has placed barriers to **class mobility**, for, in addition to one's economic status, one has to also have correct ideas about what to consume and how to consume it.

There are two things that Veblen's and Bourdieu's theories tell us about contemporary consumption. First, the idea that we consume "freely"—that is, that our choices are somehow entirely our own and are disconnected from larger social structures—is an illusion. Of course, subjectively, it certainly *feels* as if our choices are free. Nevertheless, "objectively and subjectively aesthetic stances adopted in matters like cosmetics, clothing or home decoration are opportunities to experience or assert one's position in social space, as a rank to be upheld or a distance to be kept" (Bourdieu 57). Second, these theories tell us that one of the primary social meanings of consumption is social distinction and differentiation. Juliet Schor writes:

> Bourdieu argues that class status is gained, lost, and reproduced in part through everyday acts of consumer behaviour. Being dressed incorrectly or displaying "vulgar" manners can cost a person a management or professional job. Conversely, one can gain entry into social circles, or build lucrative business contracts, by revealing appropriate tastes, manners, and culture. Thus, consumption practices become important in maintaining the basic structures of power and inequality which characterize our world. (457)

Bourdieu has claimed that "there is no way out of the game of culture." For this reason, he has sometimes been criticized for theorizing consumption in a way that stresses structure(s) at the expense of agency. Is it always the case that our choices necessitate the adoption of a position in social space? How then do societies changes and develop? While Bourdieu does have his own theory of the relationship between structure and agency, at their most extreme his views can start to seem like those of Horkheimer and Adorno that we discussed in Chapter 4. "Choice," that is, starts to look completely determined by our own location on an intricate social grid. We need not take Bourdieu or Veblen as being totally correct about consumption in order to find a great deal that is useful in their descriptions of the symbolic meaning of consumption. Indeed, one of the things that Bourdieu asserts in *Distinction* is important to our discussion in the next section of this chapter. For Bourdieu, there is no more or less legitimate form of consumption: whatever difference there might be between watching Italian opera on PBS or watching *Dancing with the Stars* lies not in the intrinsic value of one television program over the other, but in the way that these choices are mobilized socially. The next section will explore why it is important to see the meaning of consumption as being produced through the uses to which agents put the things they consume.

CONSUMPTION, DESIRE, AND PLEASURE

It is extremely easy to dismiss consumption as wasteful, pointless, without purpose, and so on. As we suggested at the outset of this chapter, consumption is both a normal part of contemporary societies and yet also a social practice accompanied by feelings of ambivalence, guilt, and uncertainty. When social critics write about the ills and traumas associated with consumer society, the image they project is of a present peopled by indistinguishable drones mystified by the electronic buzz of advertising, grimly doing their duty by dragging themselves through malls and filling up shopping bags with slick-looking black leather shoes, wafer-thin cell phones, and flavoured popcorn bought by the bucket—none of which they need! In a nutshell, many critics portray consumer society as a form of Technicolor totalitarianism—the grey dreariness of life in the Soviet Union, only lit up by neon lights and the smiling faces of Gap employees.

Not only do these views miss much of what takes place in consumption, they also presume what consumption means without ever investigating or considering that its meanings may be multiple and vary from place to place. Is contemporary life really so grim and empty? Not at all! Or, at the very least, since life is experienced very differently depending on "an individual's participation in consumption or their practical freedom to exercise choice" (Lury 6), the landscape of consumer culture can't in any simple way be equated with a gulag of the soul. Through consumer culture, individuals enact their desires and develop new ones; consumption is also a source of enormous amounts of pleasure—especially the consumption of entertainment, whether this involves reading Jonathan Franzen's *The Corrections* or watching any one of Adam Sandler's sublime and sophisticated (!) comedies.

Of course, it is possible to point out (as we will in the next section) that there are rather serious consequences of this kind of pleasure and this system of desire. And it is also possible to assert that the desires and pleasures of consumer culture are not ones that are particularly worth having, or are at best degraded remainders of more lofty and serious feelings and dispositions—the ones that a small subset of humanity experienced at some point in the past while the vast majority of people were engaged in endless labour in terrible conditions.

A more effective rejoinder that doesn't rely on positions that are difficult to substantiate, or arguments that reenact the legitimation of tastes that Bourdieu criticizes, insists on consumerism as a system that is inscribed in our most intimate pleasures and desires. Richard Ohmann paints the following picture of the consumer in mass culture at the beginning of *Selling Culture*:

> The advertiser can sell Bill Black an image of himself as a carefree male ... because he has already learned from a million other commercials to fill vacancies in his life through commodities, because advertisers have long since inscribed that nexus on his mind, because *they* have to expand sales to cope with the productive capacity that manufacturers have achieved partly by making Bill's job mechanical, which in turn makes him long for autonomy and market-free social relations, which desire has over decades been fixed to an image of the home as a place of care and refuge, which image drew him into a marriage with impossible hopes, and the burden of these hopes on his wife, along with her own ad-inflated aspirations to be super-woman, has made her resentful and no fun to be with. . . . And so on and on. (12–13)

In this system, there is no space for "real" or "authentic" desires. And this is probably right: all of us are now born into a culture that is consumerist through and through in such a way that renders appeals to "authentic" desires or pleasures as suspect as our desire for pure, unconstrained agency. Still, what such accounts are never able to explain is why consumer culture "fails" so frequently and why advertisers have to constantly re-evaluate their audiences and reconsider the ways in which they might reach them.

To put this slightly differently: "if consumption was simply a reflex of production, what need would there be for design, advertising or marketing expertise?" (du Gay et al. 85). One of the errors in thinking about consumer culture is to assume that it is total in the way that Ohmann suggests here—that there is no excess, slippage, or contradiction that breaks up the smooth operation of consumerism, or at least produces other forms and moments of social interaction and meaning. To question the absolute power of consumerist ideology does not require a return to "real" or "authentic" desires; rather, what it means is that we need to consider the ways in which individuals create social and individual meaning through consumption—however problematically, however incompletely.

Making Meaning in Use

In the words of the authors of *Doing Cultural Studies*, du Gay et al., consumption needs to be understood to some degree, and in conjunction with our discussion of structure above, as a process of "**appropriation** and resistance," "an ongoing cycle of *commodification* —where producers make new products or different versions of old products as a result of consumers' activities—and *appropriation*—where consumers make those products meaningful, sometimes making them achieve a new 'register' of meaning that affects production in some way" (103). Consumers don't passively accept the meanings that supposedly come prepackaged with the things that they consume—or at least they

In the movie *American Beauty*, plastic bags dancing in the wind become an image of beauty for the character Ricky, highlighting the unpredictable intersections of commodity culture and creativity.

don't *always* do so. Rather, consumers help to *make* culture in a variety of complex and contradictory ways. First, consumers engage in a process of distinction and discrimination through the things that they choose to consume or not to consume. The landscape of consumer society is littered with products and services that didn't hit their mark: it is estimated that more than 80 percent of consumer items introduced each year fail. Second, consumers produce meaning at the intersection of the wide range of experiences, practices, and relationships that they are or have been engaged in. The unpredictable connection of these elements creates new possibilities and meanings that can fall outside of the structures of consumption.

It is possible to overstate the agency that individuals engage in through their practices of consumption. Cultural studies has at times gone too far in creating a "vision of consumption practices as inherently democratic and implicitly subversive" (du Gay et al. 104). Nevertheless, the fundamental point of insisting on even the possibility of consumer activity (as opposed to passivity) can be substantiated by looking at actual practices of consumption as they occur in specific social situations. (The discussion of McDonald's in Chapter 10 is one example.) To decide that we know the meaning of every situation of consumption from the outset doesn't help us to understand either the ways in which consumption has changed over time or the politics of consumption—that is, the larger social issues that we need to consider whenever we investigate consumption.

THE POLITICS OF CONSUMPTION

The most common critical responses to consumer culture have been *normative*: consumer culture has been assessed on the basis of its supposed innate value. Put most simply: is it good or bad for us? Thumbs up or thumbs down? Bran Flakes (=healthy) or Frosted Flakes (=unhealthy)? For all the boosters who celebrate consumers and consumption as engines for economic growth and the spread of democracy, others decry consumerism and consumption more generally as innate social evils. On the one hand there are those who say that television (for instance) educates and amuses people, democratically opens up the range of possibilities available to them, puts them in touch with the whole society or even the whole global village, makes them informed citizens, helps them to improve their material lives, and so keeps the economy going; and on the other, those who say television creates illusions, destroys literacy and the English language, isolates people from one another, puts them in debt by making them want things they don't really need, and turns them into political zombies. (Ohmann 11–12)

The former position tends to be held implicitly, except at times when—as in the post–9/11 crisis—consumers need to be reminded again of the duty and joy of shopping. The latter position is part of a long tradition of normative critiques of mass culture dating back to Matthew Arnold's worries in *Culture and Anarchy* (1869) about the eclipse of an interest in spiritual values through the "vulgar" pursuit of material wealth during the rapid **industrialization** of Britain in the nineteenth century (see Chapter 2).

Writing in the 1920s, Samuel Strauss spoke directly about the problems of what he referred to as "consumptionism," "a philosophy of life that committed human beings to the production of more and more things—'more this year than last year, more next year than this'—and that emphasized the 'standard of living' above all other values" (qtd. in R. Robbins 3). The decline of all other values at the expense of consumer values was criticized in the 1950s by former advertising executive Vance Packard, who drew attention to the psychological tricks of advertising that led to overconsumption. Every new publishing season brings a raft of critiques of consumer culture more or less along these same lines (such as Robert D. Putnam's *Bowling Alone: The Collapse and Revival of American Community* or, in a different vein, Judith Levine's *Not Buying It: My Year Without Shopping*). Consumerism seems to be a perpetual problem, and a problem that a century of both scholarly and public criticism seems to have done little about.

Shopping and Women

Debates about whether consumerism is a force for good or ill have frequently centred on the subject of shopping and gender. Specifically, many critics have explored the question of whether shopping, an activity claimed—whether justifiably or not—as primarily the domain of women, has worked to enslave or empower them. From the time when critiques of consumerism and shopping first began to appear with regularity toward the end of the nineteenth century, they were often framed in terms of gender. All of the negative qualities connected with shopping—its association with leisure and frivolity, as opposed to work; its emphasis on outward appearances at the expense of deeper, spiritual values; and, worst of all, its erosion of shoppers' powers of discrimination as they succumbed to mindless acts of consumption—were traditionally coded feminine, in opposition to the masculine world of work, substance, and rationality. These generalized attacks on shopping as a threat to masculine values were accompanied by more specific attacks on the relatively new and alarming figure of the woman shopper.

As we noted in Chapter 2, an important aspect of the bourgeois ideology that grew up around the industrial revolution was its delineation of separate spheres of home and work—the public world, or the world of men, and the domestic space of women. Though women, particularly working-class women, crossed these boundaries all the time, the ideology of separate spheres served to create a mythological distinction between the feminine ideal—the "angel in the house"—and her evil sister, embodied in the figure of that notorious homewrecker, the prostitute. The advent of the department store—a kind of domestic space outside the home—confused the clear-cut divisions between public and private space, granting women a new and (from a masculine perspective) threatening kind of freedom that itself heralded the corruption of that sacred space, the English home.

Feminist Perspectives But women were equally critical of the induction of their sisters into consumer culture, if for entirely different reasons. Charlotte Perkins Gilman, a nineteenth-century advocate of women's liberation, lamented what she saw as the enslavement of women to a new cult of consumerism in which they functioned as "priestesses." Excluded from the public realm of "true industry and true art" (60), women were relegated to the world of false things in which their only role was both a passive and a destructive one as "a limitless demander of things to use up" (60). Sue Thornham places Gilman's argument at the beginning of a long tradition of **feminist** criticism of shopping as an activity that works, paradoxically, to keep women in their place even as it allows them an illusory freedom in the form of temporary escape from the home. Just as Gilman described women as "priestesses" of a new "temple of consumption," later writers extend the religious metaphor in their construction of shopping as a form of mass ritual in which women's active participation conceals their passive subjection.

For example, Betty Friedan, writing in 1965, observed that "like a primitive culture which sacrificed little girls to its tribal gods, we sacrifice our girls to the feminine mystique, grooming them ever more efficiently through the sexual sell to become consumers of the things to whose profitable sale our nation is dedicated" (qtd. in Thornham 126). The image of girls as sacrificial victims to the religion of shopping (and its associated cults of beauty and fashion) anticipates a more radical critique of the role of women in consumer society. Not only are women cast in the position of relatively passive consumers in contrast to the active realm of masculine production, but also they are themselves commodities, "disinvested" of their bodies and "reclothed in a form that makes [them] suitable for exchange among men" (Irigaray 181).

For many critics, then, consumerism is a social force whose largely negative effects have a particularly strong impact on women. From a masculinist Victorian perspective, shopping represents self-indulgence, frivolity, materialism, and irrationality. Because these are seen to be qualities to which women in particular are susceptible, succumbing to the lure of consumerism risks not only corrupting women's already precarious moral characters, but also emasculating society as a whole. From a feminist perspective, by contrast, shopping reinforces women's exclusion from the realm of production, where real social power lies. More troubling still, in its embodiment of the economic relations that characterize capitalist society in general, shopping confirms the status of women as *objects* of exchange: things to be looked at and possessed, whose **commodification** is only accentuated by their active participation in the process.

In opposition to these negative perspectives on women and shopping, another group of critics makes the counterargument that far from enslaving women, shopping actually empowers them. One strand of this argument proceeds from the same premise that so troubled nineteenth-century male critics, but takes the opposite view: shopping is an activity—the first significant activity—that allowed women to leave the home and enter the public sphere. According to this argument, the contemporary shopping mall functions in a similar way to the early department store, by blurring the boundaries of the private and the public, of work and leisure:

The consumer is allowed to wander in and out of private space to look at, handle, and try out products that she does not own. In a department store it is possible to wander through privately owned space, holding or wearing someone else's property as if it were your own, without asking to do so, often without even having to go through the usual social intercourse appropriate to being a guest in someone's place. Boundaries between public and private become ambiguous (Ferrier, qtd. in Fiske *Reading* 23).

Moreover, as shoppers women could for the first time exercise a degree of control and decision-making power in the economic realm—power that had until then been confined to their roles as household managers. Shopping, in these terms, can be viewed as a kind of *work*, in the way that women's traditional labour in the home is not. Commenting on the construction of her house as a place of comfort for its inhabitants "where no one ever runs out of the necessaries: stamps, Aspirin, pudding, tweezers, blankets," newspaper columnist Heather Mallick notes, "It isn't leisure that produced this. It was hard graft, thoughtful travelling and selection, judicious studying of bank balances. . . . And it is work that does good" (Mallick L5). Shopping's ability to fulfill what Mallick identifies as women's desire to be good, or at least to be seen to be good, by satisfying the needs of their loved ones might make it seem like a further entrenchment in their traditional roles rather than a way of moving outside them.

However, a number of critics argue that this general analysis of shopping's function doesn't pay sufficient attention to the complexity and ambiguity of shoppers' actual practices. While anthropologist Daniel Miller, on the basis of an intensive study of women shoppers on a North London street, largely concurs with Mallick's characterization of shopping as a way for women to consolidate relationships or express love, he refutes in *A Theory of Shopping* the easy equation of women's love with disempowerment under **patriarchy**, in part by highlighting the active and self-conscious nature of his interview subjects' shopping habits. Mallick, moreover, highlights the ambiguity of women's position as shoppers by her sly distinction between "being good and *being seen to be* good" (emphasis added). The activity of shopping might be largely constrained both by the material structures and by the ideologies of patriarchal society, but within those structures individuals have considerable leeway in how they perform their role as consumers.

Performance   The concept of *performance*, which will be discussed in greater detail in Chapter 6, highlights the distinction between the role of the consumer as an ideal subject of capitalist ideology and the enactment of that role by individual consumers. The image of the feminine consumer, an image that both reflects and is a critical part of the image of her as "woman," is not natural, or given, but constructed within a particular context according to particular economic relations. While it might be impossible ever to escape or refuse the image entirely, it *is* possible, feminist theorists such as Luce Irigaray (*This Sex Which Is Not One*) and Judith Butler (*Gender Trouble*) suggest, to inhabit it self-consciously, to perform it in a playful or excessive way that undercuts the authority of the system it represents. In the realm of shopping, this kind of subversive **performance** might entail the cultivation of a style that mimics ironically the image of traditional femininity. Or it might involve the combination of different styles to create a visually jarring effect that draws attention to the constructedness of style as "fashion" rather than a natural accentuation of female beauty. In either case, the emphasis in the theory of performance is on the agency of a shopper, who does not just passively inhabit, but rather participates actively in the construction of, her role as consumer and/or embodiment of a social ideal.

That construction cannot be understood solely in economic terms, either. As we discuss further below, the things we buy aren't solely commodities but also are bits of culture, resources from which we fashion meanings and pleasures that often challenge the commercial system that sold them. Women have traditionally shown particular ingenuity at subverting the profit-making goals of the retail industry—for example, by buying cheap knockoffs or even sewing their own versions of the high-fashion items displayed in shops or magazines, or by creating their own styles through the recycled resources of vintage shops (see McRobbie).

The *Flâneur*   John Fiske extends the argument about women's agency as consumers by drawing out the ambiguity of the concept of "looking," which is central to both the activity of shopping and, as we have seen in Chapter 3, the structuring of gender relations. As Laura Mulvey noted in her **psychoanalytic** analysis of Hollywood cinema, one of the ways the gender hierarchy operates is through an economy of sight, in which women connote "to-be-looked-at-ness." Accentuated in film, this relation also operates in public space. In the nineteenth century, one of the figures that became emblematic of the new urban culture was the *flâneur*, the connoisseur of the city and all its pleasures, whose principal activities consisted of just walking around and *looking*.

First described by the French poet Charles Baudelaire, the *flâneur* is a "passionate spectator" who enacts the dream of a restless romantic: "to be away from home and yet to feel oneself everywhere at home; to see the world, to be at the centre of the world, and yet to remain hidden from the world—impartial natures which the tongue can but clumsily define. The spectator is a prince who everywhere rejoices in his incognito" (9).

For the contemporary theorist Walter Benjamin, the *flâneur* is the quintessential figure of modernity. He is also, quite clearly, male. The feminine counterpart of the *flâneur*—the *flâneuse*—is, as Janet Wolff and Elizabeth Wilson have noted, the prostitute, whose freedom to look is constrained by her status as commodity. However, the economy of spectatorship is complicated by the figure of the female shopper who, while she doesn't stop being an object of the male gaze, also engages in active looking. As she window-shops, tries on dresses, or picks up produce, the customer consumes a whole raft of images, some of which she may choose to purchase and incorporate into her own self-construction. While it can be argued that the self-image she shops for is heavily deter-mined by patriarchal culture, as embodied especially in the advertising industry, the element of *choice* here is important. Moreover, the idea that women simply buy obediently into dominant myths of femininity—essentially seeing themselves through male eyes and constructing themselves accordingly—is too reductive an account of what Mulvey calls the pleasures of looking. As Fiske suggests,

> the pleasure of the look is not just the pleasure of looking good for the male, but rather of controlling how one looks and therefore of controlling the look of others upon oneself. Looking makes meanings; it is therefore a means of entering social relations, of inserting oneself into the social order in general, and of control-ling one's immediate social relations in particular. Commodities are the resources of the woman (or man) who is exercising some control over her look, her social relations, and her relation to the social order. (*Reading* 35)

Caroline Evans and Minna Thornton further question the **essentialist** reading of gendered looking, suggesting that "fashion, unlike cinema, generates images of women for women, a system of representations that one might suppose to be cut to the measure of a *female* desire" (10). While this may be true, it would be a mistake, as Evans and Thornton acknowledge, to see fashion as a zone of women's emancipation: female desire is not generated outside of culture, and thus it is necessarily shaped in part by ideology, an ideology that remains strongly patriarchal.

Having surveyed the arguments for and against shopping as it pertains to women in particular, we can conclude that it is neither wholly disempowering nor wholly empow-ering. In the nineteenth century certainly, and perhaps even today, shopping is a way for those who lack economic power as *producers*—particularly women, but we can also include other groups, such as youth or the unemployed—to exercise some, albeit limited, control as *consumers*. Indeed, Judith Williamson suggests that in our contemporary culture, which is generally unsympathetic to labour rights, consumption is one of the *only* viable ways for people to control their environments and produce their own identities (231). This somewhat depressing proposition is itself perhaps inadequate, however, to describe the complexities of shopping that, as we have suggested above, emerge most clearly in the case of *women* shoppers. One of the ways women complicate the case against consumerism is by messing up the categories on which such critiques are founded.

As Sue Thornham notes, citing the work of theorist Janice Winship on the ideology of women's magazines,

> the "split" within capitalist society between production/consumption; work/leisure; work/personal life; work/everyday life is one which operates . . . only for men. It depends on a concept of the labourer who is a "free" individual able to sell his labour—separable from himself—freely. Women, however, live out the relations of capitalism "through their femininity." (Winship, qtd. in Thornham 135)

As they play a role that combines elements of consumer, producer, and commodity, women achieve benefits from shopping that are, at best, ambiguous. However, by challenging the traditional oppositions between public and private, subject and object, and masculine and feminine on the level of both economics and pleasure, they refute essentialist arguments about female—or consumer—passivity.

As the example of women and shopping shows, the "yea or nay" approach to consumerism is not a viable way of understanding it. Though such approaches are perhaps inevitable, it is important to recognize that at least to some degree criticisms of consumer culture are themselves part of the process of distinction that Bourdieu analyzes: critics assert their own aesthetic values by dismissing **lowbrow** television (*According to Jim, Rock of Love*) and praising their more meritorious cousins (*Mad Men, House*). As critics like Thornham have shown, these distinctions have gender, as well as class, implications.

The Consequences of Consumption

Another way of approaching consumer culture frames the implications of consumerism in a somewhat different way. This is to ask: What are the consequences of consumer society? What is the price of the pleasures we can and do derive from making meanings through our practices of consumption? A response to this question can take various forms, ranging from the philosophical to the empirical. Philosophically, the capitalist system that gives rise to and perpetuates consumerism has long been seen as a fundamentally alienating system: it is a system in which the pleasures of consumption are purchased for most at the cost of engaging in forms of labour that are antithetical to our real interests and that have become more and more specialized and narrow. In other words, we get to define ourselves through the things we buy only by subjecting ourselves to jobs that in all too many cases hardly represent how we'd like to be spending our time.

Empirically, a number of critics have drawn attention to the impact of Western consumerism—a style of consumerism, it should be added, that is quickly becoming global—on other peoples and on the environment. Richard Robbins has explored in detail the global consequences of consumerism through his examination of the development of the sugar and beef industries (194–220). The Western appetite for sugar led to the expansion of the plantation economy in the eighteenth and nineteenth centuries, and, correspondingly, to the untold suffering of millions who were displaced from their homelands to serve as slaves on these plantations. The modern beef industry, to take another example, has had an environmentally devastating impact around the world, leading to environmental degradation through the deforestation that often accompanies large-scale ranching, the pollution of groundwater and the atmosphere by waste products, and the spread of disease both to human beings and to wild animal populations.

What is perhaps more telling is that we can see the same stories of human and environmental damage if we consider virtually *any* aspect of contemporary consumption, from the use of automobiles (depletion of both non-renewable resources and the ozone layer, increased human health risks due to smog and high levels of UV radiation, not to mention the widespread impacts of a warming planet) to the purchase of hip, funky clothing (almost all of which is produced in degrading sweatshop factories in developing countries, a form of labour that approximates slavery even if workers "freely" choose to work in them). At the same time, ever-expanding consumption of consumer items of all kinds has proven to be a key component of the health of national economies and of international markets. The growth of new consumer classes in countries such as China, India, and Brazil has been taken as a positive sign of the development of these nations.

In the final analysis, the fact that we are quickly approaching some very real limits in the Earth's physical resources makes it increasingly difficult to valorize some of the ways in which consumerism enables agency. To give but one example, we are close to reaching Hubbert's Peak, the point at which humanity has used up half of the entire planet's petroleum resources. Petroleum not only fuels our cars, heats our homes, and permits our factories to work, but is also used to make plastics, artificial fibres, paints, and so on. What will happen to consumption when we are sliding from Hubbert's Peak toward zero remains to be seen.

While this chapter has argued that it is important to take consumerism seriously in order to understand contemporary popular culture, it is just as important to understand the global impact of our "society of perpetual growth." When perpetual growth takes place in a world of limited natural and human resources, serious and inevitable problems will arise. Finding answers to these problems generated by consumption is one of the major challenges of this century. The greatest challenge is to try to understand how to mobilize the pleasures and possibilities of consumption, and the way in which consumption can be a place of individual and collective agency, in a manner that also addresses the increasingly terrible consequences of consumption on an accelerated, expanded, and global scale.

A Different Kind of Consumer Culture

In "Towards a New Politics of Consumption," sociologist Juliet Schor proposes a model for thinking past the either–or way in which consumption has typically been addressed. Her proposal is to reorient rather than do away with consumption (which is, as we will see in the final section of this chapter, one of the common critical reactions to consumerism: the belief that the only solution is to do away with it altogether) by addressing one of the key, if under-theorized, aspects of consumption.

Contemporary modes of consumption put untold stresses and strains on individuals. Schor believes that there is already an enormous amount of discontent with consumerism; what is lacking is a way to conceptualize it. Social well-being in a consumer society has always been linked to income levels. The assumption is that the more money

The Canadian photographer Edward Burtynsky has captured the scale of global production and consumption in several acclaimed series of photographs. *Manufacturing #17* (2005) shows the inner workings of the Deda Chicken Processing Plant, Dehui City, Jilin Province, China.

you have, the more you can spend and the more satisfied with life you will be. (This is why politicians always employ the rhetoric of tax cuts and new jobs to try to win votes.) What is lacking is a market for "alternatives to status or positional goods" (457): there is a market for things, but not for public goods or more time. In turn, since it is difficult to express one's desires for these kinds of goods in a society where achievement is measured almost solely by monetary wealth, consumer society "underproduces" goods that people find important: a clean environment (since environmental costs are not included in the price of goods), leisure (it is harder to choose more free time over higher incomes in virtually every employment sector), and all manner of public goods (since mass transit is so poor we are forced to use private cars, which in turn leads to a further decline in mass transit since it is used less and less).

A new politics of consumption would try to create a language and a political framework in which it is possible to create an economy of "less work and less stuff" (459). Schor believes that there is a strong demand for such an economy, even if it is difficult to see this because we can participate only in the forms of consumption currently "on offer" (459). She makes seven suggestions, all of which are important to our discussion here.

The first involves the revival of a discussion of the minimal social needs for every individual in society to be fully able to participate in it. Second is a focus on "quality of life" rather than "quantity of stuff," which in turn is related to the third, the need for more ecologically sustainable forms of consumption. Addressing minimal social needs has to be accompanied by more democratic consumption practices, that is (fourth), a way of "de-cooling" high-end products and changing the rules of the game of distinction. Fifth and sixth, a "vast consumer policy agenda" has to put pressure on the development of government policy, including the creation of policy to control the "cultural environment" (ad-free zones, diversity in retailing, etc.).

Seventh is a point that is absolutely crucial to any politics of consumption. Schor points out what Marx insisted on almost a century and a half ago: "Everything we consume has been produced. So a new politics of consumption must take into account the labor, environmental, and other conditions under which products are made, and argue for high standards" (461). *This* constitutes the real agenda for rethinking our consuming lives—lives whose frantic pace, absurdities, and wasted efforts, all in the name of accumulating more stuff, faster and faster, are in turn threatening to consume us. The forms that our criticisms take, however, rely all too frequently on the use and abuse of a set of concepts that seem unable to push us out of the dangerous orbit that we've assumed around the planet Consumption; we will look at these concepts below. If we continue our present trajectory, the future explorers who find our remains will only come across a tape with a single sentence recorded on it: "We had compulsions that made us confuse shopping with creativity . . ." (Coupland 11).

Authenticity and Co-optation: "The Merchants of Cool"

Rachel Dretzin and Barak Goodman's *Frontline* documentary "The Merchants of Cool" (2001) explores the hyper-commodified world of contemporary youth culture. Narrated by PBS correspondent Douglas Rushkoff, who appears in the documentary as a lonely adult figure wandering through the landscape of youth pop culture, the documentary explores a whole range of contemporary marketing and advertising practices that extend their way deep into the lives of one of consumer culture's most cherished subjects—youth.

The current generation of teenagers is the wealthiest in history. The documentary claims that in the United States in 2000 teenagers spent $100 billion themselves and influenced the spending of another $50 billion. Since teens generally don't have to pay for the necessities of life, the vast majority of spending went toward forms of what Veblen described as "conspicuous consumption"—CDs, movie passes, soft drinks and fast food, fashion, and video games. For companies involved in producing the objects that teenagers consume, there is fierce competition to secure these discretionary dollars. Dretzin and Goodman explore the forms that this competition has taken, as well as the impact that it has had on youth culture and contemporary popular culture more generally, in order to come to some conclusions about the degree to which the values of industry have infiltrated the last remaining cracks and gaps in consumer society.

Defining "Cool"   According to Goodman, teens today respond "most reliably" to "this maddeningly elusive thing called cool." Increasingly, "cool" has been understood as standing in opposition to the mainstream consumer products: something that everyone likes cannot possibly be cool. This has created a paradoxical situation for companies that produce consumer products, especially for those that target teens. In order to ensure sales of their products, they need to appeal to what teens find cool; as soon as they begin to flood the market with their products, a product that started out cool quickly becomes yet another mass-produced object intended primarily to separate teens from their money.

"The Merchants of Cool" showcases the ways in which companies have tried to search out what youth think is cool in order to capitalize on it; it also shows the transformation of something cool (and thus supposedly *transgressive,* or opposed to the dominant values of consumer culture) into a form of mainstream consumer culture. In the first instance, they focus on a variety of marketing techniques that employ forms of ethnography. "Cool hunters" are marketers who search out what youth think is cool before it becomes part of the culture at large (or even of youth culture at large). Such cool hunters visit high schools and try to track down "early adopters"—teens who are willing to take a chance in wearing radical clothing, listening to music that might be unpopular with their peers, and decorating their bodies and styling their hair in original ways. They then compile this information into reports that are purchased by large companies, which in turn use the information to try to anticipate the kinds of products and styles that teens will purchase.

The filmmakers paint a picture of a present in which marketers, by entering into the lives of teens more and more intrusively, have shortened the time between the expression of an authentic agency with respect to popular culture (teens making their own forms of cool, or reworking parts of existing consumer forms) and when this expression becomes commodified, turned into an experience or object to be bought and sold to as many people as possible. Rushkoff, the narrator, suggests that what is being witnessed in youth culture today is the intensification and extensification of a longer historical narrative of consumer culture. The fundamental "engine" of consumerism (what drives it onward and upward) that the film identifies involves the co-optation by businesses of genuine, authentic forms of cultural expression.

The worry of the filmmakers is that co-optation of authentic forms of popular expression now occurs so rapidly that youth culture no longer has any room to breathe or to develop and grow. And what this in turn implies is that consumer culture is now in danger of becoming total, with structure coming to overwhelm the few remaining sites of agency.

We are all familiar with the narrative offered in this documentary. When our favourite indie band signs to a major label or achieves unexpectedly widespread sales, or when a reputable film star begins appearing in mass-culture schlock (many fans have wondered why Robert De Niro would ever agree to star in *Meet the Parents* much less *Meet the Fockers*), we can't help but feel as though they have somehow "sold out," trading their artistic authenticity for the comfort of cold hard cash. This narrative seems to work particularly well in discussions of popular music.

Music Scene Fashion Narratives   Punk in England and grunge in Seattle emerged out of local situations and music **subcultures** in response to specific social and political contexts. In both cases, punk and grunge style—comments on consumer culture's fascination with fashion (punks ripped and defaced their clothing, reassembling items with staples and safety pins; grunge musicians adopted working-class clothing, specifically the iconic lumberjack shirt)—quickly crossed over to the mainstream, or at the very least were transposed to other cultural and subcultural settings. British soccer star David Beckham saw fit to wear a version of the mohawk in the qualifying rounds leading up to the 2002 World Cup; in North America, youth living outside the Pacific Northwest quickly started wearing lumberjack shirts and listening to Nirvana and other examples of the Seattle sound. The narrativization of these kinds of cultural movements implies an early, non-commodified, non-consumer moment of authenticity, followed by an inexorable process of commercial and cultural **assimilation** of apparently threatening or oppositional **discourses** into mainstream culture.

But while this may be a familiar narrative about the dynamics of contemporary consumption, it is one that passes over a number of issues that we have tried to emphasize here. First, there is a way in which (as with so many other examples of cultural criticism directed toward consumption) this narrative translates into political stasis: since genuine expressions are fated to be assimilated into mainstream discourses, it's pointless to even *try* to make your own forms of popular culture. And, since being popular means being co-opted, it is more or less structurally impossible to spread (say) an anti-consumerist message as widely as possible, as many bands have wanted to do, since once everyone is into something it must be "bad."

More significantly, this narrative assumes the solidity of two categories that should be seen as both more porous and more incomplete than the "co-optation thesis" implies. The claim that the products of youth culture are *ever* authentic in the first place—or at least, authentic in the way that "The Merchants of Cool" implies, outside of consumer culture and in opposition to it—positions youth culture in an impossible place. Punk didn't come suddenly out of nowhere: it was itself already part of a pop-culture discourse and has to be seen as "inside" rather than "outside" of consumer culture. (How else would one ever have the idea that you could cause a social and/or cultural revolution by playing your guitar?) Finally, the co-optation thesis displays little faith in the uses to which people put consumer objects. Co-opted culture is imagined as a culture bereft of agency, a position that we explored and challenged above in the section on desire and pleasure.

Counterculture Narratives One of the most important challenges to the view that consumer culture involves the co-optation of real, genuine, or authentic forms of culture is found in Thomas Frank's analysis of the supposed co-optation of the politics of the 1960s into consumer culture, a transformation that turned the sixties' hippies into the eighties' yuppies. In *The Conquest of Cool*, he focuses on the supposed absorption of the energies of the sixties counterculture into the language of advertising. He writes that "at the heart of every interpretation of the counterculture is a very particular—and very questionable—understanding of corporate ideology and of business practice . . . business was the monolithic bad guy who had caused America to become a place of puritanical conformity and empty consumerism" (7).

But an examination of fifties and sixties business culture gives us a very different vision of things: in many cases, business saw the **counterculture** not as an enemy, but as a symbolic ally in their own efforts to modify and update business practices. The bureaucratized, overly rationalized business environment of the fifties was producing fewer and fewer gains. The solution was to adopt a model of flexibility and creativity that mirrored the values inherent in the counterculture. Indeed, Frank even suggests that advertisers adopted a critical position on mainstream culture before the radicals of the sixties. Like the hippies themselves, advertisers and businesses were responding to the fact that "the mass culture critique was, if not populist, enormously popular … by the middle of the 1950s, talk of conformity, of consumerism, and of the banality of mass-produced culture were routine elements of middle-class American life" (11).

What Frank's analysis shows us is that the standard co-optation model, which places the values of the dominant culture and the counterculture (or youth culture) into strict opposition, offers a far too simplistic understanding of both. The popularity of this model, its presence as a cultural commonplace that we all turn to all the time to explain changes in popular culture, has correspondingly skewed our own understanding of it, reinforcing both the overwhelming power and solidity of the structures of consumer culture (the forces of co-optation) and the uncritical presence of those authentic experiences or expressions that are then co-opted.

SUGGESTIONS FOR FURTHER READING AND VIEWING

Bocock, Robert. *Consumption.* New York: Routledge, 1994.

Clark, David B., Marcus Doel, and Kate M.K. Housiaux, eds. *The Consumption Reader.* New York: Routledge, 2003.

Cook, Daniel Thomas. *The Commodification of Childhood: The Children's Clothing Industry and the Rise of the Child Consumer.* Durham, NC: Duke University Press, 2004.

The Corporation. Dir. Mark Achbar and Jennifer Abbott. Prod. Mark Achbar and Bart Simpson. 2003. Canada: Big Picture Media Corporation.

Czech Dream. Dir. Vit Klusák and Filip Remunda. 2004. Czech Republic.

De Graaf, John, David Wann, and Thomas H. Naylor. *Affluenza: The All-Consuming Epidemic.* San Francisco, CA: Berrett-Koehler Publishers, 2001.

Gottdiener, Mark. *New Forms of Consumption.* Lanham, MD: Rowman and Littlefield, 2000.

McCracken, Grant. *Culture and Consumption.* Bloomington: Indiana University Press, 1988.

Princen, Thomas, Michael Maniates, and Ken Conca, eds. *Confronting Consumption.* Cambridge, MA: MIT Press, 2002.

Scanlan, Jennifer. *The Gender and Consumer Culture Reader.* New York: New York University Press, 2000.

Schor, Juliet B. *Born to Buy: The Commercialized Child and the New Consumer Culture.* New York: Scribner, 2005.

———. *Do Americans Buy Too Much?* Boston: Beacon Press, 2000.

———. *The Overspent American: The Unexpected Decline of Leisure.* New York: Basic Books, 1998.

Schor, Juliet B., and Douglas Holt. *The Consumer Society Reader.* New York: The New Press, 2000.

Chapter 6

Identity and the Body

INTRODUCTION: IDENTITY—A NECESSARY FICTION?

In the 2005 film *Transamerica*, Bree, a 40-something-year-old transsexual woman, goes with Toby, a teenaged hustler, on a road trip from New York to Los Angeles. Along with a number of standard elements of the Hollywood road movie (dodgy transportation, encounters with wacky but sympathetic strangers and stereotypical mid-Western conservatives, frequent fights and misunderstandings), the plot offers a more unusual premise: Toby is Bree's son, fathered by him during a brief encounter when he was a man. Bree knows this, but Toby doesn't, believing instead that the prissy middle-aged woman who sprung him from jail is a Christian do-gooder hoping to convert him on the cross-country journey to find his father. Bree has undertaken the trip at the insistence of her therapist, who won't sign the papers giving authorization for her sex-reassignment surgery until she confronts this recently discovered and very awkward part of her past. Much of the critical commentary on this film focused on the theme of transsexuality, which as yet had received little attention in mainstream cinema, and on the surprisingly impressive performance of actress Felicity Huffman, best known for her role in the television series *Desperate Housewives*, playing a biological man playing a woman. These novel elements aside, the film is interesting as a paradigmatic exploration of the traditional Western theme of **identity**.

The transsexual aspect of Bree's character accentuates conventional questions about the relationship between identity, behaviour, and biology, as well as the political charge these questions have always carried. The film also approaches questions about the role of genetics in defining identity from another traditional angle: the relationship between parents and children. Toby clearly feels rightly or wrongly (mostly wrongly as it turns out) that solving the mystery of his birth father will help him resolve confusions about his current life path. The role of the past in defining identity is clearly key to Bree's quest as well, if we accept her therapist's expert advice that she cannot move on and become the person she wants to be until she has somehow dealt with the things she did and the person she was. Finally, the film is interesting for the way it addresses and fails to address a question that has emerged in different forms from the eighteenth century until the present: to what extent are identities made up and/or constructed (and perhaps even make-believe) and to what extent are they natural? Are our identities anchored by factors such as sex, gender, and sexual orientation, or are they free-floating, subject to change? In the following two chapters we take up these along with some even more basic questions: What is identity? Why is it so important in contemporary society? What is at stake in the **representation** and production of identities, individual and collective?

That something *is* at stake is clear to see from the many kinds of popular culture that derive at least part of their meaning from the significance of identity. From magazine ads that appeal to our sense of ourselves as unique individuals, to **subcultural** styles that allow us to create resistant identities (see Chapter 8), popular culture testifies to the centrality of identity in producing meaning and pleasure in our everyday lives. In this chapter we explore ideas about identity that tend to take up a position somewhere between the poles of **essentialism** and **social constructivism.** Essentialist theories posit identity as a fundamental, unchanging core of meaning that precedes and transcends culture and politics. Identity derives its sense and legitimacy, according to these theories, through its grounding in nature and/or history, where "history" is seen as an unbroken line of development whose truth is unquestionable. Social constructivist theories, on the other hand, emphasize the cultural and political circumstances in which identities are produced. Social constructivism takes issue with the essentialist premise of identity as something inherent within an individual or group, foregrounding instead the complex *process* through which narratives of identity express broader social relations, including and especially relations of power. Those relations remain invisible to the extent that identities are naturalized or essentialized—that is, represented as outside or prior to particular historical circumstances.

Over the course of the last century, developments in the field of psychology, political theory, and philosophy have highlighted some of the logical and practical problems with essentialism, while offering variations on constructivist models of identity. Recent advances in genetics have swung the pendulum back to theories based on biology or "nature" that seek to explain how we are who we are. Without discounting these theories, much of the discussion in this chapter explores the role of social and political forces in constructing narratives of identity. Genetics might establish broad parameters for what we can do, think, or feel, but it is culture that gives us the ingredients to establish the story lines of who we think we are. To see identity as a form of narrative or story—something made up, rather than given—does not lead us to suggest it is insubstantial or dispensable. Rather, this chapter demonstrates the symbolic and material weight of identity, both as an **ideological** force that inserts us into particular roles we may or may not have chosen in a social script we do not ultimately control, and as a platform for self-expression that may allow us limited forms of rewriting. The fluid and contradictory nature of human experience further means that we cannot be defined by any simple mechanism of identity—or even multiple identities (e.g., sister, friend, student, musician, bartender); there will always be parts of us, conscious and unconscious, that exceed the narratives that at various times work to explain or confine us.

A critical issue in debates about the significance and limits of identity is the role of our bodies in determining who we are. The assumption that has prevailed in Western thought since the time of René Descartes (1596–1650)—that mind and, by extension, self and identity were fundamentally distinct from the crude materiality of the body—has been increasingly confounded, in science and in popular thought, by a recognition of the inseparability of mind and body. A sometimes confused vacillation between the two perspectives—mind versus body and mind and body (or, to use a term we define later, *embodied subjectivity*)—characterizes contemporary practices such as health and fitness regimes and forms of body modification such as tattooing, piercing, and plastic surgery, which view work on the body as a means of self-enhancement. The perception of the body as almost infinitely malleable to our individual specifications, a perception that is in line with broader beliefs about the role of choice in consumer society, is complicated by the recognition that the capacity to fashion ourselves and our bodies is not equally available to everyone. The persistence of categories of gender, sexual orientation, and **race** as markers of identity and social power highlights the complex relationship between culture and physicality, whereby material differences are invested with cultural meanings that in turn have material effects, in the form of unequal pressures and opportunities encountered by members of different groups in their quests for self-definition.

The relationship between identity and **agency**, or the capacity each of us has to shape our own life, is a critical problem that informs many of the concerns we explore in this chapter and the following one. Thus, while many of our discussions focus on the way identities function as stories or create meaning, of central importance is the way these meanings operate to produce particular kinds of power and pleasure.

Suggested Activity 6.1

As you read this chapter and the following one, think about the identities that define you—or that you choose to be defined by—and how these identities fit into the bigger symbolic and material networks that articulate the society you live in. When and how do these identities conflict with one another?

THE HISTORY OF IDENTITY—SOME DIFFERENT THEORIES

The seeming obviousness of the concept of individual identity belies the fact that, until relatively recently (up until the eighteenth century), nobody gave much thought to it. The idea of the individual as a unique self, with deep psychological needs and preferences, held no currency in a social context in which the meaning of an individual life was subordinate to the issue of the survival of society as a whole. Who you were was prescribed not by your own internal qualities or will, but by the role you occupied in the institutions of family, church, class hierarchy, and so on. So why has individual identity come to have such importance in contemporary society? One dominant explanation is that society simply evolved to a point at which people were liberated from tradition-bound structures, and the unique identities of individuals—which had been there all along—suddenly leapt out of their straitjackets of class and religious conformity to claim their fundamental value and significance. It is certainly true that, from the late eighteenth century on, increasing attention was paid to the issue of identity and to debates over the role of nature or nurture in defining it. All of these debates were concerned with the meaning, not just of individuals, but also of society, as the issue of the role of birth or environment in shaping personality had critical implications for social policy relating to medicine, education, and the treatment of criminality.

Identity and the Unconscious

One of the first major bodies of work to concentrate on—and, ultimately, to unsettle—the grounds of identity was the field of **psychoanalysis**, pioneered by Sigmund Freud (1856–1939) in the early part of the twentieth century. Through his work on adult psychiatric problems—essentially, identity disorders—Freud developed a theory, later elaborated upon by others, of the stages of identity development that are a critical precondition for the individual's integration into society. Significant to Freud's theory is the emphasis on the way in which identities are not pre-given, or natural, but rather *produced* in order to manage chaotic fears and desires whose expression is socially forbidden. Babies, psychoanalytic theory suggests, have no coherent identities to speak of. Their inner world is defined by an unorganized collection of primal drives and instincts, with no conscious sense of themselves as separate from the world around them. A baby's eventual realization that the world—most significantly his or her mother—is not merely an extension of himself or herself but a separate being is both a traumatic break and the beginning of the process of socialization, marked by the management and containment of powerful, contradictory impulses toward "the other."

Freudian Theory of Psychosocial Development   Two key moments in the process of psychosocial development are (1) the recognition of sexual difference, which hinges on the presence or absence of a penis (symbolically expressed in Freud's theory as "the phallus"); this recognition imposes social meaning on our early desires, directing us, via fear of paternal authority, away from the forbidden love object of our mother's body, and (2) the acquisition of **language**. As a symbolic system that manages and mediates our relationship to the world, language is an important part of the social machinery that works to channel our desire into acceptable forms of adult sexual orientation and gender identity.

In Freud's formulation, these early moments in development, framed by the so-called Oedipal triangle of mother–father–child, lay the groundwork for two distinct ways of orienting the self in relation to others: the first, which comes later to be associated with sexual feeling, involves the desire to possess, or to *have* the other; the second—what Freud called identification—involves a recognition of a similarity between oneself and the other that inspires the desire to *be* the other. These two drives, which Freud suggests are biologically rooted, are organized, in the process of the resolution of the oedipal conflict, to reflect "proper" gender identification and sexual orientation: the young boy learns to identify with males and to desire females, while girls, lacking phallic agency, learn to *be* desirable to males, and to identify with women. These patterns of desire and identification are reinforced culturally, by the dominant institutions of education and family as well as by popular culture (see our discussion of Laura Mulvey's theory of Hollywood cinema in Chapter 3).

However, sexual drives are by nature chaotic—"polymorphous" in Freud's words. So-called civilization demands that we repress socially unacceptable fears and desires into the unconscious. Here they are inaccessible to our waking selves except through occasional chinks in our rational consciousness, where they appear in disguised form as dreams, fantasies, and verbal accidents (or "Freudian slips"). Because they cannot be articulated, these unconscious currents continue to create troubling ripples in our emotional lives, making the stability of both gender identification and heterosexual orientation precarious. The complex mix of love, fear, and aggression that characterizes our relations with others—particularly those closest to us—testifies to the impossibility of ever fully resolving the tensions enacted through the Oedipal conflict. The determination with which we cling to our identities—particularly gender and sexual orientation—is partly a reflection of an unconscious fear of the consequences of acknowledging the ambivalence that underlies them.

Identity and Ideology

The key lesson in Freud for understanding identity is not that it has no grounding in reality; rather, it is that the stable and coherent selves we articulate to the world and to ourselves are constructions, a bit like dams built to control and manage the torrent of chaotic drives and impulses that cannot be assimilated to society. Later psychoanalytic theorists, particularly **feminist** theorists, emphasize the importance of culture in defining psychosexual development, stressing that both the Oedipal complex and its resolution assume the shape they do in Freud's theory not because they represent natural or obvious stages in individual development but because they are already over-determined by the values of a patriarchal, capitalist culture that lays stress on the nuclear family, on the possession of phallic authority, and on the development of the individual.

Marxist Theories of Identity   The suggestion that not just the shape but also the very concept of individual identity is determined in particular cultural, historical circumstances informs the theories of Karl Marx (1818–1883), who, like Freud, understood the construction of identity as a response to underlying forces of which the individual is largely unconscious. For Marx, as for Freud, identity could be understood in one sense as a kind of mythical armour people assumed as a way of coping with the gap between their needs and desires and the social economy. While repression, for Freud, was the mechanism that shaped identity while concealing its own origins from it, for Marx the primary force in producing identity and consciousness as a kind of empty protective shell was **ideology** (see Close-Up 2.1). Ideology, you will recall from earlier chapters, is a form of knowledge or belief that is shaped by, while serving to conceal, powerful interests through its representation as natural or common sense. In the system of industrial **capitalism** that was gaining force during the time Marx wrote, ideology played a hugely significant role in securing the acceptance of an exploited working class by promoting a belief in the naturalness of the capitalist order and in the freedom of the individual within it.

In Marx's theory, ideology is the (disguised) expression of underlying economic relations. Later theorists, particularly the French theorist Louis Althusser, revised Marx's theory in order to emphasize the centrality of the social structures—what Althusser termed **ideological state apparatuses (ISAs)**, through which ideology is reproduced. Rather than being absolutely determined by the economy, the realm of culture and ideology, as it is disseminated through institutions such as schools, universities, and the media, comes to have a semi-autonomous or independent role in shaping individuals and society. The new importance accorded to culture means its effects are more pervasive than Marx suggested: while earlier concepts of ideology saw it as a kind of "false consciousness," which could be enlightened by seeing through it to the *real* economic conditions it concealed, Althusser's revised concept, which was strongly influenced by psychoanalysis, emphasized the impossibility of ever totally liberating identity from ideology.

In particular, Althusser focused on the process he termed "**interpellation**," by which individuals are compelled, through a mix of individual psychological and social imperatives, to identify with social roles offered them. This happens in a variety of contexts: for example, in the university setting, the architecture of the classroom, modes of academic discourse, and signs and ads around campus all combine to construct a set of relationships between different people. In order for the institution to function, it requires individuals to take up their assigned places in those already established relationships, not through a system of elaborate rules but through each individual's recognition of, and *identification with,* his or her role.

Suggested Activity 6.2

Think about how the educational institutions you have attended work to interpellate you into particular roles as a student and member of society. Elements you might consider include specific, material structures of authority, such as the arrangement of the classroom in which the professor sits or stands at the front while students sit together in a body, as well as the broader institutional structures that shape your expectations of what kind of social position your education, in conjunction with other social forces such as family and class, prepares you to assume.

Following psychoanalysis, particularly the work of the French theorist Jacques Lacan, Althusser locates the roots of this process of identification in the early stages of socialization, in particular the acquisition of language. Particularly critical in this process is the moment Lacan identifies as the *mirror stage,* which corresponds to the child's recognition of himself as a separate being. The mirror stage describes the moment in which the child sees his reflection in the mirror (which can also be read as a metaphor for the eyes of his mother and the world outside himself) and identifies with that image. What's particularly significant about that moment of recognition, Lacan suggests, is that it's actually a *misrecognition*: the stable, unified figure the child sees in the mirror—more stable and unified, in fact, than the child himself, whose body and its sensations are still relatively uncoordinated—is a reflection, a pleasing image of integrated selfhood that the child can never fully inhabit. The moment of identification, then, is actually a moment of splitting, in which the promise of wholeness is haunted by the impossibility of fulfillment: identity is always characterized by lack. This lack creates the potential for challenging the terms of identity, something we take up later in this chapter.

All Selves Are Not Created Equal

Of course, because the possibilities for identification are defined and limited through their production within unequal social systems, they hold out much more promising opportunities for some people than for others: in other words, identity may be an illusion, but it is an illusion that *works* for some people in a way that it doesn't for others. This inequality is highlighted explicitly in Marx's theory, which shows that the stakes of ideology are different depending on what position one occupies in the class structure, and more implicitly in psychoanalysis, where sexual difference determines what identities and authorities are available to whom, based on physiological sex characteristics.

According to both Freud and Marx, then, the process of socialization into a patriarchal, capitalist society not only establishes identity as a crucial focus of self-organization; it also prescribes and delimits what kinds of identities it is possible to adopt. Identity formation is thus both enabling and disabling—*how* enabling or disabling depends largely on the place one is assigned in social hierarchies defined by gender and class.

Feminist Theories   Feminist theory has taken up the insights of Freud and Marx while also showing the limits of psychoanalysis and Marxism in understanding the mechanisms and the politics of gender identity. The concepts of the unconscious and ideology help to explain how gender identity is socially constructed, and why it is so firmly entrenched. They explain, in other words, both why it is important to challenge so-called "natural" patterns of identification and desire and why it is so difficult. Forged in an intricate amalgam of biology and culture, women's self-perception as the "other" of male desire can't be undone by a simple political assertion of equality. Neither is it possible to counter ideological constructions of femininity with some "real" essence of femaleness, since the very notion of gender is shot through with ideology, experienced by each of us at the most basic level of self-perception.

Paradoxically, it is through the inherently fractured nature of women's self-perception that it becomes possible to mount a challenge to conventional ideologies of gender. Assigned a role in culture that is defined not as autonomous or self-sufficient but as always in-relation-to—"other" than—the normative category of man, women do not inhabit the **myth** of identity as comfortably as men generally do. They are, in the words of feminist Luce Irigaray, "the sex which is not one," a phrase that sums up the construction of women as negative, *less than* whole, desiring subjects, and as irreducible: not "one," but always split between the myth of stable identity and the reality of its fragmentation and flux. While this condition of always-incomplete self-affirmation can be seen as disempowering, it also arguably offers a lever through which to tear apart the whole fiction of identity on which **patriarchy** is based. That is, rather than aspiring to the ultimately empty idea of coherent selfhood—an idea that is always haunted by the shadow of the inferior, incoherent, other—feminine identity actually exposes the emptiness of the edifice that has served to shut women out.

Race—The Empty Signifier

The function of race as a marker of identity did not enter Freud's theory, at least not in an obvious way. While masculinity was the explicit standard by which to analyze normal human development, whiteness operated *im*plicitly in the same way: an assumed norm whose claims to universalism betrayed the **Eurocentrism** of early practitioners of psycho-analysis. Frantz Fanon, a Martiniquan psychiatrist who practised in Algeria during the dying days of the French colonial regime, challenged psychoanalytic theory to take account of the role of race, and the associated practice of **racism**, in defining identity. His 1952 book *Black Skin, White Masks* showed how, in the cultural context of **colonialism** and its aftermath, racial minorities are driven to define their identities in split and fractured forms. Where fully human identity is characterized by the "unmarked" race of whiteness, being black presents an untenable choice: become fully human by iden-tifying with what you are not and never can be, or be your "self"—in effect a non-self, defined only by difference and negation. At best, this dilemma leads to a strongly conflicted sense of self and community; at worst, it can lead to forms of psychiatric illness. Although Fanon was not overly sympathetic to feminism, his interventions shared with feminist critiques the insistence that identity—along with what becomes defined as mental disorder—must be understood in the context of relations of power. Fanon's insights inform the work of contemporary cultural theorists such as Stuart Hall, who analyze the discursive construction of race (a subject we discuss in detail in Chapter 7).

Hegemonic Masculinity

The whole concept of identity is anchored to a mythic masculine norm. However, the perceived solidity and stability of this ideal doesn't straightforwardly extend to real men—even white men. Particularly in the last decades of the twentieth century, economic changes associated with **globalization** issued a new challenge to conventional ideas of masculinity in North America. The movement of industry (and with it many working-class jobs) offshore has contributed to what is often called the "feminization" of labour—a phrase that refers not just to the influx of women into the global workplace, but also a shift in the kinds of work available, from manufacturing to service jobs in developed countries, and from agriculture to manufacturing and service in developing countries (Kanji and Menon-Sen). In developed countries in particular, the move from traditionally masculine industrial labour to softer, so-called women's jobs has been accompanied by a loss of wages and job security (service sector jobs are far less likely to be unionized), thus threatening the sense of autonomy that undergirds myths of masculinity. While her study has been faulted for unconsciously reinscribing myths of natural white middle-class male authority (see Walzer), Susan Faludi's *Stiffed* offers a lucid account of the new sense of precariousness experienced by American men in the late twentieth century as a result of lost productive capability. In addition to the real erosion of workers' rights accompanying the decline of the manufacturing industry, Faludi documents the identity crisis men suffer as they move away from the sphere of production toward what has traditionally been regarded as the girlie terrain of **consumption** (put simplistically: shopping).

Faludi's thesis finds many echoes in late 1990s popular culture, perhaps most famously in the film *Fight Club*. The iconic scene of the narrator sitting on the toilet, poring over an IKEA catalogue with guilty excitement, expresses what is supposedly every man's secret fear, of becoming "a slave to the IKEA nesting instinct." What seems at first to be an elegantly simple solution to this problem—a club in which members heal their wounded masculinity by bare-knuckle fighting—doesn't ultimately offer immunity from the curse of being owned by things, as the club becomes a franchise and then a kind of brand—like the idea of traditional masculinity itself. However, culture critic Latham Hunter makes a strong case for seeing in *Fight Club* and a host of similarly themed 1990s films (*Very Bad Things, Office Space, Falling Down, The Big Kahuna, American Beauty*) a reassertion of the conventional power structures that the fight club so crudely symbolizes. She suggests that, as they mourn the suffocation of the masculine soul within the smooth, bland space of the office cubicles, these films endorse, perhaps even more insistently than 1980s *Rambo*-style action films did, a **hegemonic** model of masculinity characterized by "amorality and aggression" (Hunter 72).

This model is "hegemonic," critic Robert Connell explains, in the sense that it confers positive value on one exclusive idea of maleness, and because its reinforcement of certain characteristics ("force," and "competence," in particular) "stabilizes a structure of dominance and oppression in the gender order as a whole" (Connell 94). Like other hegemonic ideals (we discuss hegemony in detail in Chapter 2), the persistence of myths of masculinity is not assured, but must always be shored up against resistant myths and realities. Popular men's magazines, for example, convey a mix of macho back-slapping "You go, boy!" confidence and anxiety about the emasculating effects of everyday life. One issue of *Men's Health* contains an article entitled "Yes, You Were Born To Run" that compares recreational

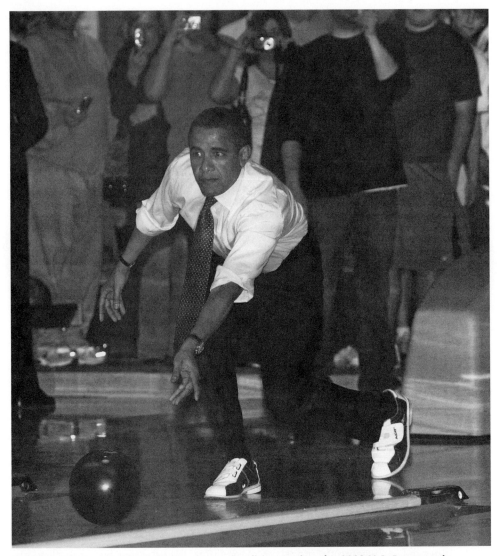

Gender codes are highly visible in electoral politics. During the 2008 U.S. Democratic primary, candidate Barack Obama was mocked for bowling "like a girl," while his rival, Hilary Clinton, downed whiskey shots in a bar and visited the Indianapolis Motor Speedway. Looking like "one of the boys" still seems to be a requisite for political success in North America.

runners with African hunters in the Kalahari (Conniff). In the same issue, a quasi-medical report explaining the physiological hazards of sedentary life (i.e., sitting around too much) tries to restore some virility to the desk jockey with an account of the cool things readers likely do while sitting: "watching *24*, tracking your NCAA pool results, or doing pretty much anything on, say, a Bowflex" (Scott).

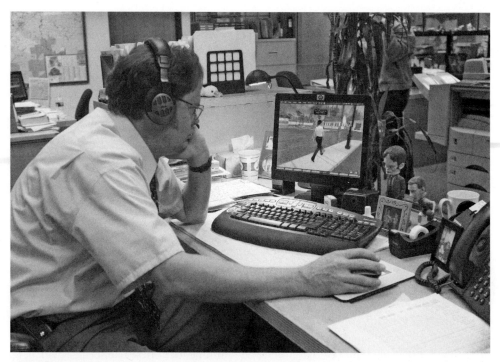

Dwight Schrute expresses his deluded impression of himself as a modern-day superhero through the online game *Second Life,* where his avatar, "Dwight Shelford," "was also a paper salesman . . . absolutely everything was the same. Except I could fly."

Other forms of popular culture lay bare the crazy incongruity of traditional ideas about "real" men and the circumstances of contemporary men's lives. The television series *The Office,* for example, satirizes conventional ideas of masculine power through characters such as Dwight Schrute, whose fantasies of empowerment contrast sharply with the smallness and drudgery of his life as assistant regional manager in a paper company.

The implausibility of Dwight's performance of super-potency offers a very crude example of the process whereby the strength of conventional gender identities is undone by their anxious and exaggerated reinforcement. The more extreme the enactment, the less solid the original idea appears. Of course one risk of parody is that the standard that one is playing with or trying to ironically undercut is actually reinforced through its repetition. The over-the-top guy culture in films like *Old School, Superbad,* and *Knocked Up* is an example of the ambiguity of satire. In each film, a supporting cast of immature, sexist guys highlights by contrast the slightly more progressive main character. The optimistic explanation for the huge appeal of these movies among men and women is that we enjoy rooting for the nice guy, and we're laughing *at* rather than *with* his boorish friends. Ironic humour is never that simple, though, and the idea of masculinity represented in these films is complicated by the persona of actors such as Will Ferrell, Seth

Rogen and Jonah Hill, none of whom possess traditional Hollywood leading-men looks. When damaging gender **stereotypes** are enacted by cartoonish versions of gender extremes (this works clearest in actual cartoons; think: Gaston in Disney's *Beauty and the Beast*), it's easy to dismiss them; however the fat and/or boyish bodies of many of the actors in the current crop of comedies can make their offensive behaviour seem goofy and endearing. As critic Scott Stoneman puts it: "How do you make masculinity seem innocuous? Make it fat. Nonetheless, as innocuous as the characters Jonah Hill and Seth Rogen play seem, the things they say are straightforwardly misogynist" (Stoneman). The **realism** of these films (unlike *The Office*, which is clearly satirical) increases the likelihood of our sympathetic identification with the characters, and unquestioning acceptance of the conventions they embody.

Performativity

Some gender theorists employ the concept of **performativity** to challenge widely held assumptions of a natural connection between biological sex, sexual orientation, and gender identity (in its crudest formulation, the assumptions look something like: "If you have a penis, you will be sexually attracted to women, and will enjoy hunting, playing sports, and watching *24*"). With its connotations of the theatre, in which actors play scripted roles, performativity, formulated most extensively in the work of Judith Butler, is an apt metaphor for the enactment of masculine and feminine identities. The script—which, in broad social terms, would refer to mythologized gender ideals (for a discussion of **mythology,** see Chapter 3)—is naturalized through its repeated performance. At the same time, the whole concept of performance, which is based on re-presentation—*playing*, not being—throws into doubt the solidity of the identity on which it is supposedly based.

While departing from the script is not an option—*all* selves reproduce to some extent socially prescribed roles—the recognition that it *is* a script disables its authority. For those whose identities have always been precarious—women, gays and lesbians, transgendered people, and racial minorities—the anti-authoritarian potential of performativity is always implicit. Their identities challenge the mythological norm whether they realize it or not, no matter how tightly they try to conform to their assigned roles. A more significant challenge is mounted by such self-conscious performances as the hyper-feminized display of drag queens or the assumption of typical "butch" or "femme" lesbian identities. These performances, by re-presenting gender norms to excess, draw spectacular attention to their artificiality.

As critics of Butler have suggested, however, it is easy to exaggerate the subversive power of performativity. In a cultural context in which the manipulation of conventional gender *style*—in the form of clothes, accessories, hair, and so on—has become an element of high fashion, the political implications of gender–role playing can't be assumed in advance. This is particularly true given that the capacity to play around with sex and gender depends a lot on one's social position, including one's race, culture, and class. The stakes of "passing"—conforming convincingly to accepted ideals of beauty, behaviour, and belief—are not the same for everyone. The 2000 film *Boy's Don't Cry* shows the limits of theories of the liberating potential of performativity. The film adapts the real-life story of Brandon Teena—a.k.a. Teena Renae Brandon—who was born female, but identified as a heterosexual male. While Brandon's performance, portrayed in the film by Hilary Swank, was by all accounts convincing—"he" managed to pass as male with a number of girlfriends—the discovery of "her" biological gender resulted in his/her rape and murder. Gender identity may be performative, something that we *do* rather than what we *are;* however the social stage on which we perform these identities still forcefully restricts possibilities for improvisation.

Identity and Power/Knowledge

A critical premise informing psychoanalytic and Marxist thought, foregrounded by feminism, is that identity is defined by and through power.

Michel Foucault   French philosopher and social critic Michel Foucault (1926–1984) devoted particular attention to that relationship, showing how power both constrains and produces social meaning, especially that privileged site of meaning that is individual identity. One of the crucial ways Foucault's theory departs from that of Marx is in his understanding of how power operates in society. While traditional Marxist theory conceives of power as belonging to, or wielded by, a ruling class (similar to the assumption in early feminist theory that power rests primarily in the hands of men), Foucault saw its function in a much more nuanced way.

Moving beyond the obvious critiques that Marxists and feminists could direct at one another—that class is complicated by gender and vice versa, so power could never be said to rest in the hands of a single, identifiable group—Foucault suggested that power is not possessed at all; rather, it circulates continuously throughout society, concentrating in different places at different historical moments and constituting particular meanings and identities as it does so. Foucault's theory does not contest Marx's point that power is unequally distributed; rather, it questions the stability of that distribution, emphasizing its fluidity and the ambiguity of its effects. One of Foucault's most significant insights is his observation that power shapes society productively rather than repressively. This does not mean that all of the effects of power are good; it means, rather, that power takes the form not only of regulations restricting people's freedom to be, speak, or act a certain way, but also of **discourses**—whole systems of thought, speech, and knowledge *production* that structure institutional and social practices (see Chapter 3).

Foucault was particularly interested in the period of the late eighteenth and early nineteenth centuries (not coincidentally, the same period that Marx's work focused on), a period in which cultivation of the *self* took on a new urgency. As we have mentioned above, before the eighteenth century the idea of individuals possessing complex and meaningful interior lives did not hold much interest. The idea began to gain currency not because people were finally free to "be themselves," but because, in an industrial-capitalist society, characterized by the fragmentation of old social hierarchy and the burgeoning of a middle class whose entrepreneurial energies translated into new forms of wealth and freedom for individuals, new forms of social discipline were required to maintain order. As Freud, Marx, and others had already clearly shown, discipline need not take the form of physical force or punishment, or even law; it works most effectively through the largely unconscious internalization of ideas, values, and modes of discrimination that are represented as natural, or "common sense." Thus "discipline," in Foucault's sense, combines what are usually seen as two separate meanings of the word, the first associated with methods of training or techniques designed to enforce obedience, and the second with branches of knowledge (e.g., science, modern languages, philosophy) characterized by particular rules or methods.

By highlighting the connection between forms of knowledge and the exercise of power (significantly, "discipline," when used in this second sense, can be either a noun or a verb), Foucault emphasizes the material consequences of knowledge as it becomes classified into different discourses—medicine, for example, or the law—that are enacted, or put into effect, through institutions such as hospitals, schools, and prisons. These institutions play a critical role in the reproduction of social hierarchies, and in the shaping of individuals through technologies of treatment, training, or punishment. Foucault's work on prisons in particular led to particular insights into the way technologies of discipline that were developed in the eighteenth century led to new forms of self-regulation and management.

An important architectural innovation in eighteenth-century prisons was the *panopticon,* a structure comprising a tower erected in the centre of a courtyard with cells arranged all around it (see Figure 6.1). All the cells were visible from the tower and—more importantly—the tower was visible from all the cells. The special disciplinary power of the panopticon lay not so much in the power it gave guards to keep an eye on the prisoners, but rather in the effect it had on the prisoners themselves, who had a sense of being constantly under **surveillance** whether there was anyone in the tower or not. The prisoners' internalization of the disciplinary gaze of the tower represents a concrete model of a more general process, intensified throughout the nineteenth century, in which individuals came to subject themselves to a kind of social scrutiny. They developed, in other words, what Foucault termed "technologies of the self," modes of conscious self-construction devised in response to naturalized systems of social power. Central to this process of self-construction was an awareness of the physical body, whose control and management is always the ultimate end of power.

The History of Sexuality

The need for a disciplined labour force in an industrial economy, combined with the unstable conditions of life in industrial society—crowded slums, the decline of traditional institutional checks on individual behaviour, along with new opportunities for leisure—led to a heightened focus on the body as a critical site of social regulation and discipline. Sexuality thus became a preoccupation in the latter half of the nineteenth century, with a host of moral codes, laws, medical theories, and treatments designed to investigate and

Figure 6.1 Panopticon

Jeremy Bentham's panopticon worked to maintain the effect of constant surveillance whether the central watchtower was occupied or not.

manage it. The idea that the Victorians were obsessed with sex is, of course, nothing new. Where Foucault's theory departs from conventional assumptions is in his insistence that sexuality, as a unified collection of drives, fantasies, and behaviour, is not a natural foundation of human identity repressed in the nineteenth century and now liberated; rather, sexuality as a coherent idea emerged in the nineteenth century *at the same time, and as a product of* its construction as an object of discourse.

Of course, that does not mean that sex did not exist before the nineteenth century, only that it was not constituted as an object of knowledge in the way that it came to be in the nineteenth century and still is today. People obviously had feelings about sex and engaged in sexual activity; these feelings and acts were subject to discussion and representation in literature, popular media, and pornography, and, occasionally, to legislation. What differentiated this earlier view was the indistinguishability from other aspects of daily life of those behaviours and characteristics we now associate with sex. Only in connection with the production of "sexuality" as a subject of discourse did it come to assume its significance as a critical component of identity.

The historical production of "normal" sexuality as an idea does not precede, but actually coincides with, the emergence of the concept of *homo*sexuality as a way of classifying a form of sexual deviance. As with other forms of classification whose historical emergence Foucault traces (e.g., the concept of madness, along with its particularly gendered form of hysteria), homosexuality is not an actual condition or mode of being but rather what Foucault terms a "regulatory fiction," produced as part of a system of social control that works on the basis of drawing a distinction between "normal" and "deviant" identities. This key distinction, which is reproduced through the discourses mentioned above—medicine (particularly psychiatry) and law—underwrites a whole network of practices that work, through treatment, punishment, and exclusion, to enforce social conformity. The reasons for the production of homosexuality as an object of discourse at a particular juncture in history are complex, stemming in part from the need to secure the integrity of the newly emerging institution of the nuclear family as a place for the reproduction of bourgeois social values; thus, the regulatory fiction of sexuality is closely tied to the regulatory fiction of gender.

The critical point to emphasize here is the entanglement of identity—specifically, that highly charged component of identity that we have come to define as sexuality—with power. Power should be understood here not as a mechanism of repression or oppression, as the theories of Freud or Marx would seem to imply, but rather as a force whose impulse to control and regulate is facilitated by its productive capacity, its ability to bring into being new objects, new knowledges.

It is this productive, generative aspect of power that makes it so ambiguous and volatile. The concept of homosexuality, Foucault suggests, did not just underwrite the production of new systems of social control: "it also made possible the formation of a 'reverse' discourse: homosexuality began to speak on its own behalf, to demand that its legitimacy or 'naturality' be acknowledged, often in the same vocabulary, using the same categories by which it was medically disqualified" (101–102). In other words, while the "invention" of homosexuality serves institutional interests, embodying a new object of knowledge and by extension a new tool of social regulation, it also opens new possibilities for modes of identity formation and associated pleasures.

Summary of the Key Theories of Identity

Foucault's insights into the operation of power—that it is all-encompassing, circulating throughout the whole social body rather than remaining in the possession of particular groups, and that it works not by restriction but by the production of new meanings, new identities, new objects of knowledge—build on the insights of Freud and Marx to tell us some key things about identity: (1) it arises not from within individuals or groups, but from the complex social structures—and, in particular, the relations of power—in which those individuals and groups are situated; (2) it is historically specific, such that some aspects of identity—**individualism**, for example, or homo/heterosexuality—emerge as particularly significant in the context of particular social or economic arrangements; and (3) it is both imaginary and real: imaginary in the sense that its apparently essential qualities are ideologically or discursively constructed, and real in the sense that those constructions have material consequences in the form of laws and policies, beliefs and actions.

Ideologies of individualism are concretized in laws relating to private property, freedom of expression, and human rights, while discourses of sexuality are implicated in regulations and practices that seek to police or treat so-called deviant forms of sexual behaviour (regulations and practices that sometimes conflict with the laws designed to uphold the rights of the individual). The embodiment of the concept of identity in legal, educational, and medical institutions firmly entrenches it as a fundamental principle in Western society. It is not merely those institutional imperatives that make identity so compelling to us as individuals; rather, it is also the way in which our own needs and desires are interpellated, or addressed by those institutions, which leads us to internalize a sense of identity as something we simply cannot do without.

KEEPING THE STORY STRAIGHT? REPRESENTING HOMOSEXUALITY ON TV

Identity, says cultural theorist Iain Chambers, is "a labour of the imagination, a fiction, a particular story that makes sense" (25). We began this chapter with a cinematic example of the way stories of identity function in our culture. Here, we will expand on those earlier comments by looking in more detail at an example of a television program that highlights some of the complexities and ambiguities of identity.

Sexuality is a particularly highly charged area for the production of identity. The strong feelings surrounding sexuality are especially evident in discussions of homosexuality, a concept which, Foucault has shown, emerged as the deviant "other" of a socially regulated (patriarchal, monogamous, married) heterosexuality. In the last few decades, great strides have been made in popular and political culture toward a more inclusive vision of sexuality. Changes in the laws regulating sexual behaviour, including the rights and privileges surrounding cohabitation and marriage, have been accompanied (and arguably influenced) by more positive representations of homosexuality in the media. Looking at an example of

In the last decade of the twentieth century, homosexuality assumed an accepted and increasingly prominent place in television shows such as *Will & Grace* and *The L-Word* and movies such as *Brokeback Mountain*. While some shows, such as *Dawson's Creek*, took an explicitly didactic or moralistic tone, others, such as *Queer as Folk*, were hailed (or condemned) by critics for their out-and-out, often graphic, celebration of homosexual relationships.

one such representation can help us to see some of the tensions and anxieties that still inform the construction of gay—and, by implicit extension, straight—identities.

Coming Out on Dawson's Creek   In 1999 *Dawson's Creek* aired a series of episodes that were remarkable at the time for their unusually sensitive portrayal of a teenager's coming to terms with his homosexuality. One of the main elements in the episode, a feature inherent in the coming-out story, is an emphasis on affirming homosexuality as an *identity*, an essential part of a person's character that is repressed by a homophobic society. Drawing on the idea that truth is revealed through art, Jack's sexual orientation is first hinted at by a poem he reads aloud to his English class. Counselled by Dawson to "listen to yourself . . . I mean, poetry is your chance to give the world a peek at the innermost, private part of yourself that you'd otherwise stifle," Jack writes a poem describing a male figure and an "inner fear" ("To Be or Not to Be"). Before he can finish reading it, he bursts into tears and runs from the classroom. The poem sparks a fire of speculation among his friends—not least his girlfriend, Joey (Katie Holmes)—about whether or not he is gay.

Besides Jack's strict and stereotypically patriarchal father, the character who reacts most intolerantly to his declaration is Ty, the Christian boyfriend of the much more liberal Jen (Michelle Williams). Ty's angry comments about the deviance of "the homosexual lifestyle" are strongly countered by Jen's defence of sexual freedom. The show clearly asks us to reject Ty's views—which, however sincerely motivated, spring from a lack of understanding compounded by guilt and confusion about his own sexuality. Interestingly, though, we are not encouraged to endorse the idea of absolute sexual freedom—not quite—as can be seen from the reaction of another character on the show.

Jen's friend, Abby, is the series' "bad girl," whose selfishness and sexual promiscuity stand in stark contrast to the more morally upright, thoughtful, and self-disciplined characters of Dawson and Joey. (Indeed, Joey expresses her uncertainty about Jack with the comment that she can't "read his eyes" the way she can Dawson's ["And That Is the Question"].) In a show that admits much moral murkiness, being honest and true to oneself is a primary virtue.

Given the questions the show casts on Abby's constancy and integrity, we inevitably respond with suspicion when she advises Jack (in classic *Dawson's Creek*–style academic-speak), "Gay . . . is just a name people came up with to persecute the normal inclination to go both ways. We're all bisexual, don't you think? We're all just sexual animals under God. This . . . society would make us think our natural impulses are something to be ashamed of, when really it's those kind of attitudes that are the embarrassment" ("Be Careful What You Wish For"). The moral dangerousness of her comments—highlighted by a quick cut to a scene in a bar in which Dawson and Jack's sister, Andie, are getting drunk—is confirmed by Abby later kissing a confused Jack, just as Joey walks in. The clear implication of an encounter that serves ultimately to convince Jack that he really *is* gay is to emphasize the importance of clear-cut, straightforward identities versus a more fluid, uncertain terrain of desire that is shown to lead only to pain and social disorder.

The importance attached to the consistency of identity is highlighted by fans and critics who criticized Jack's coming out as "unconvincing and insincere" (Nos4a2). Noting that "there wasn't a hint of his homosexuality before his secret was revealed during February sweeps" (Fretts), they dismiss the coming out as "a plot device on a soap opera" (Nos4a2). There is no doubt truth to the charge that the timing of Jack's revelation of his homosexuality was prompted by a commercial drive for ratings; we might also speculate about whether an increase in audience viewership of the episodes in question reflects acceptance or prurient curiosity—that is, does it speak to a perception of homosexuality as normal or deviant? However the issue of whether the portrayal is convincing or not speaks to different concerns, about the failure of the show to convey "real life."

The constraints of the weekly television drama that require the simplification and concentration of dramatic situations so they can be presented and resolved within a 45-minute time slot make it easy to respond—as the fan quoted above does—by acknowledging "maybe I shouldn't take stupid TV shows seriously" (Nos4a2); however, dismissing *Dawson's Creek* and its portrayal of homosexuality ignores the role of television as part of a larger network of ideological state apparatuses that inform and *mediate* the way we understand ourselves and others. Rather than condemning the representation of Jack because it is less coherent and consistent than "real-life" homosexual identities, it is useful to think about television as one of the many resources that help to define who we are. Thinking about the production of stories on television can prompt us to start thinking about the broader networks of production in which our own "stories," the building blocks of our identities, are implicated.

Current Debates on Homosexuality   *Dawson's Creek* illuminates some of the larger stories that define the meaning of homosexuality in North American culture. In particular, it self-consciously addresses a number of critical debates about the meaning of homosexuality, including the issues of whether homosexuality is a matter of nature or choice, and whether sexuality is defined by the binary poles of hetero- or homosexual orientation or operates on a continuum, with most people falling somewhere in between the two extremes in being attracted primarily to one sex or the other. With respect to the first debate, *Dawson's Creek's* clear insistence on the biological basis of sexual preference, a thesis generally supported by the medical community, earned widespread approval from members of the gay community and other media commentators. By emphasizing the *naturalness* of homosexual attraction, the show effectively refuted the thesis, advanced by anti-gay crusaders, that homosexuality represents a deviant lifestyle *choice* that can be altered through faith and willpower. It further advanced the important goal of naming and claiming homosexual identity as a source of pride and personal fulfillment, not shame and alienation: later episodes depict Jack as a happy and well-balanced young adult, enjoying a loving sexual relationship.

In considering the implications of this representation of homosexuality, however, it is worth recalling Foucault's discussion of the historical production of a concept of identity centred around sexuality. Though sexual identity can offer a route to a positive sense of self and social integration, it also enables the operation of systems of discipline and social control. Significantly, these systems operate regardless of whether the characteristics they seek to classify and manage are seen as biological or learned. The perils of theories of biological essence emerge clearly in women's struggles to overcome stereotypes of "natural" feminine weakness or intellectual inferiority. Even more disturbingly, claims for the biological basis of certain aspects of identity do not preclude their regulation and control—just think about the technological and ethical debates surrounding the possibilities of genetic engineering.

In sum, looking at representations of identity, particularly those that focus on the fraught issue of sex, reveals the stakes of **identity politics** to be more confusing than they might initially seem. Affirming a **minority** identity can be an important way of bolstering a sense of worth that has been denied by mainstream society, as well as of asserting moral and legal rights. At the same time, by insisting on the qualities of individualism, binary categories ("you're either straight or you're gay, no two ways about it"), and consistent adherence to the conventions of a particular identity, such affirmations also work to preserve the status quo of a social order that is still defined by the regulation of self-expression and activity, particularly in the realm of sexuality. In Chapter 7, we will explore the implications of upholding and challenging the concept of identity in relation to racial and cultural differences.

DIFFERENT BODIES, DIFFERENT SELVES?

As the discussion of sexuality above makes clear, questions of identity cannot be pursued very far without reference to the body. The relationship between identities and bodies is the subject of this section, which asks questions such as: What role does the body play in the production of the self? Can we even define a "self" as distinct from the body? To what extent are our bodies the products of nature, and to what extent are they the products of our individual control? How are our bodies shaped or constrained by culture and vice versa? The answers to these questions all have significant bearing on the issue of *agency:* our power to act independently in the world, to determine our own meanings, our own actions, our own pleasures.

Embodied Selves

Descartes's famous formula, "I think therefore I am," informs the modern notion of identity as defined by the preeminence of mind (consciousness) over matter (the body). Descartes' elevation of the rational mind as the faculty that gives meaning to human life, granting it supremacy over other, non-rational forms of life, informs a dualist philosophy characterized by a series of closely overlapping oppositions—spirit versus matter, mind versus body, reason versus passion, nature versus culture—that map out relations of being and, more significantly, relations of power. Besides laying the groundwork for laws surrounding the protection of private property, this framework has underwritten such dubious social practices as slavery and the subjugation of women on the grounds of a division of living beings into knowing subjects—"man"—and knowable (and possessable) objects.

Postmodernist thought has posed significant challenges to the dualisms that inform the modern concept of identity—and indeed much of modern Western philosophy (see Close-Up 6.1). In particular, postmodernism has blurred the scientific and/or philosophical certainty of distinctions between subjects and objects, consciousness and matter that allow us to know the world while remaining abstracted from, superior to it. The destabilization of philosophical dualisms associated with postmodernist thought is reflected by the more general breakdown of structure and hierarchy associated with contemporary social life. As old hierarchies dissolve—and with them any clear sense of identity based on birth, breeding, or old notions of class—the body becomes an increasingly important site for the negotiation of social meaning. In some ways, the new attention focused on the body reflects a move away from seeing bodies as simply containers for identity and toward recognition of the ways in which the self is embodied—at once natural and cultural, physical and psychological.

Postmodernism

It has been said that postmodernism has come to have so many meanings that it is impossible to offer any simple definition. In the words of the critic Peter Brooker, postmodernism is "annoyingly elusive in its range of reference and attributions whether in academic debate or across the arts and culture" (174). Such variation in meaning has led many people to dismiss the term.

Generally, postmodernism refers to a phase in Western history that coincides with the information revolution and new forms of economic, social, and cultural life. Postmodernism names a period—the current era—and points to the fundamental differences of this era from even the recent past (i.e., modernism, ranging from roughly the mid–nineteenth to the mid–twentieth century).

The Human Body: Natural or Cultural?

Once we start to explore the entanglement of nature and culture in relation to the body, it becomes harder and harder to determine where one ends and the other begins. The body may be a material phenomenon, but the way we experience it is determined by culture. Concepts of health and disease are one case in point. Anthropologist Emily Martin has investigated the role of myth and metaphor in the way science understands the human body—for example, by looking at it as a kind of machine, or by employing metaphors of war to describe the operation of the immune system in maintaining health. Thus, we "fight" disease; our white blood cells "seek out and destroy" pathogens. The metaphorical construction of the body has especially interesting social implications in relation to the representation of reproductive processes. Think, for example, of what it might mean for conventional gender mythology if we were to replace the familiar, almost cartoonish image of eager sperm competing to *penetrate* the docile, receptive egg—an image comically rendered in Woody Allen's 1972 movie *Everything You Always Wanted to Know About Sex (But Were Afraid to Ask)*—with what some scientists suggest is a more accurate image of a tiny wiggling sperm being *enveloped* by the much larger egg (E. Martin). (See Figure 6.2.)

One of the major changes in contemporary society lies in the character of the global economy. Rather than being based on the production of new things, economic transactions increasingly involve non-material **commodities**: stocks, information, the arts, and services (health care, fast food, tourism). The economy, then, is increasingly fuelled by culture, and culture, by extension, has become increasingly defined by economics. It is this development that Fredric Jameson refers to in his definition of postmodernism as "the cultural logic of late capitalism."

Figure 6.2 A Traditional Image of Conception

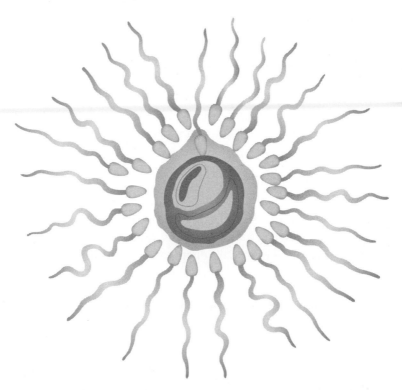

Traditional images of conception owe less to scientific accuracy than to metaphorical representations of gender stereotypes.

The economic circumstances Jameson highlights, along with recent historical developments such as decolonization, civil rights, and feminism, have all contributed to intellectual and cultural changes now described under the heading of postmodernism. The concept is often used to describe a broad shift in approaches to truth and knowledge, away from the rationality and truth-seeking that emerged out of the Enlightenment. Since the late 1950s, the existence of such truths or laws has been challenged. Postmodernism views the search for truth as a project whose real aim is achieving social power and control, and is suspicious of any "grand narratives" or theories that seek to provide the single explanation for how human beings act (such as Freudian psychoanalysis) or how societies function (Marxism, for example).

The general public seems to share this skepticism to some degree: where only a few decades ago people had faith in specialists (such as doctors) and their political leaders, now there is widespread skepticism toward those who claim great expertise—as in Britain in February 2003, when the public simply did not believe what Prime Minister Tony Blair had to say about the threat posed by Iraq.

Postmodernism also refers to styles and movements in arts and culture that express this skeptical attitude, characterized by self-consciousness, formal and stylistic borrowing, irony, pastiche, parody, recycling, sampling, and a mixing of high and low culture. Films and novels today frequently highlight the fact that they are cultural constructions. For example, in the 2006 film *Stranger than Fiction*, the main character (Will Ferrell) is trapped in a story being narrated by someone else, a woman (played by Emma Thompson) whom he eventually meets. Cultural products today make self-conscious use of older forms to create new culture, such as Todd Haynes's film *Far From Heaven*, which mimics the fifties melodramas of Douglas Sirk. Beginning with Andy Warhol, contemporary art has drawn on advertising (Jeff Wall), consumer culture (Jeff Koons), film (Cindy Sherman), and television. Irony and parody characterize the dominant modes of address on television, including "news" shows such as *The Daily Show* and *The Colbert Report* and animated series such as *The Simpsons* and *Family Guy*.

For the French critic Jean Baudrillard, postmodernism is characterized by the culture of the "simulacrum" (1), a copy without an original, or a sign without a referent, defining a world in which representation quite simply is reality. Many find this disturbing, signalling the "emptying out" of history, the disappearance of nature, and the impossibility of defining a platform of belief from which to launch individual projects or political movement. For others, the erosion of traditional concepts of identity translates into exciting possibilities for the construction of new, multiply defined selves. In general, the way we respond to the breakdown of the old structures of meaning depends on whether our particular identities, defined by the traditional markers of class, gender, race, sexuality, and so on, were empowered or excluded by those structures.

Some theorists suggest that the biological category of sex itself is not a natural given, but determined by culture. This is not to say that the physiological differences we refer to in assigning sexual identity do not exist; rather, that they operate much more variably and diffusely than the division of humans and other animals into mutually exclusive categories of "male" and "female" suggests. For example, the designation of sex hormones as male (testosterone) or female (estrogen) does not account for the fact that both hormones are released by men *and* women (Shilling 75).

Moreover, the presence of those hormones—along with other secondary sex charac-teristics such as the size and function of reproductive organs, facial hair, voice, and physique—alters with age and in response to environmental factors such as nutrition and stress. Even the seemingly clear-cut genetic markers of XX (female) versus XY (male) chromosomes are complicated by the presence of other genes influencing physique and behaviour, not to mention the range of conditions that can affect the "normal" correspon-dence of genes to physiological characteristics. In short, humans are characterized by biological variances relating to reproductive capacity; however, the reduction of those variances to the fixed, bipolar categories "male" and "female" comes about not through nature but through *culture*. The cultural basis of fundamental sex differences is highlighted by the different values and meanings accorded those differences in different times and places. In pre–eighteenth-century Europe, for example, women were viewed as biologically inferior to, but not fundamentally different from, men. The view of sexual difference as one of kind rather than degree arose in conjunction with the need to reconcile the continued disenfranchisement of women with new views about the universal rights of "man" (Laqueur 19).

Learned "Body Techniques"   But culture does not influence only the way we understand bodies; it also becomes inscribed on bodies themselves. As sociologist and anthropologist Marcel Mauss (1872–1950) noted, the way we conduct such basic activities as sleeping, eating, sitting, walking, having sex, and giving birth should be understood not as natural, but as a series of "body techniques" that are *learned* in particular social contexts and are hence culturally and historically specific. One of the most striking examples Mauss provides is French women's characteristic style (or technique) of walking, which changed in the 1930s with the arrival of American cinema: the movies carried with them a whole repertoire of fashion comprising ways not just of dressing, but also of comportment, of holding and carrying the body.

While French women's imitation of styles of movement associated with Hollywood film might be prompted by an association of the U.S. with images of energy and freedom, most body techniques serve a much more utilitarian function in relation to the demands of a smoothly running society. In most societies, this means that considerable effort is expended in what Mauss calls "education in composure . . . a mechanism inhibiting disorderly movements" (474). Thus we learn not only how to move, but also how and when to inhibit movement, techniques that differ significantly by age and gender.

The Self-Controlled Body   The idea that culture exerts a shaping and restraining effect on the body is carried further in the work of sociologist Norbert Elias (1897–1990), who documented the process by which centuries of Western civilization produced the modern, individualized, self-controlled body. In Volume 1 of *The Civilizing Process,* Elias uses the concept of "civilization" not in the sense in which it is often used, to imply the progressive movement beyond the "backward" ways of the past, but rather to describe a series of specific historical changes in Europe, from the hardscrabble social world of the Middle Ages to the court society of the Renaissance, whose influence shapes our present-day culture. In particular, Elias focuses on the shift from a way of life in which physical strength, aggression, and indulgence of appetites were necessary to survival to one in which "polite society" defined by the court dictated increasingly complex social rituals, successful observance of which played a significant role in determining one's social status.

One of the critical aspects of this shift is a move toward interdependence, such that existence had to be negotiated with an increasing awareness of the effects of one's behaviour on others. Thus the civilized body is one that is subject to an expanding set of taboos and social codes, demarcating it sharply from the physical environment and from other bodies. Practices that were once widely tolerated, such as defecating in public or sharing beds with strangers, were subjected to increasingly strict social sanction as a new model of appropriate bodily conduct emerged. This new model was characterized by a broad repertoire of gestures—manners—that signified an observance of social relations, including an overall tendency toward self-restraint and a clear sense of separation between private and public.

Physical Capital and Social Status

Of course, body techniques and codes of civilized behaviour vary from social situation to social situation (for example, what's acceptable at a rave differs considerably from what's appropriate at your Great Aunt Ethel's tea party) and depending on what position one occupies in society (class, gender, etc.). Sociologist Pierre Bourdieu (1930–2002) sheds light on these differences by expanding Mauss's concept of the *habitus.* A term connoting both living space and habit, **habitus** describes the way in which particular social environments are internalized by individuals in the form of dispositions toward particular bodily orientations and behaviours.

The concept of habitus thus allows us to talk about the way in which social differences are reproduced at the level of the individual body. Class, Bourdieu suggests, plays a determining role in the development of bodies by influencing such factors as social location and taste (learned habits of discrimination influencing choice of lifestyle—discussed in Chapter 5), as well as more physical aspects of habitus. These differences in turn contribute to the production of different kinds and degrees of social value attached to different kinds of bodies. Value corresponds more or less closely to class, with working-class bodies possessing less value than dominant-class bodies—value here is determined principally by the ability to translate what Bourdieu terms physical capital into other forms of capital: economic (money), cultural (education), and social (networks of belonging).

Of course, the different kinds of capital don't map perfectly onto one another: professional sport has traditionally offered a venue for men from underprivileged circumstances to convert physical capital into economic capital in a fairly direct way. However, the heavy toll professional sport—like most forms of physical labour—exacts on the body, combined with its relatively restricted access as a career path, diminishes its significance as an exception to the rule that "white-collar" bodies tend to enjoy more privileged access to forms of economic, social, and cultural capital than do "blue-collar" bodies.

A somewhat crude example of the relationship between taste and habitus and social and economic capital can be seen in the 1988 film *Working Girl,* in which Tess (Melanie Griffith), a secretary, employs her brains and ambition to land an executive position and an attractive, financially successful husband (Harrison Ford). An important component of her social and economic advancement is her successful cultivation of her appearance, voice, and gestures in order first to impersonate, and then truly to embody the image of a female executive. One scene has her pedalling frantically on an exer-cycle while trying to imitate phrases and intonations of speech from a tape of her boss (Sigourney Weaver) giving a speech. Perhaps the clearest sign of her progress—besides her successful business negotiations with and seduction of Harrison Ford—is the increasingly striking contrast throughout the film of Tess to her best friend (Joan Cusack), whose permanently entrenched position in the secretarial rank is signalled by her big hair, caked-on blue eye-shadow, and vampish clothes.

Premised on outrageous class (and gender) stereotypes, *Working Girl* clearly can't be read as a sociological comment on how **class mobility** operates in "real life." However, its tremendous popularity, particularly among women, illustrates the pervasiveness of cultural myths about the role of physical appearance and behaviour in achieving—and, even more importantly, deserving—social and economic status.

In an interesting contrast with *Working Girl,* the 2002 movie *Maid in Manhattan* is much less conscious about the ways in which class and social position are articulated through bodily disposition or habitus. Unlike in *Working Girl,* where Tess has to unlearn her natural speech, gestures, and tastes to play the role of someone of a higher class, all it takes to transform Marisa (Jennifer Lopez) into a credible imitation of a rich socialite is a Dolce & Gabbana pantsuit. While both movies follow a fairytale format, *Working Girl* was arguably more realistic about the barriers to social mobility—barriers that are ingrained on the body.

Ingrained Habit—Culture Becoming Nature

One of the most obviously mythical elements of films such as *Working Girl* and *Maid in Manhattan*—besides the stereotypes—is the assumption the films make that, through a combination of pluck and intelligence, it is possible for anyone to transform her or himself, mentally and physically, into whomever she or he wants to be. *Maid in Manhattan* was perhaps less wildly unrealistic in this respect: while Tess catapults from secretary to senior executive, Marisa just rises through the ranks of the service industry, from maid to manager. This difference may simply reflect a change in ideologies of identity and work, particularly with respect to gender, from the late 1980s to the early twenty-first century.

While the message conveyed by *Working Girl* was a strongly feminist one, inflected by the emphasis on individualism and corporate success in Ronald Reagan's America, *Maid in Manhattan* offers a view of ideal femininity that, depending on your perspective, is either less progressive (economic equality with men isn't really important so long as you're feisty, beautiful, and a good mom), or more so (identity is not defined by work). Both movies, however, arguably downplayed the physical consequences of occupying particular social categories—consequences measurable in terms not just of appearance, but also of one's biological capacities, including health and bodily function. In many instances, learned behaviours have real physical effects that come to actually conform to the stereotype on which the behaviour was initially based.

For example, in an essay entitled "Throwing Like a Girl," Iris Marion Young identifies a tendency in Western industrial societies for girls to move in ways that are more limited and constrained than the ways in which boys move. In effect, responding to a learned physical orientation that Young calls "inhibited intentionality" (145), girls and women are not inclined to use their bodies' full potential range of strength and motion. Thus what is often regarded as women's "natural" lack of physical strength and coordination is at least partly attributable to the way in which their bodies are socialized to move (or not) in particular ways. These learned behaviours, ingrained into habit, contribute to the transformation of women's bodies into the stereotypically "weak vessels" they were already imagined to be.

Nature and culture, then, are inextricably connected in the production of the body as a site of identity formation. Naturally occurring biological variances are simplified and reduced to signs of absolute cultural difference, which themselves come to take on the appearance of nature. The ways in which we conceive of the body influence the way we look at, treat, and inhabit it. Most significantly, cultural influences on the body come to assume physical significance, both at the level of the individual physical body and of the social structures in which individual bodies are placed. Possibilities for modifying and even transcending the body thus become a highly charged cultural and political issue.

ALTERED STATES

While people at all times and in all places have sought to change their bodies in different ways, advances in science combined with the unique pressures of a consumer culture highly biased toward the visual have contributed to a growing trend toward body-cultivation and modification. Body modification describes practices that include "piercing, tattooing,

Our culture's fascination with the not-yet-quite-mainstream phenomenon of extreme body modification is exploited by reality television shows such as *Dr. 90210*, about Beverly Hills plastic surgeons and their patients.

branding, cutting, binding and inserting implants," as well as less invasive practices such as exercise and diet, that seek to alter "the appearance and form of the body" (Featherstone 1). Whether these practices are motivated by health or by **aesthetics**, whether they uphold or challenge prevailing social norms, and whether they aim toward the accentuation or transcendence of the body—and few can be so simply classified—they demand examination in relation to the more fundamental questions of how they contribute to the production of individual and social meaning, identity, and power.

Enhancing/Producing the Healthy Body

At the beginning of the twenty-first century, Western cultures have come increasingly to see health as a matter of individual control and responsibility. This trend is reflected in such developments as increasingly stringent legislation on food labelling. Laws requiring uniform labelling on all packaged food (and on restaurant menus in some U.S. states), listing information such as fat content and potential health benefits, makes the assumption that health and fitness are largely dependent on wise consumer choices. A variety of factors have contributed to this development: individuals tend to have much more knowledge and confidence about health-related matters than they did a generation ago, leading to a much more proactive stance in managing their own health. At the same time, both fuelling and responding to this trend, a massive consumer industry has sprung up around personal health care, promoting everything from so-called "nutraceuticals" (drug-enhanced foods) to fitness clubs.

Finally, the rising costs of an increasingly technology-based medical system have led governments and insurance companies to search for ways to encourage less reliance on the system and greater responsibility on the part of individuals in addressing their health needs. This pressure is particularly acute in countries, such as Canada, that have a public health-care system. The idea that health is a human right that should be protected by the entire community through taxation is increasingly hard to sustain in the face of a growing emphasis on the individual as largely in control of, and responsible for, his or her own health. Thus questions about whether individuals who smoke or don't wear seatbelts should be entitled to free health care have begun to appear with some frequency in the media. Increasingly, then, issues surrounding health are being shaped by rhetoric about consumer choice at the same time as they convey more moralistic messages about individual responsibility.

The ambiguity of these messages is reflected in practices surrounding diet and fitness, where the general goal of "health" is overlaid with the complex and often contradictory values of physical and sexual attractiveness (generally associated with pleasure) and moral well-being (frequently defined by discipline and self-denial). In these mixed motivations can be detected the ambivalence about the relationship between self and body discussed above. While the pursuit of exercise as a form of self-improvement might imply on one hand a recognition of an integral connection between body and identity, many practices associated with exercise, including dieting (and its more extreme pathological form, anorexia) are inspired by the idea of the body as an alien thing, separate and requiring discipline from the self.

What's Natural/Normal?

Many health practices are founded on ideas about a natural physical state, which regimes of diet or exercise seek to enhance. These ideas are troubled by the burgeoning popularity of cosmetic surgery that clearly aims less to preserve a "natural" state of health than to produce a "cultural" convention of beauty. Crossing the line from medicine to aesthetics, cosmetic surgery sheds unexpected light on the reliance of both discourses on concepts of *normalization.* Celebrated by many as a technology of self-expression that allows them to convey an outer image that is more in tune with their inner selves, cosmetic surgery is condemned by others as a biotechnological reinforcement of oppressive gender norms (Balsamo).

The operation of such norms is most clearly evident in such forms of cosmetic surgery as liposuction and breast enlargement. While these procedures may be seen—and, more importantly, may actually *work*—to enhance the self-confidence of those who seek them, they do so at the expense of conscripting them more fully into the prescribed roles of a patriarchal social order.

Some forms of body enhancement work more ambiguously. For example, female bodybuilding seems in one sense to challenge conventional gender codes by rejecting a feminine ideal of almost-anorexic thinness. Maximizing instead of minimizing the body—replacing weakness with strength—bodybuilding represents a form of physical feminine empowerment. On the other hand, the maxed-out body is achieved at a cost of punishing discipline and "self"-denial that, at its extreme, actually compromises the goals of health and fitness.

Of course, bodybuilding is about more than health and fitness: like most fitness practices, it is also about display. For women, whose relationships to their bodies have always been mediated by social codes that define them as objects-to-be-looked-at (see Mulvey in Chapter 3), display is at best an ambiguous form of empowerment (Grosz 224). At the same time as it accentuates strength, the culture of bodybuilding still draws attention to the female body as the repository of female worth. As this example demonstrates, body-modification practices may challenge social norms, but they cannot avoid negotiating them. Most practices, like bodybuilding, take place in complicated conversations with our historically ambivalent conceptions about mind and body—conceptions that are inevitably tied to ideas about gender and power.

The Politics of Body Modification   Body modification practices also raise other issues of power and agency. As with highly gendered forms of body modification, the practice of surgically altering black or Asian features to give them a more Caucasian cast can be understood in terms of its promotion of empowerment and/or subjugation. The practice of blepharoplasty, in which a fold is inserted to give the eyes a more rounded, open appearance, gained notoriety in Canada after the death of one patient from a botched,

Disability

Questions about "natural" and "normal" bodies assume particular significance with respect to disability. Over the last few decades the concept of ability has come to replace the language of "normal" versus "abnormal." This generally positive move—a shift from categorizing people according to what they *are* (implying degrees of humanness) to what they can or cannot *do*—has not eliminated practices of discrimination. Disability theorists and activists highlight the way that conventional ways of looking at disability employ discourses of science and medicine to mask aesthetic and societal factors (e.g., **neoliberal** ideologies of individual success; institutional constraints; cultural anxieties about vulnerability and mortality) that privilege the economically productive body. Understood this way, disability is "not so much a property of bodies as a product of cultural rules about what bodies should be and do" (Thomson 6). Without discounting the value of medical interventions, disability activists and theorists work to challenge conventional ideas of disability as lack or inferiority, ideas that reinforce material barriers to disabled people's participation in society. Disability studies echo the concerns of cultural theories of race, gender, and sexuality that challenge the practices of minority exclusion. With respect to disability in particular, the increasing capacity for geneticists to identify (and treat or eliminate) so-called abnormalities in utero highlight what's at stake in definitions of "normal" identity and ability.

illicit operation. The incident sparked an unusual degree of media commentary on the powerful and damaging effect of myths of white normativity. A more nuanced perspective on the subject is expressed in Korean-Canadian Ann Shin's documentary "Western Eyes," which mixes a critical analysis of racialized aesthetic conventions in pop culture with interviews with women who have undergone the procedure. The women emerge from the film neither as victims of the dominant culture nor as models of self-empowerment, but as individuals struggling to define their identities through conflicting codes of physical beauty and normality.

These codes are not "natural"; neither are they solely cosmetic. The complexity of the issues surrounding medical and/or surgical body modification is evident in relation to sex-change procedures, in which transsexual individuals—those whose gender *identity* (masculine or feminine) conflicts with their chromosomal and physiological characteristics—undergo a series of surgical and medical treatments to transform them from male to female or vice versa. While aspects of gender are largely culturally determined, they are sufficiently deep and pervasive that gender identity disorders are considered by the medical community to constitute threats to physical health. Sexual modification blurs the distinction between culture and nature in the determination of what constitutes a "normal" identity. It also demonstrates the ambiguous political implications of body modification: fuelled by dominant codes of sex and gender identity, sex reassignment surgery also throws those codes into confusion, challenging society's deepest prejudices about what constitutes normal.

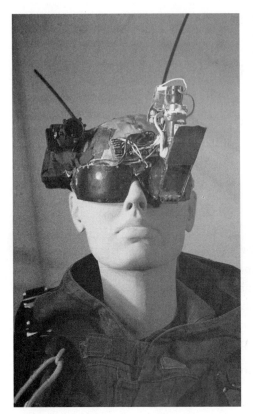

Designed by University of Toronto professor Steve Mann, "WearComp," the first wearable computer technology, blurs the line between human and machine.

Transcending the Body?

The possibilities of body modification are taken to their extreme, at the same time as they are critically challenged, in the work of performance artist Orlan, who has subjected herself to nine plastic-surgery operations—including the implantation of horns in her forehead—in order to explore (and explode) classical notions of beauty. Orlan's is a self-conscious parody of more conventional versions of plastic surgery (which themselves assume an extreme form in the more than 20 operations undergone by American talk show celebrity Cindy Jackson in an eerily successful bid to look like Barbie). Declaring "I don't want to be the Barbie Doll" (qtd. in Goodall 160), Orlan seeks instead to expose the arbitrariness, the unnaturalness, of the standards of beauty that have come to define Western femininity. She does this not in defence of the so-called "real" body, but in order to expose its nonexistence. The body, Orlan observes, "is obsolete. It is no longer adequate for the current situation. We mutate at the rate of cockroaches, but we are cockroaches whose memories are in computers, who pilot planes and drive cars that we have conceived, although our bodies are not conceived for these speeds" (qtd. in Goodall 151).

Orlan's comment reflects the **posthumanist** position that the concepts "man," "self," and "body" that underwrite traditional ideas of human identity have become untenable as society confronts the inextricable entanglement of nature and technology, human and machine. This is not to say that the body *used* to exist in a more or less natural state that has been disrupted or corrupted by technology, but that the increasing difficulty of drawing distinctions between the human and/or natural and the technological highlights the inadequacy of the once-intelligible myth of an autonomous human identity.

Sport is one area where arguments over the almost sacred integrity of the human body are highly charged. Efforts to police the boundary demarcating natural from unnatural bodies result in situations like the attempt on the part of the International Association of Athletics Federation (IAAF), the world track-and-field governing body, to exclude South African sprinter and double amputee Oscar Pistorius from the Olympics on the grounds that his prosthetic legs would give him an unfair advantage. According to his coach, Pistorius (who has broken speed records for disabled sprinters but whose times did not end up meeting the qualifying standards for the 2008 Olympics) faces a number of challenges running with prostheses. If he does perform better than other runners, it is only because he works harder (in Pistorius's own words: "I train harder than other guys, eat better, sleep better and wake up thinking about athletics. I think that's why I'm a bit of an exception" [qtd. in Longman]). An IAAF spokesperson defended the organization's argument for excluding Pistorius: "With all due respect, we cannot accept something that provides advantage. . . . It affects the purity of sport. Next will be another device where people will fly with something on their back" (qtd. in Longman). The line between acceptable and unacceptable body modification is constantly shifting. Performance-enhancing drugs are mostly banned (yet widely used), and so far no restrictions have been placed on golfers or baseball players who undergo laser eye surgery to improve their vision (see Saletan). Given the impossibility of ever establishing an objectively correct standard, the question of who can participate in what athletic activities and under what circumstances has to be approached from a different angle. With respect to the Pistorius case, Robert Gailey, an associate professor of physical therapy at the University of Miami Medical School who has studied amputee runners poses a question for the IAAF: "Are they looking at not having an unfair advantage? Or are they discriminating because of the purity of the Olympics, because they don't want to see a disabled man line up against an able-bodied man for fear that if the person who doesn't have the perfect body wins, what does that say about the image of man?" (qtd. in Longman).

Cyborgs   The figure of the cyborg, an amalgam of human and animal and/or living organism and machine, is not simply the imaginary creation of the producers of cyberpunk novels and movies but an everyday reality, embodied in our use of computers and machines. In a significant way, we have not only come to inhabit technology, but technology has also come to inhabit us, as theorists such as Paul Virilio have pointed out; he cites as one example the medical use of micro-machines to view, diagnose, treat, and enhance the body. Such innovations have the potential to be socially useful, but also scarily invasive. University of Toronto professor and inventor Steve Mann highlights both the possibilities and the dangers of cyborg technology with wearable cameras and computers that turn the tables on such routine uses of surveillance as store security systems.

For many people, the prospect of an ever-closer relationship between humans and machines invokes utopian ideas of a virtual reality in which individuals and communities are able to transcend the limits of nature and their bodies to enjoy ever-greater freedoms. For others, the prospect of a progressive erosion of the integrity of principles such as

The International Association of Athletics Federation's argument for barring (eventually overturned) Oscar Pistorius from Olympic competition on the grounds that his prosthetic limbs give him an unfair advantage raises questions about how we define a natural human body.

"humanity" and "nature" is deeply disturbing, heralding a nightmarish world like the one represented in *Blade Runner,* in which the complexity and beauty of our existence is transformed into a bunch of animate machines.

As athletes such as Oscar Pistorius, artists such as Orlan, and cultural theorists such as Donna Haraway and Steve Mann have shown, however, neither of these visions is ultimately viable. The techno-utopian dream, an extension of the Enlightenment project of harnessing the physical world to human need, relies, like the techno-pessimist vision, on the old idea of a separation between body and mind, nature and culture, that is simply not sustainable. Both the technological and the natural ideal are myths forged out of culture, whose ideological frames limit the possibilities for human liberation.

Contrary to the promises of technophiles and purveyors of cosmetic miracles, "identity has not turned into a free option for all subjects in all situations and all contexts" (Klesse 20). Prevailing structures of gender, class, racial, and sexual inequality mean that everyone does not enjoy the opportunities for self-fulfillment. The limitations on our freedom to define ourselves as we will is also compromised by the fact—of which we are periodically reminded, by environmental catastrophes (some of them human-caused) and by the inevitability of death—that we are not just *in,* but also *of,* nature. The critical issue, which we have tried to stress throughout this chapter, concerns not whether our identities are born or made, or whether they are defined through or against our bodies, but what they mean in terms of our ability to enhance our own and others' power to act in a world not entirely of our own making.

SUGGESTIONS FOR FURTHER READING

Bordo, Susan. *Unbearable Weight: Feminism, Western Culture and the Body.* Berkeley: University of California Press, 1993.

Butler, Judith. *Bodies that Matter: On the Discursive Limits of Sex.* London: Routledge, 1999.

Connell, R.W. *Masculinities.* Berkeley: University of California Press, 1995.

Davis, Lennard J., ed. *Disability Studies Reader.* London: Routledge, 2006.

Featherstone, Mike. *Body Modification.* London: Sage, 2000.

du Gay, Paul, Jessica Evans, and Peter Redman, eds. *Identity: A Reader.* London: Sage, 2000.

Giddens, Anthony. *Modernity and Self-Identity.* Cambridge: Polity, 1991.

Shilling, Chris. *The Body and Social Theory.* London: Sage, 1993.

Woodward, Kathryn, ed. *Identity and Difference.* London: Sage, 2000.

Chapter 7

Identity and Community

INTRODUCTION: WHO DO YOU WANT ME TO BE?

In the pilot episode of the television series *The O.C.*, a memorable meeting occurs between Ryan, the kid from the wrong side of the tracks, and Marissa, the troubled, rich Newport Beach girl who will become his girlfriend. Marissa, who is standing at the end of her driveway waiting for her boyfriend, is stunned to see Ryan step out of the shadows, and asks, "Who are you?" His suave reply—"Whoever you want me to be," establishes his enigmatic coolness, and sets the tone for the quests for identity and connection that Ryan and the other characters embark on throughout the series. It is a scene with mythic resonance in its depiction of the arrival of a mysterious stranger into a close-knit, if deeply dysfunctional, community, whose structure is shaken but never destroyed. It is also an interesting scene with which to begin our discussion of identity and community.

Part of the interest in *The O.C.* (aside from a lot of risky sexual and other behaviours!) revolves around Ryan's struggle to fit in. The pilot episode sets up his lower class status by some clear signifiers: the shots of Chino, the town he comes from, is drab and dingy, an impression heightened by the few actions that occur there: Ryan and his brother in an alley at night, smashing the window of a car his brother has talked him into stealing; Ryan's departure from home—a beat-up bungalow with a pickup on the front lawn—after being punched and thrown out by his mother's alcoholic boyfriend; and finally, Ryan making a desperate call from a graffiti-covered phone booth outside a liquor store to Sandy Cohen, the lawyer who has offered to help him. The bleak featureless drive between Chino and the clean and tree-filled suburb of Newport Beach symbolizes the vast distance between the two worlds—a distance that the show suggests is both hard and, in some ways, weirdly easy, to cross. Although he faces some discrimination from Sandy's wife, Kristin, initially, and also from Luke, Marissa's boyfriend (who clearly has other reasons to be hostile), Ryan takes to the easy life, well, pretty easily, enacting the American popular **myth** of upward mobility. At the same time, he retains his street cred, never losing the aura of romance that comes from his working-class origins. Ryan's story raises many interesting questions that we attempt to work through in this chapter: How do individuals fit (or not fit) into communities? What are the terms of inclusion and exclusion, and how have these changed over time? How do particular identities conflict with and/or reinforce other identities, both individual and collective? How do they work to reinforce and/or undermine structures of power? In this chapter, as in the last, our underlying concern in studying the question of community identity is to explore the way in which identities function in society to help or hinder different people in their efforts to act autonomously or as self-conscious **agents**.

Before we go any further, let's clarify what we mean by community. We hear the word used in numerous contexts: local community, community work, Italian community, community values, gay community, business community, and so on. Generally speaking, a community may be defined as "a social, religious, occupational or other group sharing common characteristics or interests and perceived or perceiving itself as distinct in some respect from the larger society within which it exists" (Dictionary.com). As the examples above suggest, the criteria by which communities are defined—and the significance attached to the defining criteria—vary widely depending on which community is described and who is describing it. It is probably fair to say though that we rarely use the word community in a neutral way, there is usually some explicit or implicit *value*, either positive or negative, attached to the word. But as the last chapter showed, we also attach a lot of value to the idea of the individual. It is therefore not surprising to find in our investigation of popular culture that communities and individuals operate in complicated tension with one another.

This is the case in *The O.C.* In one sense, as the name of the series implies, this is a show about community—a particularly exclusive community, as it happens, whose security is maintained by a literal gate. Part of the show's appeal undoubtedly stems from its **representation** of popular fantasies of how the super-rich live—fantasies that include envy/admiration of their luxury goods, endless leisure, and impossibly hot bodies, as well as *schadenfreude* (a useful German word that means enjoying someone else's bad fortune) at the scrapes they get into, which tend to be bigger and badder than the screwups of ordinary people. It probably doesn't matter much to the audience that it isn't a particularly realistic representation of the community it's supposed to depict: contrary to popular belief, not all rich people are stunningly good looking! More seriously, in the real O.C., in 2005, Asians made up 16.1 percent of the population of the O.C. and Latinos, 32.7 percent (Kelly), while the characters in the television series are overwhelmingly white. Surely if the show focused primarily on community, some effort would be made to get the demographics right. But then, you could argue that the show isn't really all that interested in community in *that* sense—the sense of the **identity politics** of **race**; it is just about individuals, getting into and out of relationships and, especially in the case of the teen characters, asserting their independence and figuring out who they are. There is a sense in which the journey Ryan embarks on in the first episode, from the moment he is kicked out of his family's house to where he's standing on the Cohens' expansive driveway telling Marissa that he can be "whoever she wants him to be," is simply a more literal version of the kind of journey of self-discovery that everyone undergoes in one form or another. And although the characters encounter some pretty spectacular roadblocks, from addiction to infidelity to bankruptcy, the general sense of the show conforms to the myth Ryan embodies of the individual as a free agent who enjoys pretty much complete social mobility. Following the time-tested formula of television and movie drama in which "the glamorous impersonates the ordinary" (Mulvey 326), Seth Cohen, Marissa Cooper and their friends are represented as pretty typical teens. Their neighbourhood might be gated, but, so the myth goes, given a little luck and the right attitude, anyone could be a part of it.

Of course, *The O.C.* is just a television show. But as we note in Chapter 3 ("Representing Popular Culture") and elsewhere in this book, television shows and movies reflect—and also *affect*—our values, fears and fantasies, as well as our sense of identity and community. While *The O.C.* portrays an image of community made up of radically autonomous individuals united by their lavish lifestyle (and, of course, the money to enjoy that lifestyle), a different picture of the relationship between individuals and communities emerges in the Canadian television series *Little Mosque on the Prairie*. Set in the fictional prairie town of Mercy, Saskatchewan, *Little Mosque* focuses on the relations between a small and close-knit group of Muslims in the town and their non-Muslim neighbours. "Community" in this show is therefore not defined by zip or postal code as it is *The O.C.* but by religious affiliation. Interestingly, aside from a vaguely defined Anglicanism associated with the church in which the local mosque rents space, the religion of the non-Muslim characters is neither here nor there. The main community boundary in the show is the division between Muslims and non-Muslims. There are however lots of sub-boundaries with*in* the Muslim group—including one literal separator in an episode that features a debate over whether a partition should be erected in the mosque to separate female from male worshippers. The focus on conflict and complexity between Muslim characters reflects the producers' desire to show non-Muslim audiences that "[the Muslim] community has the same foibles and quirks that any community does" (Dube).

The relationship between individuals and community is very different from that depicted in *The O.C.*, as can be seen in the pilot episode that also centres on the arrival of a stranger. Unlike Ryan, who enters the Cohens' neighbourhood under somewhat dubious circumstances, Amaar Rashid (Zaid Shaikh) arrives in Mercy for entirely legitimate reasons: he has accepted the position of Imam at the local mosque. In keeping with the romantic outsider motif, Rashid is impossibly good-looking. But where Ryan is able to retain his mysterious allure with his enigmatic reply to the question, "Who are you?" Amaar has no such luck. After being interrogated at the airport when a woman overhears him using the words "suicide," "Allah" and "bomb" in a totally innocent phone conversation with his mother, he arrives by taxi in Mercy to be accosted immediately by a reporter who asks him (in a tone not nearly as friendly as Marissa's in *The O.C.*), "Who are you?" By the time Amaar has patiently provided his name, the purpose for his visit, and assurances that he is not a terrorist to the clearly-still-suspicious reporter, a crowd has gathered, creating further confusion that Amaar must once again patiently dispel. Where Ryan in *The O.C.* is granted the power and anonymity of being just a guy—"whoever you want me to be," Amaar is forced to identify himself in order defend his legitimacy against prevailing **stereotypes** of non-white Muslims—a community to which he is inextricably linked, whether he likes it or not. *Little Mosque on the Prairie* challenges those stereotypes, including an assumed association between Muslim faith and a dark, or "Middle Eastern–looking" complexion, with a cast that includes a black Muslim from Africa and a white Muslim convert by marriage. It also depicts the joys and tensions of belonging to a religious community whose laws are subject to debate and controversy from within as well as from without. Conflicts are drawn within and across the Muslim and non-Muslim communities along lines of gender and sexuality. In short, the program treads a precarious line between depicting the "foibles and quirks" that define individuals, and recognizing the ties that bind communities from within and without, by choice and by imposition.

The O.C. and *Little Mosque on the Prairie* are clearly very different shows, in content and genre: *The O.C.* is classified as drama/romance, while *Little Mosque* is a comedy with serious undercurrents, inspired by the experiences of the show's creator, Zarqa Nawaz, living as a Muslim in Regina, Saskatchewan. Both shows contain elements of **realism**. However, the point of comparing them is not to determine which is more true-to-life. In an interview, Nawaz commented that "it rests on my shoulders to get the balance right between entertainment and representing the community in a reasonable way. . . . You have to push the boundaries so you can grow and evolve as a community" (qtd. in MacFarquar 1). One conclusion we may draw from this comment is that cultural producers from **minority** groups (where "minority" is defined not by numbers but by cultural power) feel and/or are held accountable in ways that members of dominant groups are not to the communities they come from for the way they represent those communities: they are more likely to be asked, not just "Who are you?" but "Where are you from?" and "What are you doing?" Shows like *Little Mosque on the Prairie* challenge the myth of liberal **individualism** in favour of a focus on how community boundaries, variously constructed, enable and constrain our actions, identities, and relationships.

Unlike *The O.C.*, *Little Mosque* makes visible the structural, institutional obstacles to achieving the principle of individual equality. Ultimately, though, the show endorses the principle that, as one Muslim viewer put it, "we're all the same at the end of the day" (Kamal Nawash, qtd. in Dube). What does that mean, exactly? Some cultural commentators argue that the **humanism** that underlies such statements tends to work to normativize, or establish as a default, the experience and perspective of the dominant group. This perspective tends to flatten out the beliefs, traditional practices, and historical experiences of minority groups in favour of a superficial affirmation of different styles of dress and cuisine as colourful accessories that liven up our otherwise uniform, "normal" way of

Shows like *Little Mosque on the Prairie* highlight obstacles to achieving equality in hopes of eliminating them.

social interaction (think "Diversity Day" on the television show *The Office*).

Identity politics, or the strategic assertion of a racial or cultural unity, is one response to the marginalization and/or invisibility of minorities that this seemingly universal perspective produces. Unlike the exclusivist identity claims of majority groups, which operate often invisibly to secure existing power imbalances, identity politics challenge the status quo in their explicit bid for recognition and the extension of majority rights to minority groups. The term "identity politics" is often used in a negative way to describe what some critics see as loud demands for special treatment by minority groups. Others, including some members of those groups, contend that *all* rights claims and struggles over power emerge from particular locations and particular constellations of identity; identity politics just makes visible the lines of exclusion and belonging. Identity politics can work strategically as assertions of legitimacy and value by groups who have traditionally suffered oppression or marginalization by the dominant culture. A strict emphasis on group belonging can also work negatively, to define meaning by a more or less explicit process of exclusion, as we discuss below.

"THE PEOPLE WHO ARE OURS"

In a 2002 survey commissioned by the Northern Ireland Community Relations Council, a sociologist interviewed Catholic and Protestant children between the ages of three and six to find out their views on the political situation there (see Close-Up 7.1).

When asked "What do you know about Catholics?" one Protestant child responded, "They're bad. . . . Catholics are different from ordinary human beings because they are badder." In response to the question, "What do you know about Protestants?" Catholic children provided similar responses: "They want to kill all the Catholics. They're like Catholics. They do the same things only they're stronger."

These children's perspectives on Irish cultural identity are interesting for what they reveal about the politics of identity in general. First, they highlight the extent to which group membership, like all forms of identification, is defined by the terms of *sameness*

Bad and Badder

The following is excerpted from a report commissioned by the Northern Ireland Community Relations Council, published in June 2002, entitled "Too Young to Notice?" Paul Connolly, a sociologist at the University of Ulster, interviewed 352 Catholic and Protestant children from Northern Ireland about their attitudes toward the political situation there. All of the children were between three and six years of age.

WHAT DO YOU KNOW ABOUT CATHOLICS?

They rob.

They're bad. They batter Almond Drive people. Almond Drive—that's where I live.

Catholics are different from ordinary human beings because they are badder. The police come after them. They make petrol bombs, get petrol at garages, throw them, and they blow up.

WHAT DO YOU KNOW ABOUT PROTESTANTS?

They want to kill all the Catholics.

They're like Catholics. They do the same things only they're stronger. Protestants would take people hostage. The police give them their weapons and make a deal to get the hostages.

Catholics don't like Protestants, and that's why they don't like them. They're bad.

WHY DO YOU LIKE OR NOT LIKE THIS FLAG?

[After showing the Protestant children an Irish Tricolor flag.]

Northern Ireland flag. You put it up in July. It annoys people when it's waving. A Drumcree flag is the good one and that is the bad one.

It's the Fenian flag. It's only bad people that have that color of flag and that's all I know about that flag.

WHY DO YOU LIKE OR NOT LIKE THIS FLAG?

[After showing the Catholic children a Union Jack.]

I don't like that flag—a sad one—'cause it's bad.

It has red and blue and white. They burn them, down at a club. Put Union Jack on grass and burned it. All bigguns throw stones at British Police. Just don't like that one.

WHAT DO YOU KNOW ABOUT THE PEOPLE IN THIS PHOTOGRAPH? WHY DO YOU LIKE OR NOT LIKE THEM?

[After showing Catholic children a picture of a Protestant march.]

Sometimes they march when they're attacking other places and sometimes when somebody's dead.

They're holding up stuff. They're Orangemen. Because they're going to kill us. They wanted to kill us anyway.

They came to our road and my daddy said they're Orange bastards!

Because they're bad. They're police.

'Cause they be fighting.

Because they're not friendly.

They're Orangemen. People tried to kill the Orangemen because they don't like them.

They're dangerous men. They're evil. They steal money.

They're not my favorite because they've got all the colors that I hate.

They're Protestants. They want to march so that they can get the Catholic area.

I like the people who are ours. I don't like those ones because they're Orangemen. They're bad people. Mummy told me they were bad.

and *difference*: Catholics are defined by virtue of their difference from Protestants, by their **essential** "otherness."

What is particularly significant in the first example is the implied norm against which "Catholic" is defined: "Protestant" identity is not mentioned, but is assumed, in its absence, to be synonymous with "human beings." A key characteristic of group identity, particularly though not exclusively in the case of dominant groups, is the **ex-nomination**, or failure to acknowledge the distinguishing sign or particularity of that identity. Not mentioning a distinguishing characteristic—like whiteness, say, or, in the case of Northern Ireland, Protestantism—implies that it is just ordinary, the norm. Difference, within this framework, is never neutral; rather, it is conceived as deviation from a standard.

While this form of discrimination can sometimes seem relatively value-free (for example, the phrase "non-white" to describe blacks or Asians looks innocuous enough until we start to think about why we rarely hear whites described as "non-black"), it works implicitly—and sometimes explicitly—on the basis of hierarchy. Hence, the others are "badder" than we are. Critical to the operation of the hierarchy is the operation of stereotype, in which a group or individual is reduced to a few fixed, unchanging characteristics (again, in implicit opposition to the more complex and fluid "normal" identities we ascribe to ourselves and those identified by a child in the survey as "the people who are ours").

Like Us, Only . . . Worse

What's striking in the stereotypes that are used by the children in this interview—and what's true of stereotypes generally—is that, regardless of what group is being described, they tend to sound a lot alike. Though some allowance must be made in this example for the age of the interviewees—a four-year-old has a limited vocabulary to describe deviance—the terms in which they describe "otherness" resonate remarkably with the terms used by adults. "Badness," or treachery, an absence of morality, and a tendency toward the illegitimate use of violence (as opposed to the *legitimate* use of violence by one's own group) are standard terms of condemnation that establish the place of the other outside the bounds of civil society, while asserting, again by implicit comparison, the moral integrity of "us."

The children's comments also illustrate another interesting thing about stereotypes: one Catholic child's remark about Protestants—"*They're like Catholics. They do the same things* only they're stronger" ("Bad and Badder" 21, emphasis added)—points to the emergence of stereotypes through the tension between difference and *sameness*. Recall the discussion in Chapter 6 of Freud's theory about the contradictory drives that inform relations between "self" and "other": the traumatic separation that marked our entry into the social world means that the stability of our identities always hinges on a tension between the desire for connection with the other and the fear of being consumed by the other. The ambivalent self-construction that underlies the production of stereotypes leads to a representation of the dominant group as simultaneously vulnerable and powerful in relation to an "other" who is both threatening and weak. Thus Protestants "do the same things [as Catholics] only they're stronger" because "the police give them their weapons." The moral superiority of the Catholics lies in their victimization at the hands of established power structures. On the other hand, claims to virtue frequently rest on *appeals* to traditional authorities—the law, God, or, in the case of children, parents: "Mummy told me they were bad" (21). The ambiguous positioning of authority as a site of identification (the thing that confirms our status) or source of victimization (the thing that shuts us out) again reveals the precarious foundations of the construction of the self.

Cultural Symbols, Material Contexts

Of course, frequently—as is the case in Northern Ireland—a tendency to ally oneself with or against established powers (and to construct those powers accordingly as legitimate or illegitimate) has a historical basis. As a consequence of centuries of British occupation, an occupation that, in spite of a formal cessation of hostilities between (mostly Protestant) Unionists and (mostly Catholic) Nationalists in 1998, is still rejected by some Nationalists, most of the police force is English—that is, largely Protestant.

The ambiguous role of the police in the stories of the children in the interview demonstrates the complex interplay between symbolism and society in the formation of the structures of power. The Protestant child infers the badness of the Catholics from the fact that "the police come after them" ("Bad and Badder" 21). As in most attempts to draw a link between race, culture or **ethnicity**, and criminality, this equation is confused in its attribution of cause and effect: the inference of guilt on the basis of pursuit or arrest is based on an assumption of the objectivity of the police. This objectivity is called into question by the Catholic children's reference to an alliance between the police and the Protestants. Regardless of its accuracy, the reference serves as a reminder of the **ideological** context in which power always operates. The role of ideology in determining identity is particularly clear to see in the case of children: we are not surprised when the shaping influence of "Mummy told me" appears behind the veil of personal conviction.

Nevertheless, it is important to resist the temptation to see children as the innocent victims of ideologies that are variously deployed and/or seen through by the rest of us who know better. As we argue in Chapter 3, no one, not even the supposedly impartial administrators of justice (nor, for that matter, the cultural critic!), escapes the **discursive** networks through which "truth"—including the "truth" of stereotypes—emerges as a function of power. The terms by which group identities are defined are always shot through with ideology, their mythological character highlighted in the arbitrariness of the symbols that convey their substance—for example, the Irish tricolour flag and the Union Jack, which Protestant and Catholic children characterized, not surprisingly, as "bad" and "the colors I hate." As empty of real significance as these symbols may be, however, we cannot dismiss their power, just as we cannot underestimate the material force of ideology as it is expressed in the beliefs and actions of individuals, police, and armies.

Collective Identity and Crisis

Within the context of what have come to be labelled "The Troubles" in Northern Ireland, it is easy to see how group identity comes to take on massive significance. As Kobena Mercer notes, "identity . . . becomes an issue when it is in crisis, when something assumed to be fixed, coherent and stable is displaced by the experience of doubt and uncertainty" (43). It would be a mistake, however, to assume that identities don't matter outside situations of obvious "trouble." The tendency for dominant groups to ex-nominate the signs or myths that designate their specialness means that it's possible for members of those groups to have, or at least to believe that they have, very little invested in belonging to a particular group. They are able to bracket questions of identity because the balance of social power allows *their* identity to pass as universal, unmarked. It is only when the balance of power shifts that it becomes necessary to haul out the symbols, to remind themselves and others what it is that makes them unique.

Particularism versus Universalism   Such a collective identity crisis arguably occurred in the wake of the September 11, 2001, terrorist attacks on the United States, when it suddenly became necessary to reassert the specific meaning of "America," all the while continuing to insist on the universality of that identity. The tension between particularism ("we are like this, we stand for these beliefs, ideas, practices") and universalism ("we are all human beings . . . except for those who don't do or believe as we do") underlies all definitions of group identity, with the fiction of universality being comfortably indulged in when times are good, and the defence of singularity being invoked when one's position of strength is threatened.

At these moments, as in the crisis following September 11, people are generally more willing to surrender *individual* civil liberties, such as freedom of speech—liberties that under other circumstances are seen as natural—in order to gain the greater security perceived to be associated with the defence of the group. These defences take multiple forms, including the tightening of physical or territorial borders, the intensification of policing activity, and the dissemination of myths or ideologies that work to bind the group together and to enforce the exclusion of outsiders.

Looking at identities in crisis serves to remind us of conditions that are more or less critical to the maintenance of *all* identities. Designated through particular practices of representation in which differences are more or less highlighted, identities are always rooted, in the last instance, in relations of power and force. A recent *Globe and Mail* story about the arrest of a suspected terrorist carried the headline "Muslim Militant or Family Man: Terrorist Has Many Faces." At times of crisis, practices of **racist** stereotyping become more widespread, with boundaries between "us" and "them" expressed in the form of **binary opposition.**

Suggested Activity 7.1

Try to find recent media examples of the representation of *difference* defined by group identity. In what contexts do these representations occur? In what situations are the identities of specific groups promoted (and/or ex-nominated) or stereotyped?

MODERN IDENTITIES: NATION, EMPIRE, AND RACE

One of the principal ways of defining identity in the modern world has been through the idea of the **nation.** Historically connected to European practices of colonialism between the sixteenth and nineteenth centuries, nations and **nationalism** remain significant today, both as symbolic guarantees of identity and security and as obstacles to more global connections. Associated with such positive ideals as patriotism, loyalty, and collective strength, nations and nationalism also work—traditionally and today—on principles of exclusion based on race, gender, and sexuality. Beginning with a specific example of how the nation functions in popular culture today, this section goes on to locate those contemporary resonances in a broader historical context.

The success of Molson's 2000 "I Am Canadian" ad campaign can be measured by the range of pop cultural sites in which references to it—even mocking ones—continue to appear.

I Am Canadian

In the Molson Canadian ad that came to be known as "The Rant," a young man in a plaid shirt—"Joe"—stands with a microphone in front of a huge crowd and offers a simple, powerful declaration of what it means to be Canadian (see Close-Up 7.2).

Introducing himself with a stereotypically Canadian, self-effacing "Hey," Joe begins his speech with a few negations of common American stereotypes of Canadians and concludes, positively and triumphantly, by proclaiming "My name is Joe and I AM CANADIAN! Thank you." The ad's instant popularity, measured by increased sales and a flurry of media and popular discussion, was widely attributed to its having expressed, simply and appealingly, the essence of Canadian national identity. Leaving aside the question of whether the ad was an accurate or positive representation of Canadianness (some people, including Ontario's Minister of Consumer and Commercial Affairs Bob Runciman, worried that it constituted "America-bashing" [see "I Am . . . an Asshole?"]), "The Rant" is useful to look at as a particularly powerful example of how **nationalist** discourse operates, both in the Canadian context and more generally.

On a general level, one of the first things the ad tells us is that having a national identity is not just a matter of being a citizen of a particular state. It is also a strongly felt personal investment in being part of a special community—one defined by particular loves (hockey, beer, nature), and beliefs: in peace, for example, or in social justice.

Joe's Rant

"Hey.

I'm not a lumberjack or a fur trader.

I don't live in an igloo or eat blubber or own a dog sled.

And I don't know Jimmy, Sally, or Suzy from Canada, although I'm certain they're really, really nice.

I have a prime minister, not a president.

I speak English and French, not American.

And I pronounce it "about," not "a boot."

I can proudly sew my country's flag on my backpack.

I believe in peacekeeping, not policing.

Diversity, not assimilation.

And that the beaver is a truly proud and noble animal.

A tuque is a hat, a chesterfield is a couch,

and it IS pronounced zed, not zee, zed.

Canada is the second largest landmass, the first nation of hockey, and the best part of North America.

My name is Joe, and I AM CANADIAN!

Thank you."

Belonging to a particular nation is not just a passive kind of subjection to an external, predetermined state structure, then, but a form of belief and action that is itself *constitutive*— a defining part of that nation.

Identity as Difference   But at the same time as Canadianness, by Joe's reckoning, seems to be a specific, deliberate thing, there is another sense in which being Canadian—or any nationality—doesn't mean anything in particular in and of itself. It signifies only insofar as it defines a particular *relationship*, one that is defined by connection with other Canadians and—equally importantly—by a *difference* from non-Canadians. The Canadian identity promoted by "The Rant" is one informed by self-conscious awareness of Canada's place in a world of other nations—nations toward which Canada assumes a particular political stance (peacekeeping vs. policing), and whose otherness is critical to the definition of the Canadian self.

Of course, the principal "other" in Joe's rant is the United States—or, more specifically, a mythical "America"—whose dominance, and implied aggressive indifference to Canada, is what turns this speech into a rant rather than a simple declaration of patriotism. Like all nationalist statements—indeed, more explicitly than most—Joe's rant is a deliberate act of boundary-drawing, establishing what, and more importantly who, belongs inside, and what belongs outside.

The urgency of defending what is often, as here seems to be the case, a fairly vulnerable boundary between "us" and "them" means that the arbitrary, or accidental, aspect of being a part of a particular national community needs to be played down in favour of an image of the nation as an organic whole. One of the chief ways this effect of incorporating all national citizens into a single coherent body is achieved in this ad, as in many nationalist statements, is by using the figure of a single individual to stand in for the nation as a whole.

Joe's status as a prototypical Canadian is highlighted by the series of images played on a screen behind him—the Parliament buildings, the flag, a set of individual faces of different races, and a waving crowd (Joe's audience?). By virtue of his placement on the stage, and his possession of a microphone, Joe is the spokesperson or representative of the community represented by these symbols. The choice of "Joe"—a good- but ordinary-looking guy in his late twenties who loves hockey and beer—as that individual is, of course, not accidental, since the target market for Molson Canadian beer is young men between the ages of 19 and 29. Though his name is no longer mentioned, Joe's spirit clearly inspires the television ads that ran during the 2008 Stanley Cup playoffs explaining the "unwritten code in Canada." If you follow the code, the ads explain, "chances are . . . you've left your coat on some pile and knew it wouldn't get stolen; you've never made a move on your buddy's girlfriend;" and "you've grown a beard in the off-season." And (of course) Molson Canadian is your beer ("The Code").

The question of what Joe represents (an alpha male with a sense of irony?) becomes much more interesting when framed in terms of his supposedly exemplary Canadianness, bolstered by the stereotypically masculine symbols of beer and hockey. Associated with a broader collection of mythological images of the nation as a rugged Northern climate, settled by bold pioneers who survived through teamwork and toughness, these symbols create an unmistakably gendered image of the representative Canadian. The picture of Canada and Canadians is also fleshed out in ways that are both more obvious and more subtle: Joe's proud declaration that he speaks "English *and* French," in contrast to implicitly monolingual Americans, draws on the idea of a bilingual and bicultural Canada—an idea that is supported, but also complicated, by his invocation of the idea of *multi*cultural diversity. Though the ad speaks powerfully to the values of inclusivity and difference as central components of Canadian identity, the voices in whom that symbolic "diversity" actually exists do not speak—except in disembodied and homogenized form, *spoken for* by Joe, as the generic (white, male, anglophone) Canadian. How might "The Rant" have signified differently (more or less effectively?) if Joe's words were spoken by a teenaged girl, an old woman, a black man, an Asian woman, a person in a wheelchair?

Suggested Activity 7.2

Though some elements of national myth persist over time, others change in response to events, processes, and conflicts within and outside the nation. Assuming it had not been done before, how would an ad along the lines of "The Rant" work today? What changes would be necessary in order to draw a positive audience response? Looking at parodies of this ad on websites such as YouTube offer an interesting window into the ongoing struggle over national meaning (See, for example, "I Am Not Canadian").

Authentic versus Commercialized Culture   When Canadian Heritage Minister Sheila Copps aired "The Rant" at an International Press Institute conference in Boston to demonstrate what culture means to Canadians, some commentators criticized her for confusing "authentic" culture with its corrupt *commercial* form. Copps herself made a distinction between deep and superficial, authentic and commercial in her assertion that "for Canadians, culture is not just another good. It's not just entertainment. It's the expression of the soul and identity of who we are." Leaving aside for a moment the issue of whether and/or how "culture" differs from "entertainment" (an issue touched on in Chapters 1, 2, and 4 of this book), Copps's presentation, and the response to it, raises questions about the relationships between national identity, culture, politics, and economics.

The principal critiques directed at Copps's use of the Molson ad—that it invoked a contrived or made-up identity in place of a genuine one, that it exploited the theme of Canadian identity in order to achieve partisan political goals, and that it ignored *authentic* national culture in favour of a commercial substitute—all miss a critical fact about **nationalism,** which is that it is, by definition, informed by a combination of spontaneous feeling and conscious construction. Even more crucially, it is inextricably tied to political and economic concerns, which it helps to influence even as it is in turn shaped by them. These complex relationships are easy to see when we look at **nations** and **nationalism** in a historical context (see Close-Up 7.3).

Nations and Nationalism

The dynamics of nations and nationalism are important to understand in the context of discussions of identity. Not only is the nation one of the most globally significant forms of collective identity, but the very concept of modern identity, in its individual and collective forms, is in significant ways tied to the historical emergence of the nation in eighteenth-century Europe.

Much as contemporary economic, technological, and political changes are throwing old identities into confusion, changes in eighteenth-century Europe associated with the industrial revolution, developments in technology and communication, and political conflict had a powerful impact on traditional identities.

Nations and Nationalism

As a form of what Benedict Anderson terms "imagined community," the nation is both example and instigator of the process by which identities that are constructed or imagined come to assume the force of *nature*. One useful way to approach the significance of the nation as a source of modern identity is to think about the relationship between nations and nationalism.

Our usual, common-sense way of understanding the relationship is to see the nation—a people defined by collective belonging to an extensive community, usually defined in relation to a specific territory—as primary, with nationalism as a frequent though not inevitable byproduct. Recent theories of the development of nations (Anderson, Gellner) suggest that the relationship might best be understood as working the other way around: that is, nations are how the ideological impulse of nationalism is legitimated and given concrete shape.

Simply put, the changes associated with modernity reconfigured strongly hierarchical or "vertical" medieval empires, framed by the ordering principles of dynasty and religion, into a more chaotic collection of "horizontal" states, characterized by their secular, more fluid political and economic organization. As a form of mythological solidarity that transforms a population into a "people," the nation was an important correlate of the modern state brought into being by state force at the same time as it fleshed out the meaning of the state, giving it a *sense* of purpose and natural rightness. As sociologist Zygmunt Bauman puts it, "the state supplied the resources of nation building, while the postulated unity of the nation and shared national destiny offered legitimacy to the ambition of the state authority to command obedience" (683).

Imagined Community, Invented Tradition

Thus, nations can be defined in relation to the machinery of particular states and to the territories they command. This is not a necessary relationship, however, as can be seen by contemporary examples of stateless nations such as Palestinians or Kurds. In fact, the nation, as a concept, derives its historical significance not so much through its grounding in a specific material polity or place, but rather through its unprecedented power to command connections between people spread out over vast distances. Unlike traditional civic groupings defined by village or even city-state, the nation demanded an imagined relationship between a vast body of people, most of whom had never met.

In the eighteenth century, as today, popular culture functioned as an important vehicle of nationalism. The nation became possible in part, Benedict Anderson suggests, because new forms of media such as the daily newspaper helped to create a large group of readers, linked by their capacity to imagine themselves as part of a whole network of unknown others. These readers form the basis of a community, informed by a collection of stories that, through their assemblage in the form of a single text, contribute to the creation of a coherent narrative of the world—a *national* point of view. Language and literacy play critical roles here, too: the rise of print capitalism that spurred the growth of newspapers corresponded with a decline of the privileged status of Latin as the sacred *written* language to which all vernacular or spoken languages were secondary. The production of written texts in the everyday languages spoken by people throughout Europe hastened the breakup of religious empires, while granting real and symbolic significance to the communities defined by distinct vernaculars. Of course, the "community" facilitated by print was strongly linked to literacy, and its contours therefore shaped by the social as well as the economic interests of educated elites. Nationalism, understood in this way, is inevitably a top–down phenomenon.

Sports, heralded as a way of bringing people together, can also exacerbate national tensions. French soccer player Zinedine Zidane's infamous head-butt, levelled at Italian player Marco Matterazi in the 2006 World Cup final, elicited a torrent of nationalist feeling on both sides. To complicate matters, the speculation that Zidane was responding to a racist taunt emphasizes the tensions operating *within* European nations that still cling to myths of ethnic homogeneity.

Like other modern structures of identification, the nation can be understood as both empowering and restrictive (see Chapter 6). Fuelled by the spirit of revolutionary movements against absolutist regimes, expressed most dramatically in the French Revolution of 1789–99, nationalism was based partly on the idea of the rights of "the people" to govern themselves. This ideal became a defining principle in the French and American constitutions. Its democratic appeal masks the function of the nation as the legitimating ideology of the *state*, whose territorial boundaries are regulated internally and externally by instruments of force—police and military agencies, legal and educational institutions, and political organizations. The two meanings of the nation—as an expression of the ideal of equal citizenship, and as an alibi for state power—function simultaneously, the never fully realized promise of popular democracy working to justify the disciplinary force of the state while concealing the gaps in social and economic power that separate the mass of "the people" from the ruling elites. The compelling symbolism of "we" operates only to the extent that it is supported by forgetting that some of "us" own greater stakes in our collective project than others.

The nation's capacity to *work* as a collective project depends in large part on its ability to **interpellate** its members as citizens, enlisting their active and voluntary submission to the greater community. To this end, the idea of the nation must be embodied in a powerful narrative that grounds the present in the past. The principal mechanism for this grounding is what some historians have described as "invented tradition": "a set of practices, normally governed by overtly or tacitly accepted rules of a ritual or symbolic nature, which seek to inculcate certain values and norms of behaviour by repetition, which automatically implies continuity with the past" (Hobsbawm *Industry and Empire* 2).

A contemporary example is the controversy that has arisen in many Canadian communities over the public use of the phrase "Merry Christmas." Every year, a flurry of angry letters-to-the-editor and radio call-ins has greeted the use of secular alternatives such as "Season's Greetings" or "Happy Holidays" on billboards and in other public venues. The gist of these complaints was that these bland greetings are threatening to destroy the tradition of Christmas, a key part of Canada's Christian heritage. History suggests, however, that not only is celebrating Christmas a relatively recent practice in this country, long predated by Aboriginal spiritual traditions, but also that secularism lays equal claim to being a Canadian tradition. As historian Alan MacEachern noted in a letter to *The Globe and Mail*, the "Happy Holidays" that adorned the front page in December 2007, was not an example of "political correctness run amok" but rather a variation of a tradition begun in 1925. The letter went on to quote the words of a 1965 editorial explaining why *The Globe* continued to wish readers "Season's Greetings" instead of "Merry Christmas":

> We reach out to each other, for each other is what we depend upon. And so many of our cards now tactfully say, Season's Greetings, for it would not be polite to say Merry Christmas to a Jewish friend or an agnostic friend or an unbelieving-in-anything friend. And they are wanted at the party. It is lonely in this scientific, pragmatic, abundant world. (qtd. in MacEachern)

These sentiments, expressed more than 40 years ago, challenge the idea of Christmas as an essential Canadian tradition that has recently come under attack from non-Christians immigrants, cheerleaders of **multiculturalism**, or cranky secularists: while many people have celebrated Christmas since the arrival of the first European settlers in the country that eventually became known as Canada, the holiday is not simply a unifying national tradition but rather part of a history of conflict and negotiation about what it means to live together as Canadians.

National conflicts are often mediated by the struggle over *competing* invented traditions, whether "tradition" is defined by religion or by the much looser concept of "culture." Whether it signifies Matthew Arnold's version of high culture as "the best that has been thought and said" (see Chapter 2), or a more grassroots **folk culture**—and often it's a combination of the two—"culture" works within nationalist discourse as a powerful emblem of belonging. Both high and folk culture myths of nation work through principles of exclusion, the former by stressing qualities of taste, discrimination, and linguistic competence or "breeding," and the latter through birth, or indigenous attachment to the land.

The first step towards lightening

The White Man's Burden

is through teaching the virtues of cleanliness.

Pears' Soap

is a potent factor in brightening the dark corners of the earth as civilization advances, while amongst the cultured of all nations it holds the highest place—it is the ideal toilet soap.

Nineteenth-century British ideologies of race and nation are reflected in advertising of the time. While messages like this one would never appear today, advertisements continue to be a potent site for the reproduction of mythologies of collective identity.

The Nation and Its Others

Culture plays an important role in mediating one of the fundamental functions of the nation, which is its capacity to draw clear distinctions between who belongs and who doesn't. One of the nation's defining features is that its unity is marked off by specific boundaries and borders: "The nation is imagined as *limited* because even the largest of them, encompassing perhaps a billion living human beings, has finite, if elastic boundaries, beyond which lie other nations. No nation imagines itself coterminous with mankind" (Anderson 7). The corollary of this imagined limit to the nation's reach is that some parts of humankind are excluded from the nation; indeed, their exclusion is fundamental to the way the nation defines itself.

The critical role of borders in defining the nation can be understood in political terms by considering the constitution of states as battles for territory and resources. It can also be understood in psychic terms if we recall, from Chapter 6, psychoanalytic explanations for how we come to define ourselves around the crucial poles of "self" and "other."

The Narcissism of Minor Difference   Historian (and Canadian Liberal Party leader) Michael Ignatieff employs Freud's concept of "the narcissism of minor difference" to explain why seemingly small differences between nations come to take on such enormous significance in the process of self-definition. The narcissist defends the integrity of his or her own sense of self by projecting all the negative or unruly elements onto the other. The precariousness of this sense of self can be guarded only through the most vigilant policing of the boundaries between self and other. The most crucial boundaries in this respect are not those that mark obvious differences, but those that separate the self from the not-quite-self. A clear example of the mobilization of these distinctions was the persecution of the Jews in Nazi Germany. At a time of deep economic crisis, Germans took refuge in a hysterical defence of national identity whose unity could be maintained only by the purging of "foreign" elements within. Ignatieff notes:

> [Hitler's] language of purity and cleansing, so widely echoed today, is the most elemental language of narcissism: the reduction of all difference to the distinction between cleanliness and dirt. Cleanliness distinguishes the human from the non-human, the valued from the despised. This is the trajectory, the path toward moral abjection to which the narcissism of minor difference can (though it need not always) lead. (50)

Nationalism is not always based on, nor does it inevitably lead to, fascism or the violent elimination of those deemed "impure." However, it does rest on an assumption of unity, maintained not only by the accentuation of minor differences that are seen to separate the nation from other nations, but also by the *suppression* of the more significant differences and inequalities that shape the lives of its individual citizens.

Nation and Gender

As the contemporary example of "The Rant" suggests, the exemplary national citizen has traditionally been gendered male. Not surprisingly, then, the language of nationalist discourse tends, implicitly if not explicitly, to reflect a **patriarchal** ideology. However, the privileging of male interests does not mean that women have no place in nationalist discourse. On the contrary, the relationship between essentialized notions of masculinity and femininity are critical to the construction of the nation (see McClintock).

As with other aspects of nationalist discourse, this emphasis on gender operates both as a reflection of, and an influence on, the role of the state as regulator of economic and social relations. With the rise of industrial **capitalism,** the family was a critical site for the reproduction—both physical and cultural—of a society dominated by bourgeois interests. As the linchpin of the family, female sexuality was subject to vigilant oversight and discipline, both through regulation and law (in relation to marriage and ownership of property, for example) and through ideology. The myth that the health of the nation hinged on the moral propriety of its women is a typical example of the way in which the discourse of patriotism aided in the suppression of female sexuality. This myth assumed even greater significance in relation to issues of nation and race, discussed further below.

The enlistment of women as emblems of the nation's integrity produces an interesting iconography in which, while the exemplary citizen is always male, the nation itself is often figured as female. The personification of the nation as woman has both political and quasi-spiritual resonances that emerge particularly clearly through the connection that is often made between women and the land. As in many other national anthems, the land in "O Canada" is personified: "True patriot love, in all thy sons' command." While the gender of Canada is unstated, conventional codes of national iconography invite us to read the nation as a maternal rather than a paternal figure. Regarded as territory to be conquered and possessed, the land (like "woman") also signifies the embodiment of Nature. This almost sacred designation works, bizarrely, to *naturalize* the masculine conquerors' claims to nationhood, while consigning the land, along with women, to the status of property. The gendered and sexualized image of nation as a male soldier guarding (or cultivator plowing) the female earth strongly contradicts the mythology of a community defined by "deep, horizontal comradeship" (Anderson 7). It also shapes the material operations of the state, contributing to a long delay in women's—and others'—achievement of equal civil rights.

NATION AND EMPIRE

We have tried so far to show how, while identity in a general sense is predicated on difference—the community of "us" dependent on an excluded "them"—this is particularly true for nations as a consequence of the historical circumstances in which they emerged. Both nationalism and nation-*states* are products of the industrial revolution, as discussed above. The industrial revolution was itself dependent on the resources of distant regions of the world, which supplied it with raw materials as well as capital in the form of gold and silver. These regions were not themselves industrialized, and were not to enjoy the benefits of **industrialization** for a long time, even though they came to assume a crucial role as markets for the products of industry. The economic development of European nation-states, in other words, was fuelled by the *under*development of other parts of the world—Asian, African, and American colonies, exploited for their resources and their labour while they were prevented, through trade regulations backed up by military force, from becoming full partners in the generation of wealth (see Blaut).

The construction of European national *identities* was similarly dependent on the non-European world. The process of secularization and scientific enlightenment that contributed to the breakup of the old religious dynasties was strongly connected to the voyages of exploration undertaken by Spain, Portugal, England, France, and the Netherlands during the fifteenth and sixteenth centuries. As much as these travels were undertaken in search of wealth, they were also driven by a quest for knowledge, and ultimately served to shape an understanding of the physical world and its human inhabitants as more vast and complicated than had previously been imagined. As Europeans came into contact with other, previously unknown peoples, two things happened: on the one hand, other places and cultures were translated and distorted—made to fit, positively or, more often, negatively into categories of the already-known, thus consolidating the universality of European ideas and values. On the other hand, contact with otherness led, in innumerable local circumstances as well as more generally, to a recognition of a multitude of radically different worlds. National identities were shaped by both of these responses to difference: the recognition of **cultural relativism,** whereby, in contrast to the religious view of a single universal truth, differences in belief and practice were seen to be inevitable and perhaps even desirable, and the consolidation of singular **sovereign** identities characterized by an imperative to safeguard and even to extend their sovereignty, by force if necessary.

The West and the Rest

Colonialism was not just an economic and political undertaking in which European nations competed for dominance through the exploitation and settlement of overseas colonies. It was also, importantly, a cultural project, in which these nations sought to extend throughout the world their concept of civilization, defined by the Enlightenment values of scientific rationalism and liberal humanism: the imperative to conquer the non-European world was tempered (but, importantly, not contradicted) by the will to save it.

Refining and complicating the explicit *universality* of the colonial vision, according to which all of humanity was marching in the same direction along a single, historically determined road to **progress**, was its grounding in principles of identity and difference. The humanistic thrust of colonialism, which sought to impart the idea of the natural sovereignty and brotherhood of man, was more seriously undermined by the fundamental principle of *in*equality that structured the whole colonial and civilizing project. Like the mission of the "rational recreationists" (see Chapter 2), which sought to improve the working classes of England by enlisting them in middle-class programs of education and recreation, the colonial project reflected two connected but irreconcilable assumptions: that of a fundamental equality between humans that could be advanced through education, and that of a fundamental and hierarchical difference between groups that justified the material and ideological domination of the inferior group by the superior one.

One expression of this ambivalence was the nineteenth-century Britain fascination with live performances by colonials. While poetry readings by Aboriginal Canadian Pauline Johnson (Tekahionwake) were a far cry from the sideshow displays of nude or partially clothed African women such as Saarti Bartman (nicknamed "Hottentot Venus"), both events functioned to some extent as performances of stereotypical otherness, the colonials offering audiences "primitive" (savage and/or innocent) reflections of their "civilized" European selves.

Orientalism—Then and Now

That process of anxious drawing and redrawing of boundaries impels the operation of colonial discourse, which produces forms of knowledge and ways of talking about "the other" as a way of securing the identity of the imperial "self." Edward Said uses the term **orientalism** to describe a dominant form of colonial discourse in which a mythologized East, or "Orient," becomes a site for the projection of Western fantasies of otherness as well as a mechanism for Western domination of actual non-Western cultures.

Based on Foucault's formulation of a nexus between knowledge and power, orientalism consists of a repertoire of images and ideas that *produce* "the Orient" as an object of Western knowledge and control. Disseminated through a variety of institutionalized forms (travel writing, civil service briefs, government policy documents, journalism, and even so-called "innocent" forms of culture such as art and literature), orientalism played a critical role in European—particularly British—domination of non-Western cultures. It draws on a bank of stereotypical (and frequently inconsistent) qualities—

Pauline Johnson (Tekahionwake) achieved fame not just for her poetic talents but also for her stage persona that played self-consciously on romantic stereotypes of Indians.

inscrutability, deviousness and treachery, religious fundamentalism and immorality, violence, and excessive delicacy and effeminacy—in order to construct "the oriental" as a fixed, unchanging other, lacking subjectivity or internal variation and condensed in binary opposition to Western consciousness and culture. At the same time as orientalism serves to mark the absolute otherness of Eastern people, thus shoring up the integrity of Western identity, it is also a way of making the foreign familiar, of turning other cultures into objects of Western knowledge.

Like all discourses, orientalism emerged out of particular historical circumstances in which it served a number of specific functions. The term can seem somewhat confusing to us today, because the term "Orient" has come to refer specifically to the Asian Pacific (China, Taiwan, Japan, Korea), whereas its eighteenth-century meaning was much broader, covering the areas now referred to as the Middle East (Turkey, Iraq, Iran) and South Asia (India, Pakistan, Bangladesh, etc.). In part, the change in terminology can be seen as the product of a more sophisticated understanding of global cultures: the West has come to recognize critical differences between and within non-Western societies.

Contemporary Orientalism   It's easy to dismiss both nationalism and orientalism as products of unsophisticated cultures or bygone eras remote from our contemporary world. However, both persist in Western popular culture in forms that, like other myths of collective belonging, show up more obviously in times of crisis. The term "orientalism" may not signify precisely what it used to; however, the discursive practices it refers to continue in different forms. Long after it became unacceptable to typecast black or Native characters as the bad guys, and particularly in the wake of the September 11 attacks on the World Trade Center, films and television shows ranging from Disney's *Aladdin* to the television series *24* continue to draw on stereotypes of the Middle East and/or Arabs as evil and barbarous.

Accompanying the rapid circulation of racist stereotypes and ensuing violence in the present context, a new academic and popular-knowledge industry for the production of knowledge about Eastern, specifically Islamic, cultures has grown up seemingly overnight. Like the eighteenth-century European scholars of the East (actually called "orientalists"), a host of Western experts began appearing on talk shows, producing new books and articles and reviving old ones that purported to explain the "essential" qualities of Islamic culture (see, for example, Huntington, and, in a somewhat more sympathetic vein, Lewis).

Like their eighteenth-century forebears, these new forms of "knowledge" homogenized a number of vastly different, complex cultures into a single, static classifiable entity, defined by implicit contrast with a more variegated, fluid West. Read in the context of a generalized Western anxiety about the non-West in general, and Islam in particular, the bulk of these studies reinforced an image of Muslim culture as fundamentally different from, and threatening to, Western culture, while also serving to legitimate Western initiatives to *contain* and *manage* the threat. While they might seem remote from acts of racist violence, these discursive forms of "cultural profiling" assume material significance in the form of new customs and immigration, policing, and legal regulations in the United States and Canada that make it easier to detain and deport, arrest and imprison people on the basis of race or national origin.

Race and Identity

Lurking in the background of much of the preceding discussion is the significance of **race** (see Close-Up 7.4), which, for the last two hundred years, has been a particularly highly charged means of defining collective identity.

When it first appeared in English around the beginning of the sixteenth century, the word "race" had a fairly neutral meaning, referring simply to different kinds of people or things. By the late eighteenth century, the term was used increasingly to designate fixed, biological, and hierarchical differences between groups of people. It became, in other words, caught up in the currency of power.

Race

Simply defined, race is a concept that delineates categories of human beings based on physically, biologically, and genetically distinct types. Linked implicitly or explicitly to psychological and intellectual characteristics, these "types" become the basis for drawing hierarchical distinctions between groups. Race, then, is inextricably linked to **racism**—to the extent that, as with nations and nationalism, we can gain a clearer understanding of both terms if we think of them as developing in a direction that is opposite to how we usually think of them. By this reckoning, "'racism' is not so much a product of the concept of race as the very reason for its existence. Without the underlying desire for hierarchical categorization implicit in racism, 'race' would not exist" (Ashcroft et al. 198). One of the critical premises this statement illustrates is that "race" is not a natural, pre-given category, but one that assumes significance in particular historical circumstances to suit particular purposes.

A number of historical circumstances combined to ignite the charge around the concept of race. First, the European Romantic movement stressed, among other things, the idea of natural, essential qualities of beings that defined distinct peoples and established their primordial claim to particular places. Though not itself based on an idea of race, this foundation of popular nationalism drew on the ideas of "blood and soil" that were to become fundamental to racist theories. Second, the development of biological science, proceeding from a very narrow reading of Darwin, tipped the balance of heredity versus environment debates in favour of a new preoccupation with genetic inheritance. Specific branches of (what is now recognized to be) "pseudoscience"—such as phrenology, which added more precise quantifiers such as skull measurement to crude delineations of race based on skin colour—contributed to a growing consensus on the significance of a correlation between specific categories of physical characteristics and moral and intellectual qualities.

Put together with the political and social missions of colonialism, these developments contributed to the modern sense of race as a critical marker of essential human differences and inequalities. The metaphorical appropriation of Darwin's theory of natural selection (evolution) into a model of social *progress* legitimated the domination of certain groups on the basis of their alleged genetic "backwardness." It also paved the way for programs of social and biological "improvement," whereby those inferior races might be raised up or cultivated to a higher level, while fuelling fears about the possibility of the degeneration of the dominant white race through miscegenation (interracial sexual intercourse).

Manifested, among other ways, in the obsessive myth of a vulnerable white woman being threatened by a predatory black man, this fear highlights the way in which categories of power and identity such as race and gender are inevitably mixed up with one another. It also shows how the construction of race, like other identity formations, is shaped by the confused tangle of fear and desire that defines the interface between "self" and "other."

Race-Based Identity   The concept of race was challenged first in the debates that led, finally, to the abolition of slavery at the end of the nineteenth century, and again following the Second World War (which confirmed the alarming congruence of the ideas of nationalism and racism) and the decolonization movements of the fifties and sixties. Scientific debate continues over the existence of significant genetic differences corresponding to traditionally defined race. While they have identified a correlation between the physical characteristics of race and some patterns of disease, the majority of geneticists continue to stress that genetic differences *within* racial groups outweigh the differences *between* groups.

Many commentators argue that race has diminishing significance in North America as a force for social division and discrimination. The 2008 election of Barack Obama as the first black American President Barack Obama might be cited as evidence that the U.S., at least, is evolving into a "post-racial" society (Chang). However, even leaving aside the way race figured in media coverage of the U.S. primaries (if only in repeated observations of the election of a black president as evidence of the nation's progress), it continues to dominate the popular cultural landscape in sometimes startling ways. The 2006 season of the television show *Survivor*, which pitted race-based teams against one another, was just one example of how a supposedly outmoded way of classifying people still resonates. Critics generally didn't buy producers' claims that the decision to use racially segregated teams was part of an effort to boost minority participation and success on the show. Noting the program's reflection of increasingly segregationist practices (such as race-based schools) in society at large, critic Jonathan Turley laments the return of the "separate-but-equal" rationale that legitimated racist discrimination in the pre–civil rights era. He suggests that *Survivor*'s Cook Islands season was "repellant not because it looks too little, but too much, like our society. It is a reality that many are likely to watch, but few want to recognize" (Turley).

Whether or to what degree it exists in a natural, biological sense, it is inarguable that race, like other markers of identity, *matters* in a cultural, political, and economic sense, affecting not just the way different people are represented based on the group they allegedly "belong" to by virtue of skin colour, but also economic opportunities, social freedoms, and even mortality. Forged in the context of colonialism, it continues in subtler but still powerful ways to shape contemporary *post*colonial culture.

POSTCOLONIAL IDENTITIES

Beginning with India/Pakistan in 1947, most of Britain's former colonies became independent in the three decades following the Second World War. In a technical way, then, the period from approximately 1950 through the end of the twentieth century can be referred to as **postcolonial.** Once we start to think about that concept in more detail, however, it becomes apparent that many of the structures of power and identity that characterized the colonial period still have a firm grip on us today. Not only do forms of colonialism and **imperialism** persist (take, for example, the situation of First Nations peoples in Canada, the United States, and Australia), but the terms in which formerly colonized groups shape their demands for *post*colonial autonomy inevitably also bear the mark of those earlier signs of European dominance: nation and race. Rather than see the hangover of colonial vocabularies and structures simply as signs of a colossal failure on the part of contemporary society to free itself from oppressive tradition, we can look at postcolonial reformulations of nation and race as evidence for the continuing attraction and danger of forms of collective identity that inevitably signify both more and less than what they claim.

Postcolonial Nationalism

In one of the more infamous events of the last age of empire, representatives of the dominant European powers met—in the spirit of cooperation—over a period of a couple of months in 1884–85 to divvy up the territory of Africa among themselves. As a result of what became known as the Berlin Conference, more than 30 newly created states, "superimposed over the one thousand indigenous cultures and regions of Africa," were parcelled out among France, Germany, England, Italy, Spain, and Portugal (Rosenberg). There were no African representatives at the conference. Some 75 years later, much of Africa successfully won liberation from Europe, via independence movements mounted in the name of the "nations" that had so recently and arbitrarily been imposed *by* Europe. This situation illustrates the paradox of postcolonial nationalism, whereby the discourse former colonies take up to defend their own unique identities and right to sovereignty is freighted with the legacy of colonialism from which the modern nation was born.

New Players, Same Game   African and other colonial subjects face the challenge of framing their calls for liberation in the language of a project from which they have been excluded by definition. Postcolonial nationalists in Africa faced this challenge in a couple of ways: first, by calling up an image of a mythic African past around which the idea of a present nation might be articulated. This project of reviving the precolonial past played a critical role in refuting colonialist assertions that Africa had no history, nothing that might be deemed a culture, before the arrival of the Europeans.

However, since the European invention of African states carved up societies along arbitrary boundaries, separating groups that had once functioned as coherent communities and forcing together others with no common traditions or even languages, the project of defining "authentic" national cultures was especially daunting.

Thus, what was implicit in European nation-building was, in African and other postcolonial nations, more obvious: traditions were, to a large degree, invented, reflecting not a unified past, but current—and almost always contested—cultural realities. Not surprisingly, postcolonial nationalist ideologies often reflected the interests of the dominant group, a group consisting of largely European-trained intellectuals and civil servants who attempted to give their imported ideas legitimacy by dressing them up in the language of the people. Once again, the contradictions inherent in the very idea of the nation, as it first evolved in Europe, have emerged with particularly painful clarity in the postcolonial context: the dependence of nationalist discourse on the concept of *identity*—an unchanging, homogeneous essence—denies the possibility of fulfilling the nation's promise to reflect the living will of the people, in all their diversity.

The revival and/or invention of the past was not the only trajectory of postcolonial nationalism. Many nationalists tried to define a vision of nationhood in which the European myth of *universal* and *equal* humanism might truly be realized. Such a nation would be the ultimate realization of the natural rights of man. This ideology of nation— embodied most explicitly in the dominant nationalist tradition of the United States (itself a former colony!)—emphasized not roots but mobility and liberty through which national belonging could be imagined to be something freely chosen.

As with other postcolonial nationalisms, however, American nationalism was influenced and ultimately constrained by its reliance on the Enlightenment ideal of humanism, with its inherent tensions between universalism and binarism such that the human was defined by what it excluded (rational vs. irrational, civilized vs. primitive, etc.). Thus, at the same time as the idea of "nature's nation" tends naturally toward imperial expansion (formalized in American policy in the idea of Manifest Destiny, by which it was deemed to be the natural right of the United States to control the whole continent), it also sanctions the "natural" restriction of rights to those seen to embody the characteristics of rational man—a category that, until comparatively recently, excluded women and blacks.

Finally, to the extent that nations work to legitimize the political boundaries of particular states, their universalist myths are necessarily grounded in specific territorial claims. In settler–invader societies such as the United States and Canada, in which colonizing populations displaced indigenous cultures, these myths inevitably involve the justification and/or erasure of their violent origins. This is often accomplished by the transformation of a history of conquest by force into a story of natural inheritance or romantic conjoinment. Such is the case in Walt Disney's *Pocahontas*, in which the violence of colonialism (translated, in the film, into an unfortunate instance of cultural misunderstanding), is ultimately overshadowed by a love story that signals the possibility of a new race of "Americans" defined by the harmonious blending of (masculine) Europe and (feminine) Indian (see *Mickey Mouse Monopoly*).

As Canadian As . . .   Because their "founding" populations are the direct descendants of colonizing groups, settler–invader societies expose the contradictions of national identity in particularly obvious ways—which takes us back to "The Rant." In the absence of a revolutionary mythology of freedom like that of the United States, Canada—due in part to its Loyalist heritage and in part to the presence of two founding/invading groups, French and English—assumes a national identity that has been described as peculiarly **postmodern** (Hutcheon *Canadian Postmodern*).

The dilemma is presented in a 1988 *Canadian Forum* article that asked readers to think about how they might complete the phrase "As Canadian as . . . ," the idea being to come up with a simile comparable to "as American as apple pie" to capture Canadian identity. The most appropriate answer, the article suggested, would be that given by a woman in response to a recent survey: "As Canadian as . . . possible under the circumstances" (qtd. in Hutcheon *As Canadian as Possible* 9).

The assertion of Canadianness as something definable only in the negative—an assertion that is echoed in Joe's articulation of Canadian identity as, above all, not American (and not what Americans think it is)—reflects a sense of the provisionality and constructedness of all founding mythologies. Identity in this context becomes ironic, expressed in terms that are more or less false, not quite right. Joe's rant is rife with irony, including the playing of the British imperialist "Pomp and Circumstance" in the background of the humble performance of a guy in a lumberjack shirt, the assertion and negation of indigenizing mythologies ("I don't live in an igloo, I don't eat blubber"), and finally the tension between arrogance and humility ("I AM CANADIAN. Thank you.") that characterizes Joe's speech.

Some Canadians lament what they see as the uncertainty and impotence of what amounts to a national identity defined by non-identity. Given the problems inherent in strong and monolithic nationalisms, this concern would seem to be misguided. However, it is also a mistake to **idealize** the self-conscious slipperiness of Canadian national identity as a model of pluralistic tolerance. As "The Rant" reveals, the foregrounding of "difference" does not make nationalist discourse immune to the dangers of speaking for, or over, other groups. It can, rather, exacerbate those dangers by appearing to have recognized and dealt with them, and/or disguising cultural chauvinism with an ironic, self-deprecating demeanour.

As anthropologist Eva Mackey has observed, "the project of Canadian nation-building has not been based on the erasure of difference but on controlling and managing it" (148). Differences are allowed—even celebrated—to the extent that they conform to a *singular* vision of happy pluralism. A show like *Little Mosque* certainly challenges the myth of nationalist uniformity embodied in the figure of Joe Canadian. However even it sticks fairly closely to the **liberal** ideology that contains fundamental differences and inequalities within a pleasant veneer of well-intentioned, generally good-looking, prosperous folks just trying to get along. As national myths go, niceness can be particularly insidious in its strenuous denial of conflict and opposition.

In sum, postcolonial claims to national identity and autonomy can appear to be more or less legitimate (the "more or less" determined in part by what role the dominant national force played in the history of colonization). They are, however, prone to the pitfalls of European nationalism, which they expose and magnify. Partly for this reason, it is easy today to dismiss the validity of *all* nationalism, particularly if one happens to be part of a strong nation-state such as the United States. The nation remains viable as an idea, however, because the ideals of political sovereignty and cultural autonomy that it embodies—ideals that many still strive for—don't seem to be attainable in any other form. For indigenous groups in particular, who remain subject to forces of formal colonialism, the framework of nationhood remains a powerful cultural and legal mechanism for securing basic rights to self-determination.

Diaspora and Cultural Hybridity

Most obviously in relation to the indigenous cultures defined as First Nations, connection to place remains an important determinant in national identity. One of the most powerful forces shaping contemporary identities, however, is the unprecedented *movement* of people throughout the globe, sparked by colonialism and more recent forces of globalization (see Chapter 9). The term **diaspora** refers to the dispersal or scattering of a people, by choice or by force (and often those motives are blurred), from their homeland to diverse geographical regions. Colonialism itself was a diasporic process, as it involved the movement of millions of Europeans across the globe. For some, such as the convicts transported to Australian penal colonies, the trip was far from voluntary. In the case of many of the colonial settlers, comprising largely poor, marginalized members of their respective societies, relocation to the colonies in search of opportunities was a choice only in the most technical sense.

Arguably the most traumatic process of migration, and one that has become central to contemporary theorizations of diaspora (see Gilroy *The Black Atlantic*), was the forced exile of thousands of Africans as slaves, who constituted the primary labour force in the American colonies. The new cultural forms that evolved out of that massive uprooting had a profound effect on postcolonial society, particularly in the Caribbean where indigenous populations had been virtually wiped out. The process of global migration initiated by colonialism has accelerated in the years following decolonization, as people from the former colonies have migrated to metropolitan centres, including the settler–invader societies of the United States, Australia, and Canada.

These movements have fragmented traditional place-bound communities at the same time as they have created new ones, shaped by complex dynamics of memory, movement, and encounters with new places and cultures. These new cultural forms demand new ways of understanding identity beyond the traditional singular markers of class, race, and nation. In *The Black Atlantic*, Paul Gilroy suggests that the metaphor of "roots" by which identity—particularly black identity—has traditionally been understood might usefully be replaced with "routes"—the lines of movement and exchange that connect Africa, England, and America, historically by slave ships and more recently by the migrations of people, money, and culture across the Atlantic. The identities that emerge from these movements cannot be easily located; they exist, rather, between cultures, and even between contrary impulses, toward return on the one hand (even if the "homeland" is largely imaginary, as it is for the descendants of African slaves) and **assimilation** on the other (Gilroy "Diaspora" 329–330).

The image of diasporic identities as "in between" cultures—suggesting a kind of entrapment in the "Middle Passage" of slave routes—is inadequate, however, both in its characterization of diaspora and in its suggestion of the existence of static, stable cultural poles between which diasporic peoples vacillate. In addition to being defined by conditions of loss and longing, diasporic identities can also be experienced as exhilarating and enriching forms of multiple attachment. For individuals, moving between cultures can translate into an advanced form of cultural literacy, often enhanced by knowing more than one language and a healthy sense of tolerance for others.

The Musical Diaspora On a broader scale, the dynamics of diaspora have produced new and powerful forms of cultural expression, nowhere more evident, perhaps, than in the realm of music. The dominance of musical forms rooted in ex–African slave culture—jazz, blues, rock and roll—leads one critic to take note of the remarkable situation in which "an utterly exploited and dominated group managed to colonize not European music, which is henceforth relegated to the outermost margins of 'high' culture, but Music itself" (Brown 24). Whether or not the evidence supports such a global claim, one need only look at the contemporary examples of rap and hip hop as forms that developed not out of only black, but specifically diasporic, culture. "Rap," as Paul Gilroy notes:

> is a hybrid form rooted in the syncretic social relations of the South Bronx where Jamaican sound-system culture, transplanted during the 1970s, put down new roots and in conjunction with specific technological innovations, set in train a process that was to transform black America's sense of itself and a large proportion of the popular music industry as well. (*Small Acts* 125)

Of course rap has long transcended the borders of the United States, shaping music throughout the world. Groups such as War Party and TruRez in Canada and Wire MC in Australia use rap and hip hop as a way to define Aboriginal identity, drawing on the social history of those styles to stress similarities between lives lived in the margins of the majority culture. The dynamics of diasporic culture, especially when they are embodied in forms such as music, which is boundary-crossing by its very nature, move beyond identities defined by race to illuminate and create wider, more **hybrid** communities.

A late twentieth-century buzzword that still retains some of its zing, *hybridity* is often used to describe a condition of multicultural plurality, a happy blend of cultures thrown together in a gigantic global jam session (see the discussion of a Bell Canada ad in Chapter 9). As theorized by contemporary critics such as Homi Bhabha, however, hybridity describes not just a movement between identities, but also an agitation *within* the notion of identity itself whereby, through cultural exchange, we are forced to recognize the "other" within ourselves. That is, contemporary movements of cultural exchange don't just break down singular identities into multiple and conflicted forms; rather, they reveal that identities were multiple and conflicted all along. At the same time, it would be a mistake to extend the concept of diaspora so far that it becomes simply a loose metaphor to describe contemporary cultural identity *in general*. To suggest, as some theorists have done, that we are all more or less diasporic now risks glossing over the important differences between degrees and kinds of movement, as well as the importance of place in shaping identities, particularly in the context of indigenous cultures.

Old Allegiances, New Alliances It is also important to avoid the temptation to idealize the material conditions of diaspora as necessarily leading to greater tolerance, equality, or political progressiveness. One consequence of celebrating fluidity, in the form of immigration or the kind of flexible identity assumed to arise from racial and cultural hybridity, is the re-marginalization of those groups who are unwilling or unable to "move with the times." This category potentially includes diverse minority groups, including the elderly, disabled people, the poor, or those whose physical characteristics don't conform to the prevailing **aesthetic** codes of racial blending (codes displayed in Caucasian-featured black Barbie dolls, for example [DuCille]). Moreover, celebratory accounts of hybridity often gloss over the dynamics of power that shape contemporary cross-cultural relations. Those conditions, and responses to them, can serve to entrench rather than dissolve identities in a form of macho self-assertion.

Rap music is one example of a cultural form that has produced controversial forms of community, in part because its politics are so ambiguous. At the same time as it expresses a sense of collective anger and alienation at the racist structures of dominant society, rap also has a strong affinity with mainstream cultural aspirations of individualism and material success, along with extreme forms of patriarchy and homophobia. This politics has produced some odd alliances across race and class—demonstrated, for example, by the huge success of white rapper Eminem, who is popular not just among white youth, but also with blacks, who respect both his talent and his (often ironic) self-consciousness about race, and also identify with the themes of suffering and resistance in his music. Less positively, Eminem has been characterized as drawing a community of fans, black and white, united by a generalized anger against "society" that is stoked by songs that evoke fantasies of violent revenge (Holloway).

Thus, the forces of diaspora, and the forms of cultural hybridity they enhance, powerfully influence the formation of contemporary group identity. As well as reconfiguring the identities of those who have experienced migration in a direct way, the politics of diaspora has shaped the production of community more generally, creating greater fluidity—and sometimes conflict—between collectivities defined by race, class, and cultural tradition. We need to be cautious, however, not to read the story of identity and community as a tidy linear narrative that moves from enclaves of race and nation to a more open and cosmopolitan global culture shaped by diaspora and hybridity. Identity and/or community formations in the contemporary world are characterized by strong foundations in traditional models of belonging that are constantly being broken, modified, and in some cases reinforced in response to the pressures of **globalization** (see Chapter 10).

POST-NATIONAL IDENTITIES: MELTED, FROZEN, RECONSTITUTED

Consumerism, Identity, and Resistance As we have noted above, the breaking up of traditional identity categories has been accompanied by the resurgence of new forms of nation and identity politics. Many of these movements are informed by strong histories of marginalization that cannot be addressed by a new rhetoric of inclusivity and the erasure of distinct identities. As with all such collective identity projects, they are also beset by problems of exclusions and the suppression of internal differences, such as those explored in *Little Mosque on the Prairie.*

An additional problem with the assertion of more or less homogeneous group identities rests in the danger of **commodifying** difference—that is, of turning it into an exotic spectacle that not only lacks political agency, but also further disenfranchises minority groups by objectifying them for consumption by the majority. This danger is accentuated in our intensely visual culture, which tends to operate through the *aestheticization* of difference, in which meaning is reduced to pure visual effect. This form of signification is more or less harmful depending on the power of the group whose identity is being portrayed, the context in which that portrayal occurs—how it is represented, and how and by whom it has been produced.

Through the commodification of culture, "objects and images are torn free of their original referents and their meanings become a spectacle open to almost infinite translation. Difference ceases to threaten, or to signify power relations. Otherness is sought after for its exchange value, its exoticism and the pleasures thrills and adventures it can offer" (Rutherford 11).

The Marketing of Difference   Difference has become a major marketing tool, functioning not just to increase profits by appealing to increasingly narrow **market segments,** but also to reproduce a particular ideological vision that harnesses the happy image of unity-through-diversity to an individualist ethic of **consumerism**. Represented most famously in 1980s Benetton ads, which promoted an idealized racial diversity through the presentation of stereotypically white, black, and Asian models dressed in different-coloured sweaters, the strategy of difference also defines more recent ad campaigns by companies such as Gap and Nike. These ads convey a message of corporate social responsibility while carefully abstracting the images they present from any complicating historical contexts. Thus, "difference is stripped of all social and political antagonisms and becomes a commercial symbol for what is youthfully chic, hip, and fashionable" (Giroux 15).

These representations of difference interact in complicated ways with actual group identity. On the one hand, advertising depends on extensive research in which consumers are polled in an attempt to identify genuine group identities, which then become the basis for the images portrayed in ads. As our discussion of **consumption** in Chapter 5 emphasizes, however, marketers ultimately do not find so much as they *create* their ideal consumers, **appropriating** forms of identity, meaning, and pleasure that are based on memory and lived experience into superficial categories of "lifestyle"—in which being part of a particular tribe (or switching from one tribe to another) is as simple as changing one's shirt or listening to a different band.

This is not to suggest that there is a simple distinction between "real," lived identities and those produced through commercial media; indeed, as Benedict Anderson shows, modern identities are inseparable from the structures of the media and the capitalist economy. Just as forms of early print media such as the newspaper played an instrumental

UNITED COLORS OF BENETTON.

With their in-your-face violation of cultural taboos surrounding race and sexuality, Benetton ads have been read as both socially progressive and crassly exploitative of the minority groups represented in them.

role in the creation of national identities, more recent forms of electronic media have helped to shape postmodern identities. The so-called 500-channel universe of television, with its abundance of specialty channels, has arguably helped to reinforce identities based on age, religion, culture, and ethnicity, while facilitating the production of new, increasingly narrow identities based on taste and lifestyle. The development of more interactive television, in addition to the much greater capacity of Internet technology to increase user autonomy, has further served as a means for new and flexible constructions of community.

That many of these communities are initially constructed as fan groups, brought together by their participants' love for a particular celebrity or media form, does not mean we should dismiss them as shallow or insignificant. The collective mourning by members of an opera e-group for a woman in the group who died in the September 11 attacks, for example, demonstrates that the pleasures of fandom can be a catalyst for more substantial forms of emotional investment (Wiltse "Globalization"). Interpellated as consumers, the members of these groups frequently translate the pleasure and emotional connection they derive from a particular manifestation of celebrity or entertainment culture into deeper forms of belonging.

Virtual Belonging

"Can we build a new kind of politics? Can we construct a more civil society with our powerful technologies? Are we extending the evolution of freedom among human beings?" (Katz 68). These stirring questions (in sharp contrast to the ironic tone of Joe's rant!) provide the lead-in to an article in the December 1997 issue of *Wired* magazine describing the emergence of a new kind of community—the digital nation. Based on a Merrill Lynch–*Wired* survey of the attitudes and beliefs of users of communications technology—cell phone, beeper, laptop, and home computer—the article set about to describe (and celebrate) the possibilities of digital citizen- or *netizen*-ship, a new form of belonging unconstrained by place, gender, race, sexual orientation, or national origin. According to the article, netizens were found to share a number of traits in common: in general they are "knowledgeable, tolerant, civic-minded, and radically committed to change. Profoundly optimistic about the future, they're convinced that technology is a force for good and that [the] free-market economy functions as a powerful engine of progress" (Katz 71). They also constitute a powerful new force in society, able to assert considerable influence over traditional political processes but, more significantly, embodying possibilities for new forms of democratic politics.

If we accept the premise of this article, the explosion of membership in online social networking sites in the decade following its publication represents a huge leap for

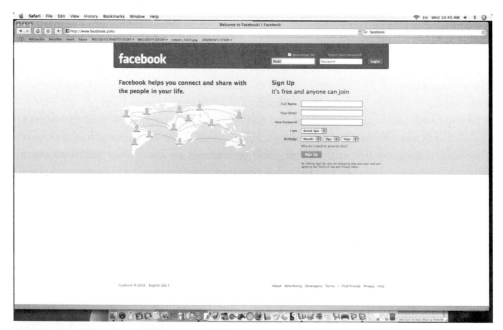

Social networking sites offer some of the same forms of support and connection provided by traditional communities along with new possibilities of flexibility. Whether they strengthen or threaten those more material connections is a different question.

democracy. In practice, the cultural and political upshot of these virtual communities is mixed. On the one hand, the extensive use of networking sites by Barack Obama team in his successful campaign for the U.S. presidency highlights the potential for virtual connections to translate into more substantial forms of civic involvement. On the other hand, the voluntary nature of web groups—participants have almost unlimited choice about the nature and degree of their involvement—doesn't do much to promote either tolerance or social responsibility. A U.K. study found that while online social networks have the potential to deliver support to the least powerful members of society,

> those at greatest risk from its pernicious effects are the young, isolated and disadvantaged—those same vulnerable groups. Similarly, online networks could be a valuable aid to community cohesion, but communities already struggling with divisions may find that online social networks inflame problems further ("Does Social Networking Boost Democracy")

The popularity of videos documenting schoolyard and locker-room fights, along with highly publicized cases of cyber-bullying, testifies to the capacity of digital technology to entrench social differences rather than contribute to their elimination.

Suggested Activity 7.3

How and to what extent is your sense of identity and community shaped by digital technologies? In your experience, does digital communication enhance and/or restrict possibilities for connection, belonging, and social responsibility?

Deterritorialization/Re-territorialization

Articles like the one cited above from *Wired* are unreservedly optimistic about the capacity for digital technology, along with other processes of globalization, to create possibilities for new identities and communities. This is a valid belief to some extent, as we note above, and discuss further in Chapter 10: the weakening of traditional borders obstructing the flow of information, goods, money, and, to a lesser extent, people has created new forms of community and made it possible to imagine the fulfillment of Marshall McLuhan's idea of a truly "global village." At the same time, the economic and social inequalities that define current global relations—inequalities that are, by most estimates, growing—seriously undercut the utopian ideas presented in articles such as Katz's. That the constituency of the "netizens" in Katz's article was exclusively American—a fact not commented on in the article—suggests the extent to which the dominant vision of global society is still confined, culturally and geographically, to a specific segment of the world's population.

The things not mentioned in Katz's article—economic inequalities, fears (whether real or imagined) of Americanization, and the existence of vast numbers of the "unconnected"—all complicate the possibilities for the achievement of a global wired community, let alone a genuinely democratic one. These factors, in combination with concerns about loss of cultural heritage, a form of historical belonging that is often grounded in the ecology of particular places, give rise to new forms of nationalism and other models of local community that rival the placeless world of the netizen. While some of these new identities clearly serve to advance the autonomy of their members, others (gated communities, anti-immigrant and fundamentalist groups) in paradoxical cooperation with the *dis*identifying forces of global capitalism that they in principle oppose, serve to further entrench inequality and conflict.

One example of a dodgy attempt to defend community values from the onslaught of globalization was a code of conduct prepared for immigrants by the council of the small agricultural Quebec town of Hérouxville. The document educated newcomers on such subjects as women's rights, noting that in Quebec a woman can "among other things, drive a car, vote freely, sign checks, decide for herself" and "dress as she sees fit respecting of course the democratic decency." Conversely, Council would "consider that killing women in public beatings, or burning them alive are not part of our standard of life" ("Hérouxville Town Charter"). Adopted in response to debates over provincial policy regarding "reasonable accommodation" of religious minorities, the code was widely criticized for its obvious targeting of Muslims. Hérouxville's status as an almost exclusively white, Catholic, francophone community with only one immigrant family (one blogger sarcastically observed: "Well that's a shock. You'd think people would be lining up to move to such a welcoming place" ["Quebec Town"]) only strengthened the charges of xenophobia.

While we can be shocked at the naked hostility of the motion (which, it should be noted, attracted some sympathy as well as condemnation), it is important to think about some of the surrounding circumstances. In defence of the document, councillor André Drouin claimed that most of the criticism came from "people of the ruling classes, the elected and the non-elected, and from people considered to be part of the intellectual elite" (Drouin, qtd. in "Bouchard Taylor"). Using **populist** rhetoric (see Chapter 1), he defends what he deems to be an expression of democratic will accountable to "'Québecois' particularities" against the powerful, unelected judiciary of English Canada. Not mentioned, but implied, are the urban elites within Quebec, in Montreal in particular, whose accommodation of minorities rarely seems to extend to poor white farmers. As Quebec journalist Alain Dubuc observes:

> We are reminded that the fragmentation of a society can take on several different forms, and that the risk of withdrawal or retreat, which can damage the connection between host society and newcomers, may also divide the host society itself. What separates the urban and rural worlds can sometimes be more important that what separates communities sharing the same urban space. . . .

> The elite—politicians, judges, intellectuals and the media—have elaborated a vision of the relationship between the majority and the various minorities,

without bothering to check if the people were following along, and pretending not to see the cracks forming in the self-righteous facade.

We must not forget this other more contentious dialogue, even though it gets a lot less attention, if we want to be able to respond to the kinds of fear and escalation that gives birth to crises such as Hérouxville. (Dubuc A17).

The image of community expressed in Hérouxville is worlds away from that of the television series *The O.C.* with which we began this chapter. Hérouxville is a real place, and "the O.C"—at least as it is depicted in the television show—is not; but it is worthwhile to compare for a moment the two visions, for what they say about the fears and fantasies that shape our imagined communities. At one end of the fantasy extreme is a world of unfettered mobility, in which concerns about individual freedom supersede concerns about cultural identity, democracy, or equality. At the other end is a world of stability and security, in which social interaction is governed by tradition. Though one appears to be more liberal than the other (the standard of "decency" governing women's dress is a bit, well, stretchier in Newport Beach than it is in Hérouxville), both represent themselves as socially progressive. In both fantasy communities, the rules of engagement are unwritten but firmly understood. In different ways, the two fantasies conceal fears of the racial tensions, forms of (post)colonial oppression and growing economic inequalities that beset real communities, including Hérouxville, Quebec, and Orange County, California.

Globalization has, however, revitalized the ideals and realities of community in important ways. With the massive demonstrations that were launched against meetings of world financial and political leaders in Seattle (1999), Washington, D.C. (2000), and Quebec City (2001), the 2001 World Social Forum in Porto Alegre in Brazil, and more recent protests against the U.S.-led war in Iraq, new and unexpected collective identities have emerged, defined by coalitions of farmers, environmentalists, students, socialists, and anarchists. Significantly, these were groups that previously had little to do with one another and that differed radically in demographics, geographical base, and even politics. They came together, however, in new and powerful coalitions, united through their critical resistance to neoliberalism. These alliances were enabled in large part through technologies such as the Internet, which, while they may not have realized the utopian dreams of some users discussed earlier, have clearly been taken up to further democratic ends far different from their initial commercial and military applications. Significantly, these coalitions work by harnessing the engines of global capitalism to more or less anti-capitalist ends. They thus point to the power of collectivities to enact substantial political change. They also point to a significant shift in the dynamics of collective identity from the relatively fixed markers of class, nation, and race to more fluid and multiple forms of definition. These activist groups both reflect and influence the generation of identities in the realm of popular culture—identities that may not be explicitly political, but that have concrete political *effects* in the way people imagine their places in the world and capacities to effect change.

SUGGESTIONS FOR FURTHER READING

Anderson, Benedict. *Imagined Communities.* London: Verso, 1983.

Bhabha, Homi. *Nation and Narration.* London: Routledge, 1990.

Giddens, Anthony. *Modernity and Self-Identity.* Cambridge: Polity, 1991.

Hall, Stuart, and Paul du Gay, eds. *Questions of Cultural Identity.* London: Sage, 1996.

hooks, bell. *Yearning: The Cultural Politics of Race and Gender.* Toronto: Between the Lines, 1990.

Mackey, Eva. *The House of Difference: Cultural Politics and National Identity in Canada.* Toronto: University of Toronto Press, 2002.

Said, Edward. *Culture and Imperialism.* London: Chatto and Windus, 1993.

———. *Orientalism.* New York: Vintage, 1979.

Chapter 8

Subcultures and Countercultures

Not a moment passes without each one of us experiencing, on every level of reality, the contradiction between oppression and freedom; without each one of us being caught up and weirdly twisted by two antagonistic perspectives simultaneously.

—Raoul Vaneigem

INTRODUCTION: THE MAINSTREAM AND OTHER STREAMS

To a large degree, the way that we have been addressing popular culture in this book has been to focus on the dominant or most prevalent forms of culture in the Western world today. By "dominant" we mean what is usually described as **mass culture**—forms of culture that are accessible, widely available, and intended for consumption by as many people as possible. There is no real mystery about the forms of popular culture that one might consider to be dominant: Hollywood and Bollywood blockbusters, pop music on the Billboard Top 40, Céline Dion, broadcast television, video games, and so on.

There are two ways in which such things might be seen as dominant. First, if we measure the prevalence of this or that form of culture by the sheer number of people that listen to it, watch it, or otherwise participate in it (whether this is measured by attendance, sales, or revenue figures), James Cameron's *Titanic* (1997) or Christopher Nolan's The Dark Knight (2008) is dominant in ways that Canadian films such as Gary Burns's *Waydowntown* (2000) or Guy Maddin's *My Winnipeg* (2007) can only hope to be. Second, dominance can refer to the core set of beliefs, ideas, and **identities** that are circulated through forms of popular culture. In this respect, *Waydowntown* might be seen as an expression of dominant culture, too. Though made on a small budget and shot in Calgary, the critique of dead-end business culture articulated in *Waydowntown* shares a great deal with other much more popular films, such as *American Beauty* or *Office Space*. Even though *Waydowntown* is an indie film, financed outside of the major studio system, formally and structurally it resembles the most common forms of movie making (*My Winnipeg*'s mockumentary style is slightly more adventurous). In this second, wider understanding of dominance, a small or limited audience isn't in and of itself a guarantee that a film or any other form of popular culture advocates or expresses views and ideas contrary to mainstream, dominant culture.

While we have tended to focus on the meaning and impact of dominant forms of popular culture, some of the ideas that we have been discussing in the preceding chapters cannot help but cast doubt on the existence of this very fact—that is, that there is anything like a single, dominant culture. In Chapter 4, we challenged Horkheimer's and Adorno's culture industry thesis, which imagines people as little more than consumers who are completely duped by the nature of the **capitalist** world in which they live; in our discussion of **consumption** in Chapter 5, we drew attention to the multiple ways in which people make meaning through their varied practices of consumption; and in our discussion of groups and identities in the previous two chapters, it is clear that identity formation, too, is more complicated than might be suggested by the idea of dominant forms of popular culture.

In the context of these discussions, "mainstream" culture looks a lot less mainstream than we generally tend to imagine when we employ this term. Or to put this another way: one of the things that becomes clear when studying popular culture is that our idea of the mainstream is sometimes less a reality than it is a cultural construction that regulates our activities through the establishment of very powerful cultural norms—norms that

Gary Burns's *Waydowntown* exposes the sterility of contemporary life through an investigation of the arid spaces of work and consumption.

everyone adheres to in some ways, but that everyone also contravenes or goes against in numerous others. No one is purely mainstream, not even the characters on *Friends* (who, for instance, revel in free pornography, engage in sexual relationships outside of marriage, and engage in other forms of behaviour that belie their otherwise straight, clean-cut image). As popular culture itself has pointed out over and over again, there is an infinity of strange and unusual things happening behind the "normal," everyday façade of white picket fences and suburban garage doors (as you can see in any episode of *Desperate Housewives*, *Big Love*, or *Weeds*). Who would have thought, for instance, that so many Canadians would support the legalization of marijuana—and even have tried it themselves?

But to say that the idea of the mainstream is a creation is not to say that there is no such thing. There *do* seem to be general, widespread patterns of social behaviour present within societies that guide both individual and group activity. As we have seen throughout this book, one of the main reasons why scholars have become interested in the study of popular culture is because of the powerful role it plays in generating and regulating social behaviour. Scholars are also interested in how popular culture has been used to work *against* dominant ways of behaving and acting, in both the minor ways in which (as we suggested above) everyone goes against the grain of the mainstream in some way, but also in more extreme or direct ways. In this chapter, we will be focusing on groups that challenge the values, ideas, and structures of mainstream culture consciously and directly through their actions and practices: **subcultures** and **countercultures**. In their actions and practices, subcultures and countercultures oppose dominant structures that they see as limiting, repressive, and/or problematic. Subcultures and countercultures are engaged in the struggle to create new and different forms of social reality. In many cases, but especially since the Second World War, this struggle has often been directed against popular or mass culture itself; paradoxically, this attack on popular culture has often come through the creation of new forms of popular culture, which are themselves often absorbed into mainstream culture in a perpetual back-and-forth that has shaped contemporary experience profoundly.

Minority–Majority Relationships

In the next section, we will establish some preliminary distinctions between these two kinds of groups. But first, we need to note that the very idea of subcultures and countercultures immediately re-invokes the idea of a dominant culture that we challenged above. The prefixes "sub" and "counter" each imply a number of things, as we will see below. One of the main things that they signify, however, is the relationship of a smaller "culture," however understood, to the larger, defining culture of a given society at a given moment. In other words, whatever else they might signal, the concepts of subcultures and countercultures opposes a **minority** group to the majority: it makes no sense to speak of a subculture or a counterculture that is "dominant."

Furthermore, this minority–majority relationship is generally an antagonistic one. While it has become common to use the term "subculture" to refer to all kinds of practices and activities that might be considered strange or unusual, we will try to use these concepts somewhat more precisely. For example, people who play Scrabble seriously enough to attend tournaments and vie for national (and even global!) championships might be interesting or unusual. But these Scrabble players do not constitute a genuine subculture. Why not? First, players of Scrabble—no matter how attentively or religiously—are, in the end, playing a popular game by its prescribed rules. This stands in contrast to, for instance, writers of "slash fiction," who express their own desires and fantasies by writing original (and often erotically charged) stories that borrow characters from popular televisions shows such as *Star Trek*. Similarly, Scrabble players don't bend a popular cultural form into a different shape—like, for example, the numerous fans who produced and distributed online "improved" versions of George Lucas's *Star Wars Episode I: The Phantom Menace* or have mocked films, videos, and television programs on YouTube. Through their actions, writers of slash fiction, the creators of the "phantom edits," and YouTube "mockumentarians" all express dissatisfaction with the limits and constraints of popular culture; the same cannot be said of serious Scrabble players, who can easily indulge their passion for the game while being otherwise upstanding, productive citizens.

Of course, the same could be said for our other two examples: a phantom editor by night could well be a university professor by day, and YouTube videomakers can be students, lawyers, doctors, or whatever. What we want to draw attention to here is that a practice shouldn't be considered subcultural unless its aim is to draw attention to the limits of majority practices and to offer new practices or cultural forms as an alternative; having an interesting hobby does not a subculture make. Subcultures and countercultures are both antagonistic; one of the ways of distinguishing between subcultures and countercultures is by looking at the precise nature of their antagonism toward mainstream culture and at the kinds of new forms that they propose as an alternative to mainstream or dominant culture.

After making some general distinctions between subcultures and countercultures, the remainder of this chapter will examine the relationship between popular culture and these groups in two ways. First, it will consider the ways in which sub- and countercultures have been *represented* in popular culture, specifically popular film. There are a few reasons why we have chosen to begin with **representations** of these antagonist cultures. One of the main ways in which sub- and countercultures are brought into contact with the "dominant," mainstream culture is through popular cultural representations of these practices. Our sense of the possibilities and limits of these groups—a sense that tends to be very different from what these groups themselves believe their aims and goals to be—is often staged within popular cultural forms. While analyzing representations of sub- and countercultures does not give us an accurate account of the practices of these groups, it does help us to understand one of the ways in which these practices become meaningful within popular culture. Starting out with representations also reminds us of the proximity of subcultures to mainstream culture. All too commonly, sub- and countercultures are imagined as being absolutely separate from and unaffected by popular culture. The opposite is in fact the case: often, popular culture has an impact on how subcultural groups stylize or represent themselves. To offer just one small snapshot: the roots of the "gangsta" tough-guy pose that emerges in hip-hop culture can be found in part in the gangster tough-guy pose of *The Godfather* films. In the mid-nineties, rapper Snoop Dogg styled himself as "Tha Doggfather," striking a very *Godfather*-esque pose on an album cover. The writers of *The Sopranos* have whimsically depicted its contemporary New Jersey hoods watching and making use of Coppola's filmic trilogy as a source for their own gangster poses; "authentic" roots sometimes have representations at their base.

Following this look at representations of sub- and countercultures, the second emphasis of this chapter is on the politics of subcultures in particular. As we will see below, countercultures are usually imagined as explicitly political; it's harder (at first) to see how a subcultural practice like skateboarding might also be political, if in a different way than an organized march down the streets of a capital city might be. For this reason, we have chosen to focus to a greater degree here on subcultures as opposed to countercultures.

Investigating the practices of subcultures and countercultures offers rich insights into the ways in which culture, especially popular culture, operates in the world today. From culture jamming (see Close-Up 8.2 later in this chapter) to the practices of religious countercultures (a category in which one might be able to include everything from Mormonism to the Raelians), from the peace movements of the 1960s to the contemporary techno-music-infused Love Parades that fill the streets of Berlin and other European cities each summer, there are numerous groups in which "culture is deeply political" and "can be used as means of resistance" (Duncombe). In the words of Stephen Duncombe, "In order to strive for change, you first have to imagine it, and culture is the repository of the imagination" (35).

SUBCULTURES AND COUNTERCULTURES: WHAT'S THE DIFFERENCE?

In what way do subcultures differ from countercultures? Are they fundamentally different, or do these two terms point to the same groups, activities, and practices, though in slightly different ways?

To some degree, the distinction between subcultures and countercultures is artificial. Subcultures and countercultures flow fluidly into one another: their boundaries are permeable. As the cultural critic George McKay puts it, "subcultures feed the counterculture—the range of subcultural movements from hippy through punk through rave and others contributes to the increasingly resistant lifestyle or perspective of counterculture" (6). Even so, it is both possible and necessary to draw a distinction between subcultures and countercultures, especially if we want to understand both the relationship that each has to popular culture *and* their impact and influence on mainstream culture. While their aims and activities are often congruent, these terms do point to different kinds of practices and activities, and should not be seen as simply interchangeable terms designating the exact same thing.

One way of gauging this difference is by considering the use of the terms in scholarly studies. A quick library search will show that the term "subculture" is used to describe things as diverse as science-fiction fans, communities in Appalachia, gay and lesbian communities, the lifestyle of singles, the practices of minority religious groups, cults, squatters, Japanese-Americans, bodybuilders, and food cooperatives. A search under the term "counterculture" pulls up a much more limited range of topics: communes, the sixties, and what have been described as "new social movements"—groups that are engaged in politics outside the boundaries of traditional political parties (e.g., women's rights, the civil rights movement, environmental groups, the anti-**globalization** movement, etc.).

Even this first, cursory attempt to separate sub- and countercultures highlights a key difference between the two terms: while subcultures may be political in their aims and activities, countercultures are *explicitly* so. The goal of countercultures is to replace the social and political values and beliefs of the majority with their own values, which they see as unjust, discriminatory, limiting, and regressive. For example, the heterogeneous groups and activities that are commonly referred to by the term "the sixties," from the hippie movement to drug culture, from the struggle for civil rights to the movement against the Vietnam War, were motivated by a common dissatisfaction with dominant social and political institutions and a desire to fundamentally alter these values. The energies that fuel countercultures come from the possibility (and hope) of radically altering the way things are. (Of course, the degree of seriousness with which this possibility is pursued varies greatly.) On the other hand, the power of subcultures comes from the tensions created by the relationship between subcultural practices and the practices of majority culture. Subcultures draw strength from the fact that their practices *are not* those of the rest of the society of which they are a part. As Sarah Thornton has put it, "the defining attribute of 'subcultures' . . . lies with the way the accent is put on the distinction between a particular cultural/social group and the larger culture/society" (5).

Subcultures

The concept of "subcultures" is a relatively recent one, developed first in the 1940s by a group of sociologists associated with the University of Chicago. These sociologists wanted to better understand the complex dynamics of contemporary Western societies. All large societies are made up of numerous smaller groups of people. While we might belong abstractly to a **nationally** defined society (Canadians, Americans, Slovenians, etc.), we do so through our participation with concrete groups of people with whom we have something in common. Such groups might include political organizations, churches, ethnic communities, sports teams, and work communities. Subcultures are also groups of people who share something in common. What makes subcultures different than other groups or communities in society is that they are (most commonly) groups that deviate or differ from existing social norms.

Subcultures are typically conceived of as "disenfranchised, disaffected and unofficial" (Thornton 2). They exist "underground," outside of the mainstream of society in minor, if not hidden, tributaries and out-of-the-way spaces that they try to secure as their own. Furthermore, subcultures are often identified with youth groups, and youth culture in particular. In contemporary societies, youth have creatively expressed their dissatisfaction with the social norms that they encounter as they enter adulthood by adopting unconventional practices, lifestyles, and attitudes. Space is also an essential component of subcultures: space within which to meet, to act, to form a community, to forge common bonds. Such spaces can range from underground clubs in semi-abandoned parts of large urban centres (CBGB in the Bowery section of New York, Yorkville coffee houses in the sixties in Toronto) to open-air festivals (the numerous large concerts held in the U.K. in the seventies, outdoor rave events in Europe and Canada in the nineties); from the use of public spaces by skateboarders (for example, the poured concrete ramps and stairs that make up the Art Gallery of Hamilton's sculpture garden) to the "space" that the Internet has made available for the creation of a wide range of virtual subcultures (for example, *Flight of the Conchords* fans, those who want to do away with **copyright**, and online gamers).

Countercultures

The concept of a counterculture is equally recent, though, as with the concept of subcultures, the term has since its invention been used to refer to groups and activities prior to the second half of the twentieth century. "Counterculture" is a term still most commonly used in reference to the politics of the 1960s, especially with respect to the art, culture, and politics generated around the protests against the U.S. war in Vietnam.

Countercultures pose an explicit challenge to the existing order of things. Put bluntly: their goal is to change the world. While this is an explicitly political goal, countercultures cannot be reduced to their political activity alone. There is an important cultural aspect to the activities of countercultures, which distinguishes them from (for example) the actions of non-governmental political organizations (NGOs) or even most contemporary activist groups. Countercultures have their

The anti-globalization movement, whose participants have held protests in Quebec City and other urban centres, constitutes one of the major countercultural forces today.

own privileged set of cultural objects (especially, forms of countercultural or "alternative" music), through which they express, articulate, and consolidate their political views (think of the link between some forms of popular music in the sixties and the activism of the period).

To perhaps an even greater degree than subcultures, countercultures express their politics culturally through a demand for a fundamental revision of lifestyle practices. After all, what makes a culture a *counter*culture is its contravention and contradiction of not just mainstream politics, but also the culture that produces these politics, which can be located in the daily, lived practices of the mainstream. If we use as an example sixties youth culture (in the U.S. as well as in much of the rest of the world), this reform of lifestyle was expressed in the adoption of communal living (group living in response to the alienation and **individualism** of capitalist culture, expressed spatially by massively expanded suburbs), vegetarianism (animal rights and healthy lifestyles), drug use (in opposition to the mainstream demands that everyone spend their lives engaged in productive labour), and open sexuality (a challenge to the restrictions of "normal" sexuality and the marriage bond). This list could easily be expanded.

Both subcultures and countercultures take culture seriously. They understand not only that culture can be a way of articulating political views and perspectives, but also that in contemporary society culture plays a crucial role in political expression. In general, both have a tendency to view "dominant" popular culture through the lens of Horkheimer's and Adorno's cultural industry thesis (see Chapter 4). One of the things that subcultures and countercultures react to is what they see as the dearth of genuine cultural expression and experience in the age of mass culture. In response, they produce their own forms of culture—their own clothing styles, music, and cultural practices—and articulate new ways of living and behaving.

Differences of Scale   The emergence of the concepts of subcultures and countercultures following the Second World War can be linked to the decline of genuine public spaces for political debate and a sense that mainstream political groups were no longer accountable to the public. With so many similarities, what distinguishes sub- from countercultures more than anything else is perhaps the *scale* of their reaction to the gradual impoverishment of contemporary political and social life, which seemed to go hand in hand with the fiscal improvement of life in Western countries; even while most people were better off financially, they felt more and more unhappy socially. Countercultures presume to act on a bigger social canvas than subcultures and are limited neither spatially to specific "scenes" or locales, nor by the dominance of youth within them. For example, contemporary anti- or alter-globalization movements include individuals and groups from around the world, and people of all ages with varying ideas about what needs to be changed and how to change it. What might be seen as loosely connecting these different actors is their insistence that "Another World is Possible" (the animating phrase of the World Social Forums).

It is important to emphasize that this difference of scale should not by itself be seen as valorizing the politics of countercultures over subcultures. That is, one conclusion that could be reached quickly is that, because countercultures work out their political commitments more explicitly and engage them more directly, they accomplish more than subcultures. Indeed, while countercultures have not been immune to criticism from any number of vantage points, it has been subcultures that are more commonly viewed (by the mainstream media, for example) as little more than self-indulgent practices engaged in by spoiled youth who will "grow out of it" soon enough, or eccentric adults who are spending their free time engaged in practices that are different from what it's imagined most people are doing. This view of subcultures tends to reduce them to something like fashion trends, which youth engage in energetically only to forget about when another trend arises. One of the main things that scholars who have studied subcultures over the past two decades have shown is that this view is mistaken. If subcultures aren't always explicit in their politics, their very existence stands as an implicit rejection of the practices and ways of life of majority culture. As we'll see below, subcultures have complex politics, too, even if these are expressed in different ways than in countercultures.

We want to stress two points before continuing. First, the goal here is not to lay out strict definitions for the purpose of setting up a taxonomic or classificatory system into which we would then place various resistant, minority groups. The aim of these distinctions is to offer a broad initial framework within which to consider the specifics of sub- and countercultural practices and actions; simply dividing groups into one or another category is only the first step in trying to understand what is going on. Second, as we already suggested above, there is considerable slippage in these categories. As McKay points out, the counterculture draws on subcultures for elements of its own cultural practices. This slippage will be evident in our discussion in this chapter, and, indeed, is endemic to the study of these groups and their practices.

Artistic Manifestoes   As an example of this slippage, it is has become common to treat artists' movements and avant-garde manifestoes as expressions of countercultural sentiments. In terms of the rough distinctions that we have drawn here, however, artistic avant-gardes seem more like subcultures. Though artist manifestoes gesture to wholesale revolutions in sensibility (as in Tristan Tzara's "Dada Manifesto" of 1918: "I am against action; for continuous contradiction, for affirmation too, I am neither for nor against. . ." [249]), they do so within a relatively restricted social sphere (relatively elite forms of artistic production) and do not always demand a complete lifestyle revolution. (That is, being both for and against contradiction does not mean that one has to give up smoking, or one's sports utility vehicle, and so on; one can be bourgeois and a dadaist at the same time.)

However, the gesture made to a total social revolution is not insignificant. In a way common to countercultures, a shift in the form and style of artistic production is imagined as having large-scale political effects. The Québécois manifesto "Refus Global" (1948) was imagined by the painter who is usually seen as its primary author, Paul Émile Borduas, as *maybe* having had an impact on painting in Canada. However, by making this aesthetic intervention through a "total refusal" of the political, social, and religious verities of its era, the manifesto played an essential role in bringing about the social changes in Quebec now described as "The Quiet Revolution." A similar categorical

Refus Global

"Refus Global" has been described as "far and away the most important text in the history of Canadian art and a signal event in the history of Québec" (Fetherling 112). Published in 1948 as a collective manifesto signed by Paul-Émile Borduas and 15 younger artists in *Les Automatistes*, its impact on Quebec society went well beyond what one might expect from a document of which only four hundred copies (only half of which sold) were produced. Relentlessly attacking the social conservatism of Quebec society and the power of the Catholic Church in social and cultural affairs, *Refus Global* helped to inaugurate The Quiet Revolution that would reshape life in Quebec.

To break definitively with all conventions of society and its utilitarian spirit! We refuse to live knowingly at less than our spiritual and physical potential; refuse to close our eyes to the vices and confidence tricks perpetuated in the guise of learning, favour, or gratitude; refuse to be ghettoed in an ivory tower, well-fortified but too easy to ignore; refuse to remain silent—do with us what you will, but you shall hear us; refuse to make a deal with la gloire and its attendant honours: stigmata of malice, unawareness or servility; refuse to serve and to be used for such ends, refuse all *intention*, evil weapon of *reason*—down with them, to second place!

Make way for magic! Make way for objective mysteries!

Make way for love!

Make way for necessities!

To this global refusal we contrast full responsibility.

The self-seeking act is fettered to its author; it is stillborn.

The passionate act breaks free, through its very dynamism.

We gladly take on full responsibility for tomorrow. Rational effort, once in its proper place, will be available again to disengage the present from the limbo of the past.

ambiguity can be seen in the case of punk. While punk is almost always treated as a paradigmatic example of a contemporary subculture, the depths of its critique of contemporary culture, which draws on a wide array of political and countercultural currents and theories, suggests that there is more at work than might be indicated by the term subculture.

One final note: As we have stressed elsewhere, it is unproductive to simply dismiss the activities of subcultures and countercultures on the basis of what we know or think we know about (for example) the incorporation of punk or sixties culture into our present-day mainstream. As we said in Chapter 4, the phrase "Resistance is futile!" doesn't turn out to be true—even for the Borg in *Star Trek*, who tried and failed repeatedly to assimilate Captain Picard and his crew into their mechanized world (a perfect allegory for how many of us see the world of contemporary popular culture: as an unfeeling mechanism intent on absorbing everything organic into its metallic confines). Why, then, should it constitute an adequate way of considering the nature of our responses to popular culture? It doesn't—which is not to say that the practices of subcultures and countercultures aren't often contradictory or that they do not have problems. They do, but so does everything else: we shouldn't demand purity of aims or **authenticity** of intent from subcultures and countercultures—in the contemporary world, it is best to imagine that everything is already contaminated, and go from there.

Suggested Activity 8.1

Given the discussion above, is it possible to identify a counterculture (or countercultures) today? Are the various political groups that oppose capitalist culture today linked by common goals and/or ideas about appropriate counter-lifestyles? How does the idea of a counterculture (or countercultures) fit with the relatively new idea of "alternative" culture (or cultures)? Make a list of subcultures and countercultures—and, for that matter, alternative cultures—and try to think about how and why we refer to these groups with these different terms. Are these categories still a productive way to think about contemporary cultural experience?

POPULAR REPRESENTATIONS OF SUBCULTURES AND COUNTERCULTURES

How do we come to understand or know about groups that lie outside the mainstream? Unless we happen to be an active part of a particular subculture or counterculture, our knowledge of it comes to us secondhand, through studies, reports, newspaper articles, and, of course, popular culture. Representation plays a crucial role in how we conceive of these sub- and countercultures. For example, for most of us, our sense of what the sixties counterculture was like and what its lasting significance has been is based on an accumulated sludge of television and film representations, *Behind the Music* documentaries, and experience with the bits and pieces of sixties "classic" rock that we play along to on *Guitar Hero*, as opposed to detailed reading of studies of the period. It is just as difficult to think about punk except through the lens of films such as *Repo Man* and *Sid and Nancy*; the music of more recent "punk" bands, such as Green Day and blink-182; and perhaps through reading the obituaries of punk luminaries such as Dee Dee Ramone and Joe Strummer (lead singer of The Clash). These popular representations influence our sense of what subcultures and countercultures are about, what they managed to accomplish, and to what degree they "succeeded" or "failed" (which is a common, if strange, way to think about these cultural forms and practices). We need to be conscious of the significance of representation not because it is possible to get the accurate, authentic "truth" about sub- or countercultures, but because we should be aware of the way that such representations shade our perceptions and interpretations.

The issue of representation raises another important point, one that we alluded to earlier and that we will discuss in more detail below. In a complex way, popular representations of subcultures and countercultures play an important part not only in how they function, but also in how we understand popular culture. Our sense of subcultures is that they are hidden from view or that their activities take place entirely unnoticed, in the dark. The truth is somewhat different, as Chuck Klosterman makes clear in his discussion of the very different reactions to the almost simultaneous deaths of two American rock musicians: Robin Crosby, lead guitarist for the early 1980s heavy-metal band Ratt, and Dee Dee Ramone, bassist for the seminal New York punk band The Ramones. Klosterman writes:

> The reason that Crosby's June 6 death was mostly ignored is that his band seemed corporate and fake and pedestrian; the reason Ramone's June 5 death will be remembered is that his band was seen as representative of a counterculture that lacked a voice. But the contradiction is that countercultures get endless media attention: the only American perspectives thought to have any meaningful impact are those that come from the fringes. (25)

Though millions and millions of people bought Ratt albums, the band is now "forgotten" in a way that The Ramones (whom no one listened to) are not. In popular culture, subcultures tend to be viewed in two dichotomous ways: either as threatening and dangerous, or as the conscience of mainstream—that is, as the "real" cultural expression of a culture that is otherwise dominated by "bad" commercial culture. (Canadians would rather have Arcade Fire than Céline Dion stand as an example of contemporary Canadian popular music, even if the latter has sold far more CDs than the former). There is another division built into this first one. When subcultures are represented as dangerous, they are often also paradoxically characterized as lacking substance: as mere style that constantly changes. Part of what is supposedly dangerous about subcultures, then, is that they attract people to engage in activities that have far less substance and meaning than mainstream culture. This is the exact opposite of what the public (or at least the media) reaction to Dee Dee Ramone's death suggests: that it is the practices of subculture that leave the permanent record for an otherwise insubstantial mainstream culture, which is defined by shifts in styles or fashion in music, film, and so on that are driven not by art but by the market. We will consider these conflicted ways of representing subcultures and countercultures by looking briefly at three films: *Forrest Gump* (1994), *Fight Club* (1999), and *Ghost World* (2001).

Forrest Gump: Subcultural Deviance

The goal of the film *Forrest Gump* is to offer an overview of the American experience following the Second World War. It accomplishes this by a fairly typical cinematic and novelist procedure, using the life of one individual, the eponymous Forrest Gump (Tom Hanks), to both highlight important events and milestones in U.S history during this period and to explore related shifts in culture and sensibility. Forrest, a fatherless, intellectually challenged Southerner, manages over the course of the film to successfully navigate his way through the real and metaphoric landmines of the past 40 years. His life passes through all of the major events of post–Second World War history, and Forrest comes into direct contact with some of the period's important historical figures. Elvis, a boarder in Forrest's home, adopts his performance style by imitating the inhibited gait that Forrest possesses as an adolescent. Forrest wins a national football championship with Alabama on a team coached by the legendary Bear Bryant; plays a crucial role in the struggle to racially integrate schools in the U.S. South; becomes an inadvertent hero as a soldier in Vietnam; becomes a champion Ping-Pong player; guests on Dick Cavett's television show (where he appears alongside John Lennon); single-handedly invents the running craze; and makes a bundle on Apple stock (he should have waited until the iPhone to sell!)—just to name a few of the symbolically charged things he accomplishes.

Forrest represents the adventure that America undergoes during this era and he navigates it bluntly, pragmatically, and successfully. For the most part, then, even as the film examines many of the difficult moments in post–Second World War American social and cultural life, it celebrates American drive and initiative and suggests that more good things are coming in the future. Forrest's life ends in that most typical place in American cinema: back at home, folded into the comforts and security of family life.

No account of the U.S. experience after the Second World War would be complete, however, without some attention to the roles played by subcultures and countercultures in creating this history. In *Forrest Gump*, the activity of subcultures is typified through the life history of the other major character in the film: the love of Forrest's life, Jenny. Through the opposition of Jenny and Forrest, it becomes clear that Forrest represents not *all* of American experience, but merely the experience of mainstream culture; Jenny represents an alternative path through recent U.S. history—the dark side of Forrest's generally blissful (or at least, blissed out) experience. The film is unambiguous in its portrayal of American counterculture. If Jenny is unable to follow Forrest's path through the major institutions of American life—college, the military, small business, sports, and so on—it is because she has been sexually abused by her father. Her immersion in the counterculture is treated less as a conscious choice than the consequences of a psychic trauma that she never gets to adequately address. Countercultures and subcultures, the film seems to tell us, are for damaged souls. Jenny drifts through the American underworld: she appears in *Playboy*; while Forrest is in the mud of Vietnam, she gets involved with hippies and peaceniks (who drive a VW van painted with rainbow colours); she becomes involved with the SDS (Students' Democratic Society) in Berkeley, which is led by her physically abusive boyfriend; she becomes suicidal after doing lines of coke as part of the early 1980s "me" generation; and, when she finally shows up again in Forrest's life to introduce him to their son, she tells him: "I have some kind of virus and the doctors don't know what it is and there isn't anything they can do about it." If Jenny's trauma leads her into the U.S. counterculture, it is her involvement with it—with *all* of it (missing nothing!) that leads to her death.

It is not difficult to see that the film suggests that subcultures and countercultures are dangerous, destructive, and misguided, especially for those involved in them. In the world narrated by Forrest Gump, happiness and fulfillment are achieved only by following the path of the straight and narrow (which in Forrest's case has the added advantage of putting him into contact with important people, like Presidents Kennedy and Nixon). Forrest's own happiness is impeded only by the fact of Jenny's death, which is the direct consequence of her alternative lifestyle. Forrest's son, who represents the future of American society, is in some respects the product of both the mainstream and the counterculture, of Forrest and Jenny. But what the film actually seems to argue is that America has a future *despite* the presence of the subculture. It is up to Forrest, after all, to raise Forrest Jr. It is not accidental that Forrest Jr. is raised in the same place as his father; for all the things that have happened, the real America perseveres, unchanged by the challenges that the counterculture and history seemed to have posed to it. Near the end of the film, Jenny suggests: "I was messed up for a long time." *Forrest Gump* exemplifies very clearly one of the dominant ways in which subcultures are represented—simply as the actions of misguided, messed-up people.

And yet, there are elements of the film that make us question its representation of American counterculture. Most obviously, it is the character of Forrest himself who causes us to wonder about the narrative we are being sold. Jenny is far more intelligent and self-conscious than Forrest; if Forrest represents the mainstream, then the mainstream is shown to be unthinking—emotional and intuitive rather than reasoned and reflective. Forrest suggests that "for some reason I fit in the army like a round peg." His successes come out of his ability to slide into preexisting systems and institutions; he challenges nothing and accepts everything. In *Forrest Gump*, the options in post–Second World War American society come down to two equally problematic positions: *either* one joins the counterculture and challenges norms and limits, but at the price of one's own happiness, health, and life; *or* one unthinkingly accepts "what is," even if this means participating in an imperialist war or raping the environment (as recorded by Forrest's enormous haul of shrimp in the Gulf of Mexico). This is a false choice, of course; we need not acquiesce to the *either/or* that the film constructs for us. Nor need we accept its **stereotypes** of the counterculture, even if we should note that it is precisely such representations of sub- and countercultures that inform the way in which many of us view their activities, as well as the people who participate in them.

Fight Club: Fight the Power?

A very different, if equally troubling, view of subcultures is presented in David Fincher's cult hit *Fight Club*. What made the film attractive to critics and audiences when it was first released was that it appeared to offer a unique, critical perspective on the values of capitalist society—in particular, the way in which consumption has come to constitute the main goal and purpose of contemporary society. While criticisms of contemporary reality are actually a quite common theme of American cinema, what made *Fight Club* appear to be different from films such as *The Cable Guy* (1996), *The Truman Show* (1998) and *The Matrix* (1999)—or even a more recent film such as *Wall-E* (2008)—was that it translated critique into action through the creation of an anti-capitalist subcultural movement whose ultimate goal is the violent destruction of the system of global consumer credit. (In the wake of the explosion of consumer credit and the crisis caused

Brad Pitt gets tough on consumer culture in *Fight Club*.

by the sub-prime mortgage meltdown in 2007–08, this would be a more popular movement than ever!)

Based on the 1996 first novel of Chuck Palahniuk, *Fight Club* narrates the story of Jack (Edward Norton), an insomniac, bored, corporate drone who finds meaning in his life through his newly formed relationship with Tyler Durden (Brad Pitt), a thrill-seeking everyman. In a number of memorable set pieces, both Jack and Tyler rail against the limits of consumer society. In order to make some connection with people in an unfeeling, individuate society, Jack begins to attend group meetings for people struggling with various diseases and ailments—none of which he has. Jack's job, which is to calculate the cost-effectiveness of consumer recalls (that is, if the cumulative cost of the lawsuits brought against the company as a result of the malfunction of a product would be less than a recall, they cynically decide against it), is depicted in all its existential horror as a brain-deadening series of unfulfilling routines.

It is only when Jack meets Tyler that he begins to "feel" again. A spontaneous fight in the parking lot of a bar leads to the creation of an underground bare-knuckles club where men can beat their sufferings out of each other and learn to feel something (even if it is pain) in a world that has crushed their sensibilities under the weight of **consumerism**. This "fight club" forms the genesis for an anti-consumerist army that is assembled by Jack and Tyler; it engages in a campaign that adopts the stratagems of culture jamming (see Close-Up 8.2) but also moves to more violent and direct assaults on computer stores and coffee shops, and, finally, on the corporate headquarters of credit-card companies, which are destroyed in the final frames of the film.

The film and book contain many rich (though problematic) strands that could be followed up and teased out, but perhaps the defining element of the narrative (which we briefly touch on in Chapter 6) is the connection that it makes between consumerism and the decline of masculinity in contemporary society. The fight clubs are an exclusively male domain: it is not just that men need to be awakened out of their consumerist lassitude, but also that by beating each other up they are re-asserting a supposedly **essential** masculine identity that contemporary culture has stripped from them. For Tyler, the real trauma in contemporary life is that men can no longer be "real" men: virile, physical, and firmly in charge of both the family and the culture at large. Contemporary experience has emasculated men and rendered them impotent. What has brought about this situation is nothing other than consumerism itself, which the film repeatedly identifies as a specifically feminine realm, in line with the long-established **ideologies** of consumerism that we discussed in Chapter 5.

In many respects, the critique of consumerism in *Fight Club* becomes an alibi for an attack on the feminine, especially of the rise of women (and minorities) to positions of power and influence in Western society. The film claims that in a world in which women have at least the potential to be equal to men, men cannot be real men. Instead of working with their bodies in factories, they have to drag themselves to "soft" office jobs and dream of the furniture in Ikea catalogues instead of the supine female bodies one finds in pornography. Changing the world for the better seems to mean putting women back

Culture Jamming

Culture jamming is the practice of turning manifestations of consumer culture—in particular, advertising images—against themselves for political ends. By parodying targeted ad images, culture jamming re-contextualizes them and offers a different set of associations through which they can be read.

Culture jamming has a double aim: to draw attention both to the problems of specific activities and practices (driving environmentally damaging SUVs, exporting the practice of smoking to the developing world, watching television, subscribing to the damaging beauty ideals promoted by the fashion industry) *and* to the limits and dangers of the larger consumerist and capitalist system that legitimates and promotes these activities and practices. One of the most well-known forms of culture jamming is the annual "Buy Nothing Day," held worldwide on the day after American Thanksgiving, which is one of the largest shopping days each and every year. Culture jammers take to the street not only to dissuade people from shopping, but also to remind them of the troubling link that has been developed between the celebration of family and belonging (everyone gathering together for Thanksgiving) and the orgy of consumerism that follows.

The Canadian magazine *Adbusters* has played an integral role in promoting and celebrating various forms of culture jamming. Examples of their campaigns and ads, as well as those of jammers from around the world, can be found at www.adbusters.org.

in their place—hardly an instance of progressive politics or a successful criticism of consumerism, which should presumably create a situation in which men *and* women could engage in consumption differently.

Unlike *Forrest Gump*, which demonizes sub- or countercultural resistance even as it highlights its lack of importance to the main script of historical development, *Fight Club* takes the activities and possibilities of subcultures seriously. Only a group outside the mainstream could shake up a world lost in consumerist dogmatic slumbers: Jack and Tyler cannot change things on their own, nor is it likely that mainstream society will change of its own accord. Nevertheless, this representation of a subculture reinforces mainstream ideologies concerning gender roles in a way that makes us question their aims and goals. Of course, in one respect, this is indeed an "accurate" portrayal of the very real limits of an engagement with gender stereotypes in many subcultures. For example, women skateboarders have had to struggle with the dominance of this practice by men, while women in punk faced similar limits and problems: even as the punks fought against the capitalist world, women punks had to fight for recognition and respect within the subculture itself. However, representational accuracy is hardly the aim of *Fight Club*: if an engagement with the politics of gender in subcultures emerges as a moral of the film, it is only by reading against the grain of its otherwise deeply **patriarchal** logic.

Ghost World: Being Ghostly

Terry Zwigoff's *Ghost World* (2001) offers one of the most compelling and original representations of subcultural practices and activities in recent film. The film's title is quite literal; it explores the ghostly world of alternative lives and practices that exist parallel to and overlap with what we generally imagine as mainstream culture. In doing so, the film also offers an incisive look at the assumptions and presumptions that constitute the mainstream, probing the very real limits that it places on individuals and groups to express their differences.

Ghost World tracks the entry of two high-school friends, Enid (Thora Birch) and Rebecca (Scarlett Johansson), into adulthood in the summer following their graduation from high school. The film begins with Enid and Rebecca's graduation ceremony and the reception that follows. Both are by-the-numbers affairs, with the valedictorian mouthing platitudes (she describes high school as "the training wheels for the bicycle of life") and the reception being typically amenable to the cool kids and torture for the geeks and nerds. From the way that Enid and Rebecca snarl and quip their way through their graduation day, it is clear that they are outsiders. For them, the utter kitschiness and predictability of the graduation exercises are a source of amusement.

Unlike typical depictions of those who do not conform to accepted models, both Enid and Rebecca are remarkably self-confident. Being at right angles to the mainstream and its expectations does not isolate them, but rather it gives them a feeling of power as they navigate their way through the clichés and stereotypes of contemporary culture. They are critical of faux enthusiasms and false emotions, without being cynical or dismissive; indeed, the falsehoods with which contemporary society surrounds itself are for them a continual source of interest and amusement. While dining in Wowsville, an "authentic fifties diner," Rebecca turns on the tabletop jukebox and out pours rap music. "Who could forget this greatest hit from the fifties!" she remarks, to the delight of both women.

Can the friends sustain this joyous, devil-may-care attitude as they make the transition from adolescence to an adult world in which there is a price to be paid for nonconformity? This is the key question around which the plot of the film revolves. Following high school, the women endeavour to find their own apartment, which immediately introduces them to a world that demands compromise and shifts in their priorities. To get an apartment Enid and Rebecca need money, which means that they need to find jobs. Rebecca gets a job in a coffee shop, and as soon as she does her sarcasm seems to become tempered by the pragmatic demands of making money and getting through the week. However, Enid's entry into the adult world is delayed by the need to make up an art class that she, a talented artist in her own right, nevertheless failed in her last term. More significantly, over the course of the summer she gets to see deep into the "ghost world" of the film's title by coming into contact with Seymour (Steve Buscemi), whom she describes at one point as "such a clueless dork, he's almost cool."

Seymour is a lonely, middle-aged man whom life seems to have beaten down. He is equally dismissive of a world made up of, at best, people Enid refers to as "extroverted obnoxious pseudo-bohemian losers." Seymour seems to have enthusiasm for only one thing: collecting rare 78-rpm records, especially of early blues music. His skill and enthusiasm for collecting music that others do not care about defines him against the mainstream, who express open admiration for the rock band Blues Hammer while ignoring the aging blues legend who opens the show that Enid and Seymour go to see.

At the same time, Seymour's interests also confine him to the ghostly, half-real world that he exists in. When Enid first sees Seymour's room, she stands in complete awe: "This is like my dream room," she says, "I would kill to have stuff like this." Seymour is dismissive: he says that he hates his collection, and suggests that collecting is unhealthy, a problem that one would be better off without.

Enid and Seymour develop a strong relationship, based as much on their common attitude toward what is supposedly the "real" world as it is on any physical attraction or emotional involvement. Up to the final sections of the film, *Ghost World* presents us with a remarkable view of the ghost world that subcultures occupy. Zwigoff successfully showed us, in his earlier filmic depiction of the life of the comic book legend R. Crumb, the world and views of outsiders in a sympathetic, though not celebratory, light. Occupying the real world's ghost world does not come without consequences: Enid and Rebecca's relationship erodes, Enid squanders a chance at a college scholarship by producing a controversial work of art, and Seymour's loneliness and isolation seems to be exacerbated rather than improved when he starts dating Dana, a real-estate agent, who buys him his first pair of designer jeans.

In the end, the film seems to imply that no matter how much power Enid's unique attitude yields over the faux–real world she inhabits, it is not enough. Abandoned by all of the people who could have constituted the community of individuals that together produce a sub- or counterculture, Enid leaves town alone on the bus that supposedly never comes. Even in this film, as surely as in *Forrest Gump*, the "real" world appears to have an ultimately irresistible power over all those who try to exist at right angles to it. There is never a firm community of dissenters established, and even where one might expect to find such a community—at Zone-O-Phobia, the comic book store Enid frequents—she and the manager are in constant conflict. "If you really want to fuck up the system," he says, "go to business school. Join a big corporation and fuck up stuff from the inside."

The goal of this section has been to emphasize the various ways in which sub- and countercultures have been represented in dominant forms of popular culture. What we can see from these three very different examples is that while subcultures are celebrated as playing an essential role in history and in social transformation, they are also almost always represented as a problem for society. Sub- and countercultures tend to be represented in relation to dominant culture either as the fringes occupied by those who just can't make it within the mainstream (which is then correspondingly valorized as the domain of "real" values, morals, and beliefs), or as the space in which genuine social discontent is voiced but in the wrong way (violently in *Fight Club*, individualistically in *Ghost World*).

Whatever position different films or television programs take on sub- and countercultures, we can see from these examples that what they in fact highlight are the views of mainstream groups on subcultures—whether dismissive or sympathetic—as opposed to the views and needs expressed in and through sub- and countercultural practices. In other words, these representations tend to present subcultures predominantly as an issue or problem for the mainstream; insofar as these groups also always make use of the **discourses** and representations of mainstream culture, this has an impact on the nature and shape of sub- and countercultural practices as well. There are two things that we should take away from our analysis of these films: first, our understanding of subcultures is affected by representations of them; second, popular cultural representation plays an important (if seemingly contradictory) role in how participants in sub- and countercultures imagine their own role and engage in their own practices, as we will see in more detail below.

THE POLITICS OF SUBCULTURES

There is no society, only individuals.

—Former British Prime Minister Margaret Thatcher

Earlier in this chapter, we suggested that even if subcultures are not explicitly political, their activities and practices always contain an *implicit* political stance—a position or attitude toward gaps and absences in the mainstream culture that individuals seek to redress through their involvement in subcultures. At a very general level, the fragmentation of contemporary societies into an enormous range of active subcultures after the Second World War points to a lack of genuine opportunities for communal or group relations *within* the mainstream. Perhaps a better way of putting this is that, since mainstream North American values tend to celebrate individuality above all else, communal forms of relation outside of the typical markers of group identity (such as **race**, **ethnicity**, or religion) couldn't exist except on the outsides or the margins of mainstream culture. There are, of course, always groups and subgroups that make up each and every society; but subcultures are something new whose very existence points to problems and contradictions in the way reality is constituted by the powers that be.

For instance, it is no surprise that the contradictory demands and stresses that contemporary society has placed on youth in particular would produce a flourishing range of youth subcultures. These subcultures aim to escape the controlling attentions of an adult society that simultaneously infantilizes youth (wants them to remain children) and encourages them to take on adult behaviours and responsibilities earlier and earlier in life. Participating in a subculture is a way of establishing one's own form of social life, with its own rules that may be very different from or even directly opposed to mainstream adult rules and values. While it may be true, as Sarah Thornton has argued, that "the vast majority of British youth subcultures, past and present, do not espouse overt political projects" (177), it nevertheless seems clear that even if their politics are implicit, such politics constitute an essential and important reason for the creation of subcultures to begin with. George McKay has described it in this way: "One of the things hippy and punk had in common . . . was an oppositional impulse, an idealism or rhetoric of idealism. For both, politics and culture were, or could be, or should be, the same thing" (5). If we are to properly understand subcultures, separating forms of cultural expression from politics proper would be a mistake.

Hiding in the Light

What are the forms that this politics takes? There are many, of course: it is both difficult and dangerous to generalize across the wide range of activities and practices that have been characterized as subcultural. However, there does seem to be one mode of politics that many subcultures have adopted—though, again, they have adopted it in many different ways. In his influential book *Subculture: The Meaning of Style*, Dick Hebdige deftly explores the dual, apparently contradictory relationship that subcultures adopt toward mainstream culture.

The effect of subcultures—both with respect to those "within" them and the majority of members of society "without"—is produced through the adoption of both invisibility *and* visibility. Subcultures hide in the shadows, where one can do whatever one likes away from prying eyes, specifically the eyes of the authorities. But insofar as it also seems essential for subcultures to be able both to mark their difference from mainstream culture *and* to engage critically with the limits of that culture, it is also important for the mainstream to be able to sit up and take notice—to be shocked, in other words, whether by the harsh social reality depicted in rap songs or by the graffiti left on the walls of their garages. Hebdige explains that

> the subcultural *milieu* has been constructed underneath the authorised discourses, in the face of multiple disciplines of the family, the school and the workplace. Subculture forms up in the space between **surveillance** and the evasion of surveillance, it translates the fact of being under scrutiny into the pleasure of being watched. It is hiding in the light. (*Subculture* 35)

The Arrival of Punk   We've already seen one of the strange consequences of the way subcultures "hide in the light." The death in June 2002 of Dee Dee Ramone, bassist for The Ramones, was widely interpreted as the passing of a significant cultural era. And yet, relatively few people ever heard him play, either live or on record, and it would be difficult to make a case that The Ramones had a major impact on the popular music that followed them. How could a supposedly minor cultural practice, hidden out of sight in dank clubs in the Bowery and in the rougher streets of London, end up as a pop culture era or touchstone? The answer: by hiding in the light of mainstream attention. For Hebdige, "subcultures are both a play for attention and a refusal, once attention has been granted, to be read according to the Book" (*Subculture* 35). There is no better example of this than the one he himself draws on: punk music and style, which flourished ever so briefly in the mid-seventies, and which has since given birth to numerous other "punk" styles.

As might be suggested by the title of Penelope Spheeris's documentary on the L. A. punk scene, *The Decline of Western Civilization*, punk represented an all-out assault on the values of mainstream "civilization." One would expect the public to recoil from punk and to respond to its challenge with diatribes against it. This is indeed what happened. In the United Kingdom, punk was treated as a pariah subculture, a dangerous movement that was colonizing the minds of some British youth and that thus had to be brought to a rapid end. But how, then, could one explain the incredible popularity and success of the group that became the whipping boy of anti-punk sentiment, the Sex Pistols? At the height of anti-punk fervour (such as it was), the Sex Pistols's "God Save the Queen" reached number two on the British pop charts, and their album *Never Mind the Bollocks* hit the top of the charts. The antiestablishment Sex Pistols and their ilk were tabloid celebrities throughout the late 1970s; by the 1980s, punk had become such a fixture of the London landscape that popular tourist postcards featured pictures of green-haired punks with ripped clothing to send back to the folks in Saskatchewan ("Greetings from London!").

As we will see in the next section, this is commonly seen as evidence of punk's *lack* of politics. But Hebdige's formula lets us see things differently: it is precisely by being available and open for display to the mainstream that the minority culture of punk was able to draw attention to the very real sources of its discontent with both the values of mainstream culture and their relationship to it. "Hiding in the light" allows subcultures to create, maintain, and nurture their own communities of belonging (by "hiding" in clubs, squats, and even the streets), while also engaging with the culture at large (exposing themselves to the "light" of public opinion by displaying their unique styles on the streets, and their music on the airwaves).

Not all subcultures engage in the same forms of display or do so to the same degree. Many subcultures prefer to remain more hidden than punk. However, secret societies, of the kind featured in Stanley Kubrick's *Eyes Wide Shut* and much beloved by scenarists for James Bond films, do not a subculture make.

Avant-Garde Punk

All that punk singers can bring to the presentations of their songs is the gesture of sexual obscenity or of impotent rage. There is a lot of caged simian gibber. . . .

—Anthony Burgess, author of *A Clockwork Orange*

You don't sing about love to people on the dole.

— Johnny Rotten (cited in Szatmary 220)

Punk has been the subject of numerous scholarly studies, popular books (Greil Marcus's *Lipstick Traces*), films (*Sid and Nancy*), and documentaries (*The Great Rock'n'Roll Swindle, The Filth and the Fury*). As perhaps the first instance of a popular cultural form that seemed to be explicitly political (to a higher and more intense degree than the music of the 1960s), punk continues to fascinate and inspire musicians, audiences, and scholars. Yet for all its influence, the era of punk was remarkably short. Less than a year passed between the British debut of The Ramones on July 4, 1976 (the event widely heralded for kick-starting punk in the U.K.) and the emergence of high-end copies of punk fashion, such as the gold safety pins sold at Saks on Fifth Avenue and the stylized rips and safety pins in the gowns designed by Zandra Rhodes for Bloomingdale's, which were already on the market by June 1977 (Szatmary 236).

As we have seen above, the way in which punk (and other subcultures) "hides in the light" makes it political in many more ways than by its subcultural "form" alone. But there are other ways in which punk is political above and beyond this form—the "down with civilization" lyrics of punk music, and the antiestablishment disposition and demeanour of punks themselves. In a way that is too seldom appreciated, subcultures of all stripes draw heavily on a stew of political and cultural ideas and ideals, especially those that have been constructed by other oppositional or subcultural groups of cultures in the past.

The Marxist Influence   One of most important of these has been the tradition of socialist and communist thought. However partially or incompletely, Marx's insistence on seeing the history of society as a "history of class struggles" has remained a core element of the way in which many subcultures understand their social status (Marx and Engels 34): as minority cultures in permanent conflict with the wealthy and their duped middle-class supporters. Subcultures need not take up explicit class-based politics in order to see themselves as belonging to those groups who are systematically disadvantaged by capitalism, nor to make use of the kinds of cultural analysis and forms of cultural practice that such political identification opens up. And socialism is just the beginning. As the example of punk shows us, there is a great deal more going on in subcultures than angry youth spontaneously rebelling against their seniors.

The familiar story told about punk is a cautionary tale that traces the rapid rise of a genuine subculture and its equally rapid co-optation by consumer culture (see Chapter 4 for a discussion of co-optation in popular culture). The threat that punk posed seemed real enough to bring the wrath of the state down on the paradigmatic punk band the Sex Pistols, even before the release of their anti-monarchist anthem "God Save the Queen" in June 1976. Denounced by Members of Parliament, attacked by the Anglican Church, banned from playing live almost anywhere in England and from having their songs played on British radio, the Sex Pistols nearly brought about the conditions that they sang about in "Anarchy in the U.K." Yet by 1980, Linda Ronstadt, Billy Joel, and even Cher were posing in punk regalia on the covers of their albums.

The quick rise and fall of punk is real enough. But what this version of the events misses is the complex political roots of punk culture. The anarchy and chaos of punk music—its fearsome, angry, and terrifically loud sound and its utter rejection of

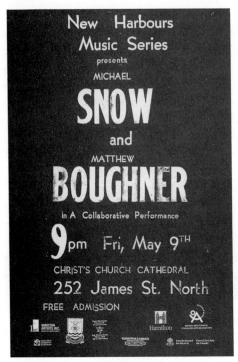

New Harbours
Music Series

presents

MICHAEL

SNOW

and

MATTHEW

BOUGHNER

In A Collaborative Performance

9pm Fri, May 9TH

CHRIST'S CHURCH CATHEDRAL

252 James St. North

FREE ADMISSION

Hamilton's New Harbour Series stages experimental and electronic music in the city's Christ's Church Cathedral.

"civilized" values—have tended to reinforce a sense of its spontaneous origins and generally unfocused politics. Punk is now often treated, as it was by a number of its detractors during the punk era itself, as little more than another blip in a long tradition of youthful rebellion expressed through pop music (falling temporally between the threatening sexuality of Elvis and the angst of Nirvana and Eminem).

But if we were to pull apart any of these forms of rebellion, we would find an enormously rich reservoir of ideas and concepts. Like Dadaism and Surrealism before it, punk understood itself quite self-consciously as a cultural form (in both its music and its style) whose aim was to *épater les bourgeois*—to pierce through the sterile drone of bloated seventies art rock (epitomized by the band Yes) and the flabby corporate culture that was increasingly coming to stand for culture as such. The New York precursors of U.K. punk music, artists such as the Velvet Underground, Patti Smith, and Tom Verlaine, drew inspiration for their lyrics from the Beat Generation (epitomized by writers such as Jack Kerouac and Allan Ginsberg); from the avant-garde centred around Andy Warhol; and, in the case of Verlaine (a.k.a. Tom Miller), from French Symbolist poetry. Though the Sex Pistols famously rejected Patti Smith's literary, avant-garde leanings, the transition of punk from New York to London interjected new political dimensions into punk even as it stripped away others.

Situationism   Malcolm McLaren, the infamous manager and midwife of the Sex Pistols, wanted to use the band to explore the "politics of boredom" first expressed in Situationism, a political movement that explored the new kinds of politics required in a society crushed not by a lack of things (i.e., too little food to feed everyone), but by an abundance of material goods. Situationism played an important role in the May 1968 student revolution in France, which began in reaction to the U.S. war on Vietnam but turned into a more general assault on the banality of a post–Second World War capitalist culture that promised so much (less work and more leisure!) and delivered so little (boring work and boring leisure!).

The philosophy of Situationism can be summarized by one of the popular slogans of May 1968: "The more you consume, the less you live." Punk carries on the tradition of Situationism, both in spirit and (as Greil Marcus shows in his history of punk, *Lipstick*

Traces) in substance, but in a political situation in which there is *neither* work *nor* leisure. If nothing else, punk responds directly to the economic chaos and high unemployment that enveloped Britain in the mid-1970s. It was civilization that was in decline and punk that was trying to save it from itself. In other words, punk was not the problem but the solution.

It would be possible to continue in this vein for some time. For instance, we have yet to mention the political roots of punk art, which was featured on album covers and posters advertising band performances. Again, the slapdash quality of this art might suggest unfocused, youthful spontaneity. But in reality, punk art drew heavily on the slogans and art of the May 1968 student revolution in Paris, as well as from the tradition of agitational-propaganda (agitprop) **aesthetics** created by the artists of the Soviet Revolution. Punk was also an importantly hybrid musical form, which drew inspiration (as well as licks) from Jamaican reggae and ska music that "lambasted the racism and capitalism that Britain had imposed on Jamaica" (Szatmary 232). In April and June 1978, The Clash and other bands played to audiences of 80,000 and 50,000 young punks respectively, who came out to show their solidarity with their black brethren against the organization of the racist National Front in Britain. It is clear that there was a whole lot going on in punk—even if most punk musicians relied on only three chords to express themselves.

The Invention of Skateboarding

So, punk is political. But what about other kinds of subcultural practices? Haven't we stacked the deck in our favour? What about a practice whose politics is somewhat more obscure, if it exists at all? What about, say . . . skateboarding?

Even though skateboarding has now become a staple of popular culture, it wasn't always a recognized sport with its own stars (like Tony Hawk), brand names, specialist magazines, computer games, ESPN tournaments, and the like. Skateboarding first emerged as a post-surfing pastime in the late 1950s and briefly surged to popularity in 1963, when the national championships were aired on television. It then died out—seemingly just another fad kids' pastime, like the hula hoop. The conditions that saw its revival in the early to mid-1970s highlight the politics that continue to be played out through this seemingly innocuous pastime.

Dogtown and Z-Boys   Stacy Peralta's documentary *Dogtown and Z-Boys* (2002) provides not only an exceptional account of the second birth of skateboarding, but also a compelling narrative of the politics that emerges out of the sport. The film explores the birth of the famous Zephyr Skateboard Team, which would later produce many of the most successful of the first wave of professional skateboarders. The Zephyr team hailed from Dogtown, a decrepit, run-down area of West Los Angeles that was quite literally built on the ruins of the American dream: the area had once sported one of the most famous of the many amusement-park piers that lined the California coast. After the park closed in 1967, the area fell into economic decline, leaving the abandoned amusement park and the area around it to "pyromaniacs, junkies and surfers." The team members grew up in this area, mostly in broken families that were never far from bottoming out. Yet, far from describing Dogtown as an urban wasteland, they describe it as a "dirty, filthy paradise."

What made Dogtown a paradise was the degree of control that the youth could exert over their space, both as surfers and then later as skaters. Dogtown was covered with graffitied signs warning outsiders to stay away: "Locals only!" "Go home!" As the Zephyr team began to develop and build skateboards to "surf" their mostly abandoned streets, they also began to stretch their claim over public space to other parts of the city. Because much of California is built on hills or in valleys, many schoolyards in the area had a landscaping quirk: in order to level out school playgrounds, landscapers had to build in walls of banked asphalt. Though these were fenced off from the public, they became the first rudimentary skate parks, which the Dogtown kids would, on weekends, bike miles and miles to get to in order to practise their new craft. During the mid-1970s, another off-limits space opened up to skateboarding. The prolonged drought in California during this time meant that the numerous swimming pools in the L.A. area were left empty. Dogtowners began to covertly enter private property in order to skate the abandoned swimming pools, and in so doing risked arrest and imprisonment.

The documentary is careful to highlight the fact that the kids who pioneered contemporary skateboarding were motivated by nothing more than having fun. There was "no promise in it," and they had "no goals, no aspirations." None of them knew what skateboarding would become or what it was accomplishing. Nor did they have a sense that by skating the streets, pools, and hidden and sealed-off spaces of the city, they were doing something more than having a good time. Of course, the consequences of one's actions can easily exceed what one believes one is doing. In a series of influential articles published in *Skateboarder* magazine in 1975, Craig Stecyk made explicit what the Zephyr team had been doing as a matter of course: making new use of the dead spaces created by contemporary culture. "Skaters by their very nature are urban guerrillas: they make everyday use of the useless artifacts of the technological burden, and employ the handiwork of the government/corporate structure in a thousand ways that the original architects could never dream of. . . . Two hundred years of American technology has unwittingly created a massive cement playground of unlimited potential," Stecyk says, "but it was the minds of 11-year-olds that could see that potential" (*Dogtown and Z-Boys*)

The disputes that continue to arise throughout North America over the uses that skateboarders try to make of public and private space for a bit of simple recreation suggests that there is something larger at stake in these practices. It might seem a stretch to equate kids interested in doing grinds and flipping their boards with anti-globalization demonstrators who take over the spaces of the city, but in a way both are making the same fundamental demand: "Whose streets? Our streets!" Skateboarding has a politics, too.

NEW FRONTIERS: SUBCULTURES IN CYBERSPACE

Subcultures and countercultures need spaces in which to meet, share ideas and live out their differences. The need for space—whether occupied legally or illegally, as through squatters movements that remain active throughout Europe—places some limits on the activities of these groups and also exposes them to the intervention of authorities nervous about the ramifications of the activities of this of that group. For example, both as a result of state and local ordinances and simple demographic realities, it can be difficult to use your BMX bike or skateboard in many big urban centres. This is why you'll encounter groups of teens popping wheelies and jumping off concrete skyscraper and freeway embankments if you take a walk in the middle of the night through the core of Shanghai or St. Petersburg, Russia: 3 a.m. is the only time you can take your BMX to meet a statue of Lenin or Mao.

The Internet has opened up new opportunities for subcultures and countercultures to do their work in a different space: cyberspace. Cyberspace creates obvious advantages to groups existing outside of dominant culture. Subcultures can exchanges ideas and make linkages to one another not just locally, but across the world, and they can connect with one another and make plans for activities in relative anonymity. And the Internet is still a place where one can "hide in the light." The websites of subcultural groups can be browsed by anyone (mostly these days, it seems, by journalists looking for a quick story on the wackiness and weirdness of the web), but access is hardly immediate. Subculture websites aren't hiding, but they usually aren't web "portals" such as Hotmail, Google, or other such entry points to the web.

The Internet has also created new conditions for countercultures to engage in political activity. The use of the Internet by the Zapatistas in Mexico to get the message out about their struggle and to mobilize international support for their cause has often been cited as one of the first instances in which the Internet was used for contemporary countercultural purposes—and on a global scale (see Close-Up 10.1). The famous protests against the meeting of the World Trade Organization in Seattle in 1999, which brought together a wide array of political and activist groups, also owed a great deal to the technology of the Internet, which made it possible to organize a demonstration whose size caught authorities largely by surprise. The number of groups that are using the web in order to advocate for social and political causes is enormous, ranging from groups who fight for the freedoms related to technology and cyberspace itself (such as the Electronic Frontier Foundation/www.eff.org) to more quixotic attempts to advocate for the independence of Newfoundland, Alberta, or Cascadia, a region made up of Washington, Oregon, and British Columbia.

Suggested Activity 8.2

Identify some online sites and networks used by subcultures and countercultures. In what ways (if any) do they identify themselves as being distinct from some imagined mainstream or dominant culture? What are the ways in which these groups use the environment and the technology of the Internet for their own purposes? What possibilities and limits do you see in the use of the Internet for these purposes?

IBM workers engaged in an online strike in Second Life in September 2007.

Though in many respects the Internet has been mainly useful for subcultures and countercultures as a new communication tool, it has also opened up interesting and original ways in which to engage in political activity. In September 2007, IBM workers in Italy staged a strike against their employers in the online environment of Second Life. They were soon joined by IBM workers across the globe in an act of solidarity. Second Life is a virtual environment in which individuals can assume digital avatars to represent them in its virtual environment. There were criticisms of the strike action by some unionists and others, who saw little point in having avatars picket IBM's spaces within Second Life. Officially, IBM, too, reported that the strike had little effect on their business operations. Nevertheless, picketing avatars did managed to block access to IBM sites in Second Life ("islands" developed by companies and others in the virtual environment can only be visited by a limited number of avatars at any one time) and there was widespread media coverage of this bizarre form of job action.

Striking on Second Life is certainly not the same as preventing truckloads of computer servers from leaving factories to go out into the world. But it would be wrong to dismiss the genuinely new political possibilities opened up by the Internet. Human rights dissidents in Vietnam have found that using Voice over Internet Protocol (VoIP) services such as Skype or Paltalk have made it difficult for authorities to monitor their activities (Gee). Police and military are able to tap phones and check up on e-mail accounts, but the digital audio signals sent out by Skype are much harder to crack—especially when typed as text. We have barely begun to scratch the surface of the possible use that subcultures and countercultures are making—and might yet make—of the new technologies that have entered our world.

SUGGESTIONS FOR FURTHER READING

Austin, Joe, and Michael Nevin Willard. *Generations of Youth: Youth Cultures and History in Twentieth-Century America*. New York: New York University Press, 1996.

Cockburn, Alexander, and Jeffrey St. Clair. *Five Days That Shook the World*. New York: Verso, 2001.

Debord, Guy. *Society of the Spectacle*. New York: Verso, 1996.

Hall, Stuart, and Tony Jefferson, eds. *Resistance Through Rituals: Youth Subcultures in Post-War Britain*. New York: Routledge, 1993.

Hebdige, Dick. *Subculture: The Meaning of Style*. London: Methuen, 1979.

Lasn, Kalle. *Culture Jam: How to Reverse America's Suicidal Consumer Binge—And Why We Must*. New York: Quill, 1999.

Marcus, Greil. *Lipstick Traces: A Secret History of the 20th Century*. Cambridge, MA: Harvard University Press, 1989.

Muggleton, David. *Inside Subculture: The Postmodern Meaning of Style*. New York: Berg, 2000.

Redhead, Steve, D. Wynne, and J. O'Connor, eds. *The Clubcultures Reader: Readings in Popular Cultural Studies*. Oxford: Blackwell, 1997.

Ross, Andrew, and Tricia Rose, eds. *Microphone Fiends: Youth Music and Youth Culture*. New York: Routledge, 1994.

Roszak, Theodore. *The Making of a Counter Culture: Reflections on the Technocratic Society and Its Youthful Opposition*. London: Faber and Faber, 1970.

Chapter 9

Spaces and Places of Popular Culture

The cities will be part of the country; I shall live 30 miles from my office in one direction, under a pine tree; my secretary will live 30 miles away from it too, in the other direction, under another pine tree. We shall both have our own car.

We shall use up tires, wear out road surfaces and gears, consume oil and gasoline. All of which will necessitate a great deal of work . . . enough for all.

—Le Corbusier, *The Radiant City* (1967; originally published 1935)

(DIS)LOCATIONS OF POPULAR CULTURE

To drive west along Wilson Street in Ancaster, Ontario, is to experience a journey along the timeline of consumer life in Canada. Wilson Street, like many main streets in small- and mid-size towns in this country, is lined with independent shoe and clothing stores, car mechanics, insurance brokers' offices, and a range of Protestant churches. In Ancaster, many of these businesses are housed in nineteenth-century buildings made of blocky stone cut in precise cubes and rectangles. Interspersed among the businesses there are franchises of some of Canada's most popular fast-food restaurants: Tim Hortons is a stone's throw from Subway and Pizza Pizza. To somebody new to this area of Ontario, the presence of the franchise restaurants can seem to be a blight on the quaintness of the town and/or a reassurance that, if you are not feeling up to taking the risk of eating at a local joint, you can always grab a slice and a double-double. For those who are more concerned that the franchises are displacing and replacing smaller locally based businesses, the presence of Tim Hortons and other franchises are a reminder that it is virtually impossible to compete with companies whose **brands** are so well known, whose products' names have become recognized substitutes for everyday consumer goods, and whose corporate mission is to dominate the essential and discretionary spending of consumers. They want your dough, morning, noon, and night.

Further along Wilson Street, where the businesses thin out and where there is still residual evidence of the farms that used to be plentiful in this region, you cross an overpass from which there is very little to engage your eye except for a few stands of trees and an empty field. On the other side of the overpass, on your left, you suddenly come upon the early twenty-first century version of Ancaster's Main Street. It is a big-box shopping development, virtually identical to ones found in Guelph, Waterloo, Calgary, Montreal, or even Budapest and Moscow. The anchor tenant of this development, sitting at the back of the development with a commanding view of the other big-box stores, is a Wal-Mart Supercentre, looking as if its vast length is holding its arms open to embrace the cars, minivans, and SUVs that move like horse-and-buggy carts up and down the painted lanes of the parking lot. Whether we work there, shop there, or just drive by, this is the landscape in which many of us spend large chunks of our lives.

It's clear to all of us that the spaces and places that we inhabit have undergone changes over time. Older cities and towns offer a visual archaeology of the kinds of spaces that we used to inhabit and the spaces that most of us tend to live in now. To many people, the shift from the old Main Street of mom-and-pop stores and houses bundled close to shops *and* to work—until relatively recently factories and other places of business were mixed in with housing and shopping—to the new main streets that run past shopping malls or along which box stores are conveniently assembled, is simply due to **progress**. More people, more cars, and more technology means that cities are spread out, highways are lengthened, parking lots are expanded, and stores are ballooned in size to house (for example) the huge number of competing LCD and plasma TVs fighting it out for market dominance. It's natural! It's progress!

Except that it doesn't feel that way to many people. After years of fleeing city cores imagined as crowded, noisy, polluted, and dangerous, many people are opting to forego long commutes to work in order to live back in the city. In Canadian cities, condominium towers are sprouting up not only in Toronto and Vancouver, but in Hamilton and Calgary. Vacation trips abroad are rarely to visit the suburbs of cities, but to either one of two poles: "unspoiled" nature in the form of beaches or mountains (we discuss these spaces in more detail below), or the heart of cities whose chief attraction seems to be that they are dense, walkable, and full of the hurly-burly of human activity—cities such as New York, London, Paris, Istanbul, and Mexico City. Increasingly, people are starting to recognize that since the Second World War, we

> have been building a national landscape that is largely devoid of places worth caring about. Soulless subdivisions, residential "communities" utterly lacking in communal life; strip shopping centres, "big box" chain stores, and artificially festive malls set within barren seas of parking; antiseptic office parks, ghost towns after 6 p.m.; and mile upon mile of clogged collector roads, the only fabric tying out disassociated lives back together—this is growth, and you can find little reason to support it. (Duany, Plater-Zyberk, and Speck x)

If this is progress, it certainly doesn't always feel like it. But what can we do about it? Are we supposed to return to a world of country lanes and small shops? Even if we wanted to, most of us couldn't afford it any longer: living in an old stone house in Ancaster or an apartment in Paris is pricey. Even though it might be all around us, space costs, and costs differently depending on how many people want it. Which is just the first of the many complicated aspects of space, a thing that we usually take for granted as simply given, as opposed to seeing it as created and re-created by human beings in different ways throughout our history.

Organizing Space and Place

What exactly is space? To begin with, space is a physical reality: the boundless container of everything known and unknown that is referred to as the universe—the "final frontier" invoked by Captain James T. Kirk in reruns of the original *Star Trek* series. We tend to think of the thin sheet of breathable atmosphere that we inhabit on Earth as also being primarily made up of space—certainly more limited and bounded than the universe, but the field in which to put stuff (cities, roads, dams, our gardens, our bedroom furniture) and in which we move around. One of the important differences between space and place seems to be that place is "made" space. Space is devoid of content, impersonal, and abstract, whereas place is filled with stuff, made into something, and clearly identifiable (not just a city, but Red Deer, Alberta; not just a room, but my brother's room). As we will see below, there is more slippage between the ideas of space and place than this might suggest; but these are some beginning points at which to look at what space and place means in and for popular culture.

Suggested Activity 9.1

What are some of the ways in which our organization or imagination of space is expressed in language? Can you think of examples of changes in how we describe space? For example, one way in which geopolitical differences were once expressed was by reference to the "West" (Western Europe, Canada and the United States, and Japan) and either the "East" (the former Soviet Bloc) or "the Rest" (the developing world or the "Third World"). Since the end of the Soviet Union, it has become more common to describe the world as divided into "North" (Western Europe, Canada and the United States, and Japan) and "South" (the developing world). What realities do such terms capture and/or obscure (e.g., how can the U.S. and Japan both be "West"?) Why do we seem to rely on such spatial divisions not only in everyday language but in organizing important political and economic divisions—so much so that they can come to be real?

The ways in which we think about space matter a great deal to how we inhabit and use places and spaces, and how we interact with people across the world—or across our cities.

Inevitably, every city has some part of it that is considered to be the "bad side" of town, a side imagined by many as dangerous and thus to be avoided at all costs. It comes as a surprise, then, that in many cases these "bad sides" have crime statistics no worse than other parts of the city; space here works to conceal or to reinforce existing **stereotypes** about **race**, **ethnicity,** and class. The process of **gentrification** is seen by many as an always positive development which transforms the bad side of town into a desirable place to live, such as Queen Street West and Leslieville in Toronto, Mile End in Montreal, Inglewood in Calgary. While "upgrading" these older spaces does make them appealing for shopping and hanging out, it also results in a change in the composition of the communities that once existed there. As often as not, the increase in property costs that comes with gentrification results in a change in the ethnic and class composition of these neighbourhoods: even if they own their own houses, poor families can find themselves challenged by the rise in taxes that comes with the increase in the rise of property values. Activists in both the Downtown East Side in Vancouver and in Edmonton (and in other cities, too) have played an important role in raising questions about the spaces and places that would remain for those disadvantaged communities "moved out" as a result of gentrification.

As we can see by this example, the symbolic and imaginative dimensions of space are closely linked to the ways in which space is *physically* organized and vice versa. In some respects, one could see human activity on Earth as little more than a relentless process by which space has been arranged and rearranged for human use. In 2002, it was estimated that humans had built up more than 32 million kilometres of roadways—more than one-third of the average distance from the Earth to the Sun (CIA Factbook). The majority of the world's rivers have been dammed, diverted and/or rerouted; levees and dikes have been built to hold out water from human habitations or agricultural plains; canals have been cut to connect bodies of water for purposes of navigation (the most famous of these being the 77-km-long Panama Canal connecting the Pacific and Atlantic Oceans, and the Suez Canal linking the Mediterranean and the Red Seas); tunnels have been carved into mountains and under waterways (such as the 50-km-long Channel Tunnel linking the United Kingdom and France); and much of the world's original environment has been re-fashioned for human use through logging, mining, clear-cutting of forests to expand agricultural lands, and so on. As these physical changes have occurred, the ways in which we experience space and imagine space have changed as well. A trip that a century ago would have taken days by train or horse can now be driven by car in a matter of hours, and jet travel makes the entire world accessible within a day's journey. Rapid communication between distant locations via the telephone and the Internet has further changed how space is organized and experienced. When **globalization** (see Chapter 10) is described as "the compression of the world and the intensification of the consciousness of the world as a whole" (Robertson 8), this is a compression that has emerged out of both the physical and imaginative reorganization of space. Even if the physical world is the same size as it has always been, the space on this world is certainly smaller than ever.

Theories of Space

Just as our understanding of the meaning and significance of space constantly undergoes changes, so, too, does the relationship of popular culture to space. The landscape was once dotted with drive-in movie theatres that offered young people a certain measure of freedom from their parents under the starry skies and the looming heads of Hollywood celebrities. Now only 50 drive-ins remain in Canada (Friesen): despite more cars on the road, movie watching has moved into basements and family rooms and onto big-screen televisions and little-screen iPods. This is just one example of how the reconfiguration of space affects not only our entertainment options, but also the way we come together (or not) in different forms of community.

The processes by which space is culturally and socially organized and the ways in which modes of organizing space have changed over time have given rise to a number of theories of space. The most important of these in terms of popular culture are connected to the rise over the nineteenth and twentieth centuries of what has perhaps become the most significant space of human activity: the city. The city as we see understand it today—a dense agglomeration of human beings engaged in multiple activities day and night—is a relatively recent spatial invention. The population of London, England, reached a million by 1800, when it was the world's largest city; by 1900 it had expanded to 6.5 million. In many respects, we are just *now* entering the time in which the city constitutes the dominant form of organized space:

> In 1950 there were 86 cities in the world with a population over one million; today there are 400, and by 2015, there will be at least 550. Cities, indeed, have absorbed nearly two-thirds of the global population explosion since 1950 and are currently growing by a million babies and migrants each week. The present urban population (3.2 billion) is larger than the total population of the world in 1960. The global countryside, meanwhile, has reached its maximum population (3.2 billion) and will begin to shrink after 2020. As a result, cities will account for *all* future world population growth, which is expected to peak at about 10 billion in 2050. (M. Davis 5)

Given the vast range of its possibilities and as well as its problems, it is not surprising that the city has generated the most sustained reflections on the organization of space, and of the significance of space for popular culture and vice versa.

Henri Lefebvre and Guy Debord

It is easy enough to recognize that how we organize space changes over time in relation to a huge number of factors: increases in population, technological developments, and changes in industry and agriculture (to name just a few). What is perhaps harder to grasp is how these changes point to larger social narratives hidden just below the surface of our experience, as well as to the deep impact that spatial developments have on how we imagine and perceive the world. The shape of North American cities, for instance, owes much to ideas we have about "proper" land use within urban boundaries. Virtually all cities (Houston, Texas, being a notable exception) engage in the practice of zoning, designating though a municipal master plan which areas are to be used for residential, commercial, or industrial purposes, and generally keeping these areas as distinct from one another as possible. The relative predictability of those cities built up mainly in the twentieth century (Calgary or Denver, for example), or the shape of suburbs and highways everywhere on the planet (whether in Shanghai or Mississauga), point to deeper narratives of control, organization, and management that guide and shape contemporary life in multiple ways.

It was the perception that daily life was becoming increasingly bureaucratic and controlled in just this way that led French philosopher Henri Lefebvre (1901–1991) and French writer and filmmaker Guy Debord (1931–1994) to investigate the structures of the contemporary city and to propose strategies for bringing about a "revolution in everyday life." Both thinkers witnessed firsthand the enormous shift in the rhythms and energies of everyday life that occurred in France in the decades following the Second World War. Paris and other French cities went through a rapid process of rebuilding, expansion, and modernization. Large pre-planned housing developments were added to cities around the country—the suburbs with which most of us are now familiar—and the texture of daily urban life was modified through the introduction of a homogenizing mass consumer culture that came to many as a shock. In France as elsewhere, the shorthand term for these modernizing developments was "Americanization." Bureaucratic, banal, emptied of life, predictable, routine: both thinkers witnessed the way "the commodity, the market, money, with their implacable logic, seize everyday life" (Lefebvre "Towards" 79), and both wanted to think about ways in which to take life back.

The great theme of Lefebvre's philosophy was the complex and messy events, objects and happenings of everyday life. He saw everyday life as the space that any philosopher should try to understand; it was there that social structures were experienced and broad understandings about the world and the possibilities of human life were generated. For Lefebvre, the long process of modernization had produced forms of everyday life characterized fundamentally by increasing alienation, lack of creativity, and an artificial separation of human activity into specialized spaces and activities: spaces to live, work, shop, have fun, and so forth. In the nineteenth century, Karl Marx had famously described alienation as the result of workers' separation from the product of their labour. For Lefebvre, this experience of alienation had become part of very stuff of life, making all experience inauthentic and full of unease. Witnessing the construction of spaces such as a new suburb in the French city of Mourenx—a place made up of "nothing but traffic lights"—Lefebvre asks: "Are we entering the city of joy or the world of unredeemable boredom?" (Lefebvre Introduction 119).

Debord shared a similar view of the world that was being put together out of the ruins of war. He is best known for Society of the Spectacle (1967), which has become an important text for scholars interested in thinking about the deep impact of mass media images on society. Though the "spectacle" is most often thought to refer to the collection of images that bombard us daily—advertising, television, movies and the like—for Debord it names "not a collection of images . . . but a social relationship between people that is mediated by images" (Debord 12). The spectacle was a form of society in which our experiences and understanding of all social relations was shaped through mass-mediated images. For Debord, spectacular society represented the deepest penetration of **capitalism** and **consumerism** into everyday life. Like Lefebvre, he saw contemporary life as deeply alienated and alienating. As he writes, "the spectacle is the bad dream of a modern society in chains, expressing nothing more than its wish for its sleep. The spectacle is the guardian of that sleep" (18).

How do these views of our present circumstances relate to our understanding of space, the city, and popular culture? It might seem as if both thinkers believe that popular culture—at least in the form of **mass culture**—is the problem that needs to be solved. As we have discussed throughout this book, it is common enough to see popular culture as a form of degraded culture—as what is left when the masses get culture, too. Though both Lefebvre and Debord have criticisms of popular culture, for them the alienating, empty feeling that comes from living in the suburbs or the experience of the consumer city does not originate in popular culture or everyday life, but in larger, structural transformations that have ensured that capitalist society and its pursuit of money are life's primary objective. For Debord, these transformations include changes to the space of the city. Though less known than his writings about the spectacle, as part of the activist art collective called the Situationist International (SI), Debord developed strategies for reclaiming the experience of the city. *Dérive* (or "drift") was a political and social practice that proposed to explore the city in ways very different than imagined or permitted by the dominant physical and social organization of urban space. To drift through the city instead of following fixed patterns (moving directly from work to home, staying only in the "good" or familiar parts of the city, staying in public spaces and avoiding the private) produces a very different view of the city within which one lives. The de-familiarization drifting generates also creates circumstances in which one can reflect on the ways in which space is organized—ways that are invisible in the routine of daily life.

In Lefebvre's later work, he also probed all the ways in which urban space had become "a space envisioned and conceived by assorted professionals and technocrats: planners, engineers, developers, architects, urbanists, geographers, and others of a scientific bent" (Merrifield 89). Little space was left that allowed for the creation of genuine differences of experience or meaning; all activity was tied into modern rhythms of work and play, with after-work leisure being little more than a preparation for more work. Throughout his life, Lefebvre was fascinated by moments in which the spaces and rhythms of "normal" everyday life were interrupted, even momentarily, from the bawdy excess of festivals to the occupation of the streets of Paris by students in May 1968. As with the SI's practices of "drifting" through the city in a manner that evaded and challenged its typical spatial organization, Lefebvre believe that these breaks in the everyday allowed for a glimpse into the **social construction** of everyday life. In so doing, the hope was that it also opened the way for a more radical reconstruction of everyday life and its spaces, and that the energy of festivals could replace the dreariness of contemporary experience on an ongoing and daily basis. Despite the apparently unassailable logic of urban space and the physical and imaginative weight of its accumulated infrastructure—streets, bridges, highways, sewers, spaces, zoned for one kind of activity instead of another—life and space could still be different.

The ideas of Lefebvre and Debord have played an important part in the explosion of interest in the space and the city in cultural theory. What their work shares with contemporary cultural geographers, such as David Harvey, Manuel Castells, Doreen Massey, and Mike Davis, is an insistence on the need to understand how we have defined the spaces in which we live and the ways in which these spaces have tended to limit or impede human possibilities much more than they enable them. The space of everyday life has "been literally colonized by capitalism" (Lefebvre "Towards" 80); changes in everyday life will require changes in the spaces we inhabit, and vice versa. And because everyday life and popular culture are tightly interwoven, the social construction of space is essential to an understanding of how popular culture works and shapes meaning.

At earlier points in this book, we have touched on some of the ways in which space and our experience of it is shaped by the social and cultural systems in which we live. In Chapter 6, for example, we discussed the ways in which the space of the panopticon—a prison designed so that prisoners feel that they might always be under **surveillance**—produced forms of self-conscious regulation and change in behaviour. Our discussion in Chapter 5 of the *flâneur*, the strolling urban figure who moves through the city to take in the

The Manchester band Get Out Clause shot a video using only surveillance cameras—an inventive way of putting devices that control and monitor to different uses.

experiences and pleasures of displays of consumer items and the bodies of other shoppers, is also an example of the ways in which space creates new forms of experience and culture. One of the clearest signs of the degree to which space is organized in ways that shape our lived experience of space *and* the shape and character of popular culture today is the divide between public space and private space; and so it is to a discussion of this that we now turn.

PRIVATE VERSUS PUBLIC SPACE

In Chapter 2 we suggested that one way to understand the development of popular culture is by way of the shifting arrangement of public and private space. The passing of Enclosure Acts in mid-nineteenth-century Britain effectively broke up what was once common land, used for grazing animals and public recreation, into parcels of private property to be used for the generation of profit by individual landholders. Enclosure is both an important example and a useful metaphor for the changes that have occurred in the distribution and use of space over the last two centuries. The commercialization of sports is one example of the impact of this process on popular culture; the loss of public land means not just fewer places to play, but also a big change in the way we play. Recreation today generally means forking out some cash for an experience that's considerably less active than the village football tournaments of nineteenth-century England.

This is not to suggest that we've moved wholesale from a society of fit and rosy-cheeked athletes to a bunch of paunchy couch potatoes wrestling over the television remote (an activity—or lack of activity—that health-care professionals actually might deem more dangerous than football!). Nor has the process of commercializing public space proceeded in a linear fashion from the eighteenth century to today. The hazards of **urbanization** that we discuss in Chapter 2, including threats to public health posed by crowding and poor sanitation, gave rise eventually to the development of an urban planning industry to manage the structural challenges of making cities work as engines of productivity and as liveable communities—goals that are sometimes hard to reconcile and whose outcome may not be what we had hoped for. Among the innovations that cities produced were parks and public swimming pools, places of leisure whose creation—like the projects of the nineteenth-century rational recreationists—sprung from a mix of middle-class motives. In addition to providing outlets for public enjoyment, it was also hoped that these sites would divert the working classes from the lures of the pub toward more wholesome physical activity.

Playing in the Park   The construction of parks in North American and European cities was a logical response to dwindling public spaces—a situation that, in 1820s New York, had led to the popularization of cemeteries as retreats from the chaos of the city. Central Park, a 7.8-square-kilometre green space (eventually expanded to 11.6 square kilometres) established in 1853 in the heart of Manhattan, became the template for a certain kind of urban oasis, imitated in many cities, though rarely on the same scale. For Frederick Law

Olmstead, the landscape architect who designed Central Park (as well as Yosemite, the Niagara Reservation at Niagara Falls, N.Y., and a whole series of parks in Boston and Buffalo), parks performed a critical social role; spending time in nature "had lasting beneficial physical, mental, and moral effects, particularly if it occurred 'in connection with relief from ordinary cares, change of air and change of habits'" (Olmsted, qtd. in Spirn 93). In contrast to British parks, which Olmsted criticized as mostly the preserve of the privileged, he hailed the creation of Central Park, "the first real park made in this century," as a "democratic development of the highest significance" ("Central Park"). Parks were to be for the enjoyment of everyone, which meant not just provision for mixed activities (in spite of occasional collisions, horseback riders, pedestrians, cyclists and pleasure vehicles circulated along the trails of Central Park) but, more importantly, the mixing of classes. Olmsted was adamant that parks should be free for all visitors, a view sustained by the condescending belief that looking at beautiful scenery would be good for working-class people's morals (Spirn 92).

The democratic, or genuinely *popular* character of parks, including Central Park, cannot be assumed or taken for granted, but is rather part of an ongoing struggle. As with many so-called wilderness areas (a topic we cover later in this chapter), the "natural" space of Central Park was achieved through the eviction of the people that lived there, mostly poor African-Americans and Irish immigrants. As contemporary cities grapple with the problem of homelessness, it seems inevitable that parks will increasingly become hotspots for conflict over the meaning of living space (in 2005 one expression of that conflict resulted in the beating death of a homeless man in a Toronto park by three drunk reserve soldiers from a nearby armoury [Mathieu]). Parks also experience the waxing and waning of the social welfare state, as their upkeep depends on the availability of public funds. In the 1970s, a lack of money and municipal will sent Central Park into a significant decline, to the point where it developed a global reputation as a dangerous place where innocent strollers were liable to get mugged. The situation slowly improved through the efforts of citizens' groups, who raised money, organized volunteer working groups, and lobbied government to repair the decaying infrastructure and rehabilitate natural spaces in the park. The park looks a lot better these days; however, struggle over its meaning as public space continues.

In 2004, on the eve of a Republican National Convention, the anti-war coalition, United for Peace and Justice (UFPJ), applied for a permit to hold a rally in the park. The city refused the application, a decision that was upheld by the Federal Court. Almost no one bought the lame explanation offered by the city—that it would "spoil the grass"; however the "real" story as represented in screaming newspaper headlines such as "Anarchy Threat to City: Cops fear Hard-Core Lunatics Plotting Convention Chaos" was equally ludicrous (qtd. in Dobbs). The rally, which drew more than half a million people, was eventually held away from the park, in keeping with the request of the organizers' that participants respect the law. However, in the press release they issued before the rally, the UFPJ reasserted Central Park's place as "New York City's town commons, a traditional public forum that belongs to all the people of this city," and declared: "The fight to restore

Central Park to public use is far from over . . . it is just beginning" (United For Peace and Justice). While the size of Central Park, combined with its location in New York City, gives it an emblematic status, the conflicts that define its history find echoes in cities across North America, as walkers, skateboarders, political protesters, dog owners, nature lovers, and wading pool afficionados assert their rights to enjoy urban green space.

Rich Kids Swim, Poor Kids Sink   In comparison with the struggle over parks as places of genuinely popular culture, the politics of swimming pools might seem trivial; however, throughout the century or so of their recent use, public pools have also seen their share of controversy. Public pools or baths—in the early years there wasn't much difference—were built in mid-nineteenth-century Britain (a few decades later in the U.S. and Canada) as part of a campaign to promote hygiene. Pools were seen as a way to promote both physical fitness and cleanliness: many people could not afford baths in their own homes, and developing medical theories about germs prompted new concerns about sanitation. Civic and medical officials alike were inclined to single out the poor as "a 'smelly' group," and the term "'the great unwashed' was often used for the working classes who were purportedly ignorant on matters of personal hygiene and hence health" (Sigworth and Worboys, qtd. in Sheard 65). There was another compelling reason to build indoor, or at least fenced, pools, which was to shield decent folks from the sight of boys splashing around "nekkid" in city rivers (not to mention protecting the swimmers themselves from hazards of floating objects like rats, condoms, and occasionally decomposing bodies [Cavett]).

If ideas about hygiene, not always well informed, were a significant factor behind the creation of public pools, they also influenced the contested issue of who got to use them and under what circumstances. Struggles over public pools mirrored broader social tensions with particular intensity, as they tended to evoke deeply held **mythological** assumptions about connections between health, cleanliness, sexuality, and morality.

Swimming pools produce a peculiar type of intimacy; as Jeff Wiltse puts it, "people who might otherwise come in no closer contact than passing in the street, now waited in line together, undressed next to one another and shared the same water" (Wiltse 3). Wiltse's book, *Contested Waters: A Social History of Swimming Pools in America*, describes how pools in the Northern U.S. became a flashpoint for turbulent race relations throughout the nineteenth and twentieth centuries. Between the wars, pools gradually evolved from spare, functional facilities segregated by sex, to lavish recreation centres where men and women would swim and lounge around in deck chairs, sometimes on fake beaches surrounded by palm trees. The erotic possibilities inspired by this environment fuelled white anxieties about the mixing of races—specifically, the proximity of black men to white women. Thus began the racial segregation of pools, which persisted until the 1950s and 1960s (consistent with the bogus "separate-but-equal" rationale of other segregation policies, the white pools got the palm trees and deck chairs, while black swimmers had to make do with more spartan facilities). Within the civil rights movement, blacks mounted a successful challenge to the whites-only rule through a combination of activism and litigation. Whatever equality resulted from that challenge was short-lived, as (mostly white) members of the upper-middle-class retreated from "dirty" and "dangerous" cities to the suburbs, where they built their own private pools. Throughout the 1960s and 1970s, a large number of public pools were allowed to sink into disrepair; some were closed for good, and some reopened as private facilities.

The state of public swimming pools has historically been, and continues to be, a microcosm of the wider North American society. As the **neoliberal** economic tide of globalization saps the public sector of money and energy, all public facilities—pools, parks, libraries, community centres—are vulnerable. In 2008, the Toronto District School Board, which controls most of the city's pools, announced plans to close many of them over the next two years to deal with a budget shortfall. According to board officials it came down to a choice between pools and funding for ESL and Special Education programs. A third option would see private companies such as Canadian Tire enter into partnerships to help keep the pools open. As with other areas of popular recreation, the cost of struggles to preserve public space are borne disproportionately by the poor and by minorities (according to the U.S. Centers for Disease Control, African-Americans drown at significantly higher rates than other races, a statistic arguably attributable in part to unequal access to swimming pools ["Water Related Injuries"]). The headline of an article in *The Globe and Mail* written by Canadian author Margaret Atwood puts it baldly: "Rich Kids Swim, Poor Kids Sink."

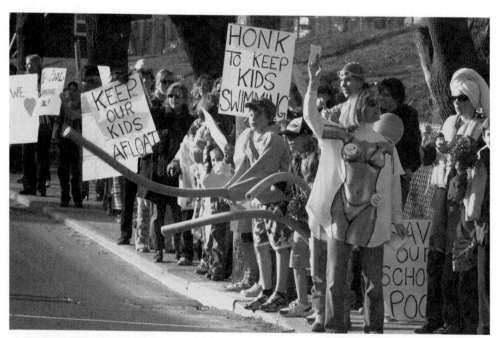

In 2008, public protests greeted the City of Toronto's announcement of plans to close public pools to save money.

Malls as Public Space?

When they first began to be built in large numbers in the 1950s, enclosed shopping malls were described by many developers as the new commons: a shared public space in which citizens could mingle and meet, encountering one another free from the heat of summer or the frigid temperatures of winter, while also shopping for yoga clothing and squeezing in a plate of Chinese at the food court. And just as in any public space, they could also take photographs of the picturesque store fronts they encountered, zip around on their skateboards, speak their minds about the Iraq War, and assemble for street protests. So why was Stephen Down being led out of the Crossgate Mall in Guilderwood, New York, in handcuffs for wearing a T-shirt saying "Give Peace a Chance"—a T-shirt that he bought from a store in the mall (Kohn 1)?

Well, in part because you can't do *any* of the things we just listed. Malls may be a place where people congregate in large numbers—perhaps even the main space in most cities in which people do get together in large numbers on a regular basis, other than sporting events. But you can't skateboard in a mall (it seems these days you can't skateboard anywhere) or march down the main strip of stores with a placard in your hand; and in many malls security guards will ask you to put away your video camera. But wearing a T-shirt!? Down was told by security that he was behaving inappropriately in the space of the mall by wearing a "peace" T-shirt on the eve of the War with Iraq in 2003. In the U.S., freedom of political expression is of course guaranteed, but only on *public* and not private property. And malls are spaces that are privately owned, as are many "public squares" adjacent to office towers, airports, apartment complexes, and even the spaces in front of many "public" buildings.

"Public" can be a tricky word, especially when it is connected to "space." Lawrence Lessing has defined the commons as goods or resources "in joint use or possession to be held or enjoyed equally by a number of persons" (19). By this measure, as Margaret Kohn points out in *Brave New Neighborhoods*, her investigation of the increasing **privatization** of public space, there is less and less space that acts as a "commons" today. "In everyday speech," she writes, "a public space usually refers to a place that is owned by the government, accessible to everyone without restriction, and/or fosters communication and interaction" (11). But right away, it is possible to see all kinds of gaps and problems in this idea of public. Not all government buildings are accessible to everyone, and even national parks are available for use only by those who can pay a fee to enter (in 2008 a daily pass to Banff National Park set a family back $19.60—before fees for camping, fishing permits, etc.). Private spaces such as malls or coffee houses can also foster communication—as long as you keep ordering lattes and bring your "I love America" T-shirt when you do.

Factories and Offices: The Spaces/Places of Work

One of the last areas of life many of us likely think of when we think about popular culture is work: unless we're lucky enough to work in the entertainment industry (a mixed blessing, to be sure), popular culture—either in its commercial or democratic sense—is what we do when we're *not* working. The discussion in Chapter 2 of this book about street football games, pubs, and music halls would seem to support this view of popular culture as distinct from work culture. It is true that in the nineteenth century, a change *did* occur as work shifted from fields to factories. Just as a space opened up between work and home (and public and private), leisure and recreation—those practices most commonly understood to be part of popular culture—were increasingly relegated to their own distinct places and times. Taking note of this shift, we include work under the broad category of popular culture for two reasons. First, in a general sense, it's impossible to draw a clear boundary between the two. Workplaces have their own cultures that express to some degree broader societal trends and in some ways are distinct from them, as we discuss in Chapter 4. Second, as we've already seen in the ideas of Lefebvre and Debord, the space—and time—of postindustrial work in North America has morphed into other aspects of life in interesting ways. As with so many other aspects of popular culture, movies offer insightful ways to understand what this shifting work space looks like.

The 1936 Charlie Chaplin film *Modern Times* offers a comical/nightmarish depiction of the Depression-era workplace. The main character, played by Chaplin, is listed in the credits simply as "a factory worker," his namelessness reflecting the depersonalized, mechanistic quality of his job. The film opens with a shot of a clock that fills the whole screen, its hands creeping to 6:00 a.m., or the beginning of the workday. Accompanied by menacing music, the scene changes to show a mass of pigs being hustled somewhere (wherever it is, it can't be nice), which then morphs into a roiling logjam of workers coming out of a subway. The workplace itself is a windowless cavern with exposed pipes, filled with vast machinery that dwarfs the humans who operate it. At the sound of a whistle, a brawny, shirtless foreman flips a lever that sets the whole factory in motion, with the workers clearly expected to fit their bodies to the rhythms of the machines. In stark contrast to the conditions on the factory floor, in an office insulated by a door with a glazed window, sits the company president, who keeps tabs on his workers through a series of closed-circuit television sets. The power structure, organized according to strict hierarchy and maintained through surveillance, seems unimpeachable.

The conflict, or the comedy, in the film starts when the character played by Chaplin, whose job it is to tighten bolts on metal parts as they roll by on an assembly line, can't keep pace with the machinery, which has speeded up, following an order from the president. Infinitesimally brief pauses to scratch an itch and brush away a fly disrupt the rhythm of the whole line, an interruption in productivity that the president responds to by ordering that the process be speeded up even more. When the worker tries to grab a quick smoke, the president's face appears on a large screen in the bathroom, ordering him to get back to work. Nor does he get any respite at lunch, as Chaplin's character becomes the involuntary guinea pig for a new device to speed up eating. Harnessed into a machine, his head is held in a kind of vice while a succession of levers spoon soup into his mouth and wipe his face with a napkin, a process that gets faster and faster until he ends up eating a bolt.

In spite of its comedy, the film delivers a powerful critique of the crushing effect of modern work and, by extension, "modern life" (the period that is sometimes said to mark the shift from working-in-order-to-live to living-in-order-to-work), which is symbolized by the physical structure of the factory. The clearest demonstration of the totally inhospitable character of the modern workplace is the scene of Chaplin's character being sucked into the machinery of the assembly line. For a few moments we see him drawn passively (and apparently quite comfortably) through a gigantic gear mechanism: he has become part of it, and it of him. His enmeshment in the machinery of work is shown by his inability to stop compulsively repeating the bolt-tightening motions of his job until well after he leaves the building. At least he *is* able to leave the building, and (following a brief period in a mental hospital), to become caught up (somewhat confusedly) in the events of the day. After accidentally participating in a political protest, being arrested a few times, and finding, then losing, a series of jobs, he walks off into the sunset with his girl into what will clearly be uncertain, but somewhat free, times.

Fast forward to the 1999 film *Office Space*, whose satirical look at contemporary office life offers a productive counterpoint to *Modern Times*. Like the earlier movie, this one opens with the journey to work. As the scurrying pedestrians of *Modern Times* are replaced by cars, the speed of the commute has paradoxically slowed to a crawl. Stuck in traffic, three drivers vent their frustration while a fourth man becomes increasingly agitated waiting for a bus, mumbling, "It's late again. If I'm there late again I will be dismissed." A fifth man drives effortlessly into a reserved spot in a parking lot, his customized license plate MY PRSHE accentuating his status (and his obnoxiousness). The journeys are emblematic of the power structure at Initech, the software company where all the men have arrived at work. The low-rise building's bland exterior and mass of cubicles present a much more benign atmosphere than the large and terrible machines of *Modern Time*'s factory. The disciplinary structures also seem less onerous: with no gigantic clock or punch cards to remind him that he is always already late, Peter, the main character, consults his wrist watch while sitting in the semi-privacy of his cubicle. The everyday annoyances of his job—Milton's (the guy at the bus stop) incessant mumbling and radio-listening, and an erratic photocopier—pale in comparison to the toll assembly-line labour takes on its workers. It quickly becomes clear, however, that the apparently relaxed atmosphere and lack of obvious hierarchy mask a power structure that is in some ways more rigid than that of the factory. The audience comes to dread, as Peter does, the appearance of his boss, Bill, casually leaning over his cubicle, camouflaging his orders (to perform seemingly useless tasks, work late, etc.) within falsely friendly colloquialisms: "Hello, Peter, what's happening? Um, I'm gonna need you to go ahead and come in tomorrow [Saturday]. So if you could be here around nine, that'd be gre-e-a-a-t. . . ."

In *Modern Times*, the instruments of the factory worker's oppression—piercing whistles, large machines, thuggish foreman, the boss's face and voice on the large screen—are obvious, if hard to resist. In *Office Space* they are much harder to see, concealed as they are behind a veneer of casual equality and the illusion of choice—"*if* you could be here around nine . . ."—as if he could choose not to be! (In fact Peter does decide to stop working, and gets promoted anyway, underlining the emptiness of the contemporary business world symbolized by Initech). Peter's final, triumphant gesture of resistance, in which he, Michael, and Samir smash the photocopier and blow up the building, seems a bit excessive as a response to the gently suffocating ambience of Initech; their rage seems all out of proportion with the innocuousness of the machines that enslave them. The scenes of destruction are also strangely cathartic, however, in part because they're so insistently physical in contrast to the immaterial economy the workers labour within.

One of the odd impressions to emerge from *Office Space* is of the overwhelmingly oppressive nature of the work environment. Even the intimidating and arguably dangerous machinery in *Modern Times* seems less menacing than the warren of portable cubicles that leave Peter and his colleagues simultaneously isolated and exposed. A dominant feature of American business architecture from the 1950s to the 1970s, cubicles were meant to embody the corporate systems they contained. Moves toward more flexible and movable walls might be seen to reflect a progressive shift toward a more open, democratic work environment. Interestingly, in Europe, where an extensively unionized work force had a consistently stronger influence on labour conditions, "open-plan" offices never did catch on; workers rejected them for the same reason they have become the butt of satire in North America; that they "represent a form of individual housing that neither provided privacy nor fostered interaction" (Christopher Budd, qtd. in Ross 111).

The absence of insulation from creepy managerial intimacy—"Hello, Peter, what's happening?"—is at the benign end of a spectrum of privacy-invading practices at work that include monitoring of computer use, video surveillance, security measures such as retina-scanning and fingerprinting, and mandatory drug tests. Less obviously intrusive, but pervasive in its social effects, is the corporate practice of eroding the distinction between workers' status as employees and their private lives. In sharp distinction from the anonymity of the factory, where the worker functions as a cog in the machinery, contemporary corporate culture goes to great lengths to validate and nurture workers as individuals. Going beyond the long-standing practice of recognizing productivity through prominently displayed photos of "Employee of the Month" (allowing some workers at least to rise temporarily above the fray), many companies now boast their commitment to nurturing their employees as "whole people." This can take the form of flex-time, allowing some workers (mostly managers) to organize their workday around other commitments, as well as more proactive efforts to cultivate workers' physical and emotional health. On-site day care programs, dry cleaners, restaurants, and gyms help to streamline workers' lives (and ensure that they spend most of them at work), while the sponsorship of newsletters, sports teams, clubs, and faith groups built around employees' own interests work to harness those aspects of individuals' lives that once found expression outside of work.

Some companies go the extra mile to fulfill workers' needs. In 2008, for the second straight year, the search-engine company Google ranked first on a list of Best Companies

More rejuvenating than a coffee break: as part of a move to unleash all the productive capacities—body and soul—of their labour force, a few companies, such as this eBay office in San Jose, have on-site prayer and meditation rooms for employees to chill out in.

to Work For, compiled by *Fortune Magazine*. In addition to flexible working arrangements and the encouragement of employee input, Google earns praise for having "special and unique benefits . . . that include opportunities, to learn, grow, travel, and have wildly zany fun during the work-day." As reported by the Great Place to Work® Institute,

> the décor of Google offices encourages much fun. Lava lamps, bicycles, large rubber exercise balls, couches, dogs, press clippings from around the world, projection screens displaying search queries or daily Google events fill the halls and offices. According to an article in the *Seattle Times* entitled "Big Google Ideas Generated Here" (06/24/06): "If the Googleplex exploded, the employees would have a hard time digging themselves out of a shower of pirate flags, action figures, t-shirts with funny sayings, leis, ironic signs, a fringed leather vest, thousands of game pieces, and giant Lego people." ("Why Is Google So Great?")

Of course perks like meditation rooms and gyms represent the top sliver of workplace benefits. The vast majority of workers labour in far less comfortable conditions. The service sector, where 75 percent of the Canadian population currently works (according to the Canadian government's Standing Committee on Industry, Science and Technology), may be less dangerous than the factory in *Modern Times*, but lack of benefits and job security contribute to the precariousness of *post*modern workers' lives. At the same time, workers caught in the net of the ever-ballooning, never-stable service industry are expected to invest significant parts of themselves in their work. *Office Space* offers the frivolous example of Peter's waitress girlfriend, Joanna (Jennifer Aniston), who is told off by her boss for not wearing the requisite 15 pieces of "flair" (suspenders, buttons, and other forms of "self-expression" that serve as crude indicators of an employee's "fun" quotient). Telemarketing companies that require South-Asian callers to adopt "neutral"-sounding American accents are a serious, real-life instance of the way the contemporary workplace (in this case, cramped offices in Bangalore, where employees facilitate the magical process of time–space compression) turns the labour force into **pseudo-individuals** while largely denying their humanity.

In *Modern Times*, the comedy in the film and our sympathy for Chaplin's character are driven by his incomplete subjection to the process of mechanization: even when, after escaping the factory, the worker continues compulsively to perform (on people's noses and women's dress buttons) the motions of his assembly-line action of bolt-tightening, he does so in the form of a crazy but graceful ballet, expressing his alienation and thereby leaving intact something of his humanity. The subjection of the contemporary worker is arguably more complete. As Arlie Russell Hochschild notes in *The Time Bind: When Work Becomes Home and Home Becomes Work*, the "balance" that many workplaces claim to endorse today tends not to mean what we might think—a balance between home and work—but rather the shifting of the things that used to be associated with home, such as secure relationships, nurturing, interdependence, recreation, into the workplace, with the result that workers willingly devote more and more time to work and less and less time to home and family responsibilities, which feel increasingly like work (Hochschild 18–21).

It seems that we have the world that writers such as Lefebvre and Debord had feared, one in which the boundary between public and private has been blurred beyond recognition—mostly in favour of the private. In the case of the provision of public amenities for all to enjoy, the struggle goes on: these spaces are easy to identity and their disappearance can quickly be seen. The spaces of work and leisure have proven far more difficult to make sense of and to keep apart from one another. We bemoan with great energy the constant demands of work on our "free" time. We just as energetically scroll through the e-mail messages streaming down the screens of our Blackberries. We crave an escape.

INSIDE OUT

On March 29, 2008, between the hours of 8:00 and 9:00 p.m., more than 24 cities across the world participated in "Earth Hour," encouraging businesses and individuals to turn off all nonessential electrical power as a step toward reducing the carbon emissions that contribute to global warming. Whether you see this as a useful event or an empty symbolic gesture, it is significant as a mark of perhaps unprecedented global consciousness of the state of the

"Nature/Industry": Maria Whiteman's photographs explore the sometimes problematic divisions we have created between nature and culture.

globe itself—a space we all inhabit, but which we can only know (in its totality as opposed to in its various smaller bits) in an abstract, mediated way. Our discussions of spaces and places so far have focused on concrete, particular zones of experience—parks, roads, offices, and so forth—where we engage with different elements of popular culture. Our focus in this section shifts to aspects of the world that may seem to be the antithesis of the space of culture: nature and the environment. We identify these areas separately not because they are practically distinguishable, but because they signify related but different ways of understanding the world around us, its non-human as well as its human elements.

Nature

It doesn't take a culture critic to tell you that nature is one of those concepts that is really difficult to define: many of us likely regard it as just one of those things that you know when you see it. Advertisers count on this fact as they market products from SUVs to shares in oil companies (many of which have pretty dodgy reputations as friends of nature) with images of sparkling lakes, mountain streams, and old-growth forests. We also see "nature" in the faces of threatened or endangered animals: pandas, tigers, or those remarkably coloured tiny frogs whose disappearance scientists tell us is a barometer of catastrophic natural decline. Other animals interest us much less: rats, coyotes, cockroaches, and sparrows appear much less frequently, if at all, as ambassadors of nature. Then there are animals such as sharks which, until recently, served as emblems for the *other* nature—the uncontrollable, even diabolical force embodied in extreme weather events such as floods, earthquakes and tropical storms. Now that they have been identified as endangered, sharks have become the beneficiaries of campaigns to rehabilitate their reputations, to show that, contrary to the serial-killer image portrayed in *Jaws* and countless other films and media stories, sharks are really big softies, more scared of us than we are of them. They thus join (with some difficulty thanks to their awkwardly large teeth) the ranks of ambassadors for *good* nature, which is almost always characterized as *fragile* nature, vulnerable to man's (and it's almost always characterized as *man's*) heedless and greedy ways. Both categories of nature—threatening and threatened—invoke a whole host of other emotions including awe, **aesthetic** pleasure, and spiritual transcendence. Thus, "nature"—even in its apparently most pared down, non-human incarnation— almost always carries a lot of baggage, which is to say that it wears its unshakeable connection with *culture* quite heavily. It is also highly unstable, as the case of the shark clearly illustrates, signifying different things in different times and different places. Rather than saying what it is definitively, or going completely (infuriatingly) in the other direction and saying that it's purely an invention of culture, we can usefully examine how ideas of nature have traditionally worked to influence our relations with others (both human and non-human).

Moral Centre, Uncivilized Chaos

As the random list of natural icons above suggests, nature, perhaps more than any other concept, lends itself to **binary opposition**, inviting mythological associations that swing back and forth between positive and negative values. This ambivalence is clear from a brief examination of two very different recent films, the animated children's comedy *Over the Hedge* (2006) and Werner Herzog's grisly documentary (excuse the pun) *Grizzly Man* (2005). Both films construct nature in a way that emphasizes its utter separateness and difference—whether positive or negative—from the human world.

As its title suggests, *Over the Hedge* is about the boundary that separates the places of human and animal habitation, and the danger—for animals—of crossing that boundary. Specifically, the hedge in the movie marks the border of a new subdivision that has sprung up while the animals (the principal characters, which include Vern, a turtle, Hammy, a squirrel, and Stella, a skunk) were hibernating. Imposingly tall and creepily green, the hedge is an object of suspicion to the animals, at least until a sleazy raccoon, RJ, persuades them to bust through it in order to find food (his plan is to use the animals as free labour, then give the food to a cranky bear who has threatened to kill RJ for an earlier theft of the bear's own food stash).

If there's a serious message to this film, it's that suburban developments have encroached onto the habitats of animals, resulting in major disruptions to the food chain. Mostly though, it's a comedy, with much of the humour of the film coming from the outrageous behaviour of the human inhabitants of the subdivision (an aesthetic and

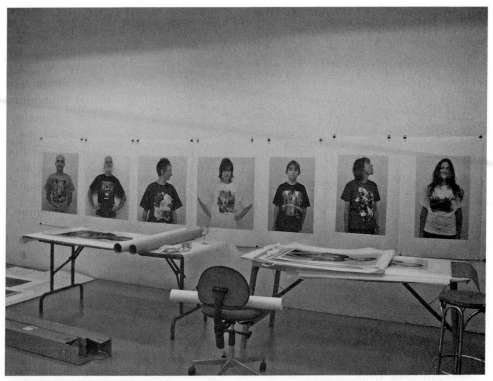

Images of charismatic mega-fauna—large ("mega") animals with crowd-pleasing charm—invoke mythologies of nature in a way that their smaller, more homely cousins do not. Artist Maria Whiteman's portraits of people in animal tourist T-shirts explore the totemic power these images continue to exert.

environmental disaster, as movie suburbs generally are). Seen from the innocent perspective of the animals, we learn that humans are greedy ("We eat to live; they live to eat"); cruel (When told by an exterminator that a particular trap is illegal, the homeowner says, "I don't care if it's against the Geneva Convention"), and lazy (Humans ride around in SUVs, RJ tells the other animals, "because they're slowly losing their ability to walk"). The human world, for which the subdivision functions as an extreme emblem, is ugly, artificial, and aggressive in its domination of nature by technologies ranging from extensive sprinkler systems to a collection of brutal animal control devices.

Most of the human vice in the movie is crammed into one comically horrible woman (Gladys, identified by the vanity plates on her SUV that read "GLADY$$") so that a caricatured idea of femininity (shrill, bossy, obsessed with domestic details) becomes part of what is evil about our side of the hedge. The animals, by contrast, aren't good in a simplistic way; under RJ's direction, they steal and—worse—become temporarily addicted to junk food, which is represented in the film not just as a nasty consequence of an industrial food system but as a kind of metaphor for degraded humanity. The animals triumph (well, except the bear, but that's another story) by overcoming their junk food addiction in favour of wholesome nuts and berries, reaffirming their work ethic and loyalty to one another, and effectively sealing off the border to the dangerous world of suburbia after dispatching Gladys and the exterminator in a particularly gruesome way. As the only humans in the movie, their fate doesn't give much hope for the possibility of reform.

While we would stop short of reading *Over the Hedge* as a serious defence of small semi-urban mammals, it would also be a mistake to write it off as a comedy that simply uses animals in place of humans to make a comment about the foibles of modern society. Neither is it a talking-animal movie like *Babe* or *Chicken Run,* whose comedy conveys uncomfortable truths about the human exploitation of animals. In fact, *Over the Hedge* is arguably not so much about the mechanics of human–animal relations as it is about the line that separates healthy and virtuous nature from the ugly, bloated, Chees-o-rama-coated goings-on of human society. While animals breach this line at their peril, the implication is that only by going over the hedge—that is, back to a more natural, pre-potato-chip existence—can humans redeem ourselves from the hell of our subdivided lives.

A version of this nature versus human philosophy guides the subject of *Grizzly Man.* Timothy Treadwell is a former athlete and sometime actor-turned-conservationist, who spent 13 summers in a national park in Alaska living among grizzly bears. Supplemented by interviews with his friends and family, most of the footage in the film is drawn from the 100-plus hours of DVD footage Treadwell shot of himself—right up to the moment of his death at the hands of the bears (we don't see or hear the tape, which was recorded with the lens cap on, though we do watch Herzog as he listens in obvious horror to Treadwell and his girlfriend Amie's final moments). Part of what is so compelling about the movie is its invitation simultaneously to sympathize with Treadwell's sentimental identification with nature and to identify with the critical editorial perspective of Herzog. While Treadwell speaks in crooning tones to the bears, to whom he's given names, such as Mr. Chocolate and Aunt Melissa, and even rhapsodizes over their droppings ("I can feel the poop! It's warm . . . "), Herzog offers a sober voice-over: "In nature there are predators. The common denominator of the universe is not harmony. It's chaos, hostility, murder." Herzog treats his subject respectfully. However his skepticism—clearly shared by the wildlife experts and park officials interviewed for the film—finds ultimate vindication in Treadwell's death (which mocks his declaration early in the film: "I will not die at their claws and paws!") that seems to support Herzog's contrary view of nature as violent and bloody. But this view is equally infused with emotion, equally mythological. For reviewer David Denby, the movie offers insight not intended by Herzog into the **ideological** opposition between the naive and optimistic American, Treadwell, and the

> hyper-cultivated European, who brings his own burden of despair to nature. Looking into the eyes of a bear that comes close to Treadwell's camera[, Herzog] discerns cruelty and mercilessness rather than hunger. Neither man, it seems, is willing to admit that a bear is a bear is a bear. (Denby)

Denby's analysis seems to make sense, but perhaps he overestimates not just the willingness but the ability of *any* of us to see nature in anything other than value-laden terms. In fact, Treadwell's view of nature resonates with many people, judging by the popularity of the workshops Treadwell ran for many years before his death. Despite Treadwell's somewhat loopy camera persona, many of his sentiments about the innocence of wild animals and the corruption of society (even the parks officials charged with protecting the grizzlies' habitat become objects of his suspicion) are widely shared by individuals and organizations a lot more mainstream than the radical Grizzly People Treadwell founded.

Out in the Wilderness

This view of nature, which is particularly strong in North America, crystallizes around the concept of "wilderness." Idealized as "an island in the polluted sea of urban-industrial modernity" (Cronon 69), wilderness is, according to critic William Cronon, actually a *product* of the social forces it is seen to offer sanctuary from. To understand that irony it is necessary to go back a few centuries to a time when wilderness still retained its biblical significance as a place of desolation, darkness and despair—the world outside the garden of Eden. Around the eighteenth century, that meaning changed. The processes of **industrialization** and **colonization** blurred the line between the known and the unknown as the entire globe was subject to systematic exploitation—for natural resource extraction, settlement, and the extension of European civilization. Within the United States, the concept of the frontier—the unsettled space at the edge of westward colonial expansion—came to embody the great hope for the American dream of democracy and freedom. In the course of contending with, and ultimately conquering, wild nature, the pioneer was seen to be reinvigorated by it, developing through the encounter the qualities of primitive energy, creativity, and independence thought to be the hallmark of the American character.

The wrinkle in this hypothesis was that by the time it was articulated (by Frederick Jackson Turner in *The Significance of the Frontier in American History* in 1893), settlement had extended to the point that the wilderness beyond it was being rapidly consumed— much like the animal's habitat in *Over the Hedge* that's shown on a map to be a tiny dot in a sea of subdivisions. Inherent in the idea of the frontier, then, was its imminent disappearance. And so the seeds were sown of the wilderness preservation movement, nurtured by the idea that in wilderness lay the antidote to the corruption and decadence of Old World civilization; in wilderness, in short, lay the possibility of the salvation of human society. Cronon points out several problems with the **idealization** of wilderness, which persists today in a form not that different from that celebrated by nineteenth-century frontier enthusiasts (the evolution of Canadian ideas of nature took a somewhat different form, stemming from a very different history of European settlement; however, the wilderness ideal has resonance in Canada—and to an extent in Europe and Australia—as well).

First, the structure of the ideal is inherently nostalgic; celebration of the wilderness tends to go hand-in-hand with a condemnation of urbanization and modern life in general. Among the virtuous pleasures associated with wilderness are solitude (in contrast to the turbulent crowds of the city) and masculine ruggedness (vs. "the comforts and seductions" and "feminizing tendencies" of civilized life [Cronon 78]). Ironically, these pleasures tended to be available only to the privileged: frontier nostalgia became a vehicle for expressing what Cronon calls "a peculiarly bourgeois form of antimodernism. The very men who most benefitted from urban-industrial capitalism were among those who believed they must escape its debilitating effects" (78). A version of this paradox persists today, whereby those who have profited most from the capitalist exploitation of natural resources are now in a position to escape from its consequences which include the genuine problems of pollution and disappearing urban green space, but also more questionable objections to sights, sounds, and smells of life in a modern city.

Authentic wilderness came to be seen as a place free from human society and economic activity in particular; this explained its particular affinity for urbanites. "The dream of an unworked natural landscape is very much the fantasy of people who have never themselves had to work the land to make a living" (Cronon 79). The view of the wilderness as home only to animals reflects disregard for the humans who lived, and continue to live and work, there. This contradiction is particularly evident in the way wilderness fantasies tend to gloss over the violent dispossession of First Nations peoples by European settlers. To the extent that the ideal wilderness contains Indians, they are generally presented as one with the land itself, romantic inhabitants because they, along with the buffalo and the forests, are seen to be on the verge of disappearance. The role of the settler/tourist in the displacement of traditional ways of life is awkwardly repressed in the construction of a sentimental image of the "noble savage" that condemns or strategically ignores the unromantic economic conditions of contemporary modern First Nations. In more concrete terms, preserving wilderness comes to seem like a cleaner, simpler goal than addressing Native land claims, with the result that Natives who attempt to hunt and fish on their ancestral lands today are often charged with poaching.

The history of Native cultures in North America and the violence of colonial contact are rarely acknowledged in our idealized constructions of wilderness. In fact it is arguable that this erasure of history is key to the sacred appeal of wilderness, and its chief problem. The flight from history also represents a flight from present-day responsibility. Not only do we deny the reality of violence that gave birth to the myth of wilderness but also, "by imagining that our true home is in the wilderness, we forgive ourselves the homes we actually inhabit" (Cronon 81). In other words, the creation of sacred natural spaces lets us off the hook for continuing to live unsustainably everywhere else. The paradox is especially evident in ads that display SUVs in remote wilderness settings—the trick being that a weekend spent in quiet contemplation of nature (alone, of course, since the sanctity of nature would be ruined if it was also accessible to other people!) can absolve us from the excesses of civilization, including the consumption of resources involved in escaping from it. The ludicrous contradictions in this scenario illustrate Cronon's argument that "wilderness poses a serious threat to responsible environmentalism" (81).

Suggested Activity 9.2

Slovenian philosopher Slavoj Zizek has expressed worries that our "ecology of fear"—our worries about everything from the potentially disastrous outcome of biogenetic experiments to anxieties about exploitation of Earth's resources—"has every chance of developing into the predominant form of ideology of global capitalism, a new opium for the masses replacing declining religion" (439). As long as we take comfort in our fears, he believes that we are unlikely to take the serious steps needed to deal with man's impact on the planet. For Zizek, one of the big problems we face is the view of nature we have constructed for ourselves, one which has made it an ultimate, final form of order that offers security to human social life even as it disappears. Our "cultural" lives might be contingent and made up as we go along through history, but nature has an order that is always beyond us and has no relation to us. Zizek would prefer that we engage in an "ecology without nature" (439), a movement to save the Earth which doesn't rely on ideas about restoring nature's balance or bringing it back into order.

This is one of the ways in which our categories of "nature" and "environment" might create more problems for us than they solve. In what ways are these categories put to use in the public debates about our environmental future today? What role do they play in other public anxieties as well (e.g., kids play too many video games and should be out getting some fresh air)?

Environmental Awareness

Cronon's comment highlights the need to be wary of the mythological foundations of one of our commonest ways of representing nature. It does so by appealing to a different, less value-laden way of understanding the physical world, through the concept of "environment." A term with more scientific credibility, certainly, than words such as "nature" and "wilderness," environment seems to offer an objective way of characterizing non-human spaces and their contents—rocks, trees, animals, air, water, and so on. As ordinary people, even schoolchildren, have come to understand some of the causes and effects of global warming, it can be said that environmental awareness is growing; we're becoming more knowledgeable—amazingly so—about spaces and processes on a scale that we can't actually experience directly. Without diminishing the value of this knowledge, it is worth pausing to consider the cultural dimensions of this realm of existence that seems to be absolutely outside and beyond culture.

How did "the environment" emerge as a subject of popular consciousness? We can identify a few watershed moments. In 1962, marine biologist Rachel Carson's book, *Silent*

Spring, used a mix of scientific data and accessible narrative style to issue a warning about the effects of the pesticide DDT on animals and people. Part of what was so significant about her text, aside from the specific dangers of DDT (which manufacturers disputed and continue to do so), was the way it invited readers to envision the physical world as a vast, interconnected web, such that the effect of a single process, like the application of a pesticide to a farmer's field, could reverberate far beyond it in space and in time.

Silent Spring, which had been serialized in the *New Yorker* before being published as a book and went on to be featured in a 1963 CBS television special, found a large popular audience. An even more momentous contribution to the popularization of the idea of the environment was the transmission of photos of Earth from space. The 1968 photo "Earthrise," taken by Apollo 8 astronauts, was televised live, and became one of a series of images used on posters for the first Earth Day on April 22, 1970. Two years later, Apollo 17 captured the much more famous "Whole Earth" image that has come to be associated with the birth of a new awareness of the world as a single, fragile organism (Maher). Both photos feature in the lecture that structures Al Gore's 2006 documentary on climate change, *An Inconvenient Truth*, following an opening sequence depicting a traditional nature scene with trees, a gently flowing river, and the sound of birds and tree frogs. The images are woven together in a way that invites us to extend our sympathetic imagination from familiar wilderness scenes to the whole biosphere.

One of the striking elements of Gore's film is the way it acknowledges and even celebrates the role of technology in mediating our understanding of nature—the scene that bridges the river and the lecture is of Gore opening his Apple laptop computer, and images of computers feature throughout the film. This representation reflects—and maybe even produced—a new form of environmental consciousness, in comparison to which 1970s celebrations of the image of the "big blue marble" in space seem simple and childlike. The rapidly growing sophistication of visual technologies combined with unprecedented public access to the images they produce—if not to the technologies themselves—have enhanced popular understanding of and concern for spaces and places that we will never physically experience. This awareness has obvious benefits in encouraging individuals to change their own behaviour and to lobby government to create policies necessary to reduce carbon emissions. But the increasing sophistication of popular global awareness may also have another less positive ramification. The technology that gathers the data that informs our awareness, along with the perspective that interprets it, is not planetary in scope; rather, it is produced by organizations whose scientific focus is shaped and sometimes diverted by the powerful political interests. The global environmental agenda as a consequence tends to be driven by wealthy nations in the global North, but directed toward poorer countries in the global South whose development obviously consumes lots of resources. From logging in the Amazonian rainforest to heavy industry in China, environmental problems in the developing world have been the target of a lot of First World finger-wagging—at the expense of attention to the reliance of our own consumer-intensive lifestyles on unsavoury environmental practices in other places. "Thinking globally" isn't the problem, then; it is that we don't think globally *enough*, or make the connections between where we live and what is happening in other places in the world.

Locavores

In the context of environmental problems that are at least partly a consequence of our enthusiastic embrace of globalization, whether as tourists, investors, or consumers, a growing movement is underway to promote commitment to our local communities and environments. The earliest and perhaps the strongest expression of this trend is the local food movement, which encourages consumers to eat food grown and produced close to home. The most extreme form of this "locavore" approach to eating is the 100-mile diet, in which individuals commit to only eating food that has been produced from within a one-hundred-mile radius of where they live. Gaining exposure through the year-long experiment conducted by a couple in British Columbia, published online and then in a book (Smith and MacKinnon), this diet is obviously more feasible in some places than others (If you live in northern Manitoba, you'll end up eating a lot of potatoes and pickled cabbage!). The local food movement has now produced other offshoots, such as local art and local fashion. Adherents of these lifestyles are motivated by a number of concerns: the cost to the environment of shipping goods over long distances, the superior taste and nutritional value of locally grown fruits and vegetables, and a sense of responsibility to one's own community are all strong reasons to commit more energy to buying locally. At their worst, such movements can be nostalgic and reactionary defences of places and lifestyles that never actually existed. Like the cult of wilderness, localism can express anxiety about the conditions of modern life (mass production, reliance on technology, diverse lifestyles) masquerading as progressive politics. It's hard to deny, however, that among the spaces and places of popular culture, our own neighbourhoods should command a large proportion of our critical attention (See Close-Up 9.2). Developing local literacy also forces us to recognize a fact that is obscured in the concepts of "wilderness" and "environment": for all the hedges we've planted, nature and culture can't be separated; they're inextricably tangled around us and also in us.

CHANGING SPACES AND PLACES

As we will discuss at some length in Chapter 10, globalization has created enormous changes in our experiences of space and place. By way of conclusion, we want to just touch briefly here on the use of space in contemporary cinema—an example of the way in which popular culture today can make space appear to be other than what it "really" is.

Displacements: Runaway Productions

In the year following the release of *Brokeback Mountain*, the Oscar-winning story of love between two men in the 1960s American West, the Wyoming Business Council's department of travel and tourism was flooded with phone calls and Internet inquiries

Where are you at? A Bioregional Quiz

1. Trace the water you drink from precipitation to tap.
2. How many days till the moon is full?
3. What soil series are you standing on?
4. What was the total rainfall in your area last year (July–June)?
5. When was the last time a fire burned your area?
6. What were the primary subsistence techniques of the culture that lived in your area before you?
7. Name five native edible plants in your region and their season(s) of availability.
8. From what direction do winter storms generally come in your region?
9. Where does your garbage go?
10. How long is the growing season where you live?
11. On what day of the year are the shadows the shortest where you live?
12. When do the deer rut in your region, and when are the young born?
13. Name five grasses in your area. Are any of them native?
14. Name five resident and five migratory birds in your area.
15. What is the land use history of where you live?
16. What primary ecological event/process influenced the land form where you live? (Bonus special: what's the evidence?)
17. What species have become extinct in your area?
18. What are the major plant associations in your region?
19. From where you're reading this, point north.
20. What spring wildflower is consistently among the first to bloom where you live?

Scoring:

0–3	You have your head up your ass.
4–7	It's hard to be in two places at once when you're not anywhere at all.
8–12	A fairly firm grasp of the obvious.
13–16	You're paying attention.
17–19	You know where you're at.
20	You not only know where you're at, you know where it's at.

Source: Quiz originally compiled by Leonard Charles, Jim Dodge, Lynn Milliman, and Victoria Stockley for *CoEvolution Quarterly* [now *Whole Earth Review* Winter 1981]. Reprinted in *Uncommon Ground: Rethinking the Human Place in Nature*. Ed. William Cronon. New York: Norton, 1995. 369–370.

(Associated Press). The sudden interest in Wyoming is noteworthy not just because the film sparked controversy among some residents, who condemned what one woman described as the destruction of the "wonderful . . . [image] of the cowboys that settled the state and made it what it was" (Sandy Dixon, qtd. in Elsworth), but because the place the film's audience was inspired to visit wasn't Wyoming at all, but Alberta. Strangely, once informed of this fact, many of them didn't care: they still wanted to go to Wyoming. Even tourism officials weren't all that concerned with drawing distinctions between the real Wyoming and the fake Wyoming shown in the film. Before the film's Wyoming debut, Michell Howard, director of the Film, Arts and Entertainment program of the state's Travel and Tourism Division, expressed her enthusiasm: "Obviously, being housed in the tourism division, we like to have our state portrayed on the big screen. . . . I think the locations are going to be beautiful" (Associated Press). Director of Wyoming Travel and Tourism, Diane Shober, went further to suggest that place functioned as

> the third character in this movie. . . . [Audiences] fall in love with a place, and people who have visited Wyoming, and those of us who get to live and work there, you know, we're in love with that place, we have a love affair with the vast, wide, open spaces and the blue skies and the mountains and the streams. (Associated Press)

So: which place did the audience fall in love with? What is the relationship between that place and the Wyoming that inspires those who "get to live and work there"? These questions have taken on new relevance in the context of the growing frequency of **runaway films**: productions intended for distribution in one country—most often the United States—but filmed in another country. Though a foreign location is sometimes dictated by the film's script, *Brokeback Mountain* represents a trend decried by the Hollywood film industry toward "economic" runaways, films shot elsewhere in order to achieve lower production costs ("Runaway Production").

Brokeback Mountain offers an interesting way into the subject of place in popular culture for a few reasons. First, it raises fundamental questions about the relationship between popular culture and place. To understand this relationship, we need to think not just about how films or television shows *represent* particular locations, but about a more complex process of mediation whereby cultural forms help to produce and transform places—socioculturally, obviously, but also economically and even ecologically. Runaway production is an obvious phenomenon through which to view this process.

To start with, we can understand it in purely economic terms in the context of trade liberalization associated with globalization, discussed in Chapter 10. Like any other industry, the film and television business must take advantage of favourable production conditions, including relative political stability, a ready supply of labour, low taxes, and an absence of onerous regulations, in order to be profitable. Culturally and geographically, Canadian locations—Toronto (or, in a pinch, Hamilton), Vancouver, and the Alberta Rockies—are obvious choices as stand-ins for American settings. The bottom line, though, is, well, the bottom line: tax breaks and subsidies for films are the crucial factor in luring Hollywood productions north—at least they were, until a stronger Canadian dollar and the associated increase in labour and production costs sent moviemakers back to New York, L.A., and maybe even Wyoming. This industry mobility affects places in many ways. Most obviously, film production provides work for all kinds of people—actors, set designers, production crew, caterers, real-estate agents, the purveyors of soy milk lattes, and so on—whose livelihoods share more with those of factory workers than it might initially appear: precarious in any case, their jobs are particularly vulnerable to the **transnational** volatility of the industries they work in. But the presence (or absence) of film crews on a city's streets also has economic and cultural spinoff effects. In his controversial prescription for creating vibrant (read: wealthy) cities in *The Rise of the Creative Class*, Richard Florida has argued that the presence of a strong **creative class**, of which the groups of people cited above are vital members, is a key determinant of success. Leaving aside the somewhat shaky claim of a connection between a concentration of "creative" professionals, social progressiveness, and economic progress, which somehow mixes up aesthetics, politics, and economics, it is inarguable that the jobs, workers, and consumers that make up what Horkheimer and Adorno more trenchantly called the **culture industry** (see Chapter 4) drive the contemporary global economy: in this context, closing stores and shutting down streets for film shoots might in some places increasingly represent business as usual.

As anyone knows who lives somewhere that, thanks to its fine Victorian architecture (or quaint shops, or grungy alleyways and/or tax incentives), often gets used for film shoots, this form of industrial production does weird things to places. In one sense, it appears to accelerate the process of **deterritorialization** often associated with globalization, whereby social, economic, political, and cultural activity becomes increasingly detached from place. If Alberta works for film audiences as a stand-in for Wisconsin, then arguably what makes places distinctive, environmentally, culturally and socially, is receding in importance (and what can we say about Shanghai, which in films such as *Code 46* has stood in for the future!). However, as we have noted above, the processes of cultural production shape the material conditions of life in particular places, for workers in the industry, and also for the people who live there. Where a particular physical or architectural attribute is important for a place's filmic quality (e.g., heritage buildings, industrial locations, skyscraper-filled business districts), there is a strong incentive to maintain those elements—weirdly stronger, perhaps, than the voices of local conservation groups. In this way, involvement in the film or television industry can accentuate the distinctiveness of particular places, making them both more like themselves and less real at the same time. More often, perhaps, a place might be desirable for its generic "Everycity" qualities, or for its amenability to alteration. Parts of the first *X-Men* film and the sequel to the *Incredible Hulk* were shot in Hamilton because of the availability of space in a deteriorating "old"-feeling downtown core to construct building façades that could then be blown up. More generally and more disturbingly, runaway productions, in which a film crew bars access to a street in order to shoot a car chase or cordons off a park to film a baseball scene, are a spectacular but in some ways typical example of the general move toward the privatization of public space.

The Future

The peculiar kind of displacement that occurs as a result of runaway film production may one day be a thing of the past. The growing sophistication of computer-generated imagery (CGI) means that film companies now are often spared the arduous task of finding aesthetically and economically appropriate locations to shoot films; why incur the cost and bother of schlepping actors, crews, and equipment to a rundown street in the outskirts of Toronto, when you can create an even grittier, more dangerous-looking environment in the studio? While the effect of the growing use of CGI on the film industry and audiences is debatable, there's no question that virtual space enables a kind of unrestricted creativity that is impossible in real places. As trite as it sounds, it is important to remember that none of us lives in virtual reality; we still need to find a way to survive, collectively and individually, in the material world.

One of the consequences of the ways in which North Americans and much of the rest of the world have organized space is that we have left ourselves with very few options when it comes to facing up to what is perhaps the greatest challenge we have ever encountered: not just a looming ecological crises due to carbon emissions, to which governments have barely mounted any response, but also declining supplies of fuel (primarily oil) and an expanding population that is estimated by the United Nations to reach 9.2 billion by mid-century.

One response to both the declining supplies and growing expense of fuel would be to reshape cities so that more people are able to walk to work or use public transit to move around. Many Canadian cities have tried over the past decade to do just this. However, the spatial infrastructure that has been built up over the past half century, which places most homes far from urban centres and guarantees that for most people work will be far from home, has meant that mass transit strategies in Canada—and in most U.S. cities as well—are unlikely to succeed. It is one thing to expand mass transit in cities such as Paris (with a population density of 24,948 people/square kilometre) or London, U.K. (12,331/square mile), and quite another to do so in cities such as Calgary (1,360.2/square kilometre) or Edmonton (1,067.2/square kilometre—23 times *less* dense than Paris) in which the population density simply doesn't permit or enable the effective, widespread use of transit. In Calgary, some new developments have been built which mirror turn-of-the-century (nineteenth to twentieth centuries) small towns in an effort to create different kinds of communities and thus different possibilities for future living. Though the garage may have been moved to the alley and houses pushed closer together, the automobile remains king as a mode of transport even in these cases: seen from Calgary's Mckenzie Town, the city's downtown skyline appears as a distant blip on the sky. If Canada, one of the world's worst polluters per capita (20.0 metric tons of CO_2 emissions per person in 2004, as compared to Germany at 9.79 metric tons), is to address not only spiking fuel costs but also the impact of mass automobile use on its environment, it seems that the best solution would be to rethink the ways in which it organized spaces and places in the twentieth century—to do it all over again, in the best-case scenario, and to cut the freeways and the suburbs out of the picture. Since this isn't likely to happen, the challenges that lie ahead are enormous.

There are other problems linked to our organization and use of space on the horizon as well. In late 2007 and throughout 2008, experts and governments began to note with alarm rising food costs around the world, which in many countries (such as Mexico) have led to food riots protesting the increase in the price of staples such as corn, maize, wheat, rice, and cassava. In December 2007, *The Economist* reported that its global food index was higher than at any point since its creation in 1845, with prices having jumped by 75 percent since 2005 ("The End of Cheap Food"). Over 2007, the price of wheat doubled, with other food commodities being at historical peaks. In countries where families live on a few dollars a day, such increases are painful: in many cases, even basic foodstuffs are suddenly out of reach. While the reasons for this development are complex, they are linked directly to the choices that we have made about how we have used (and abused) the space available to us.

As Mike Davis notes, this will be the century of the city. Growing urbanization and the expansion of middle classes in China and India have brought about changes in diet. The average Chinese consumer ate 50 kg of meat in 2007 compared to 20 kg in 1985. Since it takes 8 kg of grain to produce 1 kg of meat, this dietary change has a huge impact on the demand for and supply of grains. The continued increase in the use of fossil fuels has led countries such as the United States to look to new sources of fuel that they can produce themselves instead of importing from abroad. Subsidies to produce ethanol, a fuel that can be produced from a wide range of cereal grains and other plant matter, to fill up gas tanks has a further impact on available supplies of grains, maize, and rice. High prices for grain have also led to ever-more forested land being converted for agricultural purposes.

Part of the rationale for increased use of ethanol is that it produces less CO_2 emissions than regular fossil fuels and so is better in the long run for the environment. When forests are cut down to grow more grains, the planet is able to absorb less CO_2, and modern farming itself requires the use of a great deal of fuel. When all is said and done, many scientists have estimated that it costs almost as much energy to produce a litre of ethanol as is contained in the litre that is produced! And then we come back around to the impact of shifting demands for meat and ethanol on the huge numbers of poor people barely managing to live from day-to-day. For them, and for the slum cities that are increasingly coming to define the shape of the contemporary urban experience, the pleasures of *flânerie* or the political engagement of drifting through the city seem very far away from being the most important issues that they face. However difficult it might be, we all need to attend to the injustices created by the spaces and places of the contemporary world.

SUGGESTIONS FOR FURTHER READING

Davis, Mike. *Planet of Slums.* New York: Verso, 2006.
Harvey, David. *Social Justice and the City.* Oxford: Blackwell, 1992.
Higmore, Ben. *Everyday Life and Cultural Theory: An Introduction.* New York: Routledge, 2002.

Jacobs, Jane. *The Death and Life of Great American Cities.* New York: Modern Library, 1993.

Kohn, Margaret. *Brave New Neighborhoods: The Privatization of Public Space.* New York: Routledge, 2004.

Kunstler, James Howard. *The Geography of Nowhere: The Rise and Decline of America's Man-Made Landscape.* New York: Free Press, 1994.

LeGates, Richard T., and Fredric Stout, eds. *The City Reader.* Fourth edition. New York: Routledge, 2007.

Lippard, Lucy. *The Lure of the Local: Senses of Place in a Multicentered Society.* New York: The New Press, 1997.

Massey, Doreen. *Space, Place and Gender.* Minneapolis: University of Minnesota Press, 1994.

Merrifield, Andy. *Metromarxism: A Marxist Tale of the City.* New York: Routledge, 2002.

Soja, Edward W. *Postmodern Geographies: The Reassertion of Space in Critical Social Theory.* New York: Verso, 1989.

Williams, Raymond. *The Country and the City.* London: The Hogarth Press, 1973.

Wilson, Alexander. *The Culture of Nature: North American Landscapes from Disney to the Exxon Valdez.* Toronto Between the Lines, 1991.

Chapter 10

Globalization and Popular Culture

INTRODUCTION: WHAT IS GLOBALIZATION?

Globalization is a term that has gained increasing prominence over the past two decades. It has been discussed with equal fervour in the halls of the academy, in the pages of business magazines, on the front pages of newspapers around the world, and on the websites and Internet discussion groups of organizations and individuals dedicated to fighting global corporate dominance. At the beginning of the 1990s, globalization was a term most commonly associated with the decline of industrial manufacturing in the "Rust Belt" of the U.S. and in eastern Canada. Unlike typical recessions connected to the cyclical downturns characteristic of **capitalist** economies, the loss of blue-collar jobs was seen in these cases as the result of an unprecedented migration of North American industries to lower wage countries, especially to the **maquiladoras** along the U.S.–Mexico border. By the end of the decade, globalization was linked to an ever-expanding range of political, economic, social, and cultural phenomena, from public demonstrations against multilateral trade and economic agreements to the potential dangers of genetically modified foods to worries over what Britney Spears' music and image is doing to the Philippines.

Though globalization is primarily the name of a *process* (just like modern*ization* and **industrial*ization***), the increasing use and visibility of the term in both the media and in public debates has sometimes made it seem as if it is the name for the particular moment in history we are now living through. Just as the **cold war** was the name for the entire set of events and processes that made up the international order between the end of the Second World War and the fall of the Berlin Wall in 1989, globalization is sometimes taken to be synonymous with the "**New World Order**" announced by (the first) President George Bush and described by the author Francis Fukuyama as "the end of history." While it does seem to be the case that the term "globalization" begins to be used with frequency only *after* the end of the cold war and the dissolution of the Soviet Union, the claims made for and against globalization can be understood only if we treat it as an ongoing historical process. Indeed, much of the debate surrounding globalization concerns questions of just what kind of processes it names, how far back these processes can be traced, and, indeed, if these processes can be described meaningfully as part of a single, worldwide process.

What kinds of processes are associated with globalization? At its most basic level, globalization is the name for the social, political, cultural, economic, and technological processes that, taken together, have created the changed conditions of contemporary existence. At the centre of these altered conditions is an enormous change in both the physical and psychological experience of time and space. Globalization has brought previously distant parts of the world together. Instead of being composed of distant and distinct places, we have begun to imagine the world as a single space in which peoples and communities are connected to one another as never before. New communications technologies, such as the Internet, cell phones, and satellite transmissions, have made it possible for people (or at least some people) to communicate with one another instantaneously across huge distances, and to receive immediate information about political and social developments in other parts of the world. The communications revolution has also helped to produce greater integration of national economies, particularly with respect to financial markets. Multinational agreements that have been ratified by most countries on the globe, such as the General Agreement on Tariffs and Trade (GATT), have changed the nature of the world economy. Today, there is more than US$1.5 trillion in foreign-exchange transactions, an increase of 2,100 percent between 1980 and 1995 (Anderson and Cavanaugh 33, 16). As recent financial crises in Mexico (1994), Southeast Asia (1997), Russia and Brazil (1998), Argentina (2002), and the United States (2007–08) have shown, economic developments in one country have an increasingly large impact on every other country in the world.

Culturally, globalization is experienced as the increased knowledge of and access to the culture and cultural products of peoples around the world, as well as the often-unwanted imposition of one especially powerful culture's values and products on nearly all the others. In the first instance, globalization can be witnessed in the popularity of world music (such as the Buena Vista Social Club or Cesaria Evora), the global interest in Japanese *manga* and *anime*, and the fascination in Eastern Europe (and elsewhere) with *telenovelas* produced in Mexico and other parts of South America. On the other hand, the overwhelming, ubiquitous global presence of films, television programs, and fast-food franchises from the United States (with the same Starbucks coffee available in Beijing's Forbidden City as in the streets of Istanbul) has been seen by many as one of the negative results of a smaller and faster world.

As this chapter will show, there is an almost endless number of phenomena associated with globalization. As a result, a strict definition of globalization cannot help but reduce the complexity that discussions of it deserve. Nevertheless, all of the processes associated with globalization can generally be related to an historically unprecedented compression of time and space (Harvey). Many of the most prominent scholars who have written about globalization have described it in similar terms. The sociologist Anthony Giddens has described it as "the intensification of world-wide relations which link distant localities in such a way that local happenings are shaped by events occurring many miles away" (64), while the geographer Doreen Massey characterizes globalization as the stretching out of social relations. Malcolm Waters has described it as "the receding constraints of geography on social and cultural arrangements" (5), and for Roland Robertson it is "the compression of the world and intensification of the consciousness of the world as a whole" (8).

Popular culture today in every part of the world exists in some relationship to globalization. Indeed, as John Tomlinson suggests at the beginning of his book *Globalization and Culture*, "globalization lies at the heart of modern culture; cultural practices lie at the heart of globalization" (1). In exploring contemporary popular culture, it is thus essential to understand the reciprocal relationship between globalization and culture. As a way of examining this relationship, we need to consider a perhaps surprising question that impacts greatly on how we perceive the effects of globalization. We need to ask: Is globalization *real*? While no one disputes the fact that there have been significant changes in every sphere of human life over the past several decades, there are disagreements over just how *new* globalization is. Whether globalization is a genuinely new development in human life or whether it is the acceleration of much longer term developments has a significant impact on how we understand its relationship to cultural practices around the world.

IS GLOBALIZATION REAL?

It is sometimes easy to forget just what life was like in North America only a few decades ago. For the few households with cable television, only a few dozen channels (comprised primarily of different local stations of the major broadcast networks) were available. Personal computers had only just been introduced and could barely manage to generate text on their screens, much less the complicated graphical interfaces that we are accustomed to today. There was no Internet, no cell phones, no personal handheld assistants, no laptops. Most of the world's stock exchanges were still populated with people (with the exception of a few exchanges, most trading now takes place electronically). Mutual funds were not a mainstream investment vehicle and few people paid much attention to the daily fluctuations of the stock market. The threat of nuclear war hung over the world, as the chill of the cold war deepened during President Ronald Reagan's bellicose administration. And if you forgot to take money out of your bank account for the weekend, you were stuck: there was virtually no such thing as a bank machine that could bail you out, and even credit card use was restricted by today's standards.

The Digital Revolution

There are numerous other differences between 1983 and 2003 that one could point to. Why these? What has made today so different than even the recent past is not the changes in the clothes we wear, the music we listen to, or the films we watch (though these too have changed), but the explosion in computer and communications technologies that has affected every part of our lives. The increasing presence of these technologies throughout North American society has changed how we work and enjoy ourselves. There are professions today that didn't exist two decades ago (from web design to network maintenance to day trading), and new modes of labouring (such as working from home, or *telecommuting*). The market for video games, both on home console systems and on computers, now exceeds the annual revenue generated by Hollywood film production. **Digitalization** has enabled a convergence of media forms (music stations available on television, the presence of music and video on the Internet), as well as the creation of entirely new forms of popular culture (electronica, raves, "surfing the 'net," Facebook communities, YouTube videos). At the same time, it has also led to the decline of some long-established cultural products (digital cameras have threatened the very existence of traditional film cameras).

Additionally, these technologies have made it easier to for North Americans to access people, products, and places around the globe. Tourism, for instance, has grown exponentially over the past several decades, becoming one of the major industries in the world today; there are no longer parts of the world that seem inaccessible by phone or air travel. At least, this is true in theory: the impact of globalization is clearly not the same for everyone everywhere, a point we will return to later.

Of course, focusing only on what has changed in contemporary culture tends to obscure not just all of the things that have stayed the same, but also the long developments that have led up to these changes. As we saw in Chapter 4, a continual emphasis on the new or "hip" is itself a feature of contemporary culture and of the practices that we associate with **consumerism**. One of the most powerful engines of consumerism is our fascination with the "new." Along with each year's new car models and fashion styles, announcements of upcoming movie blockbusters and a new season's worth of television shows fuel the purchase of items that seem entirely original, but which are in fact more of the same. When we take a longer view of many of the products that make up contemporary popular culture, we can see that things change much more slowly than each fashion season might suggest. Not only do older fashions (and even car styles) return, but underneath all the evidence of change the function of cars and clothes remains the same, as has their structural role in North American society. This is not to say that the increased use of the automobile since the Second World War, or even the increasingly popularity of particular kinds of automobiles (such as sports utility vehicles or SUVs in the 1990s and early 2000s), haven't had a broader social or cultural impact. But this impact has to be assessed and understood in the context of longer trends: suburbanization and environmental damage have accompanied the automobile since its advent.

While globalization is far from being just a passing fashion or style, our sense of how the world has changed also needs to be tempered by considering (for example) the computer and communications revolution in a historical context. In other words, rather than conceding that a *revolution* has happened, it is important to understand the *evolution* that has brought about globalization. The compression of time and space that has made it possible to imagine the globe as a single space didn't occur overnight: it is the outcome of a long and complicated history. While not all parts of this history impact directly on contemporary popular culture, understanding the historical process by which globalization has come about does allow us to better comprehend the reciprocal relationship between globalization and popular culture, and to understand the broader context within which popular culture is experienced and analyzed.

NOT JUST ONE THING, BUT A COLLECTION OF PROCESSES

Claims about the "newness" of globalization have been raised in a number of related areas, including economics, politics, and technology. Though we take each of these areas up separately below, it is important to recognize that these areas are in fact connected in important ways. As we shall see in the discussion that ends this chapter, one of the things that globalization has meant is that it is no longer possible to even make such divisions *heuristically*—that is, as a simplified model that limits the range of events and concepts that we need to investigate in order to make sense of specific phenomena.

Economic Globalization

Globalization is a term that has perhaps been most frequently discussed in corporate boardrooms and on the pages of the business press. Globalization is understood as presenting both new challenges and fresh opportunities in the never-ending quest to generate ever-greater corporate profits and to maximize shareholder value. In the eyes of the general public, too, globalization is linked to new forms of business practice. Businesses and economies were once linked to definite, national spaces, which meant that they could be controlled and regulated by the governments and citizens of nation-states. However, in the era of globalization many businesses have become **transnational**: able to relocate to whatever jurisdiction has the most favourable climate for business, and sometimes able to exist outside of any jurisdiction whatsoever. The former CEO of General Electric, one of the largest companies in the world, described the ideal location of his company as a gigantic barge that could be moved around the world as needed to take advantage of changes in economic climate (Welch). Similarly, shipping companies have increasingly registered their fleets in small protectorates such as the Marshall Islands in order to avoid taxation in the countries from which they really originate.

The ability of corporations to shift production around the world, often in order to take advantage of cheap wages and loose environmental and labour regulations in less developed countries (LDCs), has been accompanied by two other factors associated with globalization. First, many companies have become global enterprises in order to expand the range of consumer markets that they can reach. Several fast-food chains based in the United States operate in almost 100 countries worldwide, while cell phone and consumer electronics giants have established consumer outlets and the production facilities to support them on virtually every continent. In recent years, even older industrial and resource enterprises, from steel producers to oil companies, have been consolidated into even more massive global businesses. Second, globalization has enabled unprecedented flows of financial goods and services. The world's stock markets are integrated as never before, with a small fluctuation in capital markets in one country able to produce major financial shifts and swings in others. For example, anxieties about the implications of sub-prime mortgage loans in the United States caused stock markets to decline in Shanghai, São Paulo, and Toronto, as well as New York City. Today, the equivalent of the combined global **gross domestic product (GDP)** flows across borders in the form of foreign-exchange transactions in roughly eight days.

The Roots of Globalization   The contemporary world economy is truly global in scope. But in many respects, it has been "global" for hundreds of years, even if we haven't used the term "globalization" to describe this fact. While prior to the time of Christopher Columbus's journey to the Americas most food and goods originated close to where people lived and worked, even in the ancient world there was a great deal of cross-cultural contact. This contact came about through military conquest (from Alexander the Great to the Roman Empire to the Crusades), travel along established trading routes between regions and even continents, and through journeys of exploration—such as Marco Polo's travels to Asia and the voyages of the Vikings, who, five hundred years prior to Columbus, had already established a settlement in the Americas at L'Anse aux Meadows, in what is today known as Newfoundland.

The "discovery" of the Americas by Europeans initiated a process of ever-accelerating, truly global trade in and production of goods. The establishment of far-sprung colonial empires by Spain, Portugal, England, Germany, Belgium, France, the Netherlands, and Italy (followed later by Japan and the United States) produced a market in Europe for goods produced abroad (bananas, oranges, coffee, tobacco, sugar, etc.). These empires also established a global division of labour that remains with us to this day. The colonies in South America, Africa, and Asia became sites of resource extraction and agriculture production for the European market. In turn, value-added manufacturing took place in Europe, with these goods often being exported back to the colonies in an effort to maximize the size of the markets (and thus of the profits) for European goods. The once powerful textile industries of India and the Philippines (e.g., cotton) were devastated by the cheaper textiles exported from England.

This global division of labour exists in very much the same form today, with an ever-increasing range of local economies (and, thus, local ways of life) feeling the impact of new global economic arrangements. In particular, the agriculture sector of many countries has been threatened by the availability of Western agricultural products that, due to protectionist tariffs and subsidies, can be sold much more cheaply than locally produced goods. Stephanie Black's documentary *Life and Debt* (2001), for instance, examines the flood of U.S. agricultural products into Jamaica, a fertile country whose financial problems and debt crisis has meant that local farmers find it difficult to produce fruit and vegetables grown thousands of miles away.

THE FINAL MERGER

Globalization is imagined as the era in which corporations have developed global reach and achieved newfound power. But here, too, the story is a much longer and more complicated one than many debates and discussions about globalization might lead us to believe. During the cold war, a number of companies were already described as having operations that were **multinational** in scope. For example, Japanese automobile manufacturers such as Toyota and Nissan sold *and* produced cars in many countries outside of Japan during the sixties, seventies, and eighties; the same holds true for all of the major corporations in the world.

A little farther back, by the end of the nineteenth century a number of U.S. corporations had developed not just national but global **monopolies** (or "trusts"), which led to the passage of "antitrust" legislation to limit the control of trade by a few large companies. The global might of Standard Oil, Carnegie Steel, American Tobacco, and other large corporations was reined in under this legislation, which has been used subsequently to challenge the power of corporations such as AT&T and Microsoft. Even farther back, enormous corporations developed alongside the creation of the European colonies. The insurance giant Lloyd's of London has been underwriting corporations and colonial expeditions since 1688; in Canada, the Hudson's Bay Company, which has been in existence since 1670, organized trade from the new world to Great Britain and Europe.

Corporations as "Persons"   In many ways, then, the world economy functions very similarly to the way it has over the past century (if not even longer). Nevertheless, there are significant differences, as a result of developments in technology and geopolitical shifts, which have a direct impact on the shape and character of contemporary popular culture. Due in part to fears about the possibility that large corporations might relocate to other countries, the past decade has witnessed an unprecedented relaxation of government legal and economic controls on corporations worldwide.

This, too, is part of a longer history that extends back to 1886, when corporations in the United States were granted full legal rights as "natural persons," far in advance of women and **minorities**. Prior to this date, corporations were extended short-term charters, which gave the public the ability to limit a company's profits and debt (among other things), and provided procedures for a full public accounting of the company's books.

Today, nation-states around the world have less legal recourse than ever in controlling the actions of corporations, which now exist to some degree outside of the laws of nation-states altogether. This has been one of the major consequences of the international trade agreements pursued by states over the past two decades. These agreements have the effect of spreading the U.S. legal definition of corporations, as well as other aspects of corporate law (such as definitions regarding **intellectual copyright**), into other countries around the world.

As a result, the balance of power between corporations and states has shifted considerably. For example, under the provisions of Chapter 11 of the North American Free Trade Agreement (NAFTA), corporations are able to file suit against governments for infringing on "investor rights." United Parcel Services (UPS), the world's largest package delivery company, has filed a US$230-million suit against Canada Post (a public corporation), alleging that the Canadian federal government is involved in a service already provided by a private corporation in violation of NAFTA. Similarly, citing NAFTA's fair and equitable treatment rules, Vancouver-based Methanex Corp. has sued the U.S. government as a result of a California decision to phase out the use of a gasoline additive produced by the company due to environmental concerns. While NAFTA and other trade agreements have included provisions to limit their applicability to cultural issues, this has in reality done very little to limit the erosion of state control over corporate activities.

The shift in the relationship between states and corporations has taken two other forms as well. First, as a way of attracting and retaining business, governments have committed significant public monies (through tax breaks, loan guarantees, or direct transfers) to entice companies to their countries, cities, and regions. This transfer of tax revenue, which is now generated predominantly by taxes on individual income rather than on corporate profit, has occurred in almost every sector of the business world. Its most public face in North America, however, has been seen in the debates over public financing of sports franchises and stadiums (see Chapter 2).

Second, while there have been challenges to the monopoly status of some companies (such as the European Union's legal challenge against Microsoft in 2008), for the most part there has been a loosening of restrictions on the size and power of corporations. In order to gain and maintain their competitive advantage globally, corporations from across the world have been merging into larger and larger entities. In 2000 alone, according to the consulting firm KPMG, the value of cross-border mergers was CAN$643 billion. To put this in perspective, the value of cross-border mergers in 2000 was about the same as Canada's GDP for that year.

Integration and Convergence The effects of these mergers have been especially pronounced in the culture industries. Changes in legislation regulating telecommunications in Canada and the United States have permitted the development of enormous multimedia conglomerates over the past decade. Giant media corporations such as AOL Time Warner, Bertelsmann, Viacom, and Vivendi Universal have an enormous global reach. Contemporary media conglomerates not only are **vertically integrated,** like the early twentieth-century film industry (see Chapters 2 and 4), but also are **horizontally integrated,** owning several record labels, television channels, or film studios. Technological changes (especially digitalization) have also made it possible for these conglomerations to make use of programming or content produced for one medium in several others. For example, a movie produced by Warner Brothers' film studio can receive positive press in *People* magazine, be publicized on the Internet via America Online, and be screened later on television on TNT, a television "superstation" that broadcasts across North America.

A look at just some of the companies owned by Disney Corp. shows the endless possibilities that such **media convergence** provides for corporations. In addition to its famous theme parks, Disney owns

- publishing houses, including Hyperion and Miramax Books;
- magazines, including Discover, ESPN Magazine, and US Weekly;
- the ABC Television Network;
- community radio and television stations across the U.S.;
- a range of specialty cable channels, including Disney, A&E, ESPN, The History Channel, and Lifetime;
- movie production and distribution companies, including Touchstone Pictures, Pixar, and Miramax Films;
- various websites;
- Disney Interactive Studios, which produces computer games (often based on Disney movies or television shows);
- record labels, including Hollywood Records;
- Disney Theatrical Productions, which produces stage versions of Disney films, as well as Disney on Ice;
- The Muppets and Baby Einstein Products, often sold through its Disney Stores;
- travel agencies and tourist resorts, including a cruise line and an island in the Caribbean;
- and, finally—for those who prefer to stay home—the planned community of Celebration Village, Florida.

(Note that the most up-to-date source for media ownership is the list maintained by the *Columbia Journalism Review* on its website at www.cjr.org/owners/index.asp.)

While none can boast of a portfolio like Disney's, Canadian media corporations have also pursued more or less successful strategies of convergence. With its recent acquisition of media properties formerly owned by Hollinger, CanWest Global Communications Corp. now owns local television stations, a national television network, and an enormous number of newspapers in Canada (including the *National Post, Montreal Gazette, Ottawa Citizen,* and *Calgary Herald*); in Vancouver, it owns both daily newspapers and two television stations. CTVglobemedia—a company spun off from the giant Bell Canada Enterprises (BCE)—owns CTV, TSN, and a huge range of other specialty cable channels (everything from *Discovery* to *SexTV*), *The Globe and Mail,* a portion of Maple Leaf Sports and Entertainment (owners of the Toronto Maple Leafs, the Toronto Raptors, and the Toronto FC soccer club), and a huge number of radio stations across Canada. In Quebec, two corporations, Power Corp and Quebecor Inc., control virtually all media outlets in the province. The increasing control by fewer and fewer corporations of much of what we understand as contemporary popular culture has important effects and repercussions (which we will discuss in more detail below). The most obvious impact is on our very sense of what constitutes popular culture. To some degree, the concentration of media power has meant a restriction in the range of cultural objects (in form if not in quantity) produced by these culture industries, which has consequently had a significant impact on what is represented and signified in the films, television programs, books, and magazines produced today.

The culture industries belong to the sector of the economy known as *service industries,* which now constitute almost 30 percent of the total exports of the United States (World Bank 190–198). As culture becomes more closely identified with global economics, popular culture undergoes a shift. For example, the popularity of the action-film genre has much to do with the ease with which these films can be exported to countries outside the United States: dialogue is minimal and easily translated, and costly Hollywood special effects offer a spectacle that few indigenous cinemas can match. In other words, because they are able to generate enormous revenues in the global film market, action movies starring action stars such as Jean-Claude Van Damme, Steven Seagal, and Jackie Chan, or low-dialogue, high-scream horror films such as *Saw,* represent an increasingly large proportion of Hollywood productions.

Contemporary cultural industries require costly infrastructural investments in production facilities and distribution networks. They also require a high degree of technological innovation and expertise. Unsurprisingly, in a world in which the division of wealth has increased both among and within countries, only a very small number of countries have been able to participate actively in the production and export of some forms of popular culture. While the United States is the most visible of these, Canada has also aggressively marketed its cultural products abroad. This has sometimes placed the Canadian government in the awkward position of defending Canadian culture from outside influence through various cultural policies (such as Canadian content rules on television and radio), while simultaneously pushing for greater exports of Canadian-produced culture.

The global economy has developed over several hundred years, and is in many respects structurally similar today to what it was like at the end of the nineteenth century. There are, however, differences—especially with respect to the production and export of culture—that are an essential aspect of popular culture in globalization.

Suggested Activity 10.1

In what contexts have you heard the concept of globalization discussed (e.g., newspaper and television stories, books, etc.)? In these contexts, is globalization presented as an opportunity or a cost? How do different groups and organizations view globalization? Is globalization seen as just how things are, or as a political–economic project that needs to be contested and challenged? What do these differences (between, for example, Fortune 500 companies and environmental groups) suggest about the general public's understanding of the meaning of globalization, and how does this differ from what we've outlined so far (and what we go on to say in the rest of the chapter)?

Globalization and Politics

Many of the points made about the economic realities of globalization apply equally to its political aspects. Politically, discussions about globalization have tended to focus on two things: (1) the decline of the power of nation-states and the rise in power of corporations and international agencies such as the International Monetary Fund (IMF) and the World Trade Organization (WTO), and (2) the increasing **privatization** of public services and public spaces.

There is some truth to both of these claims. Especially with respect to economic decision making, nation-states face considerable pressure from foreign economic developments and are often forced to act reactively rather than proactively to current events. At the same time, the massive privatization of the economy and culture offers evidence to the contrary. Though the decisions of governments to outsource services they once provided as a public good—everything from state-run utilities, to prisons, to the education system—are often presented to the public as matters of rational logic (i.e., the private sector can do things more efficiently that the government) or of external compulsion (i.e., global competitiveness demands it), it is in fact only a strong state that could bring about such a massive change in the structure of Western politics and economics.

In other words, the claim that the power of the state has declined is in many respects little more than a ruse that has disguised a massive transfer of publicly accumulated wealth into private hands. In many cases, state spending has in fact increased more quickly than corporate growth over the past two decades, though this new spending has been directed toward different ends than in the past—policing, prisons, anti-immigrant spending, enforcement of drug politics, militarization, and transfers to business and infrastructural development that tends to benefit private corporations rather than the public at large. Nation-states continue to control the major institutions through which laws are enforced and legitimate force is exerted (armies, police, intelligence agencies, etc.).

National Identity   Not only has the decline of the power of the **nation**-state been exaggerated, but so too has the claim that globalization signals a decline in feelings of national identity or pride in national culture (see Chapter 7). Feelings of national belonging now compete with other forms of identification, which can range from various kinds of consumer **identity** (e.g., patterns of belonging derived *from* your belongings, such as occurs with Harley-Davidson or BMW owners) to identities based on **ethnicity**, sexual orientation, and political affiliations, all of which exceed the boundaries of individual nation-states. While it is true that national identity constantly interacts and competes with other forms of identification, this is true of the *entire* history of the nation, and not just during the period of globalization.

Even where new nationalities (and, indeed, new nation-states, the multiple countries that now make what used to be Yugoslavia and the Soviet Union being just the beginning of the new nations that have come into existence during globalization) are not in the process of being formed, national identity remains an extremely powerful force. Pride in national identity is still reinforced by schooling (through the playing of the national anthem and the teaching of national histories and cultures), revived during the Olympics, and crystallized during times of tension and conflict—as the reaction of the citizens of the United States to the terrorist attacks on the World Trade Center and the Pentagon showed all too clearly.

The politics of globalization are complex and multifaceted. There are new political agents and institutions involved in shaping global politics, including a wide variety of non-governmental organizations (NGOs) and institutions such as the International Intellectual Property Organization, which have been developed to manage international agreements of various kinds. Once again, however, it is best to stress continuities as opposed to a sudden, massive discontinuity in the nature of politics in the era of globalization.

The Technological Dimensions of Globalization

In 2001, Bell Canada produced a television ad it called "Online Jam." Designed to promote its high-speed Internet connection service, the ad featured a guitarist and musician who log onto an Internet server in Toronto and start playing. In quick succession, a series of other musicians join in spontaneously, including a Rasta group in Jamaica and an accordion player in Austria, creating an amazingly eclectic but harmonious world-beat sound. Whether or not such a technological feat was actually possible (some of the ad's critics claimed it wasn't), "Online Jam" offers a nice, if clichéd, image of the cultural benefits to be realized through technological globalization.

The possibility of imagining the world as one interconnected space can certainly be attributed to the global revolution in telecommunications. As with other developments we've traced so far, this "revolution" isn't all that new. The ability to reach virtually any part of the globe with phone calls, television images, and computer-based information can be traced back to the launch of the first communications satellites in the early 1960s. The ability of these satellites to change the way in which we obtain information about the world became clear by the summer of 1964, when parts of the Tokyo Olympics were broadcast live on television.

Development of a global satellite communications network proceeded very rapidly. By the summer of 1969, an estimated 500 million people were able to witness the landing of *Apollo 11* on the moon. The rest, as they say, is history. In North America today, millions of individuals own tiny dishes that provide them with television images beamed from orbiting satellites; the use of cellular phones is ubiquitous, especially among young people; and live, continuous news coverage has become the norm since CNN covered the first cruise missile strikes live from Baghdad during the Gulf War in 1991. The widespread global mourning that accompanied the death of Princess Diana in 1997, the terrorist attacks on the United States in 2001, and the massive tsunami in South East Asia in 2006, all were in some sense the product of contemporary telecommunications technologies: without these technologies, the reaction to these events would likely have been very different in character and scope.

New Communication Technologies The growth and spread of new modes of communication have had an impact on popular culture in a large number of ways. Cell phones have changed the nature of work and family life, and have introduced new cultural practices—such as the use of text messaging by teens to communicate with one another in secret or the writing of the cell phone novels now racing up the sales charts in Japan. In many parts of the world, including parts of Eastern Europe, the advent of cell phones introduced phone communication for the very first time: the high infrastructural cost of traditional phones means that in these places cell phones are the primary means of interpersonal electronic communication. As the case of the Zapatistas shows, new communication technologies have also changed the nature of political struggles in the contemporary world (see Close-Up 10.1).

The Internet has introduced new modes of consumerism and interpersonal interaction, greater flows of official and non-official information, and an astonishing number of new cultural practices, from online interactive gaming to Internet dating to the transnational bride market. The impact of these technologies has been so dramatic that globalization is often associated with these developments alone. Once again, however, current developments are the product of a process dating back at least a century: the invention of the telegraph in the mid–nineteenth century (see Chapter 2) and the laying of an underwater phone cable across the Pacific in 1902 were just two early instances of the long process of what Armand Mattelart has described as "networking the world."

It is certainly the case that contemporary technologies are both more intensive and more extensive in ways that do suggest the world has become networked in a very different way than before. For our purposes, what is perhaps most significant are the possibilities that digitalization has introduced for the dissemination of information and cultural products across the globe. Music, images, and printed text can now all be transmitted, distributed, and consumed electronically. The digitalization of popular culture has also made it increasingly inexpensive for individuals to produce and distribute to a global audience the movies and songs that they make.

The Zapatistas and the Internet

Though new communications technologies have had an impact on the cultural and political sovereignty of nation-states, they have also been used in innovative and unexpected ways in various political struggles over the past decade. The online availability of multiple perspectives on political issues has re-shaped public opinion worldwide, has enabled political groups to keep up-to-date about each others' activities, and has created new forms of political action and expression.

Perhaps the best example of this is the revolutionary struggle of the ELZN in Mexico (the Spanish acronym for the Zapatista Army of National Liberation), more commonly known as the Zapatistas. At its most basic level, the Zapatista movement is a grassroots struggle for greater social, cultural, and political autonomy for the indigenous people of Chiapas, the most resource-rich Mexican state. However, the Zapatista movement has had more far-reaching consequences than other grassroots or local struggles around the world. The subject of songs and videos by the U.S. rock band Rage Against the Machine and an inspiration for the worldwide anti-globalization movement, the Zapatistas were among the very first political movements to effectively use online discussion groups, listservs, mail lists, and websites to report on their efforts and to rally international support for their struggle.

The Zapatista struggle is rooted in local circumstances that are repeated in different ways across the world. With abundant agriculture, ranching, timber, and significant oil reserves, the state of Chiapas should be one of the richest in Mexico. The exact opposite is the case. Due to endemic political corruption and the actions of powerful corporations, the wealth of Chiapas has benefited a few at the expense of the people who live there, especially the large population of indigenous Mayan Indians. The Zapatista movement was formed in order to challenge the disenfranchisement of local peoples under the existing political order in Mexico. From the outset, this "local" movement was engaged with global politics in a way that connected their struggle with other struggles against **neoliberalism** around the world.

The Zapatistas first came to global consciousness on January 1, 1994, when they declared war against the Mexican government on the first day that the North American Free Trade Agreement took effect. For the Zapatistas, NAFTA signalled a continuation of the attack on the autonomy of indigenous peoples that began with the repeal of the article of the Mexican Constitution that protected communal lands from privatization—a precondition of Mexico's entry into NAFTA. This was part of a broader global trend that has seen the transference of public goods into private hands over the past two decades or more. Beginning with their declaration of war, the Zapatistas have challenged stereotypes that have cast Natives and peasants as technologically backward peoples by keeping up a constant stream of communiqués and information explaining their situation to Mexicans and to the rest of the world, and thereby bypassing the indifference or propaganda of state-controlled media (such as the Mexican television network Televisa).

"Zapatistas in Cyberspace" offers a comprehensive guide to the activities of the Zapatistas on the web. It can be found at www.eco.utexas.edu/homepages/faculty/Cleaver/zapsincyber.html.

Connected to this process of digitalization has been a remarkable convergence of cultural forms and products: digital music can be played on cell phones, movie clips can be downloaded to personal digital assistants (PDAs), and so on. Nevertheless, a sense of the longer history of developments in communications technologies is essential in order to temper some of the more exaggerated claims about the communications revolution espoused by magazines such as *Wired* and companies such as Microsoft and Google.

Globalization *is* real. The intent of this section has been to put globalization in a larger context so that we can see past the hype that often surrounds it. In order to understand contemporary popular culture, we will need to keep the influence and importance of all of these levels in mind—a complex but necessary procedure to make sense of the already-complicated set of positions and issues that has surrounded popular culture in the second half of the twentieth century, and the beginning of the twenty-first.

GLOBALIZATION AND POPULAR CULTURE

Given the long history of economic, political, and technological developments that have led up to globalization, it should come as no surprise that there have been all kinds of cultural exchanges between peoples and cultures for thousands of years. When we speak about globalization with respect to culture, what we often imagine is not just an acceleration of these exchanges, but a whole new set of cultural practices produced as a result of them. Inevitably, the conjunction of globalization and culture also evokes the promise and/or threat of a single global culture, a culture that would be shared by everyone on Earth for better and/or worse. Both of these developments continue to garner the attention of scholars, politicians, and members of the public alike.

One of the most important things about all the various processes associated with globalization is that they have forced us to rethink long-held assumptions that continue to inform our understanding of culture. Our changing experience of time and space opens up new ways of looking at the past as much as it offers up rich opportunities to speculate about the future. The impact of globalization on culture is thus both empirical (effecting real changes in the real world) and theoretical (producing a change in our understanding and conceptualization of just what culture is). In this section, we will look at these changes and discuss the various ways in which culture has been perceived with respect to globalization.

Culture and Space

As we have seen throughout this book, there are so many definitions of culture that it is difficult to keep them apart: **folk culture**, mass culture, popular culture—culture as the name for a whole set of practices that people engage in, or as the word that describes particular kinds of artifacts and events that people produce to express themselves. It is hard to imagine that all of these very different ways of thinking about culture might have anything in common. But there is (at least) one thing that all of these senses of culture share: the idea that culture comes from some *place*. We usually think of culture—whether as practices or products—as having a definite and unambiguous point of origin. Today, we usually think of this place as being a nation or region—either a region within a nation, or regions that are collections of nations (e.g., the Middle East, Southeast Asia, Latin America, etc.).

Without thinking about it, and almost without being able to help it, we attribute attitudes and behaviour to people based on their point of origin: Italians are loud and argumentative, Americans are brash, Japanese are idiosyncratic and technologically advanced, and so on (see the discussion of **stereotypes** in Chapter 7). This is done not only with people, but also with the ideas and culture that they produce. While we sometime realize that these attributions are oversimplifications, when they come from experts in the study of these nations or regions we are often ready to believe that the unique characteristics that make one people different from another have in fact been discovered.

There are several problems with this way of locating culture in specific places—in this case, the space of the nation. First, as we discussed above and in Chapter 7, while it continues to produce pride, along with ethnic and racial tensions, the seemingly "natural" space of the nation is a recent political invention. Second, it is very difficult to isolate distinct cultural practices or products in the contemporary world—indeed, not just difficult, but impossible. Every culture has felt the impact and influence of other cultures. In Japan and other parts of the world, rock'n'roll is often taken to be typically American. The origins of rock music are, however, quite complicated—a mix of indigenized African music (as in blues) combined with musical influences from various parts of Europe. Musical forms such as Jamaican dance hall music show even greater degrees of cultural migration: rock'n'roll begets Jamaican reggae, which has an influence on American hip hop, which in turn comes back to Jamaica as dance hall music (see Chapter 7 for a more detailed discussion of the role of **diaspora** in shaping hip hop). As the sociologist Mel van Elteren has put it, "national and other cultural identities are best grasped when seen as being constituted in and through their relation to each other, rather than analyzing cultural (or national) identities one by one and then subsequently thinking about how they are related to one another" (51–52).

Specific cultures are now connected with specific spaces so closely that it is very difficult to speak about cultural migration without using the reductive vocabulary of

Gu Xiong's photographs depict a world in which the comfort of traditional categories is increasingly blurred and placed in doubt.

national cultures. By allowing us to see these migrations and movements much more rapidly—occurring not just slowly over centuries or in the space of one lifetime but within a matter of years or months—globalization has made it possible for us to question these links as never before. This is not to say that there aren't still vast "cultural" differences between, for example, Canada and Hong Kong. At the same time, as peoples and cultural practices move around the globe, we might also want to think about the connections as opposed to the disconnections among these spaces.

For example, with more than three hundred stores, Market Village and Pacific Mall in the affluent suburb of Markham, Ontario, constitutes the largest indoor Chinese mall in North America. Given its location and the patterns of consumption that it structures and produces, it is worth considering the ways in which this mall is as Canadian as it is Chinese—just as many of the new affluent suburban houses being built in China borrow heavily from the new North American housing styles exhibited in Markham.

Global Culture and Cultural Imperialism

These points are well worth keeping in mind as we shift to the other extreme. For many, globalization represents that birth of a truly global culture, a single culture shared to varying (if ever-increasing) degrees by everyone in the world. This global culture may not yet be in existence, but its arrival seems to be only a matter of time.

The effect of globalization's acceleration of time and collapse of space is to eliminate cultural distinctions—already more plural and complex than previously imagined—that might have once existed. Coincident with this process is the simultaneous decline of the world's languages and the establishment of a few major *lingua franca*: English, Mandarin, Spanish, Hindi-Urdu, and so on. Soon we will all be sharing a wide, but common, set of beliefs and practices that are reflected in a variety of international agreements, such as the United Nations' Universal Declaration of Human Rights (available in more than three hundred different languages) or, indeed, the General Agreement on Tariffs and Trade (128 signatory countries as of the 1994 Uruguay Round). We'll also soon all be reading the same comic books, watching the same movies, drinking coffee from the same outlets . . . or so the story goes.

In its most general outlines, this *does* sound like a description of our world today—or, at least, our world as it sometimes looks like from Europe and North America. There are in fact practices that seem already to have made their way to all corners of the world, the most significant being the practice of industrial management famously codified by Frederick Winslow Taylor in 1911. But if the links between space and culture were in the past overly determinate, the belief in the possibility of a global culture overestimates the degree to which culture has or can be severed not just from space, but also from specificities of history, economics, and politics that intersect in unique ways in different parts of the globe.

Class Issues   One of these, for instance, is class. Visions of global culture are more often than not an expression of the viewpoint of a group that the sociologist Zygmunt Bauman has described as "tourists": a relatively wealthy, socially mobile middle class, which exists to varying extents in different parts of the world, that is able to travel to remote locations where they interact with others like themselves in conference hotels or tourist resorts that are more or less indistinguishable from one another. For these people, the degree of global cultural convergence might seem to be startling enough to warrant belief in a truly global culture.

For the vast majority of the people in the world, however, mobility is greatly limited—and, when movement does become a necessity, it is usually due to terrible economic, natural, or political circumstances that have generated refugee crises around the world. The UN has estimated that there are currently more than 30 million "internally displaced people" worldwide.

The *possibility* of a global culture has to be clearly distinguished from questions of its *desirability*. Interestingly, with the exception of a few American commentators who positively equate global culture with the worldwide dominance of U.S. values and beliefs (e.g., *New York Times* columnist Thomas Friedman or political scientist Samuel Huntington), very few critics, scholars, or citizens see global culture as an end worth achieving. Abstractly, the possibility of the universalization of certain "cultural" beliefs—such as human rights, freedom of the press, and democratic elections—seems desirable to most people. At the same time, everyone seems to be aware that a global culture can be achieved only through the globalization of **mass culture**—a form of culture in which the central motive of cultural production is profit and in which culture is produced primarily by "experts" (film directors, professional musicians, etc.).

One of the things that no doubt dismays Bauman's tourists even as it comforts them is the widespread diffusion of North American, European, and Japanese brand-name appliances, food franchises, clothing stores, and automobiles. One of the reasons to travel is, after all, to experience "difference" (in however problematic a form), and if every place looks like "home" (as airports and their duty free shops certainly do) the thrill of encountering "exotic" peoples and places begins to lose its appeal. Westerners have an enormous amount invested in the idea of cultural diversity. The intrinsic desirability of cultural diversity seems to be one of the "facts" of contemporary human life that can't be challenged. Nevertheless, it is something that we should consider before rushing to judgment in open condemnation of the rapid "massification" of culture worldwide.

Suggested Activity 10.2

Globalization names the increased flow of ideas, goods, and cultural products around the world. But while borders may have become more porous to images, ideas, and products, the mobility of people has in many cases become more controlled than ever. Zygmunt Bauman suggests that globalization has divided the world into two new classes of people: "tourists," for whom globalization has meant increased mobility and for whom the world is almost entirely open to exploration; and "vagabonds," those who either can't move outside of fixed boundaries (for a variety of reasons) or who are forced to move by circumstances beyond their control (civil war, famines, etc.). Make a list of groups and individuals that would fit into these two categories and consider the implications of a world divided by degree of mobility. Do tourists exist only in the First World and vagabonds only in the Third World? What roles do **race** and gender play in the politics of mobility? In what way are these categories shifting and changing (if at all)?

Cultural Imperialism   The *undesirability* of global culture (and desirability of cultural diversity) is usually expressed as part of broader worries about **cultural imperialism**. The concept of cultural imperialism has come to mean many things since it was first articulated in the 1960s. However, there are two elements that seem to belong to any usable definition of the concept. First, most generally, cultural imperialism refers to the process by which political and economic power is used by a foreign culture to spread its culture and values to the detriment of cultures that it comes into contact with. Second, cultural imperialism also points to the important role that culture played in the process of **colonialism** and imperialism in the nineteenth and early twentieth centuries.

The second use of culture has been investigated extensively in **postcolonial** criticism and literature. The first definition has been used more frequently to characterize the unequal power relations—economic, political, *and* cultural—that continue to exist between developed and developing countries even after the official end of European colonial rule in most parts of the world. In the absence of direct political control, culture, especially mass culture, is seen as one of the forms through which these unequal power relations are maintained. While the British might once have had to stick troops and administrators in their colonies, the United States has often been seen as exerting their power through the values and life assumptions embedded in their globally popular films, television programs, and even novels.

In what ways can culture be seen to maintain (and indeed, to produce) this situation? John Tomlinson has identified four main ways in which culture has been seen as abetting imperialist relations: (1) through foreign ("American") mass media, whose global diffusion manages to produce the other three conditions; (2) through the imposition of the values and beliefs of one nation on another; (3) through the imposition of consumerism and capitalism as *the* "way of life"; and (4) through the imposition of modernity on parts of the world that might be interested in developing along a very different path than that taken by the West. These four senses are very often confused and folded into one another. (*Cultural Imperialism*)

This has certainly been the case in discussions of the relationship of Canadian culture to the United States. The massive presence of U.S. mass media in Canada has produced continual worries about the possibility that U.S. national values will subsume Canadian ones, which has led to all kinds of government support for the production and distribution of culture. This in turn has led Canadians to overestimate the degree to which they stand outside of capitalism, consumerism, and modernity (even going so far as to imagine it to be socialist!), which has tended to be far too exclusively associated with the United States alone.

From our discussions of the **discourse** of the nation and of the relationship between culture and space, one should be able to see quickly that—despite its intuitive power—the concept of cultural imperialism is problematic. First, as we have emphasized throughout this book, it is difficult to speculate about *any* particular outcome of an audience's encounter with mass media. Foreign audiences make sense of foreign mass media in their own contexts and for their own purposes; foreign audiences are also hardly uniform in their composition, with different segments of the audience reacting in different ways. Tomlinson suggests that "the simple notion of an immediate ideological effect arising from exposure to the imperialist text" is both "naïve and improbable" (*Cultural Imperialism* 47).

Second, the idea that cultures are neatly divided into national units and possess characteristics that can be communicated in any easy way is one that can no longer be sustained, for all of the reasons we outlined earlier in this chapter. The third and fourth claims about cultural imperialism are more interesting to consider, and we take these up in the following sections.

The Noble Savage versus Ronald McDonald

For many, the most alarming aspect of globalization is the potential it represents of imposing the Western values of consumerism, capitalism, and modernity on cultures to whom these values are not only foreign, but also hostile. In one sense, fears of the dilution of cultural diversity are real—borne out, for example, in the accelerated extinction of hundreds of indigenous languages in the face of the dominance of English. But it is also important to note that many of these fears do not actually arise out of the problem of cultural imperialism as it is normally framed: the imposition of one culture's forms and values on another. Rather, what is being expressed here is a more general worry about the value and viability of mass culture, not so much in foreign contexts but in North America itself. Until the past decade or so, such worries didn't seem to have too much applicability to the rest of the world.

In addition to making North American mass culture more globally available, what contemporary communications technologies have done is to allow North Americans to take note of the shape of the rest of the world—a world with skyscrapers, freeways, and shopping malls on every continent (except Antarctica, of course). For a significant part of the group who fit the description of Bauman's "tourists," this vision is both comforting and depressing: comforting in that it attests to the universality of "our" culture, and depressing in that it fails to offer the temporary escape that the tourist craves. However, it is important to remember that what seems like a threat to Westerners may look very different in other parts of the world. As Tomlinson points out, the "the Kazakhstani tribesman who has no knowledge of (and, perhaps, no interest in) America or Europe is unlikely to see his cassette player as emblematic of creeping capitalist domination" (*Cultural Imperialism* 109).

The Western concern with preserving the cultural uniqueness of non-Western cultures has effects on those cultures that are in some cases more damaging than the imagined effects of global mass culture. For example, New Age celebrations of a romanticized Native American tradition have the effect of freezing real, living Native cultures outside of time, thus denying them the **agency** and opportunity to negotiate their way in the global economy. Ironically, the fantasy that there is something outside that economy is a luxury that is really available only to those who are firmly inside it.

But just because there are no insides or outsides to the global economy, just as there are no purely local, **authentic** cultures outside the network of global culture, does not validate the darkest visions of cultural imperialism. That global culture is both more fluid and more uneven in its effects than is represented either by its champions or its critics is clear if we look at an example that is often cited by both: McDonald's. For many people, the fast-food giant McDonald's has become a powerful cultural symbol of globalization. With more than 20,000 restaurants in more than one hundred countries worldwide, McDonald's is a truly global company whose products represent more than quick meals at low prices.

The first appearance of a McDonald's in small towns across North America is seen by some as a sign not only of a community's economic development and growth potential (since McDonald's is careful to build its restaurants only in places where it is certain to make a profit), but also its emergence into the mainstream of contemporary culture. News of openings of new McDonald's restaurants in Moscow and Beijing made headlines in the United States, as it was taken as a sign of the global victory of free-market values. Some commentators have gone even further, to see McDonald's as an ambassador of world peace: as *New York Times* columnist Thomas Friedman notes, no two countries possessing a McDonald's outlet have ever gone to war against each other (qtd. in Burkeman).

McDonald's as a Target   In contrast to these positive views of McDonald's, the ubiquitous golden arches that make up the restaurant's logo have also been seen as a symbol of the dangers of the globalization of culture. The attacks on McDonald's storefronts during anti-globalization protests around the world, the dismantling of a McDonald's in Millau, France, by the Peasant Confederation (headed by activist José Bové) as a protest against genetically modified foods and corporate globalization, and the protests that greeted the announcement of a plan to build a McDonald's in Niagara-on-the-Lake, a small, well-preserved nineteenth-century tourist town in Ontario, all share the same commonly held view of the restaurant as a symbol of a global **monoculture**. The way in which the prefix "Mc" has come to be used suggests the same thing: "McWorld," "McAmerica," "McDonaldization"—these labels have become synonymous with the dark side of globalization that it seems everyone wishes to avoid.

When we speak about globalization as cultural imperialism, McDonald's immediately comes to mind. As anyone who has taken a long-distance trip can attest, the ubiquity with which McDonald's restaurants (and other franchise stores and services) dot the landscape at highway interchanges can seem depressing, especially because travel is often undertaken precisely to discover different places and ways of living. In part because McDonald's spread to other countries so early (to Japan, Germany, and Australia in 1971), it has come to be seen as the leading-edge and primary example of a much larger trend in which U.S. popular culture is exported to other parts of the world to the detriment of local cultures and practices. McDonald's has been followed by Starbucks in the "real" world and by Google, which seems to have extensions in every country (google.ca, google.de, and so on), in the virtual one.

McDonald's is symbolic of the larger worry expressed by the cultural imperialism thesis that it is not just the choice of purchasing hamburgers that is being made available to peoples outside of the United States, but also the export of a whole way of life: American consumer society and the fantasies of the good life that accompanies it. Gaining a McDonald's franchise means losing local dietary habits, patterns of daily behaviour, and even norms of work and **consumption**—in other words, a whole range of the life activities that make cultures distinct from one another.

However, this view of McDonald's as a force that is inevitably corrosive to cultural difference is one that fails to account for the genuine complexities of culture and globalization. There is no country or culture that has not experienced influences from other cultures and nations. Even in the case of contemporary popular or mass culture, McDonald's is hardly the only form to have had an impact worldwide, though it is

McDonald's restaurants are now at "home" around the world, including countries such as Egypt.

perhaps often the most visible symbol of foreignness to many people around the world. Worries about the influence of the kinds of popular cultural practices that are at least symbolically associated with McDonald's—consumerism, the consumption of mass-produced food, **branding**, and so on—also always underestimate or fail to account for the interests of local peoples and cultures, casting them in the role of helpless "victims" who are unable to resist the allure of the golden arches. In fact, there are some suggestions that customers are beginning to do just that: after years of unchecked expansion, the chain closed 175 outlets in 10 countries 2002 and has also had to modify its menu considerably, given the spread of other "cultures" (vegetarianism, healthy eating, organic growing, etc.)

Among the culprits cited for a loss of appetite among Big Mac eaters are the BSE (mad cow disease) scare in the U.K. and Canada, concerns about the effects of a fatty diet, and political resistance to McDonald's as a symbol—like Starbucks—of all the negative effects of globalization, both real and imagined, that we have discussed above. (See Chapter 1 for more on the symbolism of Starbucks.)

The shakiness of McDonald's stockmarket share prices in recent years and its surprising ability to rally in the face of changing fashion and politics suggest that we need to develop a more complex account of the global role of popular culture than that expressed by worries over a coming "McWorld."

The Impact of McDonald's   To answer the question of whether the spread of fast-food chains around the world is helping to create a homogenous, global culture, a group of anthropologists set out to study the impact of McDonald's in five different locales in East Asia: Beijing, Hong Kong, Taipei, Seoul, and Tokyo (Watson). What they discovered was that, while the introduction of McDonald's in these countries *was* having an impact on local customs and practices, the precise nature of this impact was very different in each context. For example, before McDonald's came to their country, Japanese consumers very rarely ate with their hands; in Hong Kong, the restaurant has replaced tea houses as the most popular place to have breakfast.

At the same time, McDonald's has been adapted to local circumstances in ways that differ not only among the different countries examined, but also in relation to the role that McDonald's plays in North America. In North America, McDonald's is generally a site to pass through for a quick meal on the way to doing something else. But it is also used for other purposes: a place for seniors to meet and talk in the mornings (most restaurants offer seniors discounts on coffee); a place for small children to play, especially in winter months; and, in the evenings, a place for teens to hang out. In East Asia, too, McDonald's has been transformed, often more forcefully, into a space serving local purposes. In Beijing, Seoul, and Taipei, McDonald's functions as a retreat from urban stresses; in Hong Kong, it is a place where middle-school students spend large amounts of time studying and gossiping—the function that coffeehouses sometimes assume in North America. Throughout the region, it is a place where women go to avoid other social spaces (such as bars) that are havens for men.

What even these few examples should suggest is that it is through the constant interaction of the global and the local that contemporary culture is produced. Even this distinction is misleading, however, since both of these terms suggest that there is something identifiably "global" (usually imagined as transnational corporations) and "local" (small communities across the globe).

Corporations such as McDonald's have global reach, but at the same time the company has shareholders from many localities and, like other corporations working on a global scale, its managers and investors tend to come from the localities in which McDonald's has a presence. The anthropologists examining McDonald's in East Asia discovered that virtually all of the managers came from Korea, Japan, China, and so on. The raw materials used to produce fast food tend to originate within geographic proximity of the restaurants, and McDonald's has generally adapted its menus to suit customers and cultures across the globe (though recently it has faced enormous problems as a result of concealing the use of beef fat in products created for the global Hindu community). Though it has been often (and deservedly) criticized, in many respects McDonald's has been a far more responsible and responsive transnational corporation than many others.

The point here is not to absolve McDonald's or other transnational corporations from criticism, or to suggest that their power and cultural influence is benign. As much as it sells a set of products, like so much else in contemporary popular culture McDonald's also sells an *experience* that has had noticeable effects around the world. With its hamburgers and fries, McDonald's sells friendly service, predictability, speed, cleanliness and hygiene, and toys and cultural symbols (e.g., Ronald McDonald) to its young customers. The experience of eating at McDonald's has had an impact on the experience of eating out almost everywhere the restaurant has been introduced. These are often subtle changes, but because dietary patterns and attitudes toward food are so important to everyday life, their impact is widely felt. Almost without exception, fast food is extremely unhealthy. There is no reason to celebrate the increase in consumption of mass-produced fast food around the world.

At the same time, the typical narratives that we use to imagine the impact of companies such as McDonald's on the shape of global popular culture have to be seen as far too simplistic. The idea that globalization leads to the production of a single "bad" global culture is not supported by more careful attention to the networks and processes through which cultural products and cultural experiences are produced in the world. Large, global corporations play an important role in this, but to see them as having almost omnipotent powers over the shape of contemporary culture tends to negate the need to produce more complex accounts of culture in globalization that might in fact yield a better understanding of where we all stand today.

Defending Cultural Sovereignty: The Case of Canada

As we have suggested above, many of the fears surrounding globalization arise more from a **mythologized** image of cultural imperialism than from cultural or economic realities. However, one undeniable consequence of the expansion of the powers of global financial bodies such as the IMF has been a decrease in the power of nations and local regions to determine the direction of their own economic development. For poor nations these concerns are often directed at the policies of powerful nations such as the U.S., whose trade policies are, ironically, still not global enough in their maintenance of powerful tariffs protecting American agriculture and industry. For those countries just slightly off the crest of the wave of globalization—countries such as Canada and France—concern is more likely to take the form of vigorous assertions of cultural **sovereignty.** (This is not to say that culture is not a concern for poorer countries; only that rapidly growing material inequities have placed cultural worries lower on the agenda than they once were.)

By way of concluding this chapter, we look at a particular example of Canadian cultural policy as a way of illustrating some of the complex, and perhaps unexpected, ways that globalization shapes not just specific cultures, but also the notion of culture as a whole.

For almost its entire history, Canada's citizens and the Canadian government have worried about the cultural, political, and economic implications that flow out of the particularities of Canada's geographic place in the world. Proximity to the United States, a country with which Canada shares a great deal of history and culture, but that possesses a much larger population and economy, has been both a blessing and a curse. The late Pierre Elliott Trudeau described Canada's relationship with the United States as like being a mouse in bed with an elephant: while the elephant barely notices the mouse, the mouse has to be aware of the elephant's every shift and move lest it be crushed to death.

Smaller countries around the world have been able to maintain their sovereignty in the shadow of larger, more powerful ones. What makes Canada's relationship to the United States different than, for example, the relationship of Hungary to the Soviet Union or to Russia is that Canada and the U.S. share common origins and even (with the notable exception of Quebec) a common language. The Canadian economy is also dependent on exports to the United States, so much so that its performance mirrors the ebb and swell of the U.S. economy almost perfectly, though this seems to be changing slightly as a result of the global demand for the natural resources that Canada produces in abundance.

The constant threat (real and imagined) that the United States poses to Canadian sovereignty has resulted in an almost obsessive worry about the distinctiveness of Canadian culture and Canadian identity. One of the most important places in which this worry has been played out has been in the field of popular culture. The size of the United States has made it able to produce popular culture in large quantities, and to commit major economic resources to its production. For example, while the average budget of a U.S. feature film today (including marketing) is $76 million, Canadian films are generally produced for 2 percent of this amount—about $1.5 million.

Canada is not the only country to feel the impact of the power of the U.S. cultural industries. In other countries too U.S. films dominate at the box office, and have done so since the First World War, when production by European studios fell to a trickle. However, Canada is in a unique situation. Radio and television transmissions can easily make their way across the border, and the availability of an enormous amount of easily accessible English-language programming, music, and films has meant that even Canadian broadcast networks rely heavily on programs imported from the United States. This dominance has been mirrored in the world of the Internet, since the enormous number of sites originating from the U.S. are easily accessible by English speakers in Canada.

Government Regulation As we saw in our discussion of cultural imperialism, this reliance on foreign or imported culture is almost always perceived as a threat to national sovereignty and to the very existence of a nation-state. Just as in other countries (and internationally through agencies such as UNESCO), the Government of Canada has intervened in a variety of ways to lend support to Canadian cultural producers and to limit the amount of foreign cultural imports. Over the course of the twentieth century, the Canadian government has established agencies such as the Canada Council (1957), which allocates financial resources to cultural groups and individual cultural producers and which also provides insight into the state of Canadian culture through reports and commission findings; the Canadian Radio-television and Telecommunications Commission (CRTC; 1968, though existing in earlier forms since the 1930s), which regulates all forms of telecommunications and broadcasting in Canada; and the Canadian Broadcasting Corporation (CBC; 1936), which supports the production and dissemination of Canadian culture through its radio and television networks. Though there is substantial debate over the function of these agencies and the overall effects of their policies, they have had a role in creating and supporting Canadian popular culture. The relative vibrancy of Canadian popular music (from The Guess Who to The Tragically Hip to newer artists like Feist and Nelly Furtado) has been aided by policies that require radio stations and music television stations (such as MuchMusic) to include specified amounts of Canadian content; without the CBC, there would likely be very little television production in Canada—even less than currently exists!—other than programs produced in Canada for broadcast on U.S. networks.

Globalization has produced new challenges for attempts to regulate Canadian culture, and has also exposed some problematic assumptions that have formed the basis of Canadian cultural policy to date. For example, while the CRTC has made modest attempts to consider the possibility of regulating Canadian content on the Internet, the very nature of this new medium would seem to make it almost impossible to regulate what Canadian companies can display on their websites, much less where Canadians choose to go as they surf the web. The **deterritorialized** nature of contemporary culture might be nowhere so evident as on the Internet. But the current problem of regulating the "Canadianness" of the Internet should also draw our attention to the fact that, as we discussed above, cultural forms have *always* crossed borders from one country to another, mixing with indigenous forms in order to produce new ones, which themselves travel to other places on the globe, and so on.

Canadian Culture Goes International Canadian literature is enjoying a period of remarkable worldwide success, with authors including Michael Ondaatje, Margaret Atwood, and Carol Shields winning major literary prizes over the last 10 years. Canadian pop music has been similarly successful: from Shania Twain to Arcade Fire to Billy Talent to Buck 65, Canadian artists have staked a claim on virtually every genre of contemporary music. However, if we consider the form of Canadian literature or music, we notice two things immediately: first, while there might be some distinctly Canadian styles, the overall form of popular culture in Canada shares broad characteristics with that of other countries and traditions: pop songs are generally four to five minutes long and use predictable instrumentation. Similarly, novels are written in well-known genres, such as literary fiction, mystery, and science fiction.

The fact that Canadian popular culture belongs to a broader Western cultural tradition doesn't mean that it isn't valuable or significant to Canadians in particular ways. Our intention here is simply to point out that what the Canadian government has tried to defend as *Canadian* culture is already the product of many different cultural influences and traditions—as every culture is, for that matter. Policies to defend Canadian culture are about the need for the nation-state to legitimize its political role as much as a question of economic policy—of producing the conditions for Canadians to be able to participate in the global cultural industries, an increasingly important and highly competitive industry worldwide. This belief in the significance of the cultural or creative industries to Canada's economic future has been given a boost by the popularity of Richard Florida's ideas about the need to support the activities of the country's "creative class."

Split-Run Magazines   In Canada, the new conditions for the production and regulation of popular culture in the era of globalization can be seen in the recent controversy over the government's support of magazine publishing. In an effort to support the development of the Canadian magazine industry, in the 1960s the government introduced measures designed to limit the distribution of "split runs" of American magazines in Canada. This was done on both financial and cultural grounds. Split runs are magazines that combine the editorial content of a "parent" issue of a magazine—for instance, the version of *Time* produced in the U.S.—with advertising solicited from Canadian companies.

For the publisher, split runs are a way of generating new advertising revenues while acquiring few or no additional editorial costs. The articles have already been written anyway, so they might as well try to sell the magazine in as many national markets as possible. Since the ad revenue of a split-run magazine constitutes a source of "extra" (or unanticipated) profit, U.S. publishers are able to compete for Canadian advertising dollars by offering ad space at a lower cost than comparable Canadian magazines (in the case of *Time*, a news magazine like *Maclean's*). Without sufficient ad revenue, Canadian magazines would be unable to generate enough money to publish, which is an economic and cultural loss, since the publishers of split runs are under no pressure to deal with issues of particular interest or relevance to Canadians.

In 1965, the federal government passed legislation that (among other things) introduced tax penalties intended to dissuade Canadian companies from advertising in split-run magazines (*Time* and *Reader's Digest* were granted an exemption from these rules because they were already distributed in Canada). These policies made it possible for a Canadian magazine industry to develop. Over the past 10 years or so, the legitimacy of these policies has been challenged by the United States. There is a long and complicated history of Canada–U.S. disputes over Canadian cultural policy, and over magazine policy in particular. The most recent of these offers us perhaps the best insight into the challenges that globalization has introduced into attempts to regulate cultural policy.

Trade Agreements   Over the past decade or so, a wide range of Canadian government policies have been reassessed as a result of Canada's involvement in a number of new international agreements. The most important of these are the North American Free Trade Agreement (NAFTA) and the General Agreement on Tariffs and Trades (GATT). Globalization is often identified with the concerted global push to establish rules governing trade that will result in the elimination of tariffs and other trade barriers and lead eventually to the establishment of global free trade.

What this has meant is that all policies that provide protection or support to local industries against foreign competition have come under increasing scrutiny. Though both the original Free Trade Agreement between Canada and the U.S. and NAFTA have clauses that are intended to exempt culture from this scrutiny, in practice cultural policies, too, have been subjected to pressure.

In the case of Canadian magazine policy, the U.S. government challenged Canadian legislation on two different occasions in front of a World Trade Organization dispute panel. The WTO agreed with the U.S. argument that Canadian policies unfairly affected the ability of U.S. publishers to compete in Canada. The final outcome was new Canadian magazine legislation that permitted increasing levels (up to 18 percent) of Canadian ad content in U.S. magazines to be phased in over several years. The impact of this decision on the Canadian magazine industry is expected to be disastrous enough that, in 2001, the Canadian Heritage Ministry announced plans for $150 million in aid to Canadian publishers.

In one respect, this is the latest in a long story of the challenges faced by Canadian culture. However, the details of the WTO case offer insights into some of the significant changes that popular culture has undergone as a result of globalization. As much as the U.S. case was about unfair trade practices, it was also about what constitutes culture today. The Canadian government argued that Canadian magazines and U.S. split runs were not "like products," and so should not be governed by the same laws:

> Magazines are distinct from ordinary articles of trade. Magazines are intended, by their very nature, for intellectual consumption as opposed to physical use (like a bicycle) or physical consumption (like food). It follows that the intellectual content of a cultural good such as a magazine must be considered its prime characteristic. . . . Editorial material developed for the Canadian market reflects a Canadian perspective and contains specific information of interest to Canadians. The content is qualitatively different from editorial material copied from foreign publications. What has been said of the essential properties of magazines is equally applicable to their end-use. The end-use of a magazine is not simply reading: it is transmission and acquisition of specific information. (World Trade para. 3.6.1, 3.6.3)

For most of us, this sense of what constitutes a "cultural good" sounds right: the most important thing about a Canadian magazine lies in what it communicates to Canadians about the Canadian experience. The United States presented a very different argument about what a magazine "is":

> The type, texture, color, thickness, and even the perfume of the paper can be important factors to market appeal. The dimensions of a magazine, the manner in which its pages are bound, the typesetting, and the appearance of the ink, can also be significant. The type, appearance, and frequency of advertisements may be a factor in a consumer's purchasing decisions as well. All of these attributes— including editorial content—combine to form an *overall package*. . . . For the Canadian and U.S. magazine industries, editorial content generally represents substantially less than 20 percent of the cost of producing a consumer magazine. (World Trade para. 3.7.8)

The WTO's ruling in favour of the U.S. position does not mean that we should now see culture as being just like every other **commodity**. It does, however, point to larger structural and institutional forces that are reshaping our sense of what culture is and what we expect it to do. This offers us perhaps the clearest way of understanding what globalization has meant for popular culture.

Globalization is the moment that mass culture becomes globalized. The cultural theorist Richard Ohmann has defined mass culture as "voluntary experiences, produced by a relatively small number of specialists, for millions across the nation to share, in similar or identical form, either simultaneously or nearly so; with dependable frequency; mass culture shapes habitual audiences, around common needs or interests, and it is made for profit" (14). The collapse of time and space has resulted in new forms of culture and new **countercultures**—and, in the midst of the new, residual forms of culture (for example, cultural practices related to religious practices) continue to exert an important influence.

Even so, and even though the effects of globalization have been unevenly distributed, it is increasingly difficult to understand contemporary popular culture except as a mass culture that has been distributed across the face of the globe in increasingly intensive and extensive ways.

OTHER ISSUES IN GLOBALIZATION AND POPULAR CULTURE

Globalization has produced many new forms of culture and has changed older forms in significant ways as well. The fact of globalization has also changed *how* we talk about culture. The recent collapse of time and space that we associate with globalization has led to a reconsideration of the ways in which we once imagined that time and space kept cultures and people apart; while the discourses of nationalism may have in fact done so, there has been considerable cultural interchange for a very long time. Globalization has also led to a reexamination of the divisions that we have used to study contemporary societies—divisions established initially for heuristic purposes, but which have since come to seem as if they were formed in response to actually existing divisions in the real world. The discussion in this chapter is an example of how globalization has made it impossible to discuss economics without politics, politics without culture, culture without economics, and so on.

What globalization hasn't produced (at least not thus far) is a comparably new way to think about both the mass culture that we now experience (unevenly) at a global scale *and* the new cultural forms, events, and movements that have appeared in the last decade of the twentieth century and the beginning of the twenty-first. Our attempt to make sense of the complexities of a mass culture that has become globalized seems to be arrested in the discourse of cultural imperialism. Attempts to understand the political and cultural significance of the coalitions of groups that make up the anti-globalization movement also seem to be confined by the terms of older discourses that don't properly describe them. Policymakers appear particularly out of step with historical developments. Through its involvement in the International Network on Cultural Policy (whose aim is "to facilitate dialogue on issues related to cultural diversity in the context of globalization, and suggest leads for solutions" [www.incp-ripc.org/about/index_e.shtml]) and other similar organizations, the Canadian government has been leading the attempt to re-establish strong national cultures in the context of globalization. That national culture is by its nature an exclusionary idea seems to have escaped the 45 governments involved in this quixotic task, as has the real source of their discontent: a mass culture that is identified confusingly with American national culture alone.

In all of the discussions surrounding globalization and culture—which now includes such diverse issues as the devastating impact of the culture of consumption has on the natural environment and the future of the planet, and the economic importance of creating urban spaces attractive to the members of the "**creative class**" who (according to Richard Florida) generate new wealth—the one thing that we seem to be no longer asking is: what hopes and dreams do we have for culture today? What do we see as the future of culture— and, indeed, if the connections and interconnections that we have described here are correct, the future of the social world itself? These are important questions to pose as the world becomes both a smaller and a more uncertain place in which to live for all of us.

SUGGESTIONS FOR FURTHER READING

Appadurai, Arjun, ed. *Modernity at Large: Cultural Dimensions of Globalization.* Minneapolis: University of Minnesota Press, 1996.

Barlow, Maude, and Tony Clarke. *Global Showdown.* Toronto: Stoddart, 2001.

Bauman, Zygmunt. *Globalization: The Human Consequences.* New York: Columbia University Press, 1998.

Giddens, Anthony. *Runaway World: How Globalization Is Reshaping Our Lives.* New York: Routledge, 2000.

Gray, John. *False Dawn: The Delusions of Global Capitalism.* New York: New Press, 1999.

Hardt, Michael, and Antonio Negri. *Empire.* Cambridge, MA: Harvard University Press, 2000.

Harvey, David. *A Brief History of Neoliberalism.* New York: Oxford University Press, 2005.

Held, David, Anthony McGrew, David Goldblatt, and Jonathan Perraton. *Global Transformations: Politics, Economics and Culture.* Stanford: Stanford University Press, 1999.

Jameson, Fredric, and Masao Miyoshi, eds. *The Cultures of Globalization.* Durham, NC: Duke University Press, 1998.

Klein, Naomi. *The Shock Doctrine: The Rise of Disaster Capitalism.* Toronto: Knopf, 2007.

Scholte, Jan Aart. *Globalization: A Critical Introduction.* Basingstoke, UK: Macmillan, 2000.

Zemans, Joyce. "Canadian Cultural Policy in a Globalized World." *Canadian Review of American Studies* 27.3 (1997): 111–125.

Glossary

Compiled by Nicholas Holm, Carolyn Veldstra, and Tim Walters

Aesthetics: The branch of philosophy concerned with sensory perception and appearances, especially as pertains to art, beauty and notions of taste or judgment. Classically, aesthetics was thought to refer to an idea of universal beauty that exceeds personal tastes, but modern conceptions of aesthetics connect our tastes in art and culture to our class, gender, and racial backgrounds. To engage with an object or text in terms of aesthetics can also mean to consider how it appeals to your senses—how food tastes, music sounds, or a painting "looks."

Agency: The ability of individuals to act as self-conscious, willful social actors, and to exert their will through involvement in social practices, relationships, and decision making.

Appropriation: The process by which often innovative or resistant cultural forms are taken up, incorporated, and commodified by the culture industry. One of the most frequently cited examples is that of punk, which, though it developed as a dissident movement in working-class England, was quickly marketed by major fashion designers, music labels, and other producers of mass youth culture. In analysis of popular cultural forms, appropriation is often viewed pessimistically as evidence of the power of late capitalism to absorb dissent into itself and turn it around for a profit; however, it is important to remember that resistance continues to circulate and change in form, even as its products are co-opted by a dominant culture.

Assimilation: Also known as *acculturation*, this term refers to the sometimes forced integration of an immigrant or subordinate group into the dominant culture of the host community through the absorption of the host's cultural practices and history. This stands in opposition to the idea of **multiculturalism**, which suggests that different groups can coexist on an equal basis.

Authenticity: A positive quality of genuineness and originality attributed to objects, practices, or ideas, often in order to demonstrate the extent to which an initially authentic phenomenon has been compromised or drained of its value. The notion of authenticity has been critiqued for its **ideological** grounding in a nostalgic vision of a more "real" cultural past now sullied by rank commercialism.

Binary Opposition: An analytical system that uses specific examples of symmetrically opposed pairs, or mirror opposites, which, although mutually exclusive, generate meaning through their difference and describe a complete, if extreme, system of understanding. For example: "us–them"—in forming group identities, people are categorized either as part of the group ("us"), or outside of it ("them"). Binary oppositions can be dangerous in that they work to repress the ambiguities that exist between the two terms by positioning the binary as natural and any other forms of identification as deviant. In addition, binary terms often carry a positive–negative value assumption; for example, "we" are "safe, good, blameless," while "they" are "dangerous, bad, evil."

Branding: An economic trend that developed in the late 1980s and early 1990s wherein companies shifted their resources from producing goods or services to producing a corporate image defined by abstract emotional or spiritual qualities. Critics of this process have suggested that the reallocation of resources and the marketing strategies it entails contributes to trends such as the rise of child and sweatshop labour in developing nations, a decline in the number and quality of available jobs in North America, and a disturbing new invasiveness on the part of corporations into our lives and minds.

Capitalism: See Close-Up 1.1 on page 11.

Class Mobility: A characteristic of societies in which it is possible for an individual or a family to move from one social class to another, and thus alter their social status and economic standing. For example, modern Western societies have greater class mobility than the rigid aristocratic societies that preceded them, which had firmly defined and immobile class boundaries. The idea of class mobility can also act as an ideology that paradoxically maintains the status quo. Even in Western societies, it remains difficult for the majority of people to change their class standing.

Cold War: A phrase that popularly refers to the tense, hostile relationship between the communist (U.S.S.R.) and capitalist (U.S.) superpowers and their respective allies from the end of the Second World War until the collapse of the Berlin Wall in 1989. Although marked by bitter animosities fuelled by ideological differences, a similarly voracious desire for world domination, and numerous moments of near-disastrous military escalation (for instance, the Cuban Missile Crisis), the cold war was known as such because it was fought largely by diplomatic and economic means rather than by sustained and overt acts of aggression. Though the cold war spawned numerous proxy wars in Third World countries, the U.S.S.R. and the United States never came to blows directly.

Colonialism: The historical process through which dominant groups have assimilated, dominated, and subjugated less powerful ones. Distinct from **imperialism**, which can also be used to describe non-territorial kinds of control, colonialism involves physical settlement along with the military, political, and economic conquest of a people.

Commodification: Rendering any artifact, action, object, or idea into something that can be bought or sold. Popular culture is often maligned for its commodification of formerly more **authentic** cultural forms, with the assumption that through commodification things lose their implicit value.

Commodities: Objects and services produced for consumption or exchange by someone other than their producers. Although humans have always exchanged the goods that they produced for other goods, in the nineteenth century a new focus on the consumption of an increasingly diverse array of commodities by greater numbers of consumers was partly responsible for the gradual shift to a consumer culture. Marx employed the term **commodity fetishism** to describe the almost magical value attributed to objects in a capitalist economy—value derived not from how they are used or the labour that produced them, but from the price they command on the market. The most significant, and most damaging, aspect of commodity culture from a Marxist perspective is its tendency to attribute value to things and the relations between them rather than to people and human relationships.

Commodity Fetishism: See Commodities.

Conspicuous Consumption: A pattern of behaviour, initially observed by Thorstein Veblen, that began in the nineteenth century as a result of increased incomes and leisure time along with the growth of marketing. "Wasted" consumption (that which exceeds what is strictly necessary for life) began to be *used* by members of different classes in a way that was "conspicuous"—obvious, noticeable, visible—in order to signal or symbolize social distinction.

Consumerism: The name for the complex set of dominant values and practices produced by and arising from life in a consumer society: a historically unique form of society in which consumption plays an important, if not central role. Central to consumerism is the (generally implicit) belief that the organization of life around the purchase of commodities is the optimal way to address the needs and wants of individuals, and even to allocate social goods.

Consumption: See **Conspicuous Consumption**.

Copyright: See **Intellectual Property**.

Counterculture: Groups that express antagonism toward the existing social and political order, and propose alternative ways of organizing society. The term counterculture is most commonly used to refer collectively to the alternative politics expressed by a variety of groups in the 1960s (feminist, civil rights, and anti-war activists, etc.). More generally, "the" counterculture describes all those groups that challenge and contradict the "common sense" of everyday life with the aim of creating a better society.

Creative Class: A controversial term coined by urban studies theorist Richard Florida to describe a new social and economic class of artists, intellectuals and "knowledge workers," a group that encompasses engineers, scientists, architects, and lawyers. In Florida's conception, members of the creative class are liberal, artistic types who act as the major force of economic growth in postindustrial cities through their production of new ideas, technology, and **intellectual property**.

Cultural Imperialism: A term describing the ideological infiltration of the cultural products of dominant nations (typically, the United States) into less globally powerful ones at the expense of some aspects of indigenous culture. Globalization theorists have cast some doubt on the concept of cultural imperialism, pointing to its problematic assumption of a passive, colonized global audience, as well as its simplistic reading of actual processes of global production and consumption.

Cultural Relativism: The acceptance of difference across a range of cultural activities, with the understanding that different cultures, individuals, and groups hold different values, all of which are of equal merit. This idea often works together with a postmodern refusal to accept fixed meanings or explanations and opposes **essentialist** assumptions about culture, race, gender, and so on.

Cultural Studies: See Close-Up 1.2 on page 14.

Culture: Culture has been described by critic Raymond Williams as "one of the two or three most complicated words in the English language." The term has a wide and diverse range of meanings and associations that cannot easily be reduced to a single definition. In contemporary usage, the term carries three main significations: (1) a description of a whole way of social life (as in the idea that humanity is comprised of numerous, distinct cultures); (2) the name for "serious" works of literature, music, fine arts, film, and so on, and the activities involved in producing these kinds of works; and, finally, (3) as an extension of the latter definition, culture can be used to refer to a wide range of signifying and symbolic works and activities, whether these involve everyday social practices (e.g., **folk culture**) or the objects and practices of popular culture (e.g., detective novels as well as serious literature, television as well as film, etc.).

Culture Industry: A term first introduced by Max Horkheimer and Theodor Adorno in *Dialectic of Enlightenment* (1947) to describe the new conditions of cultural production in the twentieth and twenty-first centuries. In contrast to earlier periods, culture is now mostly produced and distributed in an industrial fashion and on a mass scale like any other **commodity**. Cultural industries (in the plural) include the music and film industry, advertising, television, and professional sports, among others. The concept of cultural industry (in the singular) draws attention to the overall social consequences of such a cultural-commodity system, including the dominance of **instrumental rationality**.

Culture Wars: A series of disputes, primarily taking place in the U.S.A., that attempt to reframe politics in terms of "values," especially as it pertains to contentious issues such as abortion, homosexuality, and public morality. Closely allied to the legacy of the 1960s **counterculture**, in universities the culture wars showed up in part as a conflict between traditional notions of literary value, often pejoratively linked to the writing of "Dead White Males," and a growing recognition of the overlooked contributions of **minority** and women writers and popular texts to the development of contemporary culture.

Deconstruction: A method of analysis initially articulated in the work of Jacques Derrida that involves exposing the submerged philosophical assumptions that underpin texts and concepts. Derrida asserted that all Western thought is founded upon countless sets of **binary oppositions** (black and white, speech and writing, man and woman, etc.) wherein one term is invariably considered to be superior to its "opposite," a valuation with vast cultural consequences. Deconstructionist readings attempt to discover how such unarticulated ideologies underpin seemingly straightforward surface meanings.

Deterritorialization: The weakening of ties between a culture and a place so that a location becomes detached from the historical and social circumstances that produce it as a unique site. Deterritorialization leads to an emphasis upon the generic rather than specifically local qualities of place, with the result that deterritorialized spaces, such as hotels and shopping malls, are often perceived to be interchangeable.

Diaspora: From the Greek word for "to disperse," diaspora refers to the voluntary or forced migration of peoples from their homelands to new regions. In areas that are greatly affected by large diasporic movements (i.e., in the West Indies via colonization and the slave trade), distinct, or creolized, cultures have developed, which blend indigenous with homeland cultures. These unique diasporic cultures challenge **essentialist** models of culture or the **nation**.

Digitalization: The translation of any kind of data (text, images, sounds, etc.) into an electronic language that can be used by a computer or other digital system for purposes of storage, distribution, or manipulation. Depending on one's perspective, digitalization is either an empowering tool with which to create and share diverse forms of information more democratically, or a practice that threatens more authentic (or "real") forms of cultural production and challenges **copyright** protection laws. Because it offers unprecedented possibilities for the manipulation of sounds and images, digitalization also raises important issues for practices of **representation**.

Discourse: A concept articulated by Michel Foucault to describe the way speech and writing work in conjunction with specific structures and institutions to shape social reality. Discourse refers to distinct areas of social knowledge (typically, broad subjects such as law, science, or medicine) and the linguistic practices that are associated with them, but also establishes rules about the context of this speech or writing, such as who is permitted and authorized to address these subjects. Knowledge, according to the concept of discourse, *is* power, since it comes into being through the operations of power and also exercises power by determining what truths will be endorsed. Discourses thus have immediate, material effects on the way a culture operates.

Distinction: The condition of being set apart and considered different or special, usually through the achievement of a specific honour, and connected to value. In the study of popular culture, distinction is often linked to consumption, with the implicit idea of a capitalist system being that one can achieve distinction through one's purchases.

Essentialism(ist): The belief that categories, or individuals and groups of human beings have innate, defining features exclusive to their category (e.g., the belief that different races have inherent characteristics that differentiate them from other races). Essentialism has been challenged by **social constructivist** theories that point to the ways in which identity and meaning are culturally produced.

Ethnicity: Ethnicity is a broad social category that addresses one's perceived membership in a larger group based on characteristics such as religious, cultural, or national background. Whereas one's **race** is generally "determined" by specific physical traits, ethnicity typically implies a somewhat more conscious and flexible affiliation with a particular group. Like race, however, the concept of ethnicity has often been used to discriminate against groups based on **stereotypical** perceptions of their common attitudes or attributes.

Eurocentrism: A critical term for any world-view that focuses upon European philosophies and practices to the detriment of non-European perspectives. Eurocentrism is often thought to imply a tacit assumption that European ways of understanding the world are either superior to other beliefs, or the norm from which other non-European cultures can be considered divergent. Eurocentrism is deeply implicated in the processes of **colonialism** and **racism**.

Ex-nomination: A term used by Roland Barthes to identify one of the ways in which the dominance of the ruling class goes unexamined precisely because *it is not named as such*: the process of ex-nomination ensures that we see the values or attributes of dominant groups not as the product of particular class interests, but simply as apolitical, intrinsic *human* values that are, therefore, as unsuitable for critique as a grapefruit or any other "real thing." Ex-nomination also works to legitimate the dominance of specific racial and cultural groups by failing to acknowledge or "mark" their distinctive qualities (e.g., white, heterosexual), thereby assuming their universality.

Feminism: The name for a diverse range of political movements and approaches to the study of culture and society that concern themselves with the role played by sex and gender in the unequal distribution of power, particularly as concerns women. There are multiple feminisms: some promote gender equality, others seek to dispense with the concept of gender entirely, while still others seek to emphasize and value gender and sexual difference.

Folk Culture: Those cultural products and practices that have developed over time within a particular community or socially identifiable group, and that are communicated from generation to generation and among people who tend to be known to one another.

Fordism: A highly mechanized and standardized manner of production, pioneered on the assembly lines of auto-maker Henry Ford in order to improve worker efficiency by duplicating the specialized precision of a machine. Fordism now refers not only to a seminal development in the history of industrialization that enabled hitherto unimaginable levels of mass production/consumption, but also to a type of culture (or a particular aspect of a culture) that displays similar—generally negative—qualities of uniformity and conformity. Fordism has been supplanted in much of the North American economy by **post-Fordism**.

Frankfurt School: See Close-Up 4.1 on page 116.

Gentrification: The movement of relatively affluent middle-income individuals and families into poor, urban neighbourhoods. Though often considered, especially in official civic discourse, as an improvement of underused or "run-down" space, the process almost inevitably displaces previous lower income residents and is often thought to disrupt or destroy the character of local communities.

Globalization: An (arguably) recent, complex shift in the relationship between the world's many cultures fuelled by complex economic, political, and technological factors. Its central effect is that temporal and geographic distances are no longer as divisive as they once were. Although seeming to possess enormous potential for improving the conditions of some of the world's poorest regions, globalization is increasingly seen as being primarily profit-driven, and is closely allied with the remarkable ascension to power of massive transnational corporations and with the connected phenomenon of cultural imperialism. Some critics of globalization argue that it is little more than a process of further concentrating wealth and power in the hands of those who already have it, and that its effect on the indigenous cultures of developing nations is devastatingly corrosive. Others distinguish between different aspects of globalization (economic, political, technological, cultural, etc.) and point to the potential for new forms of cultural expression and new democratic alliances that are facilitated by a more globally connected world.

Gross Domestic Product (GDP): The total monetary value of all the goods and services produced within a nation's economy during a one-year period, a figure often used as an indicator of a nation's financial well-being. The GDP's value as a diagnostic tool to measure the health of a country is often critiqued because it fails to account for the value of such activities as domestic work and volunteering, and attributes positive value to those transactions that produce profits but reflect a decline in social well-being (e.g. a boom in the divorce industry, the growth of prisons). Increasing concern about the inadequacy of the GDP has led many economists and some countries to supplement or replace it with an alternative measure of national value, the GPI (Genuine Progress Indicator). The GPI can be said to present a more accurate picture of national welfare by measuring previously unaccounted costs and benefits (e.g. to human health or the environment).

Habitus: Concept outlined by Marcel Mauss connoting both living space and habitat that describes the way in which particular social environments are internalized by individuals in the form of dispositions toward particular bodily orientations and behaviours. The habitus we occupy radically affects such basic activities as sleeping, eating, sitting, walking, having sex, and giving birth, all of which should be understood not as natural, but as a series of "body techniques" that are *learned* in particular social contexts, and are therefore culturally and historically specific. Pierre Bourdieu extended this concept to talk about the relationship between habitus and social class.

Hegemony: See Close-Up 2.2 on page 53.

"Highbrow"/"Lowbrow": A colloquial reference to "high" and "low" culture—a distinction that is made on the assumption that high culture holds some sort of greater innate intellectual or moral worth, while low culture is base and degrading to those who partake in it. The distinctions between these two groups become unclear with, for example, pop art, which borrows images from "low culture" (i.e., Campbell's soup cans) and displays them in a venue for "high culture"—the museum. The term "nobrow" has been used recently to describe images, objects, or experiences that can't easily be classified into high or low. In fact, the quotation marks that often surround mentions of "high" or "low" culture suggest that these categories are not only constantly shifting, but also arbitrary, often deployed as a means of legitimating class hierarchy.

Horizontal Integration: A **synergistic** venture wherein one company acquires (and integrates with) another company that is making the same kind of product or providing the same kind of service in order to increase the purchasing company's presence in (and power over) a given market.

Humanism: A collection of philosophies that espouse that human life has an inherent worth and dignity that must be valued above all else. Humanism teaches that there exists a universal human condition that binds all of humanity together and that all people experience regardless of their **ethnicity** or culture. Consequently, humanists advocate that a concern for humanity needs to be the foremost concern of all culture, and political and philosophical projects. Some critics have attacked humanism as a "speciesist" **ideology** that encourages the exploitation of non-human life.

Hybridity: In horticulture a term that means to graft two different plant types together in order to create a third, unique plant; in cultural studies a term, generally associated with **diaspora** and **postcolonialism**, that refers to the blending of two or more cultures. The "third culture" that results from this interaction is not simply a combination of the two, but a space of possibility in which differences both between and within individual cultures express themselves.

Idealization: To idealize an object, person, or social movement is to fail to critically account for its actual existence, holding it instead to impossibly high standards while ignoring the possible or potential flaws the idealized object might have. Idealization involves the forgetting of the actually existing material conditions in which relations occur and objects exist.

Identity: An individual's unique personality or self (i.e., "who we are inside"). The concept of individual identity is complicated by the fact that, rather than inhabiting a single identity, we all assume multiple identities that are defined by particular circumstances and relationships. Marxist and psychoanalytic theories further challenge the concept of identity, showing how it is constructed by largely unconscious processes of **interpellation**. More recent theories of **performativity** offer possibilities for challenging the rigidity of the traditional identities on offer—identities that are founded in **essentialist** notions of gender, race, and sexuality.

Identity Politics: The strategic assertion of unity, defined by characteristics such as **race**, **culture**, **ethnicity**, or sexuality. Identity politics challenge prevailing power structures by demanding recognition and the extension of majority rights to minority groups.

Ideological State Apparatuses (ISAs): Term coined by French Marxist Louis Althusser to describe those social structures/organizations that indirectly (i.e., not by direct coercion) ensure that individuals subscribe to the ideology of the state or ruling class. Unlike repressive state apparatuses (for instance, the police or the military), which explicitly enforce the laws of a culture, ISAs work via the process of **interpellation** to compel individuals to conform to particular, class-specific social roles.

Ideology: See Close-Up 2.1 on page 44.

Imperialism: Imperialism refers to the extension of rule over different countries, territories, or peoples, usually by force, for the purposes of economic gain. Imperialism continues today through trade regulations that inhibit development in poor countries, or that tie the course of their development to the economic agendas of wealthier nations. See also colonialism and **cultural imperialism**.

Individualism: The belief, closely allied to **liberalism**, that the individual is the basic moral and political unit of society, and that the interests of the individual should take precedence over those of the community. The individual in these conceptions is thought to possess complete **agency**. Individualism promotes a society in which individual choice is not restricted by external constraints and in which individual members should practice self-reliance and responsibility.

Industrialization: The movement within a culture or economic system toward an increased emphasis on large-scale/mechanized industry rather than agricultural/small-scale commercial activity. Although initially conceived as a primarily economic process in its broadest sense of organization, capitalization, and mechanization, industrialization has sweeping social and cultural implications. As well as determining the manner in which things are produced (and, therefore, what kinds of products are available), the process of industrialization also affects the way labour and other resources are divided up within a culture.

Instrumental Rationality: See Close-Up 4.2 on page 119.

Intellectual Property/Copyright: Intellectual property refers to one's legal ownership of an idea or any other kind of original creative work. This ownership may be protected by trademarks, patents, and copyright. Largely as a result of recent sweeping advances in technologies that can be used to reproduce or disseminate digital information, converting even the genetic material of living things into readable "code," intellectual property has become a hotly disputed issue.

Interpellation: A term coined by the French Marxist Louis Althusser to describe the process by which an individual is addressed, or "called on," by ideology to assume a certain identity. Critical to the success of interpellation is the degree to which an individual recognizes and identifies with the roles she or he is assigned by the dominant culture.

Language: A term that in cultural studies refers to more than literal words, language can be broadly applied to describe all forms of communication (or **sign** systems)—visual, oral, aural, physical. In the study of culture, the units of any type of language are a focus for study, as societal values, relations, and power distribution are reproduced through a culture's language(s).

Liberalism: A school of political and philosophical thought that holds the individual is the basis of society and takes individual freedom to be the ultimate ethical and political goal. Liberalism, often considered to be the dominant **ideology** of the "West," emphasizes the importance of universal equality before the law, the existence of inalienable human rights, and electoral democracy. Two major forms of liberalism can be distinguished: social liberalism, which emphasizes the freedom to choose one's own lifestyle and the duty of the state to provide a certain quality of life to individuals; and economic liberalism, which emphasizes private property rights, the role of market forces, and non-interference by the state.

Maquiladoras: Spanish term describing the thousands of factories that have sprung up along the U.S.–Mexico border in the wake of NAFTA (the North American Free Trade Agreement). An inexpensive source of labour for **multinational** corporations, maquiladoras are known for meagre wages, brutal management practices, dangerous working conditions, and widespread environmental violations.

Market Segmentation: Beginning in the latter half of the twentieth century, a paradigm shift in the marketing world that involves gearing cultural production toward increasingly narrow segments of the public with the express goal of better catering to a consumer's specific tastes.

Marxism: A wide range of political and cultural philosophies that draw their inspiration from the work of Karl Marx. Marxist approaches to society and culture emphasize the primacy of economic relations and structures in determining all other social activity. In particular, Marxism emphasizes the exploitative foundations of **capitalist** systems of economics. The notion of **ideology** arises out of the Marxist tradition as a way to account for how the dominant economic class controls the production and distribution of ideas in society.

Mass Culture: A form of culture produced for profit by a vertically integrated factory system, for a large and diverse audience. Mass culture, though in some ways more pervasive than ever, is also breaking down as a result of economic processes of **market segmentation**, cultural developments such as **identity politics**, and the growing accessibility of technologies that allow "the masses" to produce culture for themselves.

Materialism: There are two understandings of materialism. The first is as an unhealthy, undesirable or vulgar attachment to the **consumption** and ownership of material goods, or **commodities**, which equates happiness with owning a lot of things and distracts from the "finer" spiritual or intellectual aspects of life. The second understanding of materialism is a philosophy that stresses the importance of physical objects and the actually existing conditions of life, over ideas.

Media Convergence: The combination of "new media" (primarily, cable and the Internet) with older media forms (radio, television, film, and newspapers and books), primarily by large corporations, with an intent to realize greater profits through the **synergistic** sharing of resources.

Minority: In cultural terms, any relatively small and/or powerless group of people who differ from the majority, or dominant, culture in ethnicity, religion, language, political persuasion, and so on. Minority politics are linked to movements by groups to gain certain political, economic, or social rights that they have been denied because of their minority status. In cultural studies, minority culture may also refer to **highbrow** (serious, intellectual) culture, as opposed to **lowbrow** (mass) culture.

Monoculture: From the agricultural term for the cultivation of a single crop, in cultural studies the idea of monoculture is linked to **globalization** and refers to the concept of a single world culture shared by all. This term has negative implications in that it suggests the destruction of local and cultural diversity. It is often implied that monoculture is synonymous with American or consumer culture.

Monopoly: An economic situation in which a single supplier controls the market for a particular product or service. This situation puts the producer in a position of unchallenged dominance from which it can inflate price to cover more than just necessary costs (including a return on capital). Governments often legislate to restrict the emergence of monopolies, since they are usually detrimental to the consumer and the economy.

Moral Panic: See Close-Up 3.2 on page 80.

Multiculturalism: A sociopolitical concept (and, in some countries, a government policy) that describes the coexistence of many different cultures in one place. As it is linked to national politics, multiculturalism recognizes that there is no essential or unified definition of a national culture, but rather emphasizes an idea of the nation as one of cultural freedom (i.e., Canada). Nominally a celebration of all cultures as equal, multiculturalist policies can often gloss over substantial power inequalities within a nation.

Multinational (Corporation): Any firm that extends itself outside of national boundaries by operating branches in many different countries simultaneously.

Myth(ology): A term coined by Roland Barthes to describe the ways in which sign systems work ideologically to reproduce and legitimate particular social relations. Myth is a mode of signification that works to express and surreptitiously to justify the dominant values of a given historical period. Unlike the relatively simple level of denotative or literal meaning, in which a word or image corresponds to a single, straightforward definition, myth brings into play a whole chain of associated concepts (e.g., tree–nature–goodness) by which members of a culture understand certain topics, and which help to shape their collective identities.

Nation/Nationalism: See Close-Up 7.3 on page 233.

Neoliberalism: A political movement, originating with the policies of Margaret Thatcher in the U.K., Ronald Reagan in the U.S.A., and Brian Mulroney in Canada, that attempts to remove all government influence in economic matters through the **privatization** of state functions, deregulation of trade, and reduction of welfare spending. Neoliberalism is associated with economic **liberalism**, rather than social liberalism. Critics of neoliberalism argue that it radically increases inequality and poverty, and places greater importance on free markets than on public well-being. In recent years, neoliberalism has come to be seen as the dominant **ideology** of **globalization**.

New World Order: A phrase associated with the **postcolonial**, post–**cold war** configuration of world power, which remains dominated by the West, and particularly by the United States. Coined by former U.S. President George H. Bush, the phrase describes genuine shifts in the geopolitical order, but also covers up long-term continuities in the global power and capitalism (i.e., not everything is "new" in the New World Order).

Orientalism: Refers to the way in which "the Orient" was and is constructed by the West as a means to claim authority and exercise control over Eastern cultures. The Orient is not a fact, or a specific geographical place; rather, it is the complex layers of knowledge and **mythology** that have been constructed around Western ideas about the non-West. For example, the way in which North American media characterize the "Middle East" as a place of repressive government regimes and fundamentalist religion glosses over the vast cultural differences between different groups of the region and contributes to the Western assumption that domination of these "backward" nations is legitimate and necessary.

Patriarchy (Patriarchal): A social system in which men hold power in the family and in the social structure. Patriarchy has more recently been used as a term in feminist criticism to describe the total system of gender relations in which male dominance has historically worked to dominate and disempower women. The challenge in trying to dismantle this system is that it has been historically naturalized to seem as though the social position of both genders has been biologically determined.

Performativity: Developed most extensively in the theory of Judith Butler, performativity refers to the process by which identities are enacted through repeated performance rather than inherently possessed or inhabited. The idea of performativity works on the premise that roles such as sex and gender are produced within an **ideologically** determined social script. While it's not possible to throw away the script—to be "oneself" instead of playing one's assigned role—the theory of performativity, by highlighting the tension between the scripted ideal and its embodied performance, offers possibilities for resisting the straitjacket of traditionally defined identities.

Populist: A political philosophy or rhetoric that claims to represent the interests of "the people" over those of "the elites." The term tends to be (but not always) used pejoratively, and is thus rarely used for self-description. Populist politics can be either left wing or right wing.

Postcolonial(ism): *Postcolonial* refers to the period after the formal retraction of colonial rule in the developing world. This period varies considerably, but in the case of the former British colonies, it refers to the period after the Second World War. *Postcolonialism* is a term that refers to the working through of the effects of colonization on a society or culture. The study of postcolonial culture examines the various mechanisms of **colonialism** (e.g., political rule, economic exploitation, colonial education systems) and their long-term, embedded cultural and social implications. While many former colonies are now independent states, postcolonial studies insists on the need to recognize and understand the ways in which colonialism's effects persist in the social, cultural, and political life of former colonial states today.

Post-Fordism: A mode of economic organization characterized by smaller, more flexible, and decentralized networks of labour and production, catering to more specialized ranges of consumer demands. Post-Fordist economies shift jobs away from manufacturing and toward the service sector, such as hospitality, tourism, and cultural production.

Posthumanism: A philosophy that questions concepts that underpin the tradition of humanism, such as identity, subjectivity, consciousness, and the soul. While humanism is based on ideas of human beings as unique individuals, and of humanity as a clearly defined, superior life form, posthumanism rejects the autonomy of "the human" in favour of the cyborg—a being defined by a combination of human and machine and/or animal characteristics. Posthumanism has been taken up in different ways by feminists, for whom it represents a way of challenging biologically essentialist views of sex and gender, and by proponents of genetic engineering, who support the idea of designing "better," more powerful humans through technological enhancement.

Postmodernism: See Close-Up 6.1 on page 204.

Preferred Reading: Any given text (be it a novel, film, image, or song) can be interpreted in a theoretically infinite number of ways depending on the perspective and experiences of the reader. However, the preferred reading is the particular interpretation that emerges as the most obvious to the greatest number of people based on prevalent and culturally specific modes of understanding (e.g., it is the reading that in many cases strikes interpreters as being "common sense").

Privatization: The process through which ownership of a public enterprise or the responsibility to enact a state function is transferred from government or community control into the private corporate sector and run to generate profit. Privatization is a key aspect of **neoliberalism**, and arises from a belief that the market can fulfill state functions more efficiently or cheaply than the government. State functions that have been privatized in some countries include education, television broadcasting, telecommunications, and even water supply and law enforcement. The reverse process, whereby a government takes ownership from the private sector, is called nationalization.

Progress: An understanding of history, often considered to have arisen out of the Enlightenment, which holds that human conditions and society have steadily improved and will continue to do so, and that the future will invariably be better than the past due to advances in technology, politics, economics, or culture. Following the devastation and barbarity of the Second World War and the Holocaust, some social critics began to question the notion of progress. However, the idea still defines most Western accounts of history and everyday understandings of the direction the future will take.

Pseudo-Individualization: Along with **standardization** (which it facilitates), one of the primary characteristics of the products of the culture industry as described by Max Horkheimer and Theodor Adorno. Pseudo-individualization refers to a mode of capitalist production wherein, although virtually identical, cultural products are superficially varied to enable them to seemingly speak directly to a consumer's sense of individuality, their unique taste, and apparent freedom to choose.

Psychoanalysis: A body of ideas that derive their inspiration from the work of Sigmund Freud, specifically his work on the unconscious mind and its role in identity formation. Psychoanalysis seeks to account for individual behaviour and social structures, such as gender and sexuality, through reference to a fundamental conflict between primal drives and desires and the need to repress and organize those drives for the purposes of social life.

Race: A constructed category that is widely used to distinguish among various groups of human beings based on inherited biological or physical characteristics (such as skin colour or facial features). Although seemingly a neutral descriptive tool, race has functioned historically as a way to draw spurious connections between specific physical characteristics and the possession of certain behavioural traits assumed to be shared by all members of the race. The idea of *race* is therefore inseparable from the discriminatory attitude and practices of *racism*.

Racism: The systematic practice of stereotyping and persecuting people on the basis of their race. Racism remains a central form of ideology today. Cultural studies has focused on the ways in which racist attitudes and stereotypes are both reinforced by and challenged in popular representations, and institutionalized in a variety of popular cultural practices.

Realism: See Close-Up 3.3 on page 86.

Representation: The social production of meaning through sign systems (i.e., words, images, gestures, etc.). Involves making meaning by creating links between conceptual and linguistic or signifying levels of meaning, links that are established through codes shared by members of a culture. Inseparable from the socially specific processes of **ideology** and **mythology**, representation constructs the world in particular ways that have significant bearing on the organization of society.

Runaway Film: A motion picture that, although intended for primary distribution in one country (usually the U.S.), is filmed in another country for economic or creative reasons (e.g., tax breaks; scenery or directorial preference). Historically, a majority of such films have been shot in Canada instead of the United States, due to its proximity and lower costs as a result of currency disparities and government subsidies. The filming of *The Lord of the Rings* trilogy in New Zealand is an example of both an economic and creative runaway film.

Semiotics: See Close-Up 3.1 on page 73.

Sign: The smallest unit (such as a word, image, or sound) of communication to which meaning is attached. In order to be a sign, the unit must meet three criteria: it must possess a physical form, it must refer to something else, and it must do so in a way that is recognizable to others. The sustained and large-scale interconnection of signs facilitates the construction of shared sign systems that enable individuals to communicate with other members of their culture in a comprehensible manner. See also **representation**.

Social Constructivism: A way of explaining the production of meaning, identity, and value. (often in explicit opposition to **essentialist** explanations). Social constructivists believe that identity is not inherent within an individual, group, or thing, but is instead largely a creation of cultural, political, and historical forces.

Sovereignty: The possession of legal control and governance over a specific geographic territory. Sovereignty once rested in the body of the monarch, who possessed supreme power over his or her kingdom. In the modern context, sovereignty has been located in nation-states. Globalization has been understood by many scholars as having complicated and undermined the sovereignty of nation-states. The growth in the political power of international organizations (e.g., United Nations, World Trade Organization) and the rise of non-governmental organizations has redistributed nation-state sovereignty to a multiplicity of local and global sites and political levels.

Standardization: Along with **pseudo-individualization**, one of the primary characteristics of the products of the culture industry as formulated by Max Horkheimer and Theodor Adorno. Standardization refers to a widespread similarity between cultural products. Both a method of production and a manner of consumption, standardization not only dictates the kind of cultural products that will be manufactured but also inscribes in the consumer a shared mode of passive, apolitical, and disengaged reception.

Stereotypes: A form of representation that reduces people to a few simple, essential characteristics that are represented as fixed by nature. Stereotyping is predicated on the simplistic notion that an individual's membership within any given social group (based on, for instance, class, gender, race, age, or sexuality) invariably predisposes him or her to possess certain personality characteristics, attitudes, or behaviours.

Structuralism: An analytical approach characterized largely by a shift in focus from interpreting a text in order to unveil its hidden meaning to identifying and interrogating the ways in which meaning is brought into being *structurally*. Structuralism is a diverse approach encompassing numerous methodologies, connected by this concern with the ways in which the structure of any given text is implicated in the production of its meaning. Although it has been subject to intensive critique (focusing, for example, on its inability to take account of historical change), structuralism's once-radical emphasis on the role of relationship and context in determining meaning has been enormously influential in many disciplines.

Subculture: A term that describes groups or communities that deviate or differ from existing social norms. Subcultures are typically conceived of as groups of individuals who come together around shared practices and ideas that are rejected or treated with suspicion by official, mainstream culture. By creatively expressing their dissatisfaction with existing social norms and practices, subcultures challenge and modify what counts as normal, everyday life. Subcultures are often identified with youth and youth culture in particular.

Subliminal Advertising: A form of advertising that tries to persuade by having an impact on the subconscious or unconscious. Subliminal advertising passes underneath the threshold of the senses (sub-*limen*). Such forms of advertising hope to generate a desire in consumers to purchase a product or service without their conscious awareness of having been influenced to do so.

Surveillance: The practice of monitoring persons, locations, or situations in order to gather information about the environment that is being observed. In Cultural Studies, surveillance is often understood, with reference to the work of Michel Foucault, as a means of ensuring that behaviour remains within the bounds of established norms. Surveillance technologies have become much more advanced and their use much more widespread in recent decades with the implementation of government security programs following the events of September 11, 2001.

Synergy: A strategy of synchronizing and actively forging connections between directly related areas of entertainment. For example, the merger of media giant Time Warner with Internet giant AOL was intended to allow content developed for one communication medium (e.g., television) to be reused, recycled, and reinforced in different media (e.g., film, Internet, etc.).

Transnational (Corporation): A firm that operates on a global scale and works, to a greater or lesser extent, outside of national jurisdictions. For example, former General Electric CEO Jack Welch's fantasy of operating the company from a permanently floating barge in order to avoid all national trade regulations and laws would be an example of a completely transnational company—it would operate worldwide without operating from within any specific country.

Urbanization: The long-term but increasingly intensifying shift of human populations from the country to the city. In nineteenth-century Britain, urbanization contributed significantly to the reduction of open spaces available for recreation as land was expropriated for the building of industrial infrastructure. By 2007, more than 50 percent of the world's population lived in cities. Urbanization is associated with the production of new cultural forms, and also with problems such as crowding and the loss of agricultural land, green space, and species habitats.

Vertical Integration: A **synergistic** venture wherein one company acquires the means by which a particular product or service is manufactured, distributed, *and* sold. Its aim is to increase a corporation's control over its own products by diminishing its reliance on other companies. Vertical integration is considered by some to be responsible for a reduction in the diversity of available cultural products.

Works Cited

Adorno, Theodor. "Excerpt from 'On Popular Music.'" *A Critical and Cultural Theory Reader*. Ed. Anthony Easthope and Kate McGowan. Toronto: University of Toronto Press, 1992. 11–23.

———. "The Culture Industry Reconsidered." *The Adorno Reader*. Ed. Brian O'Connor. Oxford: Blackwell, 2000. 230–238.

Akin, David. "From Igloo to Internet: First Nations Gain Entrée to the Electronic Age." *Hamilton Spectator* 22 Sept. 1997: B1.

Althusser, Louis. *Lenin and Philosophy and Other Essays*. Trans. Ben Brewster. London: New Left, 1971.

"And That Is the Question." *Dawson's Creek*. The WB, Global, Toronto. 17 Feb. 1999.

Anderson, Benedict. *Imagined Communities*. London: Verso, 1983.

Anderson, Sarah, and John Cavanagh. *Field Guide to the Global Economy*. New York: The New Press, 2000.

Arnold, Matthew. *Culture and Anarchy*. 1869. Ed. J. Dover Wilson. Cambridge, UK: Cambridge University Press, 1990.

Ashcroft, Bill, Gareth Griffiths, and Helen Tiffin. *Key Concepts in Post-Colonial Studies*. London: Routledge, 1998.

Associated Press. "Brokeback Mountain Could Inspire Wyoming Tourist Boom." *USA Today* online edition. 30 Jan. 2006 <http://www.usatoday.com/travel/destinations/2006-01-30-brokeback-tourism_x.htm>.

Atwood, Margaret. "Rich Kids Swim, Poor Kids Sink." *The Globe and Mail* 19 April 2008: M1.

"Bad and Badder." [Q & A]. *Harper's Magazine* Sept. 2002: 21–22.

Bailey, Peter. *Leisure and Class in Victorian England: Rational Recreation and the Contest for Control, 1830–1885*. London: Methuen, 1978.

Balsamo, Anne. "On the Cutting Edge: Cosmetic Surgery and the Technological Production of the Gendered Body." *The Visual Culture Reader*. Ed. Nicholas Mirzoeff. London: Routledge, 1998. 228–233.

Bangeman, Eric. "I Sue Dead People." *Ars Technica* 4 Feb. 2005 <http://arstechnica.com/news.ars/post/20050204-4587.html>.

Barthes, Roland. *Mythologies*. Trans. Annette Lavers. London: Granada, 1973.

Baudelaire, Charles. *The Painter of Modern Life and Other Essays*. Trans. Jonathan Mayne. London: Phaidon, 1965.

Baudrillard, Jean. *Simulations*. Trans. Paul Foss, Paul Patton, and Philip Beitchman. New York: Semiotext(e), 1983.

Bauman, Zygmunt. "Soil, Blood and Identity." *The Sociological Review* 40.4 (1992): 675–701.

"Be Careful What You Wish For." *Dawson's Creek.* The WB, Global, Toronto. 7 Mar. 1999.

Benjamin, Walter. *Charles Baudelaire: A Lyric Poet in the Era of High Capitalism.* Trans. Harry Zohn. London: New Left, 1973.

———. *Illuminations.* Trans. Harry Zohn. New York: Schocken, 1968.

Bennett, Tony. "Putting Policy into Cultural Studies." *Cultural Studies.* Ed. Lawrence Grossberg, Cary Nelson, and Paula Treichler. London: Routledge, 1992. 23–37.

Berger, John. *About Looking.* New York: Pantheon, 1980.

Best, Geoffrey Francis Andrew. *Mid-Victorian Britain, 1851–1875.* London: Weidenfeld and Nicolson, 1971.

Blaut, James M. *The Colonizer's Model of the World: Geographical Diffusionism and Eurocentric History.* New York: Guilford, 1993.

Borat: Cultural Learnings of America for Make Benefit Glorious Nation of Kazakhstan. Dir. Larry Charles. Prod. Sacha Baron Cohen, Jay Roach. 20th Century Fox, 2006.

"Bouchard Taylor Commission." *Herouxville Town Charter.* 1 Nov. 2007 <http://herouxville-quebec.blogspot.com/>.

Bourdieu, Pierre. *Distinction.* Trans. Richard Nice. Cambridge: Harvard University Press, 1987.

Branston, Gill. *Cinema and Cultural Modernity.* Philadelphia: Open University Press, 2000.

Briggs, Asa. *Mass Entertainment: The Origins of a Modern Industry.* Adelaide: Griffin, 1960.

———. *Serious Pursuits: Communications and Education.* Volume 3 of *Collected Essays of Asa Briggs.* Champaign-Urbana: University of Illinois Press, 1991.

"Brokeback Mountain Could Inspire Wyoming Tourist Boom." *USA Today* online edition. 30 Jan. 2006 <http://www.usatoday.com/travel/destinations/2006-01-30-brokeback-tourism_x.htm>.

Brooker, Peter. *A Concise Glossary of Cultural Theory.* London: Arnold, 1999.

Brown, Nicholas. "The Music of the Sphere." *Content Providers of the World Unite!* Ed. Susie O'Brien and Imre Szeman. Globalization and the Human Condition Working Paper Series. Hamilton: McMaster University Institute on Globalization and the Human Condition, 2003. 23–28 <http://www.humanities.mcmaster.ca/~global/wp/Content.pdf>.

Burke, Peter. "The 'Discovery' of Popular Culture." *People's History and Socialist Theory.* Ed. Raphael Samuel. London: Routledge, 1981. 216–226.

Burkeman, Oliver. "Not So Big, Mac." *The Guardian Unlimited* online edition. 22 Nov. 2002 <http://www.guardian.co.uk/media/2002/nov/22/marketingandpr.usnews>.

Butler, Judith. *Gender Trouble: Feminism and the Subversion of Identity.* New York: Routledge, 1990.

Carey, James W. *Communication as Culture: Essays on Media and Society.* Boston: Unwin Hyman, 1989.

Carson, Rachel. *Silent Spring.* Greenwich, CT: Fawcett, 1962.

"The Case for War." Editorial. *The Economist* 1 Aug. 2002: 9–10.

Cavett, Dick. "The Swimmers." Review of *Contested Waters: A Social History of Swimming Pools in America.* By Jeff Wiltse. Sunday Book Review. *New York Times* 3 June 2007 <http://www.nytimes.com/2007/06/03/books/review/Cavett-t.html?ref=review>.

"Central Park." Citimaps.com <http://www.citimaps.com/centralpark/history.html>.

Certified General Accountants Association of Canada. *Where Does the Money Go: The Increasing Reliance on Household Debt in Canada.* Certified General Accountants Association of Canada, 2007.

Chambers, Iain. *Migrancy, Culture, Identity.* New York: Routledge, 1994.

Chang, Jeff. "The Ongoing Evolution of Obama's Post-Racial Politics" *Huffington Post* 12 Feb. 2008 <http://www.huffingtonpost.com/jeff-chang/the-ongoing-evolution-of-_b_86312.html>.

CIA Factbook. "Rank Order—Roadways." <http://www.cia.gov/library/publications/the-world-factbook/rankorder/2085rank.html>.

Clairmont, Susan. "Road Hockey Sparks Conflict." *The Hamilton Spectator* online edition. 4 Jan. 2002 <http://www.hamiltonspectator.com/clairmont/516812.html>.

"The Code." Molson Canadian TV Spots. Accessed 15 Nov. 2008 <http://www.molsoncanadian.ca/tvspots/index.html?file=the_code.flv&title=TheCode>.

Cohen, Leah Hager. *Glass, Paper, Beans: Revelations on the Nature and Value of Ordinary Things.* New York: Doubleday, 1997.

Cohen, Stan. *Folk Devils and Moral Panics: The Creation of the Mods and Rockers.* London: MacGibbon and Kee, 1972.

Connell, Richard W. *Masculinities.* University of California Press, 1995.

Conniff, Richard. "Yes You Were Born to Run." *Men's Health* (May 2008) <http://www.menshealth.com/cda/article.do?site=MensHealth&channel=fitness&category=cardio.activities&conitem=57a7b78301459110VgnVCM10000013281eac____>.

Coupland, Douglas. *Generation X.* New York: St. Martin's Press, 1991.

Cronon, William. "The Trouble With Wilderness; or, Getting Back to the Wrong Nature." *Uncommon Ground: Rethinking the Human Place in Nature.* Ed. William Cronon. New York: Norton, 1996. 69–90.

Cunningham, Hugh. *Leisure in the Industrial Revolution.* London: Croom Helm, 1980.

Darnton, Robert. *The Forbidden Best-Sellers of Pre-Revolutionary France.* New York: W.W. Norton & Co., 1995.

Dauvergne, Mia, and Geoffrey Li. "Homicide in Canada, 2005" *Juristat.* Catalogue 85-002-XIE. Vol. 26.6 <http://dsp-psd.communication.gc.ca/Pilot/Statcan/85-002-XIE/85-002-XIE2006006.pdf>.

Davis, Mike. "Planet of Slums." *New Left Review* 26 (2004): 5–34.

Debord, Guy. *Society of the Spectacle.* Trans. Donald Nicholson Smith. New York: Zone Books, 1995.

The Decline of Western Civilization. Dir. Penelope Spheeris. Spheeris Films Inc., 1981.

DeMott, Benjamin. "Put on a Happy Face: Masking the Differences Between Blacks and Whites." *Harper's Magazine* Sept. 1995: 31–38.

Denby, David. "Loners." *New Yorker* 8 Aug. 2005 <http://www.newyorker.com/archive/2005/08/08/050808crci_cinema?currentPage=1>.

Denning, Michael. "The End of Mass Culture." *Modernity and Mass Culture*. Ed. James Naremore and Patrick Brantlinger. Bloomington IN: Indiana University Press, 1991. 253–268.

de Zengotita, Thomas. "The Gunfire Dialogues: Notes on the Reality of Virtuality." *Harper's Magazine* July 1999: 55–58.

Dobbs, William. "400 Days Later, UNPJ Still Seeking RNC Permit." Interview with Amy Goodman. *Democracy Now* 14 July 2004 <http://www.democracynow.org/2004/7/14/400_days_later_ufpj_still_seeking>.

"Does Social Networking Boost Democracy—or Threaten It?" *Headstar.com*. 11 Oct. 2007 <http://www.headstar.com/site/scripts/news_article.php?newsID=167>.

Dogtown and Z Boys. Dir. Stacy Peralta. Prod. Agi Orsi and Jay Wilson. U.S.A, Sony, 2002.

Duany, Andres, Elizabeth Plater-Zyberk, and Jeff Speck. *Suburban Nation: The Rise of Sprawl and the Decline of the American Dream*. New York: Farrar, Straus and Giroux, 2000.

Dube, Rebecca Cook. "Muslims Laud 'Little Mosque on the Prairie.'" *Christian Science Monitor* 17 Jan. 2007 <http://www.csmonitor.com/2007/0117/p07s02-woam.html>.

Dubuc, Alain. "Fear and Ignorance: A Rural Revolt." *Vancouver Sun* online edition. 1 March 2007 <http://www.canada.com/vancouversun/news/editorial/story.html?id=2d10e22f-1e87-4faf-a6dc-15ffebaa8ab7>.

du Cille, Ann. "Dyes and Dolls: Multicultural Barbie and the Merchandising of Difference" *Differences* 6.1 (Spring 1994): 46–68.

du Gay, Paul, ed. *Production of Culture/Cultures of Production*. London: Sage, 1997.

du Gay, Paul, Stuart Hall, Linda Janes, Huch Mackay, and Keith Negus. *Doing Cultural Studies: The Story of the Sony Walkman*. London: Sage, 1997.

Duncombe, Stephen. *Cultural Resistance Reader*. New York: Verso, 2002.

During, Simon, ed. *The Cultural Studies Reader*. New York: Routledge, 1993.

Elias, Norbert. *The Civilizing Process*. Volume 1: *The History of Manners*. New York: Pantheon, 1982.

Elsworth, Catherine. "Wyoming's Macho Image Challenged by Film Story of Two Gay Cowboys." *The Telegraph* online edition. 11 Sept. 2005 <http://www.telegraph.co.uk/news/worldnews/northamerica/usa/1502571/Wyomings-macho-image-challenged-by-film-story-of-two-gay-cowboys.html>.

"The End of Cheap Food." *The Economist* 6 Dec. 2007 <http://www.economist.com/opinion/displayStory.cfm?Story_ID=10252015>.

Engels, Friedrich. *The Condition of the Working Class in England*. Trans. and ed. W.O. Henderson and W.H. Chaloner. Oxford: Basil Blackwell, 1958.

Evans, Caroline, and Minna Thornton. *Women and Fashion: A New Look*. New York: Quartet, 1989.

Faludi, Susan. *Stiffed: The Betrayal of the American Man*. New York: HarperCollins, 2000.

Fanon, Frantz. *Black Skin, White Masks.* Trans. Charles Lam Markmann. New York: Grove, 1967.

Featherstone, Mike. "Body Modification: An Introduction." *Body Modification.* Ed. Mike Featherstone. London: Sage, 2000. 1–14.

Fetherling, Douglas, ed. *Documents in Canadian Art.* Peterborough, ON: Broadview Press, 1987.

Fight Club. Dir. David Fincher. Prod. Ross Bell, et al. 20th Century Fox, 1999.

"Fighting for the Right to Play Road Hockey in Hamilton." CBC Sunday Report. *The National* transcripts. Host Alison Smith. 6 Jan. 2002 <http://tv.cbc.ca/national/ trans/ T020106.html>.

Fiske, John. *Reading the Popular.* London: Routledge, 1989.

———. *Understanding Popular Culture.* London: Routledge, 1989.

Florida, Richard. *The Rise of the Creative Class: And How It's Transforming Work, Leisure and Everyday Life.* New York: Basic Books, 2002.

Forrest Gump. Dir. Robert Zemekis. Prod. Wendy Finerman. MGM, 1997.

Foucault, Michel. *History of Sexuality.* Vol. 1. Trans. Robert Hurley. Harmondsmith: Penguin, 1984.

Frank, Thomas. *The Conquest of Cool.* Chicago: University of Chicago Press, 1997.

Freccero, Carla. *Popular Culture: An Introduction.* New York: New York University Press, 1999.

Fretts, Bruce. "Remote Patrol." EW.com. *Entertainment Weekly* <http://www.ew.com/ew/ article/0,,271178,00.html>.

Friesen, Joe. "An End to Locking Lips at Dusk." *The Globe and Mail* online edition. 11 April 2008 <http://www.theglobeandmail.com/servlet/story/RTGAM.20080411 .wdrivein11/BNStory/GlobeSportsBaseball/>.

"From the Front Door to the Classroom Door—Putting Safety and Security First." *Calgary Board of Education.* 18 Sept. 2006 <http://www.cbe.ab.ca/New/safety.asp>.

Fukuyama, Francis. *The End of History and the Last Man.* New York: Free Press, 1992.

Galt, Virginia. "Precautions No Guarantee of Safety, Officials Concede." *The Globe and Mail* 12 Feb. 2000: A30.

"Game On! Road Hockey Charges Dismissed." *CBC News* online edition, Toronto. 8 Jan. 2002 <http://toronto.cbc.ca/template/servlet/View?filename=hockey_010802>.

Gannon, Maire. "Crime Statistics in Canada, 2005." *Juristat* 26.4 <http://www.policecouncil. ca/reports/SCCrimeStats2005.pdf>.

Garnham, Nicholas. "Concepts of Culture: Public Policy and the Cultural Industries." *Cultural Studies* 1.1 (1987): 23–38.

Garratt, Cheryl. "Wake Up . . . " *The Observer* 8 Sept. 2002: Food Section: 14–15.

Gee, Marcus. "Cyberdissidents weaving along new path." *The Globe and Mail* December 6, 2007: A20.

Gellner, Ernest. *Nations and Nationalism.* Oxford: Blackwell, 1983.

Gendron, Bernie. "Theodor Adorno Meets the Cadillacs." *Studies in Entertainment.* Ed. Tania Modleski. Bloomington: Indiana University Press, 1986. 18–36.

George, Jane. "Montreal Carving Factory Churns Out the Soapstone." *Nunatsiaq News* online edition. 30 Dec. 1998 <http://www.nunatsiaq.com/archives/nunavut981231/nvt81231_12.html>.

Ghost World. Dir. Terry Zwigoff. Prod. Mr. Mudd. U.S.A., MGM/UA, 2001.

Giddens, Anthony. *Consequences of Modernity.* Palo Alto: Stanford University Press, 1990.

Gilman, Charlotte Perkins. *Women and Economies.* 1898. Mineola, NY: Dover, 1998.

Gilroy, Paul. *The Black Atlantic: Modernity and Double Consciousness.* London: Verso, 1993.

———. "Diaspora and the Detours of Identity." *Identity and Difference.* Ed. Kathryn Woodward. London: Sage, 1997. 301–349.

———. *Small Acts: Thoughts on the Politics of Black Cultures.* London: Serpent's Tale, 1993.

Giroux, Henry. *Disturbing Pleasures: Learning Popular Culture.* New York: Routledge, 1994.

Goodall, Jane. "An Order of Pure Decision: Un-Natural Selection in the Work of Stelarc and Orlan." *Body Modification.* Ed. Mike Featherstone. London: Sage, 2000. 149–170.

Grierson, Bruce. "Headrush." *Adbusters* 25 (Spring 1999): 23–29.

Grizzly Man. Dir. Werner Herzog. Prod. Erik Nelson Lionsgate, 2005.

Grossberg, Lawrence, Ellen Wartella, and D. Charles Whitney. *Media Making: Mass Media in a Popular Culture.* Thousand Oaks, CA: Sage, 1998.

Grossman, David. On Killing: *The Psychological Cost of Learning to Kill in War and Society.* New York: Little Brown, 1998.

Grosz, Elizabeth. *Volatile Bodies.* Bloomington: Indiana University Press, 1994.

Hall, Ann, Trevor Slack, Garry Smith, and David Whitson. *Sport in Canadian Society.* Toronto: McClelland & Stewart, 1991.

Hall, Stuart. "Cultural Studies and the Centre: Some Problematics and Problems." *Culture, Media, Language.* Ed. Stuart Hall, Dorothy Hobson, Andrew Lowe, and Paul Willis. London: Hutchinson, 1980. 15–47.

———. "Cultural Studies and Its Theoretical Legacies." *Cultural Studies.* Ed. Lawrence Grossberg, Cary Nelson, and Paula Treichler. London: Routledge, 1992. 277–294.

———. "Encoding, Decoding." *The Cultural Studies Reader.* Ed. Simon During. London: Routledge, 1993. 90–103.

———. "Gramsci's Relevance for the Study of Race and Ethnicity." *Journal of Communication Inquiry* 10.2 (1986): 5–27.

———. "Notes on Deconstructing the Popular." *People's History and Socialist Theory.* Ed. R. Samuel. London: Routledge & Kegan Paul, 1981. 227–240.

Hall, Stuart, Chas Critcher, Tony Jefferson, John Clarke, and Brian Roberts. *Policing the Crisis: Mugging, the State, and Law and Order.* New York: Holmes & Meier, 1978.

Harvey, David. *The Condition of Postmodernity.* Cambridge, UK: Blackwell, 1989.

Heath, Joseph, and Andrew Potter. *The Rebel Sell: Why the Culture Can't Be Jammed.* Toronto: Harper Collins, 2004.

Hebdige, Dick. *Hiding in the Light: On Images and Things.* New York: Routledge, 1994.

———. *Subculture: The Meaning of Style.* New York: Routledge, 1981.

"Hérouxville Town Charter." 24 March 2007 <http://herouxville-quebec.blogspot.com/2007/03/about-beautiful-herouxville-quebec.html>.

Hirschberg, Lynn. "The Thinking Inside the Box." *New York Times Magazine* 3 Nov. 2002: 67–71.

Hobsbawm, Eric. *The Age of Extremes: A History of the World, 1914–1991.* New York: Vintage, 1996.

———. *Industry and Empire: An Economic History of Britain Since 1750.* London: Weidenfeld and Nicolson, 1968.

Hochschild, Arlie Russell. *The Time Bind: When Work Becomes Home and Home Becomes Work.* New York: Holt, 2001.

Holloway, Lynnette. "The Angry Appeal of Eminem Cuts Across Racial Lines." *New York Times* online edition. 28 Oct. 2002 <http://www.nytimes.com/2002/10/28/business/media/28RAP.html?ex=1036838360&ei=1&en=aec9e21c86415ad0>.

Horkheimer, Max, and Theodor Adorno. *Dialectic of Enlightenment.* New York: Continuum, 1971.

Hunter, Latham. "The Celluloid Cubicle: Regressive Constructions of Masculinity in 1990s Office Movies." *American Culture* 26.2 (2003): 71-86.

Huntington, Samuel. *The Clash of Civilizations and the Remaking of World Order.* New York: Simon and Schuster, 1998.

Hutcheon, Linda. *As Canadian as Possible . . . Under the Circumstances!* Toronto: Robarts Centre for Canadian Studies, 1988.

———. *The Canadian Postmodern: A Study of Contemporary English-Canadian Fiction.* Oxford: Oxford University Press, 1988.

"I Am . . . an Asshole?" *www.egulphy.com.* 16 April 2000 <http://www.angelfire.com/rock/cpar/p2k/2kapr16paperless.html>.

"I Am Not Canadian" [video]. 6 May 2007. *YouTube* <http://www.youtube.com/watch?v=MpumYq8YRY4>.

Ibbitson, John. "Harris Vows to Rid Streets of Pushy Beggars, Squeegees." *National Post* 20 May 1999: A1, A8.

Ignatieff, Michael. "The Narcissism of Minor Difference." *Clash of Identities: Essays on Media, Manipulation, and Politics of the Self.* Ed. James Littleton. Toronto: CBC, 1996. 41–54.

Irigaray, Luce. *This Sex Which Is Not One.* Trans. Catherine Porter with Carolyn Burke. Ithaca, NY: Cornell University Press, 1985.

———. "Women on the Market." *The Logic of the Gift.* Ed. Alan Schrift. New York: Routledge, 1997. 174-189.

"I Was Canadian." *BC Free Press* online edition. June 2000 <http://www.bcfreepress.bc.ca/page129.html>.

Jameson, Fredric. *Postmodernism, or the Cultural Logic of Late Capitalism.* Durham, NC: Duke University Press, 1991.

Jenkins, Henry. "Professor Jenkins Goes to Washington." *Harper's Magazine* July 1999: 19–23.

Jhally, Sut. *The Codes of Advertising: Fetishism and the Political Economy of Meaning in the Consumer Economy.* New York: St. Martins Press, 1987.

John Howard Society. "Youth Crime in Canada: Public Perception vs. Statistical Information." 1998 <http://www.johnhoward.ab.ca/PUB/C16.htm#exe>.

Jones, Gareth Stedman. "Working-Class Culture and Working-Class Politics in London, 1870–1900: Notes on the Remaking of a Working Class." *Journal of Social History* 7.4 (1974): 460–508.

Kanji, Nazneen, and Kalyani Menon-Sen. "What Does the Feminisation of Labour Mean for Sustainable Livelihoods?" *World Summit on Sustainable Development.* Aug. 2001 <http://www.glow-boell.de/media/de/txt_rubrik_5/SuS_Kanji_FemEco_IIEDfinalpaper.pdf>.

Katz, Jon. "The Digital Citizen." *Wired* (Dec. 1997): 68+.

Kelly, David. "O.C.'s Mix of Cultures Yields Co-operation, Tensions." *L.A. Times* 24 June 2007. Posted on *American Renaissance* <http://www.amren.com/mtnews/archives/2007/06/ocs_mix_of_cult.php>.

Kenney, Kim. "Princess Diana's Wedding Gown on Exhibit in Dayton, Ohio." *BellaOnline: The Voice of Women* <http://www.bellaonline.com/articles/art29010.asp>.

Klesse, Christian. "'Modern Primitivism': Non-Mainstream Body Modification and Racialized Representation." *Body & Society* 5.2/3 (1999): 16–38.

Klosterman, Chuck. "The Ratt Trap." *New York Times Magazine* 29 Dec. 2002: 24–25.

Kohn, Margaret. *Brave New Neighborhoods: The Privatization of Public Space.* New York: Routledge, 2004.

Lacayo, Richard. "Violent Reaction: Bob Dole's Broadside Against Sex and Violence in Popular Culture Sets Off a Furious Debate About Responsibility." *Time* 12 June 1995 <http://www.time.com/time/magazine/archive/1995/950612/950612.cover.html>.

Laqueur, Thomas. *Making Sex: Body and Gender from the Greeks to Freud.* Cambridge, MA: Harvard University Press, 1990.

Leavis, F.R., and Denys Thompson. *Culture and Environment.* Westport CT: Greenwood, 1977.

Lefebvre, Henri. *Introduction to Modernity.* Trans. John Moore. New York: Verso, 1995.

———. "Towards a Leftist Cultural Politics." *Marxism and the Interpretation of Culture.* Ed. Cary Nelson and Lawrence Grossberg. Chicago: University of Illinois Press, 1998: 75–88.

Lessing, Lawrence. *The Future of Ideas: The Fate of the Commons in a Connected World.* New York: Vintage, 2001.

Levine, Lawrence W. *Highbrow/Lowbrow: The Emergence of Cultural Hierarchy in America.* Cambridge MA: Harvard University Press, 1988.

Lewis, Bernard. *What Went Wrong? Western Impact and Middle Eastern Response.* Oxford: Oxford University Press, 2002.

Life and Debt. Dir. Stephanie Black. Tuff Gong Pictures, 2003.

"Little Mosque." *Little Mosque on the Prairie.* Toronto, CBC. 9 Jan. 2007.

"Local Ad." *The Office.* Toronto, NBC, Global. 25 Oct. 2007.

Longman, Jere. "Athletics: Disabled Runner Makes Case for Competing in Olympics." *International Herald-Tribune* online edition. 14 May 2007 <http://www.iht.com/articles/2007/05/14/business/track.php>.

Lury, Celia. *Consumer Culture*. New Brunswick, NJ: Rutgers University Press, 1996.

Lütticken, Sven. "The Art of Theft." *New Left Review* 13 (2002): 89–104.

Lyman, Rick. "Black Actors Are Still Keeping Their Eyes on the Prize." *New York Times* online edition. 27 Feb. 2002 <http://www.nytimes.com/2002/02/27/movies/oscars/27OSCA. html?ex=1015827477&ei=1&en=cc19dc5fb5ed0083>.

Lyotard, Jean-François. *The Postmodern Condition: A Report on Knowledge*. Minneapolis: Minnesota University Press, 1984.

MacEachern, Alan. "Ye Old Season's Greetings. *The Globe and Mail* online edition. 31 Dec. 2007 <http://www.theglobeandmail.com/servlet/story/LAC.20071231.COLETTS31-14/PPVStory/?DENIED=1>.

MacFarquhar, Neil. "Sitcom's Dubious Premise: Being Muslim Over Here." *New York Times* online edition. 7 Dec. 2006 <http://www.nytimes.com/2006/12/07/arts/television/07mosq.html>.

MacGregor, Roy. "Here's the Skinny on Shinny: It's Starting to Pick Up Again, But Shame About Those Rinks." *The Globe and Mail* 2 Jan. 2003: A2.

Mackey, Eva. *The House of Difference: Cultural Politics and National Identity in Canada*. Toronto: University of Toronto Press, 2002.

Maher, Neil. "Neil Maher on Shooting the Moon." *Environmental History* 9.3 (2004). <http://www.historycooperative.org/journals/eh/9.3/maher.html>.

Malcomson, Robert W. *Popular Recreations in English Society 1700–1850*. Cambridge, UK: Cambridge University Press, 1973.

Mallick, Heather. "Ready, Aim, Swipe." *The Globe and Mail* 14 Dec. 2002: L5.

Martin, Emily. "Body Narratives, Body Boundaries." *Cultural Studies*. Eds. Lawrence Grossberg, Cary Nelson, and Paula Treichler. New York: Routledge, 1992. 409–423.

Marx, Karl. "Excerpt from the Preface to 'A Contribution to a Critique of Political Economy.'" *A Critical and Cultural Theory Reader*. Ed. Anthony Easthope and Kate McGowan. Toronto: University of Toronto Press, 1992. 45–46.

Marx, Karl, and Friedrich Engels. *The Communist Manifesto: A Modern Edition* 1888. New York: Verso, 1998.

Massey, Doreen. *Space, Place and Gender*. Cambridge: Polity Press, 1994.

Mathieu, Emily. "Pair Jailed 10 Years in Homeless Beating Death." *The Toronto Star* online edition. 2 May 2008 <http://www.thestar.com/News/GTA/article/420621>.

Mattelart, Armand. *Networking the World, 1794–2000*. Trans. Liz Carey-Libbrecht and James A. Cohen. Minneapolis: University of Minnesota Press, 2000.

Mauss, Marcel. "Techniques of the Body." *Incorporations*. Ed. Jonathan Crary and Sanford Kwinter. New York: Zone, 1992. 455–477.

McClintock, Anne. *Imperial Leather: Race, Gender and Sexuality in the Colonial Context*. New York: Routledge, 1995.

McKay, George. *Senseless Acts of Beauty: Cultures of Resistance Since the Sixties*. New York: Verso, 1996.

McLuhan, Marshall. *Understanding Media: The Extensions of Man*. New York: McGraw-Hill, 1964.

McRobbie, Angela. *Postmodernism and Popular Culture.* London: Routledge, 1994.

Mercer, Kobena. "Welcome to the Jungle: Identity and Diversity in Postmodern Politics." *Identity: Community, Culture, Difference.* Ed. Jonathan Rutherford. London: Lawrence and Wishart, 1990. 43–71.

Merrifield, Andy. *Metromarxism: A Marxist Tale of the City.* New York: Routledge, 2002.

Metcalfe, Alan. *Canada Learns to Play: The Emergence of Organized Sport, 1807–1914.* Toronto: McClelland & Stewart, 1987.

Mickey Mouse Monopoly: Disney, Childhood and Corporate Power. Dir. Miguel Picker. Prod. Chyng Sun. Artmedia, 2001.

Miller, Daniel. *A Theory of Shopping.* Ithaca, NY: Cornell University Press, 1999.

Modern Times. Dir. Charles Chaplin. Charles Chaplin Productions, 1936.

Mulvey, Laura. "Visual Pleasure and Narrative Cinema." *A Cultural Studies Reader.* Ed. Jessica Munns and Gita Rajan. New York: Longman, 1995. 322–332.

Nachbar, Jack, and Kevin Lause. "Getting to Know Us: An Introduction to the Study of Popular Culture: What Is This Stuff That Dreams Are Made Of?" *Popular Culture: An Introductory Text.* Ed. Jack Nachbar and Kevin Lause. Bowling Green, OH: Bowling Green State University Popular Press, 1992. 1–36.

Naremore, James, and Patrick Brantlinger, eds. *Modernity and Mass Culture.* Bloomington, IN: Indiana University Press, 1991.

Negus, Keith. "The Production of Culture." *Production of Culture/Cultures of Production.* Ed. Paul du Gay. London: Sage/Open University, 1997. 67–118.

Nos4a2. "*EW Questions DC*" <http://www.geocities.com/Hollywood/Guild/ 5740/dcbb/ gayjack.html>.

Office Space. Dir Mike Judge. Prod. Daniel Rappaport and Michael Rotenberg. 20th Century Fox, 1999.

Over the Hedge. Dir. Tim Johnson and Karey Kirkpatrick. Prod. Bonnie Arnold. DreamWorks, 2006.

Ohmann, Richard. *Selling Culture: Magazines, Markets and Class.* New York: Verso, 1996.

O'Sullivan, Tim, John Hartley, Danny Saunders, Martin Montgomery, and John Fiske. *Key Concepts in Communication and Cultural Studies.* London: Routledge, 1994.

Page, Don. "A View from the South." *Coast to Coast* 5.3 (1999) <http://www.stleonards.ca/ docs/coast/5-3/5-3.html>.

Pilot. *The O.C.* Toronto, Fox, E!. 5 Aug. 2003.

Pocohantas. Dir. Mike Gabriel and Eric Goldberg. Prod. James Pentecost. Walt Disney Films, 1995.

"Quebec Town Forbids Stoning and Throwing Acid in People's Faces." *Progressive Muslima News.* 30 Jan. 2007 <http://proggiemuslima.wordpress.com/2007/ 01/30/quebec-town-forbids-stoning-and-throwing-acid-in-peoples-faces/>.

Radway, Janice. *Reading the Romance: Women, Patriarchy and Popular Literature.* Chapel Hill, NC: University of North Carolina Press, 1984.

Rankin, Jim, Jennifer Quinn, Michelle Shephar, John Duncanson, and Scott Simmie. "Black Arrest Rates Highest." *The Toronto Star* online edition. 26 Oct. 2002

<http://www.thestar.com/NASApp/cs/ContentServer?pagename=thestar/Layout/ Article_Type1&c=Article&cid=1026146837542&call_page=TS_RaceAndCrime&call _pageid=1034935301156&call_pagepath=GTA/Race_and_Crime&col= 1034935301113>.

Reguly, Eric. "How the Cupboards Went Bare." *The Globe and Mail* online edition. 12 April 2008 <http://www.theglobeandmail.com/servlet/story/LAC.20080412.FOOD12/ TPStory//?pageRequested=2>.

Reynolds, Joshua. *Discourses on Art.* 1797. Ed. Robert Wark. New Haven, CT: Yale University Press, 1975.

Robbins, Richard. *Global Problems and the Culture of Capitalism.* Second Edition. Boston: Allyn and Bacon, 2002.

Robertson, Roland. *Globalization: Social Theory and Global Culture.* London: Sage, 1992.

Robinson, Laura. "Girls Should Take to the Streets." *The Globe and Mail* 11 Jan. 2002: A15.

Rosenberg, "Berlin Conference of 1884–1885 to Divide Africa." Accessed 18 Nov. 2008 <http://geography. about.com/ library/weekly/aa021601a.htm>.

Ross, Andrew. No Collar: *The Humane Workplace and Its Hidden Costs.* Philadelphia: Temple UP, 2004.

"Runaway Production." Director's Guild of America. Accessed 18 Nov. 2008 <http://www. dga.org/news/>.

Rutherford, Jonathan. "Identity and the Cultural Politics of Difference." *Identity: Community, Culture, Difference.* Ed. Jonathan Rutherford. London: Lawrence and Wishart, 1990. 9–27.

Said, Edward. *Culture and Imperialism.* London: Chatto and Windus, 1993.

———. *Orientalism.* New York: Vintage, 1979.

Saletan, William. "The Beam in Your Eye: If Steroids is Cheating, Why Isn't LASIK?" *Slate* 18 Apr. 2005 <http://www.slate.com/id/2116858/>.

Schivelbusch, Wolfgang. *Tastes of Paradise: A Social History of Spices, Stimulants, and Intoxicants.* New York: Pantheon, 1992.

Schnellner, Johanna. "Only Money Breaks the Colour Barrier." *The Globe and Mail* 21 Dec. 2001: R3.

Schor, Juliet. "Towards a New Politics of Consumption." *The Consumer Society Reader.* Ed. Juliet B. Schor and Douglas Holt. New York: The New Press, 2000. 446–62.

Scott, Paul. "You're Sitting on a Time Bomb." *Men's Health* (May 2008). Rpt. in *WebMD* 15 Nov. 2008 <http://men.webmd.com/features/sitting-time-bomb>.

Seabrook, John. *Nobrow: The Culture of Marketing, the Marketing of Culture.* New York: Vintage, 2001.

Sheard, Sally. "Profit is a Dirty Word: The Development of Public Baths and Wash-Houses in Britain 1847–1915." *Social History of Medicine* 13.1 (2001): 63–86.

Shears, Mary Deanne. "Our Duty: Examine All Issues." *The Toronto Star* online edition. 19 Oct. 2002 <http://www.thestar.com/NASApp/cs/ContentServer?pagename=thestar/ Layout/Article_Type1&c=Article&cid=1026146584089&call_page=TS_

RaceAndCrime&call_pageid=1034935301156&call_pagepath=GTA/Race_and_Crime &col=1034935301113>.

Shilling, Chris. "The Body and Difference." *Identity and Difference.* Ed. Kathryn Woodward. London: Sage, 1997. 63–120.

Shohat, Ella, and Robert Stam. *Unthinking Eurocentrism: Multiculturalism and the Media.* London: Routledge, 1994.

Simons, Penelope. "Human Security, Corporate Accountability and the Regulation of Trade and Investment." Canadian Consortium on Human Security, 2004. 85–86 <http://www.corporate-accountability.org/eng/documents/2004/march_2004_ human_ security_corporate_accountability_and_the_regulation_of_trade_and_investment__ by_the_canadian_consortium_on_human_security_cchs_pdf_17_mb.pdf>.

Smith, Alisa and J.B. MacKinnon. *The 100-Mile Diet: A Year of Local Eating.* Toronto: Random House, 2007.

Solnit, Rebecca. *River of Shadows: Eadweard Muybridge and the Technological Wild West.* New York: Penguin, 2004.

Spirn, Anne Whiston. "Constructing Nature: The Legacy of Frederick Law Olmstead." *Uncommon Ground: Rethinking the Human Place in Nature.* Ed. William Cronon. New York: Norton, 1996. 91-113.

Stackhouse, John. *Timbit Nation.* Toronto: Random House, 1993.

Stallabrass, Julian. "Digital Commons." *New Left Review* 15 (2002): 141–146.

Statistics Canada. "The Daily." *Statscan* <http://www.statcan.ca/Daily/English/020830/ d020830a.htm>.

Stevenson, Seth. "I'd Like to Buy the World a Shelf-Stable Children's Lactic Drink." *New York Times Magazine* 10 Mar. 2002: 38–43.

Stoneman, Scott. "Fat Masculinities." E-mail to Susie O'Brien. 12 Mar. 2008.

Stranger Than Fiction. Dir. Marc Forster. Prod. Lindsay Doran. Starring Will Ferrell. Columbia, 2005.

Suskind, Ron. "Without a Doubt." *New York Times Magazine* online edition. 17 Oct. 2004 <http://www.cs.umass.edu/~immerman/play/opinion05/WithoutADoubt.html>.

Strasser, Susan. *Satisfaction Guaranteed: The Making of the American Mass Market.* New York: Pantheon, 1989.

Szatmary, David P. *Rockin' in Time: A Social History of Rock-and-Roll.* Upper Saddle River, NJ: Prentice Hall, 2000.

"A Talk with the Producers of 'The Merchants of Cool.'" Accessed 3 Oct. 2002 <http://www.pbs.prg/wgbh/pages/frontline/shows/cool/etc/producers.html>.

Thompson, E.P. *The Making of the English Working Class.* Harmondsworth: Penguin, 1963.

Thomson, Rosemary Garland. *Extraordinary Bodies: Figuring Physical Disability in American Culture and Literature.* New York: Columbia University Press, 1997.

Thornham, Sue. *Feminist Theory and Cultural Studies: Stories of Unsettled Relations.* London: Arnold, 2000.

Thornton, Sarah. *Club Cultures: Music, Media and Subcultural Capital.* Cambridge: Polity, 1995.

"To Be or Not To Be . . . " *Dawson's Creek*. Toronto, The WB, Global. 10 Feb. 1999.

Tomlinson, John. *Cultural Imperialism: A Critical Introduction*. Baltimore: The Johns Hopkins University Press, 1991.

———. *Globalization and Culture*. Chicago: University of Chicago Press, 1999.

Transamerica. Dir. Duncan Tucker. Prod. William H. Macy. Starring Felicity Huffman. The Weinstein Company, IFC Films, 2005.

Turley, Jonathan. "Why Race-Based Survivor Makes Us Squirm." *USA Today* online edition. 14 Sept. 2006 <http://blogs.usatoday.com/oped/2006/09/why_racebased_s.html>.

Twitchell, James. *AdCult USA: The Triumph of Advertising in American Culture*. New York: Columbia University Press, 1996.

Tzara, Tristan. "Dada Manifesto 1918." *The Dada Painters and Poets*. Ed. Robert Motherwell. New York: G. Wittenborn, 1951.

Tsoukalas, Spyridoula, and Paul Roberts. "Legal Aid Eligibility and Coverage in Canada." Legal Aid Research Series. Ottawa: The Department of Justice Canada, 2003 <http://canada.justice.gc.ca/en/ps/rs/rep/2003/rr03lars-5/rr03lars-5.pdf>.

United for Peace and Justice. "UFPJ Announces Full March Route for August 29th." 26 Aug. 2004. Accessed 27 July 2008 <http://www.unitedforpeace.org/article.php?id=2572>.

Van Elteren, Mel. "Conceptualizing the Impact of US Popular Culture Globally." *Journal of Popular Culture* 30.1 (1996): 47–89.

Veblen, Thorstein. *The Theory of the Leisure Class*. New York: New American Library, 1953.

"Victoria's Secret." Prod. Marleen Trotter. Rep. Wei Chen. *W5*. Vancouver, CTV. 10 Mar. 1992.

Virilio, Paul. *Open Sky*. London: Verso, 1997.

Voynar, Kim. "Review: *Broken Flowers*." *Cinematical*. 7 August 2005 <http://www.cinematical.com/2005/08/07/review-broken-flowers/>.

Wallace, Amy. "True Thighs." *More*. Sept. 2002 <http://www.more.com/more-women/celebrities/jamie-lee-curtis-true-thighs/>.

Walzer, Andrew. "Narratives of Contemporary Male Crisis: The (Re)Production of a National Discourse." *Journal of Men's Studies* 10.2 (2002): 209–224.

"Water Related Injuries: Fact Sheet." Centers for Disease Control and Prevention. Department of Health and Human Services <http://www.cdc.gov/ncipc/factsheets/drown.htm>.

Waters, Malcolm. *Globalization*. London: Routledge, 1995.

Watson, James, ed. *Golden Arches East: McDonald's in East Asia*. Stanford: Stanford University Press, 1997.

Weber, Max. *The Protestant Ethic and the Spirit of Capitalism*. 1930. Trans. Talcott Parsons. New York: Charles Scribner and Sons, 1958.

Weiss, Brad. "Coffee Breaks and Coffee Connections: The Lived Experience of a Commodity in Tanzanian and European Worlds." *Cross-Cultural Consumption: Global Market, Local Realities*. Ed. David Howes. London: Routledge, 1996. 93–105.

Welch, Jack. Interview on CNN *Moneyline*. 8 Dec. 1998.

Wente, Margaret. "It's Okay to Hate Hockey." *The Globe and Mail* 10 Jan. 2002: A21.

———. "Today We Are All Americans." *The Globe and Mail* 13 Sept. 2001: A6.

———. "We Are All Australians Now." *The Globe and Mail* 19 Oct. 2002: A23.

"Western Eyes." Writ. and Dir. Ann Shin. *Rough Cuts*. Toronto, CBC. 16 Apr. 2002.

Whorf, Benjamin Lee. *Language, Thought and Reality*. Cambridge, MA: MIT Press, 1963.

"Why Is Google So Great?" *Great Place to Work® Institute*. 2007 <http://www
.greatplacetowork.com/best/100best2007-google.php>.

Williams, Raymond. "Advertising: The Magic System." *The Cultural Studies Reader*. Ed.
Simon During. London: Routledge, 1993. 320–336.

———. "British Film History: New Perspectives." *British Cinema History*. Ed. J. Curran
and V. Porter. London: Weidenfeld and Nicolson, 1983. 9–23.

———. *Culture and Society 1780–1950*. New York: Columbia University Press, 1983.

Williamson, Judith. *Consuming Passions: The Dynamics of Popular Culture*. London:
Boyars, 1986.

Wilson, Elizabeth. "The Invisible *Flâneur*." *New Left Review* 191 (1992): 90–110.

Wiltse, Ed. "Globalization, Fandom and Cyber-solidarity." *Content Providers of the World
Unite!* Ed. Susie O'Brien and Imre Szeman. Institute on Globalization and the Human
Condition Working Paper Series. Hamilton: McMaster University <http://www
.humanities.mcmaster.ca/~global/wp/Content.pdf>.

Wiltse, Jeff. *Contested Waters: A Social History of Swimming Pools in America*. Chapel Hill,
NC: University of North Carolina Press, 2007

Winship, Janice. "A Woman's World: "Woman"—An Ideology of Femininity." *Women Take
Issue: Aspects of Women's Subordination*. Women's Studies Group, Centre for
Contemporary Cultural Studies. London: Hutchinson, 1978. 133–154.

Wise, S.F., and Douglas Fisher. *Canada's Sporting Heroes*. Don Mills, ON: General, 1974.

Wolff, Janet. "The Invisible *Flâneuse*: Women in the Literature of Modernity." *Theory,
Culture & Society* 2 (1985): 37–46.

Wong, Jan. "Shootout at School Prompts an Eerie Attitude." *The Globe and Mail* 12 Feb.
2000: A1, A30.

Working Girl. Dir. Mike Nichols. Prod. Douglas Wick 20th Century Fox, 1988.

Wolgamott, L. Kent. "Museums Re-evaluate Display Methods." (Lincoln) *Journal Star*
online edition. 25 June 2006 <http://www.journalstar.com/articles/2006/06/25/
sunday_am/doc449991afdae48467800411.txt>.

World Bank. *World Development Indicators 1998*. Washington, D.C.: World Bank, 1998.

World Trade Organization. "Canada—Certain Measures Concerning Periodicals."
Dispute Resolution Panel Report WT/DS31/R. 14 Mar. 1997 <http://www
.worldtradelaw.net/reports/wtoab/canada-periodicals(ab).pdf>.

Young, Iris Marion. "Throwing Like a Girl: A Phenomenology of Feminine Body
Comportment, Motility and Spatiality." *Human Studies* 3 (1980): 137–156.

Zizek, Slavoj. *In Defense of Lost Causes*. New York: Verso, 2008.

Index

filmmaking
  changes in cultural production, 130–138, 146–147
  history, 55
  runaway films, 313–318
Fiske, John, 5, 13, 174
flâneur, 174–176
folk culture, 8–10, 336
Folk Devils and Moral Panics, 80
football
  commercialization, 59–64
  street, 35–37, 64–66
Fordism, 42–43
Forrest Gump, 269–271
Foucault, Michel, 76, 195–199
Frank, Thomas, 181–182
Frankfurt School, 116
Freud, Sigmund, 186
Friedan, Betty, 172
future of spaces, 317–318

G

Garnham, Nicholas, 117
GATT (General Agreement on Tariffs and Trade), 322, 348–349
gender
  bodies, differences, 206–210
  consumption, 171–176
  identity, 187, 189–195
  nations, identity, 237–238
  representation, 90–95
  sports, 66
Gender Trouble, 174
Ghost World, 274–276
Gilman, Charlotte Perkins, 172
globalization
  authentic cultures, 341–345
  creative class, 351
  cultural imperialism, 337–340
  digital revolution, 323–325
  economics, 325–331
  history, 326–327
  McDonald's, 341–345
  overview, 321–323
  politics, 331–332
  sovereignty, 345–350

  space, 336–337
  technology, 332–335
Globalization and Culture, 323
Global Problems and the Culture of Capitalism, 154–155
glossary, 353–369
Goodman, Barak, 179
Gore, Al, 312
Gramsci, Antonio, 53
Grizzly Man, 306–309
Grossberg, Lawrence, 9
Grossman, David, 98–99

H

habitus, 208–209
Hall, Stuart, 22, 24, 52, 78, 101–102
Handbook of Football, 60
Harmsworth, Edward, 56
headlines, newspaper, 75–76
health
  bodies, identity, 211–212
  impact, consumption, 176–177
Hebdige, Dick, 277–278
hegemonic masculinity, 190–194
hegemony, 52–53
Hérouxville, 254–255
history
  coffee, 28–30
  consumer culture, 153–162
  cultural spaces, 39–41
  of cultural studies, 15–18
  culture industry, 51–59
  filmmaking production, 130–138
  globalization, 326–327
  identity, 185–199
  industrialism, 41–43
  popular recreation, pre-1830, 37–38
  popular recreation, working class resistance, 46–51
  production, 42–43
  sexuality, identity, 196–199
  sports, organization of, 59–64
  street football prohibition, 37
  working class, 43–46
Hobsbawm, Eric, 42
Hochschild, Arlie Russell, 304

postindustrial culture, 22–23
postmodern
    capitalism, 11
    identity, bodies, 203–207
power
    consumption, 167–168
    identity, 195–196
    relationships, popular culture, 13
printing press, 53–54
private spaces *versus* public, 295–304.
       See also spaces
privatized media, 12
production
    changes in, 130–138
    coffee, 28
    copyright, 142–147
    culture industry thesis, 115–127
    economics *versus* art, 112–115
    filmmaking, 130–138
    Fordism, 42–43
    lifestyle marketing, 139–141
    market segmentation, 139–141
    oppositional, 122–123
    popular culture, overview, 109–111
    pseudo-individualization, 121–122
    standardization, 120–121
    Walkman example, 127–130
    working class, 43–46
product packaging, 139–140
pseudo-individualization, popular culture
       production, 121–122
psychoanalysis, 186
psychosocial development, 186–187
public spaces. *See also* spaces
    history of, 39–41
    versus private, 295–304
pubs
    community spaces, 40–41
    culture of, 57–58
punk, 277–281
Putnam, Robert D., 171

R
race
    body modification, 212–214
    identity, 190, 241–243
    marketing identity, 249–251
    representation, 90–95
    swimming pools, 297–298
Radway, Janice, 100–101
railway system, 54–55
Ramone, Dee Dee, 268–269
rationality, instrumental, 118–119
rational recreation, 46–47
Reading the Romance: Women, Patriarchy and
       Popular Literature, 100
realism, 85–86
reform, workplace, 45–46
Refus Global, 265–267
regulations, history, 55–56
relevance, culture industry thesis,
       126–127
representation
    audience, role of, 100–104
    coffee, 25–27
    contexts, 95–104
    conventions, 72–74
    counterculture, 267–276
    defined, 67–68
    discourse, 76
    ideological context, 104–106
    imagination, 99–100
    inside *versus* outside, 89–90
    manipulation of mass media, myth
       of, 96–100
    moral panic, 79–80
    mythology, 74
    negative, challenging, 92–95
    news-gathering organizations, 81–82
    newspaper headlines, 75–76
    photographs, 84–86
    political context, 104–106
    politics of, 90–95
    reading a television scene, 102–104
    realism, 85–86
    semiotics, 72, 73
    social consequences, 98–99
    structuralism, 71–74
    subculture, 267–276
    truthiness, 106–107
    virtual culture, 106
    youth, construction of, 77–78
    youth violence, mass media, 83–90
    youth violence, mugging, 78–79
    youth violence statistics, 68–71

re-territorialization, 253–255
Robbins, Richard, 154–156
Roberts, Brian, 78
rugby, 59–64
runaway films, 313–318

S

sampling, music, 142
Saussure, Ferdinand de, 73
Schor, Juliet, 177–178
Second Life, 284
segmentation, market, 139–141
self-controlled body, 207–208
Selling Culture, 160, 169
semiotics, 72, 73, 75–76, 86–87
sexuality
    history, identity, 196–199
    homosexuality on TV, 199–203
Shakespeare, William, 5
*The Significance of the Frontier in American
        History,* 309
signification, 71, 74
Silent Spring, 311–312
situationism, 280–281
skateboarding, 281–282
soccer, 59–64
social consequences, representation, 98–99
social networking sites, 252–253
social status, bodies, 208–209
Society of the Spectacle, 292–293
sociocultural differentiation, consumption, 165
software copyright, 145
sovereignty, globalization, 345–350
spaces
    bioregional quiz, 314
    defined, 289–290
    environmental awareness, 311–313
    future of, 317–318
    globalization, 336–337
    locavores, 313
    malls, 299
    nature, 305–313
    overview, 287–289
    parks, 295–297
    private *versus* public, 295–304
    public, history of, 39–41
    runaway films, 313–318

swimming pools, 297–298
    theories of, 291–295
    wilderness, 309–311
    work, 300–304
sports
    blood sports, 50
    commercialization, 59–64
    gender, 66
    mythology, 65
    organization of, 59–64
    street, 35–37, 64–66
squeegees, 86–87
standardization, popular culture production,
        120–121
Starbucks, 30–32
Stiffed, 191
Strasser, Susan, 128
structuralism, 71–74
studio system, filmmaking, 133–135
styles, films, 138
subculture
    co-optation, 180–181
    counterculture, distinction, 261–267
    culture jamming, 273
    cyberspace, 282–285
    defined, 262–263
    Fight Club, 271–274
    Forrest Gump, 269–271
    Ghost World, 274–276
    mainstream, overview, 257–259
    minority-majority relationships,
        259–261
    politics of, 276–282
    punk, 277–281
    representation, 267–276
    skateboarding, 281–282
Subculture: The Meaning of Style, 277
subliminal advertising, 157–158
Summit of the Americas, 7
swimming pools, 297–298

T

taste, consumption, 164–168
technology, development of, 52–55, 130,
        146–147, 332–335
telegraph, 54–55
telephone, 54

Credits

TEXT

CHAPTER 1

Page 29: Penelope Simons. "Human Security, Corporate Accountability and the Regulation of Trade and Investment." Canadian Consortium on Human Security. March 2004. Pg. 62–86. Found at: http://www.corporate-accountability.org/eng/documents/2004/march_2004_human_security_corporate_accountability_and_the_regulation_of_trade_and_investment_by_the_canadian_consortium_on_human_security_cchs_pdf_17_mb.pdf.

CHAPTER 2

Page 66: Laura Robinson. "Girls Should Take to the Streets." *The Globe and Mail*. Jan. 11, 2002. Pg. A15.

CHAPTER 3

Page 67/68: urbandictionary.com; Page 68: "Victoria's Secret." CTV Television Network. 2002. Found at: http://www.ctv.ca/servlet/ArticleNews/story/CTVNews/20021025/ctvnews850243/20021025/; Page 70: Maire Gannon. Statistics Canada. *Juristat*. Figure 15: Youth Crime Rate Decreased in 2005. Catalogue no. 85-002-XIE. Vol. 26, No. 4, Pg. 13; Page 72: Kim Voynar. Cinematical. Review: *Broken Flowers*. Found at: http://www.cinematical.com/2005/08/07/review-broken-flowers/; Page 80: Stan Cohen. *Folk Devils and Moral Panics: The Creation of the Mods and Rockers*. London: MacGibbon and Kee. 1972; Page 94: Laura Mulvey. "Visual Pleasure and Narrative Cinema." *A Cultural Studies Reader*. Ed. Jessica Munns and Gita Rajan. New York: Longman. 1995. Pg. 322–332; Page 96: Bruce Grierson. "Headrush." *Adbusters*. 25 Spring 1999. Pg. 23–29; Page 101: Janice Radway. *Reading the Romance: Women, Patriarchy and Popular Literature*. Chapel Hill, NC: University of North Carolina Press, 1984; Page 102: Stuart Hall. "Encoding, Decoding. Culture, Media, Language." Pg. 94. London: Unwin Hyman. 1990. © 1990 Stuart Hall; Page 107: Ron Suskind. "Faith, Certainty and the Presidency of George W. Bush." *New York Times Magazine*. Oct. 17, 2004. Found at: http://www.nytimes.com/2004/10/17/magazine/17BUSH.html?scp=3&sq= suskind&st=cse.

CHAPTER 4

Page 128: Susan Strasser. *Satisfaction Guaranteed: The Making of the American Mass Market*. New York: Pantheon Books. 1989.

CHAPTER 5

Page 167: Juliet Schor. "Towards a New Politics of Consumption." *The Consumer Society Reader*. Ed. Juliet B. Schor and Douglas Holt. New York: The New Press. 2000. Pg. 446–462; Page 175: John Fiske. *Reading the Popular*. London: Routledge. 1989; Page 176: Winship qtd. in Thornham 135.

CHAPTER 7

Page 224–225: Connolly, P., Smith, A. & Kelly, B. (2002). *Too Young to Notice? The Cultural and Political Awareness of 3–6 Year Olds in Northern Ireland*. Belfast: Community Relations Council; Page 230: Courtesy of Molson Canada; Page 235: Alan MacEachern. "Ye Olde Season's Greetings." *The Globe and Mail*. Dec. 31, 2007. Pg. A14; Page 254: Alain Dubuc. "Fear and Ignorance: A Rural Revolt." *The Vancouver Sun*. Mar. 1, 2007. Found at: http://www.lafontaine-baldwin.com/fear-and-ignorance-a-rural-revolt-2013-the-vancouver-sun.

CHAPTER 8

Page 266: "Refus Global." *Documents in Canadian Art*. Ed. Douglas Fetherling. Broadview Press. 1987. Pg. 121. Copyright © 1989 by Douglas Fetherling. Reprinted by permission of Broadview Press; Page 268: Chuck Klosterman. "The Ratt Trap." *The New York Times Magazine*. Dec. 29, 2002. Pg. 24–25; Page 277: Dick Hebdige. *Hiding in the Light: On Images and Things*. New York: Routledge. 1994.

CHAPTER 9

Page 287: Le Corbusier. *The Radiant City*. (1967; originally published 1935); Page 288: Andres Duany, Elizabeth Plater-Zyberk, and Jeff Speck. *Suburban Nation: The Rise of Sprawl and the Decline of the American Dream*. New York: North Point Press. 2001; Page 291: Mike Davis. "Planet of Slums." London: Verso. 2006; Page 303: The Great Place to Work Institute. "Why Is Google So Great?" 2007. Pg. 7. Found at: http://resources. greatplacetowork.com/article/pdf/why_google_is_no._1.pdf; Page 308: David Denby. "Loners." *The New Yorker*. Aug. 8, 2005. Found at: http://www.newyorker.com/archive/ 2005/08/08/050808crci_cinema; Page 314: Quiz originally compiled by Leonard Charles, Jim Dodge, Lynn Milliman, and Victoria Stockley for *CoEvolution Quarterly* (now *Whole Earth Review* Winter 1981). Reprinted in *Uncommon Ground: Rethinking the Human Place in Nature*. Ed. William Cronon. New York: Norton. 1995. Pg. 369–370; Page 315: Extract from AM, "Brokeback Mountain Fuels Wyoming Tourism Boom," reporter Kim Landers, first published by ABC Online, 4 March 2006, is reproduced by permission of the Australian Broadcasting Corporation and ABC Online. © 2006 ABC. All rights reserved. Further information can be found at: http://www.abc.net.au/am/content/2006/ s1583819.htm.

CHAPTER 10

Page 349 (top): World Trade Organization. "Canada—Certain Measures Concerning Periodicals." Dispute Resolution Panel Report WT/DS31/R. Mar. 14, 1997. Found at: http://www.wto.org/english/tratop_e/dispu_e/cases_e/ds31_e.htm; Page 349 (bottom): World Trade Organization. "Canada—Certain Measures Concerning Periodicals." Dispute Resolution Panel Report WT/DS31/R. Mar. 14, 1997. Found at: http://www.wto.org/english/tratop_e/dispu_e/cases_e/ds31_e.htm.

PHOTOS

CHAPTER 1

Page 3: © Patrick Andrade/Reuters/Corbis; Page 6: Tim Graham/Getty Images; Page 26: Tracy Carbert; Page 32: Source: IS2006-0270, Tim Hortons Trailer in Kandahar, Afghanistan, July 1, 2006. Canadian Forces Combat Camera, National Defence, 2008.

CHAPTER 2

Page 36: Dick Hemingway; Page 49: Reproduced by permission of National Trust of Scotland; Page 60: Rischgitz/Getty Images; Page 61: Hulton Archive by Getty Images; Page 62: AP Photo/Domenico Stinellis.

CHAPTER 3

Page 80: © Anton Vengo/SuperStock; Page 84: Peter Redman/National Post; Page 92: © The CW/Courtesy Everett Collection.

CHAPTER 4

Page 113: © The New Yorker Collection 2000 Bruce Eric Kaplan from cartoonbank.com. All Rights Reserved; Page 118: Ontario Colleges. Found at: http://whycollege.ontariocolleges.ca/en/obay.html; Page 123: Digital Image © The Museum of Modern Art /Licensed by SCALA/Art Resource, NY. ART303192; Page 145: Courtesy Copyleft.net;

CHAPTER 5

Page 156: Mary Evans Picture Library; Page 157: Quaker Oats Ltd.; Page 165: Courtesy of Diesel Canada; Page 170: IStockphoto; Page 178: Image copyright Edward Burtynsky. Courtesy Nicholas Metivier Gallery, Toronto.

CHAPTER 6

Page 192: Alex Wong/Getty Images; Page 193: Courtesy NBC; Page 200: Everett Collection/The Canadian Press; Page 210: Photo by Rex Features/Canadian Press; Page 214: Early 1980s embodiment of Professor Steve Mann's "Wearable Computer" invention, from "CYBORG: Digital Destiny and Human Possibility in the Age of the Wearable Computer". Random House Doubleday. ISBN: 0385658257 (Hardcover); Page 216: AP Photo/PA, Tim Ockenden.

CHAPTER 7

Page 223: WestWind Pictures/Little Mosque Productions IV; Page 229: Courtesy of Molson. Actor Jeff Douglas; Page 234: JOHN MACDOUGALL/AFP/Getty Images; Page 236: © North Wind Picture Archives/Alamy; Page 240: Image A-09684 courtesy of Royal BC Museum, BC Archives; Page 251: © Copyright 1991 Benetton Group S.p.A. Photo: O. Toscani. Used by permission of Benetton; Page 252: Courtesy Facebook.

CHAPTER 8

Page 258: Courtesy of Burns Film Ltd; Page 263: Caleb Huntington; Page 271: TM and Copyright © 20th Century Fox Film Corp. All rights reserved; Page 280: Matthew McInnes/New Harbours Music Series; Page 284: AP Photo/Lisa Peyton.

CHAPTER 9

Page 294: The Get Out Clause. www.thegetoutclause.co.uk.index.htm; Page 298: Colin McConnell/The Toronto Star; Page 303: Courtesy of Ebay; Page 305: Maria Whiteman; Page 307: Maria Whiteman.

CHAPTER 10

Page 327: © The New Yorker Collection 1999 Mick Stevens from cartoonbank.com. All Rights Reserved; Page 337: Ikea photography 13 × 19, 2001. Artist: Gu Xiong. Reproduced by permission of Gu Xiong; Page 343: © Thomas Hartwell/CORBIS SABA/MAGMA.

1970

1980

Theory

1971
Louis Althusser, *Lenin and Philosophy*
1973
Laura Mulvey, "**Visual Pleasure and Narrative Cinema**"
1976
Michel Foucault, *History of Sexuality*, 1976-84
1978
Edward Said, *Orientalism*
1979
Pierre Bourdieu, *Distinction*; Jean-Francois Lyotard, *The Postmodern Condition*; Dick Hebdige, *Subculture: The Meaning of Style*

1981
Jean Baudrillard, *Simulacra and Simulations*
1983
Benedict Anderson, *Imagined Communities*
1984
William Gibson, *Neuromancer*

Popular Culture and Sports

1971
Gil Kane and Archie Goodwin's *Blackmark*, the first graphic novel, is released
1972
Formation of HBO; First original cable television programming in the USA; DJ Kool Herc pioneers the music that will become hip hop
1974
Publication of Stephen King's *Carrie*; The "Rumble in the Jungle," a boxing match between George Foreman and Muhammad Ali, takes place in Zaire

1975
Jaws, the "first blockbuster," released
1977
The Sex Pistol's *Never Mind the Bollocks, Here's the Sex Pistols* enters the British charts at number one

1980
Pac-Man released; CNN launched
1981
MTV launched
1982
Release of Michael Jackson's *Thriller*
1983
Madonna releases her self-titled debut album
1985
Nintendo Entertainment System released in the United States
1986
Formation of FOX broadcasting

1987
Publication of the first book in the *Where's Waldo/Wally?* series
1989
First episode of *The Simpsons*

Politics and Society

1971
The Nixon administration ends the Bretton Woods financial system of currency exchange controls, allowing the free flow of international capital; Greenpeace founded in Vancouver, Canada
1973
OPEC embargo leads to international oil crisis
1978
Birth of Louise Brown, the first "test-tube" baby
1979
Election of Margaret Thatcher as the first female prime minister of the United Kingdom

1982
Canadian Charter of Rights and Freedoms passed; Falklands War
1985
Act for the Preservation and Enhancement of Multiculturalism passed
1987
Economic reforms known as "perestroika" begin in the Soviet Union
1989
The Fall of the Berlin Wall marks the end of the Cold War; Pro-democracy demonstrations in Beijing's Tiananmen Square are crushed by the Chinese military

Making Modern Life

1970
Phillips releases the first VCR-format recorder
1971
First Starbucks opens in Seattle
1976
First Automatic Teller Machine (ATM) installed at Barclay's Bank in London
1977
First computer for personal home use enters the market
1979
First commercial cell phones go on sale in Tokyo, Japan; Original Walkman goes on sale

1982
The first Compact Discs (CDs) released
1983
McDonald's introduces the McNugget